INDEPENDENCE PARK

Nostalgia Jewishness is a lullaby for old men

gumming soaked white bread.

J. GLADSTEIN, *modernist Yiddish poet*

CONTRAVERSIONS

JEWS AND OTHER DIFFERENCES

DANIEL BOYARIN,

CHANA KRONFELD, AND

NAOMI SEIDMAN, EDITORS

The task of "The Science of Judaism"
is to give Judaism a decent burial.

MORITZ STEINSCHNEIDER,

founder of nineteenth-century

philological Jewish Studies

INDEPENDENCE PARK

THE LIVES OF GAY MEN IN ISRAEL

AMIR SUMAKA'I FINK

AND JACOB PRESS

Stanford University Press · *Stanford, California*

Stanford University Press

Stanford, California

© 1999 by the Board of Trustees of the

Leland Stanford Junior University

Printed in the United States of America

CIP data appear at the end of the book

To the love we shared

ACKNOWLEDGMENTS

WE THANK OUR PARENTS—Chava Fink, Shalom Fink, Marlene Press, and Lionel Press—for their love. Amir acknowledges the support and encouragement of his life-partner, Yossi Maurey, who accompanied this project almost from its inception. Jacob acknowledges his lover and partner, Jaime Douglass, and his friends and inspirations Christian Haye, Denise Fulbrook, and Melissa Solomon. Ḥagai El-ʿAd and David Meiri, together with Rafi Niv, shared many of the duties of midwifery in the labor of this book. A fellowship from the late Joy Ungerleider-Mayerson's Dorot Foundation funded Jacob's first year in Israel; her generosity enriched a life. Dan Yakir, of the Association for Civil Rights in Israel, Amit Kama, formerly of the "Agudah," and Jerry Levinson, of the Jerusalem Open House, have been similarly invaluable resources. We are pleased that the cover of this book is graced by the work of Adi Nes, who proved to be as patient as he is talented; thanks also to the designer of our map, Andréa Martins. We feel privileged to have benefited from the professionalism and commitment of the staff of Stanford University Press, especially our gracious editors, Helen Tartar and Nathan MacBrien, and our assiduous copy editor, Ann Klefstad. And what would we have done without our muses and patrons, Eve Kosofsky Sedgwick and Daniel Boyarin? We owe them much; we offer our gratitude and deepest respect. Most important, we thank Shaḥar, Noʿam, Rafi Niv (again), ʿAmit, Andrei, Eli, Dan, Walid, Yossi A., Oren, Itziq, and Theo Mainz, the authors of this book.

A.S.F. *and* J.P.

CONTENTS

PREFACE

AMIR AND I have grown to love this book. For us, it will forever recall the summer of 1993, the close of our affair.

I arrived in Israel in the spring of 1991, a few days after my graduation from Harvard College. Unwilling to formulate anything so obviously necessary as long-term professional plans, I had applied for and received a fellowship from the Dorot Foundation. This enabled me to take up residence in Jerusalem, where I studied Judaism and Hebrew, and, after six months, met Amir.

The way I spoke Hebrew then, even street vendors of falafel—not generally known for linguistic hypersensitivity—would quickly and condescendingly steer our conversations into English. But not Amir. From our very first date (a blind one, courtesy of friends) he encouraged me with the patience of Job to drag my thoughts into expression along the rough terrain of irregular verb groups and through the unfathomable fogs of gendered nouns. And in the thicket of misunderstandings in which we entangled ourselves that night, I glimpsed Amir's sensitive soul, his romantic heart, and his playful mind. And he was cute, after all. We became a couple, and over the course of the next year and a half, I learned to speak Hebrew well.

Amir, along with almost all Jewish Israelis, had been drafted into the army when he was eighteen. Instead of volunteering for combat or being cubbyholed into administrative work, he, after undergoing basic training, was chosen to join the staff of the popular army-run radio station, Galey Tzahal. Here, for three years, he did his military service as a reporter, and when I met him he was, at the age of twenty-one, working as the news editor of the Haifa daily newspaper, *Qol Ḥeifah*. His career as a journalist was budding, but he loathed his work, and was planning to give it up to go to college—he had always dreamed of being an archaeologist.

For months, we conducted a long-distance relationship, commuting between Haifa and Jerusalem. Unfortunately, when he finally moved to Jerusalem to begin his studies at the Hebrew University, I moved to Tel Aviv. My fellowship money had run out; I needed to begin supporting myself; my new job was contingent upon my leaving Jerusalem. Amir and I kept on commuting. In the spring of 1993, I found out that my application for admission to Duke University's Ph.D. program in English literature had been accepted. Suddenly it appeared that I would be taking up residence in North Carolina at the end of the summer. That is a much longer commute.

Amir and I found ourselves in the position of being two people who love each other—and who know that in exactly four months they will be splitting up. This book was conceived out of these four months. The compilation of a book of the personal narratives of Israeli gay men was an excuse for us to spend time together, to teach one another, to argue, and to construct a permanent memorial to our fleeting relationship.

We appeared at most of the interviews that provide the substance of this book as a team, although Amir conceived of and asked most of the questions during the interviews. I performed the process of translation, transcription, and redaction, although Amir and I went over the resultant text together. This was a huge, huge job. Huge. But I have wonderful memories of those days: propped up on the bed in Amir's Jerusalem apartment, the computer in my lap, the afternoon breeze breathing in through the open balcony doors, the stereophonic voice of an interviewee blaring over the speakers, Amir taking a break from cooking to explain the meaning of obscure military terminology. As we counted down the days to my departure we spent every free moment together. For us, this book will forever be synonymous with that experience.

In point of fact, there is no reason why this book should not be linked with the many days, weeks, and months that followed my departure from Israel, because our work was far from done. I settled into America again, and Amir and I redefined our working habits, as well as our relationship. If during the summer we spent hours sitting together listening to the recorded voices of our interviewees, now we each sat alone, each listening to the voice of the other. In every one of my weekly recorded epistles, most of which were given over to lamentations over my exile, I included a generous helping of technical questions pertaining to this book. In each of Amir's cassettes—masterpieces of commiseration—he was diligent in providing answers. And now at last our collaboration has really come to a close. Sadly, the book is done. We hope you love it as we do.

J.P.

A NOTE TO THE READER

IDEALLY, THIS BOOK would be in Hebrew. There are many reasons why it is not. First, the English-speaking audience for a work of this sort is relatively larger than the Hebrew-speaking one. In addition, hardly any of our interviewees would have agreed to speak "on the record" if we had said that we were publishing this in Hebrew. Almost all of the men we spoke to, like almost all gay men in Israel at the time we were performing these interviews, dreaded the possibility that people they had not specifically chosen to tell would find out that they were gay. Seven out of the twelve men with whom we spoke insisted that we invent aliases for them, as well as for those who appear in their stories; three agreed to speak with us only on the condition that we send them the final text for approval, so that they could be sure they had not said anything too revealing; three interviewees asked that we alter certain details in their stories in order to further obscure their identities. Only two allowed us to use their full names.

Most of our sessions were from four to six hours long. The transcripts have necessarily undergone an extensive editing process. In the final text, our interviewees have been allowed to speak in a free-flowing monologue—this was very much what most of our interview sessions felt like. We were continually amazed at the willingness of these men to share their secrets with us, and most of them required very little encouragement in the creation of their narratives. We found that much of our work was reduced to pressing the "record" button and being rapt listeners. And flipping the tape.

Besides the ordinary—and insurmountable—anguishes of translation, we have faced the equally hopeless task of conveying spoken voices through writing. We have done our best to keep the vibrant spoken Hebrew of these men from becoming homogenized into a stagnant literary English. In addition, we have tried to preserve the distinct idiom of our speakers, each of whom has his own relationship to the Hebrew language. The voices of these men will forever echo through our minds—we hope that some residual reverberations have found their way into this text.

We have done our best to cope with the problem of "Hebrish," a fascinating linguistic phenomenon. Residents of Israel for whom English is a first language have a habit, when speaking with one another in English, of leaving a smattering of Hebrew words untranslated. Why? Well, there are some words that are just more fun in Hebrew. But mostly, Hebrew words are used to refer to phenomena that have a distinctively Israeli twist: ʿaliyah is not just any migration—it is immigration to Israel; a garʿin is not just any cooperative group—it has a socialist Zionist ideology; and so on. It has been our continuous temptation to translate these interviews into Hebrish, but we have attempted to restrain ourselves. We ask that Hebrish-speaking readers forgive us for translating miluʾim into "reserve duty," dati into "religious" (and ḥiloni into "secular"), ʿatudah into "officer candidate academic studies program," and ṭiyul into "day-trip." In many of these cases, the English sounds laughably inappropriate to our ears, but we could think of no rational justification for the retention of the Hebrew.

We have, however, been forced to preserve some Hebrew terminology, which merits explication. The Israeli work-week extends from Sunday morning to Friday at midday. The Jewish sabbath, shabbat, begins at sundown on Friday, and ends after sundown on Saturday. For religiously observant Jews, this is a time given over to family and prayer, commencing with a large meal on Friday night. Even though most Israelis are not "religious," the Friday night family dinner remains an institution with a powerful grip on the country. Among these "secular" Israelis, Saturdays themselves are often devoted to the pure pleasures of sleeping, eating, and visiting with friends and family. To us, shabbat conveys a texture so substantially different from what is normally implied by the words "Saturday" or "weekend" that we have decided to leave it untranslated. Many other terms that may be puzzling to the reader unacquainted with Jewish or Israeli culture are explained in the glossary at the back of the book. We also occasionally attempt to assist the reader with footnotes.

Of course, where we attempt to avoid getting bogged down in translation we fall headlong into the quicksands of transliteration. Hebrew has a writing system that features optional vowels, three variations on the letter "h," and a character representing a "glottal stop." Two millennia of study have not yet produced a generally accepted standard for writing Hebrew words using Roman letters. The system we use here is designed to sate two competing audiences: for readers who are unfamiliar with Hebrew phonemes, we provide a reasonable approximation of correct pronunciation, given the constraints of the Roman alphabet; for bilingual readers, we try to provide a distinct character corresponding to each Hebrew letter, so that we can also convey the precise sound and spelling of most words. Although there are exceptions, the basic system is as follows:

q = ק	m = ם	z = ז	ʾ = א
r = ר	n = נ	ḥ = ח	b = ב
sh = שׁ	s = ס	ṭ = ט	v = ב
ś = שׂ	ʿ = ע	y = י	g = ג
t = ת	p = פ	k = כ	d = ד
	f = פ	ḫ = כ	h = ה
	tz = צ	l = ל	v = ו

We follow these transliteration rules in the case of all proper names as well, unless an alternate spelling is already generally accepted among readers of English, or unless an individual has a known preference.

∾

Some factual background. A few of our interviewees refer to the June 1993 "Happening," organized by the "Agudah," or "Society"—namely, the organization then known as the Society for the Protection of Personal Rights for Homosexuals, Lesbians, and Bisexuals in Israel. Hundreds of supporters of the Agudah gathered in the park on Sheinqin Street, in bohemian downtown Tel Aviv, for live music and political speeches. More than a picnic, but not a march, this was the first such public event in Israel's history. Also, as we were in the midst of interviewing, we were heartened to learn that a work documenting the lives of Israeli lesbians was in production. It is *Lesbiot: Israeli Lesbians Talk About Sexuality, Feminism, Judaism, and Their Lives*, ed. Tracy Moore (New York: Cassell, 1995).

Our interviews also took place right around the time that "Operation Accountability" was in the news, and this may require some contextualization. Iranian-sponsored Muslim fundamentalist fighters based in the anarchy of Syrian-dominated Lebanon had been periodically launching missiles at the civilian population of northern Israel, and in late July 1993, after the deaths of two Israelis in such attacks, the Israeli army launched air attacks on the area in which the missiles were based. The Israeli strategy was to terrorize the surrounding Lebanese population into appealing to their government to appeal to the Syrians to get the fundamentalists to stop terrorizing the Israelis. At the time, many Israelis feared that the country was on the verge of becoming entangled in a full-scale war.

Perhaps the most important contextualizing fact to keep in mind in reading these stories is that during the same months when we were meeting with and recording the words of these men, representatives of Israel and the PLO were conducting secret meetings of their own, laying the groundwork for the Oslo Peace Accords. Many of our interviewees performed their military service in the West Bank and the Gaza Strip, and almost all of them speak here, some in passionate terms, against the Israeli military control of these territories. Under the Oslo Peace Accords, Israel turned over Gaza and most major centers of Palestinian population on the West Bank to the control of the "Palestinian Authority" in 1995–96, bringing this chapter of Israeli history closer to its final pages. Whether the conclusion will be tragic or comic remains uncertain.

∽

A few explanatory words about the Israeli periodical press are also in order. *Yediᶜot Aharonot* and *Maᶜariv* are Israel's two major mass-circulation daily newspapers. In addition, each urban area in Israel has a number of city newspapers, similar in format to that of the *Village Voice* in New York. In Jerusalem, *Kol Haᶜir* and *ᶜIton Yerushalayim* compete; *Haᶜir* is published in Tel Aviv; and in Haifa, *Kolbo* and *Qol Ḥeifah* (now defunct) shared the market. *Laᵓishah* is a women's magazine of tremendous national popularity, and *Magaᶜim* was long Israel's only commercial publication for gay men.

The official currency of Israel is the "new shekel," but Israelis tend to speak in dollars when dealing with large sums. References to shekels have been retained, so readers are going to have to get out their calculators—as a rule of thumb, remember that there were roughly three shekels to a dollar when we performed these interviews. On the bright side, references to meters, kilometers, and kilograms have been converted into more familiarly archaic feet, miles, and pounds.

In light of this academic superstructure, we should reemphasize here the limitations—and ambitions—of this project. We do not extrapolate from statistical data, nor have we synthesized an overarching metatheory. Our interlocutors were selected unscientifically and we have neither confirmed the historicity of their narratives nor censored the seeming errors of their analysis. The value and the interest of this work begins and ends in the value and interest of the realities created by self-expression. We believe this to be considerable.

INDEPENDENCE PARK

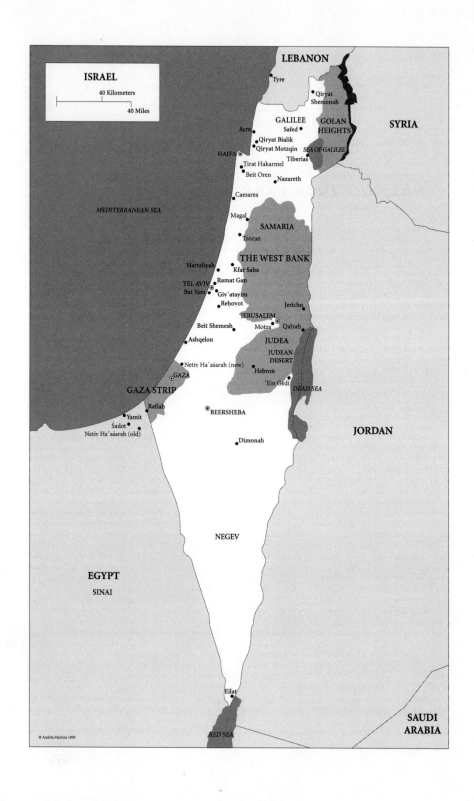

INTRODUCTION

Four Soldiers in Basic Training Had Oral Sex Party

> Four soldiers in basic training for the engineering corps were caught
> "red-handed" while engaging in an oral sex party. The soldiers, who
> according to one account are homosexuals, have been sentenced to
> prison terms of up to 24 days, on charges of shameful conduct.

This eye-catching item appeared in the August 8, 1993, edition of *Maʿariv*,
the widely read Israeli daily newspaper, merely months after the American
debate about "gays in the military" had anticlimaxed in a consensus en-
dorsement of the Clintonian closet under the slogan "don't ask, don't tell."
Imagining how a four-way gay orgy on an American military base would
have played out in the American press does not demand excessive exertion:
the Israeli "sex party" was the very nightmare/fantasy of those who had been
arguing that homosexuals were incapable of military work. Would these soldiers' names have been made public? Would their military careers have been
over? Need one even speculate? Approaching the Israeli "sex party" with this
set of expectations, the American reader of this news item can hardly help
but observe that these were very lucky soldiers: while a month in military
prison could hardly have been a picnic for them, they were to be permitted
to finish their terms of service, and they remained anonymous.

Yet the above report did not constitute the entirety of *Maʿariv*'s article.
The newspaper proceeded to report that these soldiers might have been the
victims of injustice:

The matter has been brought to the attention of the Chief of Staff [Ehud Barak] and the Defense Minister [Yitzḥaq Rabin]. According to army sources, the punishment seems too severe, and is not comparable with the punishment received by soldiers who are caught while engaging in heterosexual relations.[§]

These are amazing sentences. If we can believe our eyes, they indicate—even upon rereading—that for *Maᶜariv* this item was newsworthy not, as American readers might have supposed, because the Israeli army was allowing homosexual soldiers in its ranks, or even because those soldiers were orgying on military bases, but rather because a one-month prison term for being caught engaging in a consensual sex act seemed out of line. Viewed from the American cultural context, both the army and the press seem to have gone absolutely sane.

The story of the oral sex partiers did not end here, either. The plot thickened. Enter Yaᶜel Dayan, member of Knesset from Yitzḥaq Rabin's then-governing Labor Party, daughter of the late Moshe Dayan (the legendary eye-patched archetype of an Israeli general), and leading public ally of the Israeli gay and lesbian civil rights movement. Following *Maᶜariv*'s lead, Dayan exercised her right as a member of Knesset to request the details of the case from the military justice bureaucracy. She received a letter clarifying the actual circumstances of the incident. According to this extraordinary document, the real story was that one soldier bet another one, as a "prank," that the

> party of the first part would not be able to engage in homosexual relations with the party of the second part. . . . In order to win the above-mentioned bet, two soldiers from the division openly engaged in oral sex, in plain view of other soldiers from the base. . . . Afterwards . . . another pair of soldiers decided to demonstrate that it too was capable of engaging in oral sex, without remuneration. These relations too were performed in plain view of the others, in public, on the base.

The document goes on to state that, contrary to the account published in *Maᶜariv*, the perpetrators were not caught "red-handed"; rather, the event

[§] Yonatan Haleli, "Four Soldiers in Basic Training Had Oral Sex Party" (Hebrew), *Maᶜariv*, August 8, 1993. From the Yonah Schimmel Memorial Library Journalism Archives at the Society for the Protection of Personal Rights for Lesbians, Gay Men, and Bisexuals in Israel, Tel Aviv (hereafter abbreviated as "SPPR Archives"). Unless otherwise indicated, all translations from the Hebrew are our own.

became the subject of gossip on the base. When rumors reached the base commander, he ordered an investigation during which the four soldiers "admitted their guilt and expressed regret at their actions."

In the letter sent to Dayan, the army indignantly defended the propriety of the disciplinary proceedings taken in this case:

> The senior commander's approach, if it had indeed become clear to him that this was a case of the engagement in homosexual sexual relations in privacy by those whose orientation was thus and in accordance with the preservation of discretion, would certainly have been different, and he would have found it inappropriate to try them.

The military was quite clear on this point: it was not interested in private gay sex on the part of gay soldiers, whether off or on the base. Paradoxically— mind-bogglingly, perhaps—the military cited its concern about homophobia to justify the severity of the sentences pronounced. This is where the letter became completely surreal:

> The trying officer . . . took into account the humiliation and mental anguish that were caused to other soldiers in the division whose orientation is indeed homosexual, or who were victims of a similar sexual situation against their will, and who were in danger of being hurt or facing a mental crisis because of these pranks and because of this clowning at their expense.
>
> The commander emphasized that he is aware of soldiers serving on the base who do indeed have such an orientation, hence the damage should not be considered to be "possible" but rather as "virtually certain."[§]

The four soldiers in this case received the maximum possible sentence because the army believed that they were *not* gay; their actions were interpreted as both the products and the agents of an atmosphere of homo*phobia*, not, in themselves, homo*sexuality*. The trying officer defined the soldiers' acts as psychological assault: they deserved to be punished severely, not because of how they chose to give each other pleasure, nor even

[§] Letter from the Disciplinary Courts Section of the Legal Supervision and Direction Branch of the Chief Military Counsel's Headquarters; re: Inquiry of MK Yaʿel Dayan, August 16, 1993 (Hebrew), *Magaʿim* 53 (November 1993), p. 11.

because they chose to do it in public, but rather because of the paradoxically persecutory context in which their actions placed gay sexuality. Their crime was the placement of gay sexual expression within a mocking frame.[§]

The lives of gay men in Israel are not what you would think.

∾

Independence Park, Tel Aviv, is the best-known meeting place for gay men in Israel. Independence Park, Jerusalem, is perhaps the second best-known. And "independence," the hope, is the dominant theme in the lives of the twelve men who tell their stories here. They are Jew and Arab; they are twenty-two to seventy-two; one is a waiter, others are students or teachers, another is a prostitute, another a journalist, another a janitor; they are married to women, "married" to men, or single; their families come from Yemen, Germany, Morocco, Romania, Syria, Russia, Iran.

The Independence Parks of Tel Aviv and Jerusalem—which make repeated appearances in stories of these men—are named in celebration of Jewish national independence in the State of Israel, the realization of the Zionist dream of Jewish ingathering from diaspora and consequent auto-emancipation. Yet while Israel may have won its War of Independence decades ago, the actual meaning of independence is still being hammered out daily in the lives of all the country's citizens. For instance: if Israel is an independent entity, it should be clear what is part of the country and what is not. But even such fundamental matters as borders remain blurred: both in the literal, territorial sense of where Israel stops and its neighbors begin; and also in the abstract, larger sense of what, if anything, needs to be differently Israeli—or Jewish—about the national culture. Is it a problem that Israelis wear European clothes and watch American television? And what about running public transportation on the Sabbath, when traditional Jewish law has always forbidden traveling? The Israeli war of, for, about, and because of independence continues on a daily basis.

[§] One should note, of course, that the judge in this case displayed a bizarre degree of confidence in the possibility of accurate knowledge of the "true" sexual orientations of the soldiers involved, and in the epistemological primacy of this knowledge in the interpretation of their actions. You've got to wonder: if the judge had concluded that these soldiers were "actually" closeted "gays," would he then have suspended the sentence on the grounds that their actions were only ostensibly homophobic, and that what they were "really" doing was expressing their repressed desires in the only socially acceptable fashion they felt was available?

So it is not surprising that the theme of independence echoes throughout the lives of these twelve men. But this is not only because, as Israelis, they inevitably occupy a position in relation to Zionist aspirations. It is also because, as gay men recording their personal histories, they tell the tale of a different but analogous kind of war—the one to independently shape their lives in response to a sense of difference that separates them from others. These men narrate the gay life story as a story of auto-emancipation: born in dispersed, disempowered isolation, their rise to self-consciousness engages them in a campaign to foster personal independence through the mapping out of defensible personal borders. In other words: the twelve men who speak in this book tell the story of the gay male struggle for *sexual* autonomy in the context of a culture formed by a very similar modern Jewish struggle for *national* autonomy. It will be up to the reader to decide if, in light of all this struggling, the pastoral associations of the word "park" make the phrase "Independence Park" anything but oxymoronic. Can there be an Independence Park? When? And how?

∾

The average American newspaper-reader might consume hundreds of thousands of words about Israel over a lifetime: journalists do their duty by reporting what public consensus defines as "news," and much of it comes from Israel. But it makes no difference how closely one follows developing events. There is no chance of gaining insight into the Israeli experience from headlined accounts of terror and tears, of horror and hate. The voices of these men illuminate many of the intangible essentials of Israeli life that will never be transmitted through journalistic channels of communication—whether it be the cheapening tedium of military service or the other-worldly serenity that descends on the nation's streets on Friday evening. Inevitably, this cross-section of gay Israeli life is a cross-section of Israeli life.

Israel is a Middle Eastern country roughly the size and shape of New Jersey, with a population of approximately six million. About five million of the people in Israel are Jews, most of whom were either born abroad or are the children of immigrants: roughly two million with ancestors from North Africa and the Middle East; slightly less than two million with roots in Europe and the Americas; half a million from the former Soviet Union. There are also more than a million Arabs living in Israel, both Christian and Muslim, as well as numbers of ethnic Druze, non-Jewish immigrants from the former Soviet Union, and "foreign workers" from Romania, Africa, and the Far East.

Most of the population is concentrated in the relatively small area of the Mediterranean coastal plain surrounding the European-style cities of Haifa (population 300,000) and Tel Aviv (population 500,000, although the surrounding suburban sprawl is home to another million). The downtowns of these beachfront cities are filled with once-whitewashed rain-stained apartment buildings, most of them suffering the painfully public morning-after of modernist, utopian architecture. The inland hills in which the rosy-stone-faced dwellings of the capital city of Jerusalem and its suburbs are located are also a major center—with total population of over half a million, not counting the suburbs—but the historical character of Jerusalem, combined with its large religious and Arab population, give it a markedly different, more inward-turned, character. As one saying goes, "In Haifa you work; in Tel Aviv you play; in Jerusalem, you pray." The half of the country south of Jerusalem is a sparsely populated desert, leading to the Egyptian frontier; the landscape of the far north is lush and wooded, leading up to the borders with Lebanon and Syria. The highlands of Amman, Jordan's capital, can be seen to the east, from the outskirts of Jerusalem.

The State of Israel is the product of the philosophy of Zionism, a form of Jewish politics developed in nineteenth-century Europe which argues that the Jewish people properly constitutes a nation and that its condition of geographic dispersal is an anomaly in need of correction in the form of political autonomy in the ancient Jewish homeland. There is an entire spectrum of Zionisms, from the secularist, socialist doctrine of David Ben-Gurion and the founders of the state, to the messianically militant dogma that was part of the 1980s settler movement. Even as fundamentalist nationalists have become politically ascendant, holding the parliamentary balance of power that allowed Benjamin Netanyahu's center-right Likud party to govern beginning in 1996, increasing numbers of Israelis, particularly the young intellectuals of Tel Aviv, choose to distance themselves from nationalist discourse altogether, proclaiming themselves and their era "post-Zionist." In truth, ideology has never been the sole factor in Israeli history: most Jewish immigrants here have been as much refugees as they have been nationalists. They fled Russia, Poland, Germany during the first half of the century; Egypt, Iraq, Syria, Romania in the 1950s; the Soviet Union and its legacy in the 1970s and 1990s.

The modern history of Israel begins with the immigration of small groups of Eastern European Zionist utopians, together with a number of Yemenite Jews, during the 1880s. They joined the small indigenous Jewish community and the largely Arab population of what was, at this time, a province of the empire of the Ottoman Turks. After the First World War, the land passed into the hands of the British, who were persuaded, for a time, to allow greatly increased Jewish immigration: it was under the aegis of British imperialism, between the First and Second World Wars, that the Jews of Palestine consolidated their major institutions and became a numerically significant presence. But over time, the British became increasingly convinced that Arab sentiment would not permit the peaceful establishment of a Jewish state here, and authorities progressively sealed off the area to further substantial Jewish immigration. This policy was in effect during the years of Nazi Germany's systematic murder of millions of Jews. After the war's conclusion, the British turned the Palestine problem over to the United Nations, which resolved in 1947 to partition British Palestine into an Arab state and a Jewish state. The plan was rejected by the Palestinian Arabs, but accepted by the Zionist leadership, and on May 15, 1948, Israel issued its Declaration of Independence. When the smoke cleared from the first Arab-Israeli war, the new "Jewish state" was in control of most of the former British territory, with the exception of the West Bank and East Jerusalem, controlled by the Kingdom of Transjordan, and the Gaza Strip, occupied by Egypt. It was to these areas that, preceding and during the course of the war, many Palestinian Arab refugees had fled, and it was in these areas that, upon Israel's independence, they were forced to stay. The renewal of Israeli-Arab hostilities in 1967, and further Israeli territorial gains in this year, had the consequence of placing these remaining areas and their largely refugee populations under Israeli control. Israel also occupied Syria's Golan Heights at this time. The Golan was formally annexed by Israel in 1981, although Syria has never ceded this area. In the West Bank (also known in Israel as "Judea and Samaria") and Gaza (also known in Israel, together with the West Bank, simply as "the territories"), the Palestinian Arabs remained under Israeli military occupation until 1995–96, when, under the Oslo Peace Accords negotiated by Yitzḥaq Rabin and Shimᶜon Peres with the Palestine Liberation Organization's Yasir Arafat, Israel turned over Gaza and most major centers of Palestinian population on the West Bank to the control of the "Palestinian Authority." While many agree that Palestinian statehood is now inevitable, the assassination of Rabin in 1995, followed by the defeat of his Labor Party at the polls and the election of Netanyahu, seemed to halt constructive engagement between the Israeli government and the Palestinians.[§]

While Israel has always been a Jewish state, it has never been governed by religious law.[†] This is a difficult point for many Americans to grasp. For centuries, traditional Judaism taught that the goal of Jewish life was the attainment of righteousness through the observance of ritual and moral law as commingled and codified in holy texts. Beginning in the eighteenth century, many Jewish thinkers in Europe took the unprecedented step of proposing modifications in Jewish law with the goal of reconciling religious observance with assimilation to Western culture: the nominally religious cast of modern American Jewry owes much to these thinkers. But from its very start, the mainstream of Zionist thought, by positing the essence of Jewish identity as national peoplehood, has emphasized the political while downplaying the theological. Zionist ideologues thus parted ways from all other modern forms of Judaism, arguing for the importance of preserving the separatist Jewish community which characterized pre-Enlightenment Jewish existence, even while dismissing specifically religious definitions of Jewishness. From this point of view, then, it is a far more righteous act to serve in the Israeli army—putting one's life at risk in the name of the defense of Jewish community—than it is to observe the ritual laws of the Sabbath, even in modified form. To this day, much of Israel's cultural, political, economic, and military elite remains zealously "secularist." The most fashionable restaurants in Tel Aviv never serve kosher food.

An irony: the Zionist argument for Jewish separatism is founded upon the conviction of the necessity of Jewish assimilation of specifically Western values. According to this line of thinking, characteristic of the Herzlian branch of Zionism in particular, Western countries will never allow the Jews to achieve the desirable goal of fully normalizing their status as individual citizens, indistinguishable from others, because of the ineradicable nature of antisemitism. So the Jews must take their fate into their own hands and

[§] There are few better examples of the ideological nature of all historical narrative than the chain of events so blithely summarized above. Certainly, there is no agreement between these two editors regarding relevant facts and contexts—or even vocabulary, for that matter. For more detailed academic accounts, in English, each with its own biases, see Martin Gilbert, *Israel: A History* (New York: Morrow, 1998), Peter Y. Medding, *The Founding of Israeli Democracy 1948–1967* (Oxford University Press, 1990), or Howard M. Sachar, *A History of Israel* (New York: Knopf, 1976–87, 2 vols.).

[†] Israel's secular legal system does, however, recognize the authority of religious courts over some matters of "family law," including marriage and divorce.

withdraw from Europe, even while assimilating on the collective level into a nation indistinguishable from European nations. One of the most central themes of modern Israeli life—and one that is also an important explanation of Israeli attitudes towards Judaism—is this all-important struggle for self-assertion as a "normal" Western society. Dramatic economic expansion in the years since 1967, and a drastic improvement in the Israeli standard of living during this same period, has enabled substantial realization of this goal. Yet the precariously manufactured nature of this attainment shadows everything Israelis say and do: the Israeli elite has overcome its Middle Eastern geography and, by sheer force of will, appended itself culturally and economically to the European continent; it has done so at the cost of perpetual anxieties about being drawn back into its immediate environment.

It is this deep-rooted allegiance to what is perceived as Western that accounts for the current civil status of the category of person referred to in formal Hebrew as a "*homoseqsu̇al,*" and informally as a "*homo.*"[§] In the United States, there is a widespread and foundationless belief that Israeli gay men and lesbians must live lives of unremitting horror in contrast with the dreamy freedom enjoyed by their American counterparts. This is not the case. In fact, the political agenda of the international gay and lesbian civil rights movement has progressed further, and more quickly, in Israel than in almost any other country in the world.

A mad dash through recent landmarks: Israel kept a dormant anti-sodomy law on the books until 1988—but by December of 1991, the Knesset had passed a bill outlawing workplace discrimination based on sexual orientation. In November 1994, the Israeli Supreme Court ruled that the El Al airline was required to grant the gay partner of flight attendant Jonathan Danilowitz all domestic partnership benefits it grants to heterosexual couples. With the opening of the 1994–95 academic year, Israeli teachers of sexual education received an approved statement on homosexuality from the nation's Education Ministry, drawn up with the goal of emphasizing to instructors that "all human beings should be treated with respect and tolerance, even if their sexual orientation is different from that of the majority."[†] In September 1997, the

---

[§] There are other commonly used terms for a homosexual man, including *gay; mitromem,* a mild pejorative in the vicinity of "poofter"; and *ohel batahat,* a stronger pejorative, for someone who "takes it up the ass."

[†] The Director of Sexual Education in the Education Ministry cited in Ran Rezniq's hyperbolically headlined, "Gay Studies Will Be Required in Sex Ed Classes" (Hebrew), *Ha'ir* [undated]. SPPR Archives. The official went on to say, "We want all young people to receive current and precise information." There was no public reaction to this statement.

Supreme Court ruled that the religious Education Minister could not bar the state-run educational television station from broadcasting a teen talk show—produced with taxpayer dollars—featuring a discussion of the difficulties of being young and gay. In the court's formal decision, Justice Ya‘aqoy Qedmi approvingly described the program as teaching "that gays and lesbians are just like other young people."[§] As of 1997, there were three openly gay men in the Israeli foreign service, and their male lovers received all benefits afforded to the heterosexual spouses of diplomats. In June 1998, Adir Steiner, the gay partner of the late openly gay Colonel Doron Meisel, in settling his long-running suit against the Defense Department, received a major portion of the pension he would have received had he been a military spouse, as well as formal recognition as a military widower. Together with the relatives of other deceased veterans, Steiner will receive an annual letter of condolence from the Minister of Defense on Israeli Memorial Day. Also in 1998, Israel's newly enacted sexual harassment law included "sexual orientation" as an explicitly protected category; the Civil Service ruled that the spouse of an out lesbian nursery-school teacher will receive a state pension as a widow, should she survive her partner; and the Attorney General ruled that the Customs Department must allow the same-sex domestic partner of an immigrant to share certain of the tax benefits for which immigrants are eligible. In November 1998, lesbian community activist Miḣal ‘Eden was elected to the Tel Aviv city council, after campaigning as an advocate for "queer" constituents. Ten years ago it was unclear whether gays and lesbians in Israel even *had* an agenda; the past decade has seen demands met even as they are articulated.[†]

To understand this dynamic, we need only look a bit more closely at a sample landmark—one among so many. Though homosexual behavior or identity was never officially sufficient grounds for exemption or discharge from the military service required of Israeli Jews, for many years all gays were officially barred from access to classified information. According to a 1983 directive, every Israeli soldier known or suspected to be gay had to undergo examination by a mental health officer and the security clearance department. (In practice, enforcement of these policies was left to the discretion of unit commanders.)

On February 2, 1993, nationally televised Knesset hearings on the status of

---

[§] *Society for the Protection of Personal Rights for Gay Men, Lesbians, and Bisexuals in Israel vs. Minister of Education, Culture, and Sport,* Israeli Supreme Court Sitting as High Court of Justice 273/97 (June 24, 1997).

[†] For a more detailed analysis of the legal landscape, see Alon Harel, "Gay Rights in Israel: A New Era?" *International Journal of Discrimination and the Law* 1 (1996), 261–78.

lesbians, gay men, and bisexuals were organized under the sponsorship of Yaᶜel Dayan. At these hearings, ᶜUzi Even, chair of the Department of Chemistry at the University of Tel Aviv, spoke about being bounced out of his very senior position as a researcher for military defense in 1981, after a routine security check revealed that he was gay. The scientist appealed for the removal of all remaining restrictions on the military service of gay men and lesbians, invoking a broadly popular vocabulary of pride in national service:

> I haven't come to ask charity or pity: I have one request: remove the limitations you have burdened us with. Let us contribute to the society in which we have grown up. Let us integrate ourselves and contribute from our energies and abilities that which we can.[§]

The public response to Professor Even's challenge was overwhelmingly positive, and the following day's papers reported on him as "impressive" and "respectable." More important, Yitzḥaq Rabin—who as prime minister and defense minister had ultimate authority over military policy—took less than a week to respond publicly: "I don't see any reason to discriminate against homosexuals."[†] Rabin initiated the procedure necessary to alter the orders disqualifying homosexual soldiers from access to classified information. Today, commanding officers are still required to report on the sexual orientation of their soldiers—but there are no officially mandated consequences attendant upon the army's possession of this information, and all security clearances are assessed on a case-by-case basis.

Virtually the only public figures to speak out against the 1993 Dayan hearings were the leaders of the orthodox Jewish political parties. Yitzḥaq Levi, of the National Religious Party, issued a call to prevent the "disgrace" of the Knesset and to "forbid the entrance of homosexuals and lesbians into the Knesset compound." Rabbi Yosef Ba-gad, of the ultranationalist "Homeland" party, appealed to all members of the Knesset to participate in a "living chain" around the Knesset compound, in order to prevent the hearings from taking place.[*] But in the event, Ba-Gad's living chain never material-

[§] Ḥayim Shibi, "Out of the Closet, into the Knesset" (Hebrew), Yediᶜot Aharonot, February 3, 1993. SPPR Archives. See also Amir Peleg, "A Few Hours of Pride" (Hebrew), Yediᶜot Aharonot, February 5, 1993. SPPR Archives.

[†] Amnon Barzilay, "Rabin: I Don't See Any Reason to Discriminate Against Homosexuals" (Hebrew), Ḥadashot, February 8, 1993. SPPR Archives.

[*] Ḥayim Shibi, "Ba-gad Will Block the Entrance of Homosexuals into the Knesset" (Hebrew), Yediᶜot Aharonot, February 2, 1993. SPPR Archives.

ized, and Levi's attempt to ban the event would have needed the support of the Speaker of the Knesset, Sheyah Vais, of the governing Labor Party. Vais was not inclined to support Ba-gad. Indeed, Vais issued a public statement chastising Levi for his intolerance:

> I recognize the basic civil right to be different. In every enlightened parliament in the world this right is respected, and I do not think that the Knesset is entitled to neglect this segment of the public.[§]

In the defining rhetorical move of classical Western political liberalism, Vais characterized the mission of the politician as the defense of liberty—and not, as Levi might have hoped, the defense of virtue. Vais asserted that the liberal ideal of civil protection of difference characterizes all "enlightened" democracies—and thus it will characterize the Israeli democracy as well. Significantly, he could take for granted that his audience shared his deep concern with bringing the nation into conformity with "enlightened" political standards. Vais set himself up as nothing less than the guardian of Israel's precarious status as a certain desirable kind of nation—a status that he encouraged his audience to view Levi as recklessly endangering. In the Speaker's spin, the civil emancipation of those of minority sexual orientations was important because it had to be understood as nothing less than a litmus test for Israel's status as a modern nation.

This book emerges from the energy of these thrilling years, from the rush of events that was fundamentally transforming the politics of being gay and Israeli. Yet perhaps the most interesting characteristic of the Israeli landmarks in gay and lesbian civil rights of the early and middle 1990s is that they materialized without the help of grassroots organization or politicization on the part of a self-conscious community. What's more, the emergence of a body of gay and lesbian civil rights legislation did not instantaneously and automatically transform the daily life of very many individuals. Up until the late 1990s, large numbers of Israeli men and women who engaged in homosexual sexual conduct regularly did not identify themselves as "gay" or "lesbian." Many, many other men and women did view themselves as existing in a distinct sexual category, but expended vast amounts of energy in attempting to exert control over the access of others to this information. In other words, they were closeted. And even among those who chose to live publicly "out" lives in which their sexuality was an integral part of their personas and

---

[§] "MK Levi Appeals to Deny Homosexuals and Lesbians Entrance to the Knesset Compound" (Hebrew), *Yediʿot Aharonot*, December 24, 1992. SPPR Archives.

relationships, most were hostile to the idea that collective organization or identification had anything to offer. As a consequence, there was, historically, nowhere in Israel where you could find the kind of semi-separatist urban community that has traditionally been the sustenance of queer culture in Europe and America. Throughout the early 1990s, the scene in Tel Aviv, the undisputed center of Israeli "alternative lifestyles," consisted primarily of one exclusively gay sauna for men, one mixed cafe, and an average of two mostly gay male bars (their location and ownership frequently changing). Thanks to a number of anonymous foreign donors, a gay, lesbian, and bisexual community center in downtown Tel Aviv was opened in 1993. It is run by the organization commonly known as the "Agudah," Hebrew for "Society," and short for the Society for the Protection of Personal Rights for Homosexuals, Lesbians, and Bisexuals in Israel (now called the Association of Gay Men, Lesbians, Bisexuals, and Transgendered People in Israel), which, with one full-time and two part-time employees, was the gay community's sole social and political organization. Besides one occasionally cruisy section of Tel Aviv's beach, the public parks—particularly the parks named "Gan Haᶜatzmaᵓut" or "Independence Park," in both downtown Tel Aviv and Jerusalem—remained central institutions of Israeli gay male culture. A magazine for gay men called *Magaᶜim*—"contacts" or "touches"—printing personal advertisements, black-and-white pornographic photography, and news and feature articles, was published with varying frequency from 1987 to 1995. And that was basically it. For the entire country. So even though the men who speak in this book were living in an era of extraordinary political transformation, many speak from the heart about painfully formative experiences, seeking gay institutions in what seemed to be an airtight social vacuum.

Most recently, however, culture has begun to catch up with politics. In 1997, *Magaᶜim* was replaced by the incomparably more sophisticated *Hazman Havvarod* ("The Pink Time"), "an Israeli queer monthly" publishing news, features, a cultural and social calendar, personals, and enough advertisements to betray the birth pangs of an economically empowered subculture in Tel Aviv. The Jerusalem Open House, "a lesbigay community center," opened its doors in 1999, with a commitment to serve all Jerusalemites, including Arabs and religious Jews. Tel Aviv, Jerusalem, and Haifa have increasingly popular gay pride festivals in June of each year. And there is no missing the most sensational of the many recent cultural sea-changes: the Israeli transgender scene has suddenly and unexpectedly received a welcome spotlight. When this book was in the making, Israeli drag queens were underground and out of sight. By 1998, a cross-dressing troupe called "Pesyah's

Daughters" was hosting the most highly rated Friday-night television show. And then there was the glorious Dana International, a 27-year-old out transsexual, born Yaron Kohen to working-class Yemenite parents in Tel Aviv. This statuesque raven-haired beauty won the nomination to represent Israel in the 1998 Eurovision song contest, an annual pop competition broadcast in 25 countries to an estimated audience of 600 million. (Past winners of the contest include ABBA and Celine Dion.) And on May 9, 1998, she won the contest—with a song called "Diva," of course. Dana International has become one of Israel's most visible, if controversial, public figures—formally received in the Knesset, congratulated by the prime minister, appointed "ambassador at large," her popularity crosses social, ethnic, and generational lines. But beyond topping the charts, her Eurovision victory has allowed Dana to become, for many, the symbol of the international respect accorded a country that honors the universal dignity of humankind, and as such she has become the standard-bearer of Israeli secularism. Gil Samsonoy, chair of the Israel Broadcasting Authority committee that originally nominated Dana for Eurovision, was unequivocal about the politics of the Israeli embrace of Dana in particular and gender transgression in general, telling one journalist: "We should be seen as a liberal, free country."[§] And Dana plays her part well—the words "democracy" and "human rights" rolled off her lips in the press conferences celebrating her victory. She has repeatedly proclaimed, "I represent gays and lesbians from all over the world . . . I represent the regular Israelis, all the Arabs, the Christians . . . Everyone who wants to be represented by me." Through Dana, the Israeli mainstream seems to be marching beyond its not-so-far-gone combination of ignorance and prejudice, past the still-fresh achievements of political tolerance, and into what appears to be an appreciation of its own ability to celebrate its margins. According to Ya³ir Qedar, former editor of *Hazman Havvarod*, Dana is "the best thing to happen to the gay community here in fifty years."[†] Once, the gay men of Israel were alone in Independence Park. But the future lies with those who, a month after the fiftieth anniversary of Israeli independence, attended an open-air drag festival in Tel Aviv.[*] An estimated 10,000 people attended—in Independence Park.

[§] Allison Kaplan Sommer, "The Divine Miss Dana," *The Jerusalem Post*, May 10, 1998.

[†] Ya³ir Qedar cited in Lee Hockstader and Ramit Plushnik, "Israel's Highly Unorthodox Pop Sensation," *Washington Post*, November 5, 1998.

[*] This event took place on May 22, 1998. When police attempted to shut the festival down earlier than had originally been agreed upon with its organizers, the crowd rioted, harassing police officers and blocking traffic on one of Tel Aviv's major thoroughfares.

SHAHAR

We found our way to Shaḥar through a twisted chain of acquaintances: to be precise, a friend of mine from college shared an apartment with a classmate of a friend of Shaḥar's from the army. Word spread along this lengthy grapevine that Amir and I were interviewing gay men for a book, and Shaḥar sent word back that he would be more than willing to spill his guts. We had no objections to talking to someone who was described to us as a twenty-something super-macho farm boy who had, after years of struggle, embraced the gay scene of Tel Aviv. Telephone calls ensued, and on an extraordinarily balmy July evening Shaḥar found us—sweat-drenched—at the door to his apartment.

Shaḥar—youthful, blond, muscled, tight t-shirted and Hawaiian-shorted— could not have been a more gracious host, or a more cooperative interviewee. We seated ourselves in his living room, decorated in the makeshift aesthetic familiar to many college students. There may have been a brightly colored sheet on the couch, or a stereo resting on a milk crate. As we sipped icy water, we began to chat, the tape recorder rolling. In a neighboring apartment building, an entire family of newly immigrated Russian musicians had taken up residence, and they treated us to rather invasive classical accompaniment. Muffling the music would mean closing the doors to the balcony, and the sealing of any potential source of air was absolutely out of the question, so the strains of their squeaky strings could be heard quite clearly in the background as we spoke.

∾

My PARENTS ARE FROM HAIFA—they were born there. My father comes from a Polish family, and my mother is Russian. They didn't come from farming families. I don't know what their parents did. I guess they, you know, worked in factories. My grandmother doesn't hardly remember anything any more, so I can't even ask her. But both my parents are from a totally urban background, city high schools, like, everything in the city. They met in the army, in Naḥal, the branch of the army that combines military service with the "pioneer" life, setting up a communal settlement or something like that. So after the army, they decided they would go live on a kibbutz together with their unit. This was sometime around the fifties, the end of the fifties. They were good Zionists.

They went to Kibbutz Magal, which is between Haifa and Tel Aviv, near Caesarea. It was a new settlement then, and they were one of the first couples to get married there. And then my brother was born. And then about a year later, I was born. My first sister was born when I was, like, six, and then they decided that we were leaving the kibbutz—my second sister was born a few years after that.

I don't remember much from the kibbutz. What I do remember is the children's room. All the kids lived together in the children's room, and there was a care-giver, and when she would leave we would throw pillows at one another, really let loose. And then I remember the traumatic day when my mother came and said that we were leaving. She said that we were going to a new place, but we would, you know, come back and visit. I didn't want to leave.

It was, like, a real trip, being on the kibbutz. All the kids would sit together at night, and my father would come, and he would tell bedtime stories. We all lived together in a separate building, in the children's room. So we were all together, you know, all the time. We would shower together and sleep together and eat together and shit together—everything together. A real, like, socialist experience—together all the time. I had no idea that people did things differently in other places. This seemed the natural thing to do. It was just, you know, natural. That's the way it was.

My father really, really, wanted to stay on the kibbutz, but my mother just couldn't take it anymore. The whole family thing really bothered my mother, that she couldn't raise her own children. We had to be back in the children's house by four o'clock—you couldn't stay with your parents any later than that. And that bothered her. My mother wanted to raise her own kids. For instance, there was the whole thing with names. She had to rename us—she wanted to name me Liʾor or something like that, but she wasn't allowed, because, you know, there already was one Li'or in my age group. So she called me Shaḥar. There were all sorts of other things too, the whole way the kibbutz was put together. And she wasn't really doing what she wanted to do, either. She just worked in the kitchen. She wasn't even a housewife. She didn't even have a home to take care of. Just a room, and that was it.

So we left the kibbutz and moved to Moshav Ṡadot, in the Yamit area of the northern Sinai, in 1971.[§] It was at this time that they began to build the first Jewish settlements in the Sinai, and this was one of them. There were advertisements in the newspapers that encouraged people to go—they offered apartments there at a very cheap price, because, you know, no one wanted to live there, in that hole. It was just sand. I remember when I first got there. There was nothing but sand. Nothing. It was, like, gravel and sand, that's what there was. My parents left the kibbutz, with nothing except for three kids, and, together with some other families, built this moshav.[†] They began from scratch. They left the kibbutz with hardly any money at all. And they made the desert bloom. That's what they did. They made the place into a fucking garden.

It was an agricultural moshav, the only thing to do there was, like, agriculture. There wasn't anything else around for miles and miles. And no one knew if it was good for farming or bad for farming. In the end, it turned out that, you know, it was a terrific place for farming. Excellent climate, sun all year round, there was no winter, it was always sunny—and it wasn't that horrible desert heat that comes from the east. It was pleasant. They planted, and they built, and they made. They made a moshav.

From around ages six through ten, before I, you know, developed sexually, I really didn't have any problems with the other kids. I got along fine. At least that's what I remember. I didn't feel different, I didn't feel like I stood out, even though I remember that I was really drawn toward the girls' groups. I wanted to play with the girls, to be with the girls. I had no desire to play soccer, or all of those violent games. I liked jump rope and hopscotch.

I was around ten or eleven when I, like, figured it out. Around this time I remember that people began to call me names, faggot and sissy and so on. I was a girlish boy. And the other boys would, you know, laugh at me. And

[§] Sinai: Desert peninsula between Africa and Asia; conquered by Israel in the 1967 Six-Day War.

[†] moshav: Agricultural or manufacturing colony, modeled on the kibbutz, but capitalist and individualist in its organization—products, in most cases, are marketed cooperatively while property and profits are privately held.

then I learned these words, for the first time. I began to become more interested, to read all sorts of things, to try to figure it out. I was around eleven, something like that. Before that, it was just natural, I was with the girls, and, you know, it really didn't bother me.

Around this age I began to read all sorts of pornographic books. A kid in my class, I don't know where he got them from, he had all sorts of fuck books, stories in Hebrew, describing orgies and stuff like that. All straight of course. And we would read them, like, pass them around, you know. And then I began to write my own book. A real novelist! This book had all of my crazy fantasies, written down. It was insane—I would, like, describe these huge orgies, where I would have whole fucking brigades of men sleeping with one another. Without any women at all, only men. There wasn't a single girl. It wasn't usually military, it was more like a sort of big class trip, everyone goes out together, only the guys, and everybody fucks everybody. And I would make drawings too, of penises. I would use all this to masturbate with. I would masturbate while writing. But by the time anything was written, like, I had already used it once, and it didn't do anything for me. I had to make up new things all the time.

I didn't think that there were other people in the world who thought about these things, that there were real books that wrote about these things. I was totally cut off in that place. We would never go to the city. The closest city was Beersheba, it wasn't like, you know, you could go there just to buy magazines. I don't even think that at that time there were any magazines of that kind in Israel, at least not like today. And there wasn't anyplace I could get them from, in any case. And I really didn't even think they existed.

We had the book, *Behind the Fig Leaves*, a totally idiotic book, that book. A sex guide. For young people. I'm surprised you don't know it, I think, like, every kid in the country read that book. Every house I go to, I see that book. A terrible book, in my opinion they should have taken it out of circulation a long, long time ago. I, of course, couldn't have cared less about the other parts, I went straight to the section on homosexuality, to see what it was. And I remember that it was such a shock—it was, you know, the first of the many nails that built my closet. It said there that homosexuality was really like a sickness, a perversion, something that was wrong, and that demanded treatment. Everyone has it, all children have it, but if the condition, you know, persists and becomes more serious, you should seek professional treatment to try to change it. I really internalized that, very deep inside. And then all those names that people called me really began to bother me, all those things that the other kids would say. But I would just close my eyes and keep on going.

About a year and a half after I began writing down my fantasies, my parents found my book. And we had a very short conversation about it. "Sex is a beautiful thing, don't ruin it." And that was all. My mother said that. I was in the kitchen, and she took me aside and began saying, "Today I was looking for something in your room and . . . ," and I already knew that she had found the notebook, the second she said this, boom, my heart was pounding. Because, like, I knew that there was something wrong with what I had done. That's what I knew. It was very vulgar sex. I knew it was wrong. And then she said to me, "Sex is a beautiful thing, don't ruin it." And she, you know, said to me something like, "Where is this from, did you make these stories up, or did you copy them from somewhere?" I said I copied them. I said, "From a book, from a book, I copied it out. Don't worry, I just copied it out of some book." I, like, calmed her down by saying that I wasn't gay, basically. "I'm normal, I'm not like that." I remember that my father had a reaction, but I can't remember what it was. He also, like, tossed something off, but it was, you know, something sort of like what my mother said. Or maybe he didn't say anything at all. It might be. I don't remember. Maybe I'm repressing it.

One time, maybe a few months after she found the book, my mother, like, walked in on me when I was jerking off in my room. She just, you know, went right back out and closed the door when she realized. Afterwards, she said, "Shaḥar, it's OK, but next time, don't do it like that, do it a little more privately, quietly." Something like that, "It's totally OK, but be more careful." Along those lines.

I really loved the openness, the wide open spaces. Miles and miles of dunes. I would go off by myself, until all I would see was sky, maybe a single raven in the sky, and that's it. I would have, like, episodes of violence, but not really directed against anything. These sort of random outbursts. I would go off and shout—for no reason at all—I would go off by myself and shout at the top of my lungs, to release it all, to get it out in the open. I would shout, "I'm queer," as loud as I could. Just to, you know, get it off my chest. I would shout "faggot, faggot!" or I would shout all sorts of things at God—I would say God's name to see if I would be consumed by hellfire. I would go and shout, "Adonai, Adonai!"—bullshit like that. I would curse God.

Now I remember, I would go out there and, you know, jerk off sometimes also. It was really a kind of therapy for me, an escape. I would go out by myself, and I would do whatever I wanted. I would take all my clothes off and walk naked. It was just total emptiness. It's not just that there was no one there at the moment—it was a completely empty place. You could, like, go off, disappear on the other side of the moshav, past a few dunes, and then all you could see was sand, a little vegetation here and there, palm trees. A different world. No people, no nothing. Like totally free.

My brother was a bird-watcher. He was always, you know, looking for birds in the sky. He had binoculars, he would walk around with them around his neck all day long. And I would go with him, wandering around, looking for all kinds of birds.

But searching the sky for birds was not my thing. I preferred looking at the ground, and thinking. So looking for coins was just the thing for me. You can look for coins at the same time as your mind is occupied thinking. This area was once, you know, a trade route, and there are a lot of ancient coins there. I found, like, some Roman coins, and some from the Byzantine era. I would clean them with lemon juice—I would leave them to soak for a day or two, and then rub them with an eraser, and they were clean. I still have over a hundred, a lot of them are really tiny, very worn.

I had great eyes, I was a real hawk. I would just walk along, and they would jump out at me. No one else could find any. No one. I felt really bad about it. Sometimes, when I would take my little sister, I would bring along some coins, and I would, you know, toss them in her path just so that she could find them, so she could say that she had found them. And she wouldn't find them! I would have to say to her, like, "Look at the ground, open your eyes, I'm just sure there's got to be a coin here." And she would say, "Where, where, I don't see anything." And I would have to be like, "Here, here, it's here, look, you found a coin." Like that.

I would find all sorts of shit—pottery, jars. That was my central hobby in life. I got a lot of books about coins from my parents for my birthdays. I spent a lot of time on it. I organized them, and all that. I think it was just, you know, the first sign of greed. I loved money so much. It may be that I collected them because, you know, I really, really liked to see money. I liked money, I liked the sense that it was worth something.

I wasn't the pioneering type. I hated working in the fields. I really hated it. Real hate. They expected me to work in the fields—I was supposed to be a farmer, I was supposed to be dying to go out to the fields on Shabbat. People could stay home from school because they were working in the fields with their parents—that was totally acceptable. And if the moshav was, you know, preparing shipments or something like that, everyone would go to school late, a half hour, an hour, because we would be helping to prepare the shipments. At times like these, every morning we would prepare shipments, then go to school, and right after school it was back off to the fields. I lived, ate, and breathed the farming life. They expected it from us. To wake up on Shabbat and work. The beginning of the season, the end of the season, whenever there was pressure, we would work. The whole family, off to work in the fields.

And I hated it. I hated that agriculture thing. It was the absolute pits. You know, the heat, and the aching muscles, and the sand sticking to your knees. Terrible. Not for me. And I would always be telling my father, "I'm not going to be a farmer. When I grow up, I'm not going to be a farmer." I lowered their expectations right away, about everything having to do with farming.

My older brother, he's a farmer in his soul. I'll explain to you what that means, to be a farmer in your soul. At one point, I was, you know, in charge of a field of cucumbers. And I would get up in the morning, and I would see that my cucumber vines had grown longer, with a lot more leaves—and it would really depress me. It would, like, really fucking get me down. Because it meant that I was going to have to, you know, go around the entire field one more time, and wrap the damn vines around their stakes—when they've grown a certain amount, you have to rotate them around their stakes, so they don't fall off. And it would depress me so much. I would be like, "Oh shit, here we go again, the damn things grew again." But my brother, he would go out to the fields, and if he saw that, you know, the cucumbers grew more leaves, or the tomatoes or something, he would be all sunshine, he would just glow. He'd be really pleased—"Wow, wonderful, terrific, it grew, it sprouted. The first tomato!" and all that bullshit. He loves it. He lives it. I mean, I like it also—but not when it gets to my poor little knees. It was a total nightmare for me. And that's it. I'm not a farmer.

My first time was with a Bedouin boy.[§] You know, the Arab men, you can always see them walking hand in hand. You see it a lot, like when you're on reserve duty in the territories, for instance. They don't have a problem with it. I don't even know if it's a sexual thing for them, but, you know, in the east, the Arabs, they don't have any problem with the whole thing, getting it up the ass and all that, or walking with another guy. I would go with my father to Gaza all the time, to the open-air markets, you know, all sorts of markets. And you would see it a lot, guys hugging each other. I just thought it was the greatest

---

[§] Bedouin: Tent-dwelling Muslim desert nomads who usually migrate in a seasonal pattern, following sources of water and pasture for sheep and goats.

fucking thing in the world. I would see the boys walking arm in arm in the road in Gaza, with their flowing robes, like they were queens. It was terrific.

Sometimes, when I wandered along the shore, there would be some Bedouins wandering around there too, in their big white flowing robes, without anything underneath. You would never find a lot of them—maybe every mile or so there would be one guy, wandering around. And, like, you understood, you knew what they were doing there. So I would feel a lot more comfortable on the beach, a lot freer. And I think that was why I had my first time in the dunes. Because I felt more comfortable with them.

One time someone came over to me. He was a boy also, maybe thirteen, something like that. He just walked up to me, and I, of course, you know, went completely hysterical. He began to stroke my leg. We went over to this kind of hollow in the sand, and we fooled around. He gave me a hand job, and I came. We didn't talk at all. There was no need, no point in wasting words. I remember that he was uncut. That was also something that, like, really freaked me out. And then he wanted me to do the same for him, but I got up and ran away. He ran after me, cursing me, but I ran and ran and ran. I caught a ride back to the moshav.

And that was the first. I would see them and all that, but I don't think it ever got to physical touching again. I was, like, scared out of my wits. I always had in the back of my mind that someone from the moshav would catch me. I was totally hysterical about it. I really wanted to keep it quiet.

I felt awful afterwards. I felt like I had done something wrong. I swore to myself that it would never happen again. I disgusted myself so much. I was covered with sand and come, and I went home and scrubbed it off. Awful. That feeling was part of my life for a long time to come. To get laid, to enjoy it, and afterwards to feel, you know, evil, disgusting. That terrible feeling that you had done something wrong.

And then there was the time with the boy in the pool. This was maybe two years later, I was fifteen. We were playing in the pool, about four of us, we were rolling around in the nude. I was the oldest there. It was at night. And somehow or other, you know, we were just kidding around, we begin kind of showing off our cocks to each other. And suddenly I noticed that one of them had gotten a hard on. He was, like, eleven or twelve. So I went to him and took him aside and said, "Listen, you don't know what you're doing, the other kids are going to laugh at you, be careful, this isn't good." I basically tried to, you know, put him into the closet. "Look out, this isn't good." And he said to me, "It's OK, it's OK, don't worry. The two of us will stay here together afterwards." I said OK. And then after maybe two hours the other two left, and we were alone. We got out of the pool, and then there was, you know, a very short masturbation thing. Very quick.

And once again, as soon as I came, I got very freaked out. I began to really let loose on him. I said to him, "You don't know what you're doing, what's your problem—you should sleep with girls, it's better, it's more fun." And he looked at me, and was like, "What, you don't like it, you never tried it with guys?" It was a long time later that I found out that this boy had slept with just about all the kids there. He got everyone into his bed. I found this out later. A real slut, he was.

But I really, totally distanced myself from him after this. I wouldn't talk to him, like, nothing. I cut off all contact with him. I would see him and just ignore him. I made sure that it was totally clear to him that there was nothing gay about what had happened, that it didn't mean anything to me. And we just stopped talking to each other.

I really can't explain why it was so easy for him. I don't know. Maybe he never read that piece of shit book *Behind the Fig Leaves*. Maybe that's it.

I was around sixteen years old when the Camp David accords came along, and all of a sudden there was the possibility of Israeli withdrawal from the Sinai that fell with a big thud on the moshav and on all the moshavim in the area.[§] I began this huge flurry of activism in the Movement to Stop the Retreat from Sinai. I became involved in Hateḥiyah, the right-wing political party, which began to, you know, snowball its activities against the withdrawal—it was the only party that actively opposed Camp David.

It was the natural thing to do, from my point of view. I joined the movement as a boy who lives in the Sinai and who disagrees with this awful decree, which was basically an Israeli retreat. All of the kids on the moshav were, in one way or another, active in all sorts of things that were going on. The moshav had a few of its own demonstrations, I don't know if you remember—we closed roads, blocked traffic, things like that.

I think that all of this made me closer to my father. Because my father was very, like, fanatic about this subject, the withdrawal. So suddenly there was some communication between us, something there had never been before. Also, suddenly I got something to do, and I became a leader. People came to

§ When Prime Minister Menaḥem Begin signed the Camp David Accords in 1978, he agreed to a full Israeli withdrawal from the Sinai—including the destruction of all Jewish settlements—in return for Egyptian recognition of Israel and the formal signing of a peace treaty. The withdrawal was completed in April 1982.

me, relied on me. I met a lot of people who were older than me, I was busy all the time. I really put everything into it. This was the subject that, you know, filled most of my time. Most important, I began going to Tel Aviv for demonstrations.

I had never been in Tel Aviv until I was about thirteen. We went on a school trip, my whole class, at thirteen. And then I remember that we decided as a group where we wanted to go—everyone marked the places they'd heard about on our map. People, you know, marked the Dolphinarium, Dizengof Square, the boardwalk, and so on. And I, of course, I insisted that we go to Independence Park—"We just have to see that place," I said. I was thirteen, but, you know, I knew that Independence Park was the gays' place—that's what I knew about Independence Park. I knew that at night it was a center for gays. Don't ask me how. I think I read it in newspapers, I don't know. But I knew. So I dragged my entire class along with me, and we traipsed in. It was a very quick visit, and it was the middle of the day. We went in, and we went out. But I saw some men there, and I knew. I saw that, like, people were cruising around in the bushes. I had that knowledge, that they were like me, that they were also gay. And it really got to me. I was totally shaking all over. Afterwards, we walked down to the beach and went to the Dolphinarium. And that was my first encounter with Tel Aviv, and with Independence Park.

But now, within the framework of the Movement to Stop the Retreat, I began going to a lot of demonstrations in Tel Aviv. One time, there was a demonstration downtown, and I left the demonstration in the middle, left all of my friends, told them I was fed up, some excuse. And I went to the park. This was the first time I went to the park by myself. It was the middle of the day. I was about sixteen. So I lit up the first cigarette of my life at the entrance, and I went in.

As soon as I went into the park, someone just, you know, came up to me and began talking to me. We went into the bushes together, but the moment he pulled down my underwear, I came. We talked a little afterwards. We sat down on a bench, and he just talked to me, and I said that I didn't know what I was doing, what I wanted, that I was confused, and so on. And he just, you know, stroked my stomach and listened. And then I began to get another hard on. And he took one look at my crotch and said, "I don't see any confusion here. It's OK, don't worry, relax. You are 'like that.' You can relax." And that's it. He gave me his telephone number, and of course, you know, I didn't keep it. That was my first time in the park.

After this, I began making up all sorts of excuses to get myself to Tel Aviv at night, so I could go to the park. My grandmother still had an apartment in Haifa at the time, although she didn't live there any more, she lived in a nursing home. So I would tell my parents that I was, you know, going to the apartment in Haifa—but I wouldn't even get all the way to Haifa. I would go to Tel Aviv and meet someone in the park.

I had no strategy in the park. Each time, I had to take a quarter of an hour to pull myself together just to go there. And no matter how hard I tried, the moment I went into the park I would begin to have these sort of, you know, psychosomatic convulsions in my stomach, like I was going to puke. From overexcitement, nervousness, everything together. So I would just walk in, begin crossing to the other side, and the first one who caught me could have me. It didn't make a difference to me, how old he was, what he looked like. Nothing made a difference to me at all. Whoever took the initiative and came up to me and talked to me—and didn't walk away once he realized how hysterical I was—I would go with him. I preferred to do it in the park, but I would go to people's apartments if they wanted. I didn't care who it was, I totally didn't want to hear a telephone number afterwards, nothing. I would always, you know, get a telephone number after the screw, of course, and I would always take the telephone number, and toss it in the garbage on my way out. All I wanted was to get the hell out of there once it was done. I felt terrible every time, and I kept going back. That was Tel Aviv at sixteen.

No one knew about me on the moshav, of course. Nothing. The moshav was one world, and then, like, I had the park, which was my own, private world.

I began to move closer to what was expected of me at this time. I stopped hanging out only with the girls, I began to play soccer. I had a good friend, a guy my age. There was nothing sexual about it—I mean, we would jerk off together, but it was just, like, pals who were masturbating together. It was all in a totally straight context. We weren't doing it so we could touch each other. We were, like, doing it to masturbate, to see each other, to laugh. For the hell of it.

And then the movie *Cruising* came to the moshav's movie theater. And I sat there, like, shaking throughout the entire movie. From beginning to end. Totally hysterical. And the thought that someone might notice how I was behaving, you know, it made me even more hysterical. I was very nervous during those years. Very.

I didn't think there was such a thing as a gay relationship. I had no idea that there was such a thing as a "relationship" in that kind of life. It seemed to me that, you know, people are gay for a while, and then they get over it, they change. That it doesn't exist as, you know, a lifelong thing, where you can create something stable, that you can stay this way for your whole life. I thought that you had to get married, which could only be with a girl, and to make a family, which could only be with a girl. And that's how I saw my future. I didn't see any possibility of anything else, that there are other ways of living, different ways of life.

My older brother isn't very good-looking, and he was also always sort of an outsider, very awkward physically. He wasn't a very sexual type. His first girlfriend was at sixteen or seventeen, and he married her. They're still married. Very conventional, my brother, like, very conventional. Also in everything having to do with sex. Very, very conventional. He lives his own life, he does, you know, all sorts of things with birds. He lives in his own world, my brother. So I certainly never felt any pressure from him. The pressure was that all of my parents' expectations for girlfriends and success with sex and girls fell on me. Because my brother pretty much, you know, cut himself off from that. And I was also better-looking than him, so, like, it was natural that it all fell on me.

By the time I was seventeen, I had the image of a real free spirit on the moshav. I had a reputation as a Don Juan, girls were always calling me up. And I, you know, put on a sort of show for my parents, as a straight. I don't think they thought for a moment that it might be that I was still feeling things along the lines of those stories they found when I was a kid. But I didn't give them any reason to suspect anything. It was repressed in such an extreme way that I didn't even let myself think about it, so certainly they weren't thinking about it. I mean, I knew that I would go to Tel Aviv every now and then because I was horny and I needed to find something, I had to act on my fantasies. But, like, beyond that there was nothing. Nothing. I totally disconnected myself from this part of me. I never thought about it. I was totally removed. And I would tell my parents about, like, all kinds of girls, and sort of toss in that we were screwing, to make a kind of show for them.

I would lie. During this period I lied a lot. Well, I wouldn't lie directly, I wouldn't lie straight out. If they asked me questions about sex, I would say, you know, ambiguous things, that you could understand either way. I would give answers you could understand one way, but also differently, if you was thinking about things, aware. But because they weren't aware, because they only thought in heterosexual terms, they always interpreted what I said in the same way.

Eventually, of course, the Camp David accords were put into effect, and Israel pulled out of the Sinai. Which meant that we had to abandon the moshav, after eleven years there. We stayed, you know, right up to the end, but we didn't barricade ourselves into houses or anything like that. We didn't resist the army. After three years of pressure, of people leaving little by little, and of such hostile media—and the media really was so hostile toward us— there was a kind of psychological toll. After three years, you realize that, you know, this is the end. Except, of course, for my father, who always lived inside some kind of stupid bubble. But the rest of us saw that the withdrawal was going to happen. You could see, you know, the families leaving the moshav, one by one. You see it with your own eyes. In the end, there were only twenty families left. And that was that. But even when the withdrawal began, my father was still in his bubble, he believed that nothing would happen. He wouldn't sign on the document that said we would leave until the withdrawal was actually happening. Then he signed.

During this three-year period, the people on our moshav really, like, went to pieces. There were two suicides. And two women went crazy. The community really just crumbled. You have to remember the whole situation with the damages that we were being paid by the government to convince people to evacuate the settlement. The whole story was that you could sign for the damages, get your money, and then stay around until the time came to evacuate. So some families decided very quickly to accept the government's offer. They signed for the damages, maybe they were having financial problems, I don't know, but they signed on the document that they would leave, and took the money. It was a shitload of money, especially at that time, and especially for people who had never had anything at all. Like, a hundred thousand dollars, something like that. That was a ton of money to people. And they just didn't know what to do with themselves. So people just went batty. They began, like, traveling to Europe, and they bought all sorts of expensive cars. They threw drug parties—it was insanity, to be there at that time. People, you know, driving around the desert in sports cars. It was totally unbelievable. It was really something else. And then people began to get very depressed. What can you do? Like, suddenly you've got a shitload of money. So they, you know, went crazy.

It might be because of that, or it might be because of tremendous pressure. Only someone who lived there can know how much pressure there was that final year, from people in Israel, on the settlers there. It was like we had done something wrong, you know, "You're disgraceful, you're draining the country of money, raiding the treasury." It was a precedent then to give money to someone so that he would abandon his home. It had never happened. It was a precedent for the country. And people didn't like it. People looked down on it. In school there were all sorts of comments all the time, "millionaires' children," "children of extortionists." We were going to high school near Beersheba, we would drive there, it was about an hour and fifteen minutes away from the moshav, and the teachers would always be making all sorts of hostile comments. And Shulamit Aloni and her friends were calling us all kinds of names in the Knesset.[§] So I think it was this that, you know, made those people fall off their rockers. People really got down. Just, like, hit bottom.

Because I had three years to get used to the idea, the withdrawal really wasn't very traumatic for me or anything. But it did hurt. I would have dreams for years afterwards—to this day I sometimes have dreams about going back there. All sorts of variations on resettling the area, going back to that place, to childhood. But I don't think I have any real, you know, traumas. Or maybe I'm just not aware of it.

After we left the moshav, we lived for a three-month period at an army vacation village in Ashqelon, while they were, you know, building the new moshav where we were going. Because of all the problems the settlers from our moshav were having, we didn't manage to move as a group, to resettle together in a different place as a moshav. A lot of people didn't want to go back to agriculture, a lot of people were already too old to work in farming, so they took the money, built private houses for themselves, and went into business, or something like that. But the other big moshav that was evacuated, Netiv Haʿaśarah, did manage to stay together. My parents' lives are in farming, and they, you know, wanted to stay with that. So we joined them, because they were still an agricultural moshav, with communal cooperation and guarantees, which was very important to my father, that there should be a cooperative association on the moshav, that they would help one another out. On top of that, Netiv Haʿaśarah relocated in a very beautiful area, really very pretty, near the sea, and near a stream, and near dunes. Really a beautiful moshav, on the top of a hill. There's quality of life there. So we moved with them.

[§] Shulamit Aloni (b. 1929): Long-time member of Knesset and founder of the Civil Rights Movement [Ratz] party; best known for her vocal advocacy of human and civil rights and the return of territories conquered in the Six-Day War as well as for her opposition to the policies of the Likud under prime ministers Menaḥem Begin and Yitzḥaq Shamir.

It was a big social change. Because suddenly I was cut off from the very closed group that I was used to being with, on top of losing the surroundings that I had grown up with. And I went through a big change, like, in terms of my style. I became really close with two girls, and we became a total clique. And they were wild things. Really, you know, wild little girls. Punks. Rebels. And that was exactly what I needed at that time. I needed to rebel. They knew that we were the troublemakers on the moshav—hooligans. We would smoke cigarettes and hashish. All my political activism, my demonstrations, they weren't good enough, because while I might have been protesting the political establishment, I was totally going along with what I was supposed to be doing, so far as my parents were concerned. And now I rebelled against my parents.

This was definitely connected to my sexuality—this was my way of telling my parents that I was good for nothing, and they shouldn't expect anything from me. I made absolutely sure that they saw that they should expect no happiness from me. They should just leave me alone. Don't expect me to get married, I don't want to get married, I just want to, you know, spend my life on the road, I don't want a framework. Just love. Just peace. I was a kind of flower child—I went around barefoot, with torn clothes, all sorts of rags, bracelets. It was my way of shouting, "Don't expect me to amount to anything. I'm strange, I'm different from everyone around me, I'm an outsider, I'm not like everyone else. You've got to accept me like this." Of course, I never would have admitted that this had anything to do with homosexuality, but inside, like, I was thinking about it, thinking that this will help me in the future, this will teach my parents that they need to accept me the way I am. As someone who doesn't fit in. Like, not as a boy just like any other.

They treated it like a stage I was going through. You know, an adolescent boy who was screwing around. Of course, they were very angry. They caught me smoking hash three times. They brought a psychologist to the moshav to talk to me. It was, you know, difficult for them, like, a tragedy at home, "Oh my God, you're using drugs," all that bullshit.

I didn't even take my high school matriculation exam. By eleventh grade I had already basically stopped studying, and I pretty much left school at the beginning of my senior year, although every now and then I would still make an appearance. I spent a lot of time in Eilat, getting high, sitting in the shade all day. I was, like, totally out of touch. In my own world. I failed every one of my classes.

Socially, I had these two girls, and we formed our own little group. And then I had a whole bunch of people I hung out with besides them. I had no sex life on the moshav, nothing at all. At the same time, I would always be making these kind of, you know, raids on the park in Tel Aviv. I didn't tell anyone. Not even with these friends of mine. I felt very strongly that, like, this was something forbidden. A curse. Something that would harm me, that would do me no good. Once, they even asked me point blank, these girls. We were on the beach, and they said to me, "Tell us, are you gay?" I denied everything, I said, "No way, what are you talking about, that's ridiculous." I think they got along with me so well because they didn't expect anything sexual from me. I was like their sister. A close girlfriend.

I knew how to protect myself. I was very manipulative. I had short-term relationships with "girlfriends" as a cover, but I didn't have a single sexual encounter with a girl during this period. It was all a cover, and I did a damn good job of it. When a girl fell for me, I would, you know, get to know her, begin to become close, and then suddenly distance myself. Close myself up completely, and leave everyone else wondering what we did or didn't do. And I would say it isn't relevant, we were together, and now it's over. I was a heartbreaker.

And then I was drafted. I entered into a very particular mindset in the army. I said to myself, "You are going to perform your army service like a man." I asked to be a paratrooper, one of the more elite combat assignments. My father and my brother were paratroopers, and so, like, it was natural for me to take the same path too. They were always talking about it at home— paratroopers, paratroopers, paratroopers—and if not the paratroopers, anything but the tank corps. Paratroopers, like, all the way. But after the first five minutes of the first day of preliminary exercises and selection, I knew that this was not for me. I said bye-bye—and they put me in the tank corps. So, like, I went to the tank corps.

Of course I was really ashamed when I came home, to say that I was in the tank corps. It was a real tragedy. But my parents were, you know, really pretty positive about it. "It's all right, it's great, really, if you're happy there." As it turned out, I got a lot closer to my parents again during the time I was in the army. Especially to my father.

I didn't have a single sexual contact within the army itself. I wasn't at all worried about being gay in the army. It didn't cause me any problems, to shower with the guys, or anything like that. I knew I had no problem with that. I knew that I was going to be in a situation where I would be surrounded by other guys, but I just had the feeling that this would not be a problem for me. You have to remember, even before the army, I really forced myself into a very macho mindset. I really tried to, you know, inject myself into masculine company, and I felt like I was already enough of a man for it, that I wouldn't have any problem. I had friends, we would laugh it up, play soccer, pal around. I knew that I didn't have any problem getting along in that kind of atmosphere any more.

In the army, I suddenly felt like I was managing to do what was expected of me for the first time in my life. I was totally masculine, macho. I was a trainer—I taught about all sorts of tanks and combat techniques and things like that. I was really on this totally macho trip there, in my uniform, with my gun. A real man. I was a very good soldier. I was obedient, I did exactly what they expected.

I kept on making short trips to Tel Aviv, just to get myself laid. Period. I didn't have any other reason to be in Tel Aviv. Consciously, really, I would do it consciously. I would work out, like, a cover to go to Tel Aviv, and as the planned day got closer I would get really excited, thinking to myself, I'm going to paint the town red, I'm finally going to get some, to live out my fantasies. For me, it was living out a fantasy. But I was still, you know, deep, deep, deep in the closet. I would only go once every few months—I had maybe five or six encounters during the whole time I was in the army. And the moment I would leave Tel Aviv I would go back to my day-to-day life of the army, and I would totally cut myself off from thinking about anything else.

I jerked off with amazing frequency when I would go home for Shabbat. I think I had a pretty amazing capacity. I wouldn't do anything in the army—maybe I would jerk off while on guard duty, and that's it. But Friday and Shabbat, when I was at home, I would, like, do it practically nonstop. I had all sorts of clippings from magazines in my room on the moshav, of naked men and so on. I knew that, sexually, you know, this was what I wanted. I knew that I, for one, like, did not want a girl. I knew it. I didn't want to become close with a girl, and I didn't want any kind of a relationship with a girl. Girls were coming on to me all the time, but I wasn't interested. I knew that I wanted guys. And I knew that this was something I had to be very careful to keep as a secret.

I would say to myself all the time, "I am going to be the only one who knows the truth about myself. No one is going to know. As long as I live, no one is going to know except for me." The case was closed. I wasn't at all in doubt.

I was really hot for a few soldiers, amazingly turned on by them. I taught a training course, so every few months, a new group of soldiers came through. So there were new hunks all the time. Soldiers so beautiful you could just go crazy! And I would fantasize about them, you know, build little scenes in my head. But beyond that, nothing. Once or twice I tried, somehow, to become closer with one of my officers, but, you know, I gave that up pretty quickly.

The first time I really had anything to do with a girl was also when I was in the army. This officer friend who I had the hots for set me up with a friend of his, and one thing led to another. I found myself spending the night alone with her in her house, even though she really didn't do anything for me. Somehow, I managed to get through the night there without anything happening—we just talked and talked and then we went to sleep. But when we woke up in the morning, our friend called—and he of course asked her, "So, did you fuck?" And she told him we didn't. And he was like, "Why?" And she was like, "I don't know, it just didn't happen." And then I took the phone. He said to me, "What, you didn't fuck her?" And I was like, "No, I didn't fuck her, nothing happened." He said, "Why?" And I was like, "I don't know, it just didn't happen." So he goes, "OK, well you can fuck now." And he hanged up the telephone.

Now I was in trouble. I didn't know what I was supposed to do, but it was clear that there was no way out. I said to her, "Can I kiss you?" I had no idea what I was doing. I mean, the gay thing makes getting laid very easy. Like, you don't have to deal with any bullshit—you go to the park, and you get it. And that's the whole story. No talking, no getting to know someone. Just getting laid. And suddenly, with a girl, like, you don't know if she wants it or not. It's very complicated, all of a sudden there were all of these doubts. I didn't know what to do with this whole thing. So, you know, we kissed, and kissed, and kissed. And nothing was happening—I'm not even close to getting a hard on, I'm not even slightly turned on. These kisses aren't doing anything for me. I began getting panicked. So I got up to go to the bathroom, and, like, I tried to jerk a little, just so I could get it up. And then I went back to her, and that helped, because then I really did begin to get turned on. I, like, got excited, and began to, you know, get into the whole thing. I finally convinced myself that I wanted to get laid—and then she said that she didn't want to fuck. We just played around, and that's it, she didn't want to get fucked. That was probably just as well, because her parents came home all of sudden, a few minutes later. And that was my first time with a girl. And it went pretty well, all things considered. She told my friend that it was good, and I was pretty pleased with myself, that I had been able to get through it. But the fact that I had trouble getting it up with her did actually traumatize me for a long time afterwards. And that's it. I finished my service, and was discharged. That's it. That was the army.

I was twenty-one. I went back to the moshav for about six months and worked in the fields. I knew that I wanted to go on a trip abroad, I wasn't sure where. I thought maybe South America, but I didn't know anything definite. Then, after six months, I got married. It's not as serious as it sounds. Married women are exempt from army service, and a girl I knew was having a terrible time in the army, so she asked me to marry her. It was something that I just knew I would never do for real, and she was really suffering, so I said, what the hell, why not. My parents were totally furious. I was kicked out of the house. They said to me, "OK, you're married, so get out of the house. Go live with her." Of course, they knew that it was a sham. They knew that I had nothing to do with her, that it was only to get her out of the army. But I had to move out.

We went to Eilat for three months, we lived on the beach in Eilat, this girl and me, for three months. She was a real character. She was easy to live with, because she was a kind of a nutty type of person. She fucked the whole beach. She was kind of crazy. We each slept in our own sleeping bag, and we called ourselves a family. I never talked to her about myself. I think we were totally stone drunk for two months straight. Alcohol was my life, I was totally out of touch with everything around me. And after, like, three months of this, I went home, and my parents calmed down, and everything calmed down.

I was there for another few months, on the moshav, and then I moved to Tel Aviv, to live with two girls I knew from the kibbutz where I was born. I would hang out with their crowd, and we got along really well. And then I went traveling.

The three of us went to South America together for about three months. We were in Ecuador, Peru, and Bolivia, and then we split up, and I went to the U.S. Now, this whole time, I don't think I had a single sexual encounter. Nothing at all during those three months. I was with them, and we were all into just, you know, roaming around, kicking back and having fun. I had a great time, but I didn't have any sex life at all. I never told the girls anything. Up to this time, I still had told no one. Absolutely no one.

I went to New York to work in moving. I lived in Queens. Finally I had a few encounters, but I didn't really, you know, get involved in any kind of a scene or anything. I really wanted to go back to travel in Brazil—I could only think about going back to the Carnival in Brazil. So I worked for, like, about six months, with an Israeli company, and every now and then I would go to Central Park to meet someone. But I really cut myself off from it. I was pretty out of touch at that time. I never went to a club. You have to remember that I was working very, very hard, morning to night, seven days a week. Only work. It was the experience of being Israeli in New York. To live with Israelis, be with Israelis, not to experience New York at all, just to live there for a while to make money. That was my way of life.

After a while, my friend from the army came to join me, and we wound up going back to South America together, to Brazil. And here I began to let myself go. On this trip I finally began to relax. I began going out more often, I would go out in the evenings to all sorts of places. And Brazil is a place where the men just project this air, like they're saying that they don't give a shit who they do it with. Even though homosexuality is against the law there. The men there are, like, in this amazing mindset. You see it and you feel it. You feel it from them, that they're giving you the eye, you feel it from them, that it's totally OK. And in the Carnival, you can see all the drag queens, just all over the place, men dressed up as women. And you just accept it.

So, in Brazil I had a few really nice encounters. Somehow I began to feel freer. I met guys on the beach, in the parks. I just have an instinct for it. I would walk around, and I would find the places immediately. I would go out for an evening stroll, and I would walk, like, two feet and I would just fall into a gay meeting place. I don't know how, but I would always find the right parks. I would just immediately understand, from looking at a place, that it could be here.

I was also very stoned there, and this may have helped me feel so "free." It may be that that was also a way of escaping, to go into the whole thing of being stoned and get away from everything around me. I was high just twenty-four hours a day.

I was dying to tell my friend what was going on with me. Like, a bunch of times it was on the tip of my tongue, but he's the type that minds his own business—if you don't bring something up, he's not going to ask you all sorts of questions. And we would talk about everything except for sex. I wouldn't ask him, and he wouldn't ask me. We were close friends, but sex was, you know, a subject that had nothing to do with us. He was going out with all sorts of girls, and I had nothing like that. Eventually he went back to Israel, and I began traveling alone.

I definitely knew about AIDS, and I was pretty hysterical about it, so I was super careful. It was masturbation and that's that, nothing more. No penetration, no fucking. It was all very light sex. I knew I had to be careful, and I preferred it that way too. All of my experiences had been like that—there was never penetration. They were usually just, like, mutual masturbation. I would never do anything more, I would never agree to anything else. And that's the way it was in Brazil also with the people I met.

What was different there was that for the first time I really did keep in touch with people I met in the parks. It was more than just a one-night thing—sometimes I would see people for a week running, if I was in a certain city for that long. I met this guy from Argentina and we were together for a week. I wasn't afraid to do that, I had really, you know, let go, I saw that there were a lot of people like that. I freed myself from the whole thing in my head, and I began to understand that it wasn't so awful, that it was OK. And that's it. After about a year and a half abroad, something like that, I went back to Israel. My brother was getting married. So I was planning on going back for a month to Israel, and then going back to New York again.

I flew back by way of New York, where I stayed for a final ten days, with an old roommate who I was still close with. She was always telling me about her brother, how she thinks he's, you know, bisexual. And she wouldn't ever ask me about my personal life. She would just tell me all the time about her brother, who she thinks is bisexual. And since I was going back to Israel, I asked her to give me her brother's telephone number.

And as soon as I got back to Israel, I got in touch with him. He lived nearby here, and I went up to his apartment to meet him. As soon as I saw him, I knew. I said to myself, "This guy knows what the score is." But I wasn't absolutely sure—maybe 98 percent. I was missing that 2 percent to be, like, totally certain. And I was very frightened of coming on to him, and having him tell me that he wasn't interested. The first time we met, nothing at all happened—I found out afterwards that he was sure I was straight. But I began hanging out with him a lot because I was just living with my parents at the time. It was like, I didn't have much to do. And so I got to know him better.

He told me that he was moving to a new apartment. And the apartment he was leaving was a really nice penthouse. He was looking to rent it, and, to make a long story short, I suddenly decided that I would stay in Israel and move in there. So I did.

He came to visit one evening as I was moving in. And we talked all night long. It was about, like, six in the morning when the sexual tension in the room was just about to explode, and I decided that, you know, the first step would have to come from me. So I said, "You know what? I'd really like to fuck around with you." And that's it. We were together for three years, the two of us, together.

After three weeks, he invited me to move into his new apartment with him, and I went for it. We lived in Ramat Gan, suburban Tel Aviv. And the decision to move in with him was a very conscious decision that, this is it, I'm coming out of the closet. And it wasn't like, I'm going to live with him because I love him, or I'm in love with him, it was like, I'm going to move in with him just in order to help myself come out of the closet. I wasn't thinking about being a couple or anything like that. I'd just had enough of being in the closet, and I wanted to live my life. My trip to the U.S. and South America opened my mind, showed me that you can live that way. It's possible. And when I got to Israel, I just wanted to do that. I wanted to meet gays, I wanted to get into those circles, I was ready for it.

We lived together for a year and a few months in Ramat Gan. It was a very difficult period for me, a very difficult time. I basically just came out in, you know, one fell swoop—I told all of my close friends at the same time. Almost everybody was totally fine about it. They were more than fine—it was actually a lot of fun, a real blast. I was proud of myself, I felt good about myself. And everyone was like, "It doesn't make a bit of difference what you do, we couldn't care less, there isn't any problem at all, everything's OK." I was in a kind of euphoria, when the slap in the face came from one of the two girls I had been traveling with. "What, yuck, gross, how can you do that, are you kidding, what'll your parents say, how can you do this to your parents?" I had been in a kind of bubble, and, like, she kind of popped that for me. But I got over it.

Me and my boyfriend were a real couple, although, like, I didn't define it that way at all. We were together for a year before I began to define it. But the fact was that, you know, we were together, we fucked all the time, and I was totally faithful. I thought only about him, like, nothing else. I didn't want anyone else. Of course, at the time, I didn't know he was cheating on me. It didn't even occur to me. It seemed totally obvious to me that if we're together, we're together. I wasn't looking for anything else. I was totally dependent on him—he was everything to me, and I wouldn't make a single move without asking him. He was very much the dominant one in the relationship.

Until I met him, every time I went to the park I would have panic attacks, like it was my first time all over again. I would become totally hysterical. He slowly taught me how to feel comfortable there. We would go into the park together, and I would see that it wasn't so awful, that people were sitting, talking, laughing. We would go to the park together pretty regularly. At first it was just for the hell of it, just to go in there and see the people, and he would meet his friends all the time. A lot of people in Tel Aviv knew him— we would, you know, walk along the street, and every five feet we would meet someone who knew him. Whatever he did, he stood out. In any case, little by little, we began meeting people in the park for threesome situations. We would bring people home, and we would have a menage-à-trois. Everything was really, like, just in the context of having fun. I didn't have any problem with that. We were just having fun.

I found work in a cafe/restaurant pretty quickly, and I began studying graphic design. It was a time when I really blossomed. I began to dress, you know, elegantly. It used to be that I couldn't have cared less what I wore—I would literally dress in filthy rags. I really didn't care at all. I didn't wear deodorant—I didn't even have any idea what it was. But during this time I began to learn what it meant to dress well. I began, you know, going out to clubs. I really began to live it up. I began to have fun. I really blossomed.

After a little over a year, we decided to go to New York, together. It was really just a case of trying to run away from our problems, when I think about it now. I had already got to the point where, you know, I wanted to split up. I just didn't want to be with him any more. He's a crazy guy, all sorts of ups and downs, he's difficult to live with. And after a year I began to get tense, and I was afraid, and I didn't know if this was what I wanted, if this was really what I wanted. All my old fears began coming back to me, and I just couldn't stay in Israel any longer. I began to feel like I was losing my mind here. I began to lose what was holding me in Israel. So we talked it over, and within two weeks we were on the plane.

We lived in New York for a year. And for me that was a really good year. We lived together, we lived separately, we wandered from place to place—we never knew what was going on.

I would always be going to clubs, gay clubs, and I really began to open my mind. Really. You know, you don't have the whole family thing there. You don't have that pressure. You just have to worry about yourself, you're only concerned about yourself, you're only thinking about yourself all the time. You don't have any pressure from society, from your surroundings. You could just go out, and that was that. That was the point where I really liberated myself, and began to live. All sorts of clubs, you know, meeting people, insanity. Real fun. We would go out, looking to get laid together, and we fought nonstop. It was fabulous.

I was there during the Gulf War, in 1991. And to be Israeli in New York then was really something. It was like, "Wow, I've got to hand it to you, you're surviving." We would be in a bar, and they would find out that there were a group of us from Israel, and everybody would be very excited. It was a real attraction.

It was very difficult not being in Israel during the war. I, you know, registered in the Israeli consulate in New York, so that if they wanted to mobilize my company they would be able to find me. That was kind of going overboard—what were they going to do with the tank corps? I really wanted to go back, but of course flights to Tel Aviv were suspended. And so I said to myself, well, if I'm already here, I guess I should stay here. This way I'll be certain to survive—if they all get exterminated by chemical warfare, at least I'll survive, and me and all my friends will go back to Israel like the pioneers, rebuild the whole thing from the start. I would talk about it with all the Israelis I met, that we would go back to Israel and, you know, rebuild the state. Because from New York, it really looked like this was the end. When you're sitting there hearing about all the missiles, that they're bombing Tel Aviv, it really looked like this was the end of the road. That Tel Aviv had been destroyed and, you know, everyone was going to be gassed to death. It didn't occur to us that it was something so light—that the guy was basically just throwing huge hunks of concrete on us, and that was all. It looked like the end. So we were, like, very patriotic.

I went out all the time, then. I went out almost every night. And I also had very good work. I was a dog groomer—I worked in a sort of a dog barbershop. It was great money. I fell into the job by total chance. I had an Israeli neighbor, she was about forty—totally insane, like, a totally insane woman. She was living alone, and she was my neighbor, and she was a very well-trained dog groomer, she worked in this shop. So she came to me and said they were looking for a new groomer.

She took me to work, and she told them that I was a dog groomer who she had met at, like, a national conference of Israeli groomers, and that I was so wonderful, and skilled, and talented, they absolutely had to hire me. And they hired me. I would watch what she did, she would teach me, and after a month I began to groom the dogs. Within a few months I knew what I was doing. At one point, I actually wound up moving in with that woman. She was really something special. Like, totally off the wall.

Actually, it was because of the Gulf War that they fired me from dog grooming. After a while, I really began to despise that job. God, I hated those dogs. They climbed all over me, shitted all over me, peed on me, bit me, scratched me—they made me totally miserable. I would go home all bruised and scratched, and I would curse the day those dogs were born. But I stayed with it for eight months. And then we began having fun at work. We would bring in some pot, and we would smoke, and we would make all sorts of, you know, crazy designs on the dogs. We went kind of crazy. Like, with poodles, you know, you need to make their heads round, a kind of a little ball on top of their heads. But we would make pyramids, or heart-shapes, we would paint them pink. We just went wild. Of course, the customers, like, got very whiny. It's not a very pleasant feeling to come get your poodle, and to discover that, you know, it has a pink pyramid of a head because the groomers decided that it would look better that way. We went totally crazy.

And then the Gulf War began, and we just stopped going to work. We would sit, like, glued to CNN all day, like total idiots. It was just an excuse not to go to work. So in the middle of the war, the owner fired both of us. And my friend had been there for ten years! The owner was also Jewish, the asshole.

I was totally fed up with what was going on with my boyfriend, anyway, so I left New York, and I went back to Israel alone. I just couldn't take it any more. He was totally driving me crazy, and I didn't want anything to do with him anymore. I wasn't in love with him.

I came back to Israel determined to live the life of a gay man, without my old boyfriend. This was three years ago. I was twenty-four. I had pretty much gotten to the stage where I'm at now, like, where I said, this is who I am, and I don't want to change that. I want to live my life, my way. I don't want to always be making up stories, I don't want to deny anything, I don't want to run away from anything. I just want to, you know, live. Just to live my normal life, with this as a part of it. This is my life. Without, like, trying to escape from it.

I got into the fast track pretty quickly. I worked in bars, restaurants, cafes, where all the waiters were gay. It was an amazing life. And I began to meet people. But after three months, my boyfriend came back from New York, and we moved back in together. Our relationship was far from over. Of course, you know, all of the arguments began again. We split up now and then, and in the course of time I had a relationship here and there, all sorts of flings, nothing serious. Because I think I was still very much tied to him. I think that to this day I'm pretty tied to him, in a certain way. He'll always be a very important part of my life. He really helped me out, like, dragged me out of the rut I was in. He gave me a lot.

Now, about a year ago, things got so bad that we were getting into fist-fights. We would hit each other, because we weren't getting along. We were totally driving each other up the fucking wall. We really got to the point of just, you know, laying into each other. He was in love with me—he fell totally in love with me. But right about that time, I began to find out about all sorts of things that had happened in the past. I kept coming across old tricks of his, and all the trust I had put in him totally collapsed. I didn't want to sleep with him. I was so hurt. I didn't want anything to do with him anymore. And he had finally fallen in love with me! It was one big catastrophe, like, the whole story. I wanted him to move out, and he refused to leave. He just sat himself down in the house and refused to leave. I literally kicked him out.

And then he came to me one day, I had met someone new, and we were planning on going traveling together, this was a year ago. And then he came to me, and told me that, like, he had AIDS. He had done a test, and he had AIDS. And so, I said to myself, you know, if he's got it, I've got it—because, like, we fucked without any protection, we always fucked without any protection, freely.

The world had suddenly just opened up. The first thing I felt when he told me was that I was really angry at him. I was angry, because I felt the need to blame someone, so I blamed him. He told me that he thought it was from something he had done, that he had been with someone who had AIDS, and it was because of that that he did the test. He didn't go and do the test for no reason at all—he had a reason to think that he might be infected. So I was like, "Why didn't you say anything, we would have been careful, we would have done something"—I didn't even want to talk to him, I was so angry with him. I didn't want anything to do with him. But I was really scared, I mean, this was it. If he had it, I had it. I had absolutely no doubts. Totally convinced. And it took me about two weeks before I got tested, there was some holiday, I don't know what happened. Two horrible, horrible weeks. The worst two weeks of my life. I didn't talk to anyone, not at work, nothing. I just saw the end of my life. Of course, during this time we got closer again, we began talking again, and we got together again. I mean, we both really needed to talk to each other, to be with each other.

When I got tested, they told me that everything was OK. In fact, they told him that everything was OK with him too. He didn't have it. To this day, I don't know what the real story is. Like, I asked him, and, like, I made him swear that he hadn't lied to me, and oh boy, oh boy if I find out that he was lying. But, you know, he swears that they made a mistake when he was tested, and he really thought he had it. And to this day I don't know. I really can't say for sure if he was telling the truth or not.

We stayed together for another few months after we were tested, but eventually things exploded again. And then I had to go to army reserve duty for a month, and I took that chance to make a real break from him, and we totally split up.

About six months ago, on Purim, I was at some party, and I met a really nice guy. Things just clicked between us, and we had a great time together. We kissed a little at the party, and then I went home with him, and we talked a lot, and we talked and talked, and then we got to the point of getting into bed, we were both getting hot, and then, half-jokingly, I said, like, "Tell me, have you been tested lately?" And what's weird is that I never ask that. I'm just careful with everyone—I mean, it's a stupid question, because anyone can just say "Yes, I've been tested." So I treat everyone as, you know, a potential carrier, and I'm careful. Unless we get into a real relationship, and I go with him to get tested, and I find out that he's OK. So for me, like, he's a carrier until I get to the point where I would believe him, where I know him and I can trust him.

But in any case, I asked him, I was like, "Have you been tested?" And he goes, "Yes, I've been tested." And I was like, "And what was the result?" And he was like, "Of the last one, or the one before that?" And I went, "Get out of here—no, I want the third to last one you did. The last one, of course." And then he said to me, "I'm HIV positive."

Now. This was the first time I had ever met someone who was infected, who was a carrier, and I was really in shock. I just sat down, and I was really in a light state of shock. And I said to him, "What do you mean, HIV positive? Are you sick?" And he said to me, "No, no, I'm not sick, I'm just carrying the virus, but I'm not sick yet, it hasn't yet developed." And we began to talk about it.

At first, I just wanted to get up and leave. Just get out of there. But I stopped myself, I said, like, no, I'm not leaving, I enjoy being with him, I want to stay with him, I want to talk to him. And we sat until six in the morning, and we talked and talked. We sat in his place until the morning. It was really nice. We talked about the disease, and how he feels, and he tried to get something sexual going, but I said to him, "Listen, I'm just frightened, I'm scared to kiss you. I know you don't get infected that way, I've read articles, maybe I don't read enough of them, what I've read has been very superficial. I've never been especially interested in the subject. So it may really be that you don't get it from a kiss. If I hug you, I know that I can't get it, I have no problem with that. But a kiss frightens me. Everything beyond that frightens me." So he told me that he understood. He was so nice about it, he said it was OK, no big deal. So we sort of masturbated, each one of us, being very careful, with a porn movie, a few touches, and that was that.

And we began seeing each other. I really liked being with him, I really enjoyed being with him. He was a person with a lot to offer. A real man, mature, at peace with himself. He'd known he was carrying the disease for seven years. He really had his act together, and he knew what he wanted from life. He was really a unique person. He had a lot to give. We had a blast together. We got together almost every day, and it was real fun.

And then we began kissing, and I began to feel like I was losing control. I got a little concerned. I got to the point where I said, I may go further. But suddenly I felt my life force very strongly, so strongly, and I wanted to end it. I wanted to end the relationship. I didn't want to stay with him. And I also didn't know if I loved him. I said to him, "Listen, if I really knew you, and I loved you, and then you told me that you had AIDS, it might really be that, like, it wouldn't make a difference to me. I would say, fuck it all, I love you, I want to be with you, and I don't care if you have AIDS. But because I'm beginning this with the knowledge that you have AIDS, I already have a block in falling in love with you. It's very difficult to begin a relationship, to give of myself, to fall in love. I just have a block, I know that this is limited. Your time is limited. It may be that, like, in another year you'll fade away. And I'm also afraid for myself. I want to live. I don't want to die, I don't want to get AIDS. I want to keep on living." He invited me to come with him to visit his parents, and we had dinner with his parents, and after dinner we had a talk, and I said to him, "Listen, I want to split up. I just can't do it, this is too difficult for me." And we ended the relationship. It was only three weeks all together.

We began seeing each other much less frequently. And he began to get sick. And the depression of being sick just kind of consumed him. When we were together, I encouraged him. He was always telling me, "You brighten my life, you give me the will to live again." He began going to a health club, when we were together. I said to him, "Yes, go." And when he said it was too difficult for him, I said to him, "So go learn meditation, I don't know what, just do something, like, keep yourself busy, take some classes, do different things, enrich yourself. Just don't let that disease consume you. Don't think that way." But I ran away. It was too difficult for me.

The people around me weren't exactly thrilled with what had been going on. I had a very hard time with all sorts of people. This guy was known as having AIDS, people knew. And they saw us together. And people came to me and, like, warned me. My old boyfriend gave me a very hard time—he treated me really badly, like I had AIDS myself. He didn't want to drink from my glass. And other people said, like, "This isn't a good idea," "You really shouldn't." I myself didn't really want to, and with everything together, I just ended it. But he really needed people, and I wasn't there, and a lot of other people weren't there.

I had gone to the moshav for a few weeks, and he came to visit me, we went together to Hapaʿamon Cave, it was really fun. And then something happened, I just totally cut myself off from Tel Aviv, I don't remember what it was. Oh yeah—they fired me, I quit, I left my job then, and I found myself all of sudden unemployed and broke, and I was having a hard time. So I went back to the moshav for, like, a week to get some distance. And when I came back to Tel Aviv they told me that he had committed suicide. He jumped off a building. That's it. Very difficult.

Lately I've been taking some courses in computer animation. All sorts of things connected to computerized animation. I'm working on my final project now. I called it "Being Put Into the Closet"—it was basically the story of how society, like, puts you into the closet, as I see it. I presented it. And I came out to my class by doing that, because it was very clear, as soon as I began to talk. Afterwards, there were, you know, a lot of handshakes from the other students and slaps on the back. I was very proud. I felt really good about it, both in terms of continuing to study this subject, and also in terms of that philosophy, that you need to express what's going on inside. To speak honestly, without masks, without trying to run away.

My brother and one of my sisters, they both know about me. Today we're at the point where everything's out in the open. My brother asks me what's going on, and when I meet someone new I tell him about it. With the youngest, the subject hasn't come up. She's, like, eighteen, going into the army now. I still haven't told my parents.

I've never told anybody I do reserve duty with about myself either. I really have a block about it. I have to tell them I have a girlfriend, to keep them at a distance, to keep them from trying to set me up with all of their cousins, nieces, and sisters. I know that if the guys there found out, they wouldn't let it just slip by quietly. It's a little world of its own, there, in the army, a crowd of people I'm with only a few weeks a year, every year. When we're there, we're good friends. When we're on duty, we're brothers, really, everyone there is your brother. When it's over, I have nothing to do with any of them. I don't see them until the next time we're called. Most of the guys in my company are, you know, religious and older. I can only imagine what would happen if they found out. I wouldn't be able to stay in the company. It would just be impossible. I figure they would try to get me out, and I'd also feel uncomfortable. It wouldn't work out, it couldn't. That's what I think.

My father votes Hateḥiya, and my brother votes Hateḥiya, and my sister votes Hateḥiya, and my mother also votes for, like, something on the right.[§] I used to think like they do, but today, my political views are on the left, on the political map. I think that things are a lot clearer for gays, because it's easier for them to understand the whole thing of being an oppressed minority. I mean, Arabs are oppressed in this country, just because they're Arabs.

When I'm on reserve duty, and I'm doing the intifadah, it's something that I, when I come back, I need a month afterwards just to calm down. You know, it's very difficult to go back to normal life after a month of the intifadah. You live it day after day, and you see what goes on there. The cheapening of human life, the way Arabs are treated like dogs. And it hurts. And you see your friends, and that's the way they see things, that's the way they act. The behavior of the people around you when you're in the intifadah, it's horrible. You stand on a roof. And the Arabs throw a rock at you. And, you know, you couldn't care less where the rock came from, you shoot in every direction. You break the plate glass of store windows, you knock over vegetable carts. That treatment, that attitude—the army can do anything it fucking wants there. You're like God there.

I feel really strongly about this. I remember it just drove me crazy, once, I was in the cafe in Tel Aviv, and I saw a Border Guard jeep, a military jeep, driving down the street, and all of sudden, it just drove right up onto the traffic island, in the middle of the city, and made a u-turn. Like there aren't any laws! Now, in the army, in the territories, you do that all the time with the jeeps. You, with the jeep, can go wherever the hell you want, in whatever direction you want. There aren't any rules you have to obey, nothing. You can drive down the street in the wrong direction, you can cut into traffic, you can stop whoever you want. You're God. That's the way you act. You could block traffic, just sit in the middle of the street, make all the cars be-

<hr>

[§] Hateḥiyah: Literally, "Revival"; political party founded in the wake of the 1979 Camp David accords with Egypt, in opposition to the principle of "land for peace." Hateḥiyah disbanded after failing to receive any Knesset seats in the 1992 elections.

hind you wait. Or drive in the middle of the street, on a two-lane, two-way street—and they're the ones who have to worry about getting out of the way. But they won't even dare honk. They're scared.

I have a very hard time with this. To see those roadblocks, where they check everyone's papers, just to, you know, humiliate them. Every time I see them checking Arabs' papers I feel like shit. I remember that when I was a kid, during the evacuation, I experienced it myself. When they began preparing for the withdrawal from Sinai, they didn't let anyone into the area without identifying documents. So we would drive up to the border in the car, and they would make us all get out, and check our documents. And you feel that humiliation. They checked your papers, if you were a resident or not, they only let you in if you had an identifying document that proved you were a resident. It was just to harass us.

I began to change my political views after the withdrawal. At the same time I became a real troublemaker in my behavior, trying to, you know, rebel against my parents. They just said, "You think that way just to get on our nerves." And it's true that it began that way. But in the army, I began to understand more, and to get more angry about all sorts of things that annoyed me. To feel the pain more.

The first gay Arab I spoke to was in Argentina. It was a very strange thing. He was a Palestinian whose parents had moved to Argentina, and the moment he heard that I was from Israel, he totally went into shock. He couldn't believe he was even talking to me. He said that if his father knew he had talked to me he would just kill him. But we talked a lot. I argued a very right-wing position, just to educate him. I was like some public information center there. "This is the way it has to be."

Today I agree that the Camp David agreements and the withdrawal from Sinai and everything was a good thing, of course. Today, when I look back on it, I know it was worthwhile. You know, it isn't a terrible thing to move a person from place to place. Nothing happens. People get killed in wars—but no one gets killed by moving to a new house. That's the way I see things today. I don't see it as, like, a tragic thing, to give territory back. It's only earth. That's the way I think about it today. And that's the way I feel about the Golan also. And because I went through it myself, I think I know what I'm talking about.

I could see myself getting into gay life, in the sense of being involved politically, thinking about it, getting worked up about stuff. Take this Pride Day "Happening" that the Agudah had yesterday, on Sheinqin Street. I couldn't go, I was working. But I really wanted to go. It's important to raise consciousness. I saw the television news coverage today. I was so sorry that I wasn't there. There were pictures of people dancing, and sitting, totally free, footage that was fun to see. People weren't hiding from the cameras. People were just sitting and talking, totally normal. Totally normal. Which is the way it should be. A real trip. It was great to see, those pictures. Next year.

I talk about everything totally freely at work, even if there are straights around. If you work with me, I have no problem opening up to you. It's important to drop those psychological barriers. I'm working in a cafe now, a totally straight place. I remember one time, this lawyer came to sit in the cafe, and we got to talking, about homosexuality, and all that, about everything that has been happening lately, and he began to say all sorts of bullshit, so I just talked to him. I don't think he knew. We began arguing, I was like, "What's your problem, if you belonged to a minority group you would also be worried about these things, you would also want to change all sorts of things. Why shouldn't I be able to marry anyone I want? What's wrong with my marrying a guy? Why does it have to be this way?" I like to get really into it, all the way. To have these arguments and, you know, to get excited about it.

The biggest problem that gays have in this country, or at least in Tel Aviv, is themselves. Gays are their own worst enemy. They are full of stereotypes about gays, themselves. So a lot of the real arguments I have about gays are with other gays. If someone is effeminate, they just get laughed at, and people keep their distance. But you just need to accept these things. You want people to accept you, why can't you accept people who act in a feminine manner? Why do you avoid them? Why do you treat them like they're this strange and radical group? That whole attitude drives me crazy. And then there's the attitude that says that, like, there is no such thing as being a committed gay couple. And a lot of people think like that. That it's impossible. But why is it impossible? If you believe in it, and you try to achieve it, and you want it, it can happen. In the U.S. you see so many gay couples who live together. I saw it when I worked in moving in New York—older people who change apartments together. It was so, you know, inspiring. You see it less in Israel, there's no question about it.

Things are getting better for gays here. The age when people deal with this is getting younger as time passes. If I, at twenty-two, was just beginning to try to cope with the whole thing, after the army, today's generation begins that process before the army. They get to the army and they're already dealing with these things.

I think things are different now because things are more open. People talk about it more, you read about it in the papers, you see them talking about it on television. It's just more accessible. Without noticing, you hear about it a lot. It's not like it used to be, you know, when you never heard anything ever. The only thing I had to read was *Behind the Fig Leaves*, that stupid book. The whole approach is different today.

It's because of people like Professor ʿUzi Even, and his partner Amit Kama, who were on television and everything, and Yaʿel Dayan, with everything she's been doing in the Knesset, that things are changing here. And it's terrific. They should be really proud of what they've done. At the clubs now, it's not like it used to be, when everybody would sit inside, and everything was totally hermetically sealed. Today people stand around outside, and they sit and talk. You come on Thursday night and, like, the whole plaza in front of the club is full of people. Everyone's outside, and no one gives a fuck who sees them. People care a lot less now. If you just stop for a second and look around, you can see that there's been a meaningful change for the better lately about this whole thing.

I used to think a lot about going abroad, going to live someplace else. Now I know that I want to live in Tel Aviv, to live here. I like it here. My friends are here, like, my crowd that I hang with, they're all here, they're all working, in business. This is the city. I feel like, you know, this is my home. When I think about home, this is it.

I felt foreign in New York. I felt like that was temporary, that I was missing something. I think you could say that maybe there was something ideological in my deciding to stay in Israel. Like, this is my home. This is my language. I want to live here. But an important part of it was just family. I mean, my family is in Israel, and I really have a good relationship with them now. My nieces are here, and I just die for them, I go crazy for them. And my sister-in-law, who I really love. Everyone is on the moshav, the whole family, except for me.

I wouldn't say I'm Jewish. I'm Israeli. I never had anything to do with the gay synagogue in New York. My boyfriend would go there. He would bug me, like, all the time to go with him, but I would say to him, "I've never been to a synagogue in my life, you want me to go to a synagogue just because it's for gays?" I don't have any religious thing.

I'd like to live with someone, and know that we want to grow old together, that, like, we want to build a relationship that will last for our entire lives. But it's not like I'm out there looking for this. If it comes, it comes. I'm not hysterical to meet people with this in mind. But I'm very much ready for it. With the people I meet, when things get serious, I make it very clear what I'm looking for, what kind of relationship I want. An honest, real relationship with a guy.

I dream of raising a child together with a man I love. To meet a guy, build a real relationship, and at some point, if possible, to adopt a child. I'm aware of the fact that it won't happen. I'm aware of the fact that in Israel, if they know I'm gay, they'll never let me adopt a child in a million years. I know that it's something that I've sacrificed because I've chosen to live this way in this country. Maybe in a different place that wouldn't happen, but here it's something that I am aware of. I don't really think about it. I haven't gotten to the point where it really preoccupies me or anything.

The last year has been, like, totally normal. I meet people all the time, and I think I've got a pretty stable crowd that I, you know, hang with, by this point. All sorts, gay and not gay. We go to clubs, live it up. You've got your friends, you've got your close friends, and you've got the club you go to every Thursday night—Works. We sit, chat, meet people. There are always new people to meet. That's what's so great about the gay life in this city. You meet new people all the time, all sorts of different people. And it's just like this book—everyone has a story to tell. You can just listen to people's stories nonstop, around the clock, if that's what you want. A lot of people don't realize this, but you can go to the park just to talk and talk, to get into conversations and meet another person. And it's fun, and there's a lot in it. In addition to sex, which is also important. Actually, here nearby, on Ben-Gurion Avenue, there's some action as well. At night, there's nonstop cruising on the avenue, nonstop. I met someone here once, not long ago. People sit on the benches, they, you know, look at the trees. It's a neighborhood branch of Independence Park.

I'm pretty sure I'm going to tell my parents about me this coming Shabbat. It just has to happen, for so many reasons.

At one point I wanted to tell them, I called them up, told them I have something to say. But at the last minute I backed out. I realized that the real reason I wanted to tell them was to just kind of throw the ball into their court—"I'm gay, and I'm having a hard time dealing with it, so help me, because I'm your son, because you brought me into this world. Help me." I saw that it would be a mistake. So I made up some sort of a story, and that was it. But my parents know that, if they ask me, they'll get the real answer. That's why they're not asking. But at this point, something is really, like, crying out to happen. I'm in a good mindset right now. You know, it's amazing how I've changed—for a long time I thought that I would never talk to my parents. That was always my motto.

I just met somebody new. I was with him yesterday and today. And it's fun. I'm, like, slowly falling in love. But that's Tel Aviv—you meet people, you fall in love, you fall out of love, you meet new people. Relationships are beginning and ending all the time. You know, there are a lot of gays in this city. Really, a lot. And for me, I've found what I want.

NOᶜAM

Amir and I wanted our interviewees to be at least vaguely representative of Israeli men. This meant, inevitably, reaching beyond the circles of our acquaintance and making contact with people we would never have met under other circumstances. This was certainly the case with Noᶜam, whom we found through the newly organized Jerusalem support group for gay married men. We made contact with their representative, and asked that anyone who would be willing to talk with us feel free to call. Amir, as a journalist and Israeli—not to mention native Hebrew-speaker—was, in every other case, responsible for making the initial, invariably awkward, telephone contacts, as well as organizing the logistics, and actually conducting the bulk of our interviews. But in this case, my partner's archaeological commitments had consigned him to some godforsaken (is that blasphemous, in the Promised Land?) excavation pit for four weeks, right in the middle of our summer. For the time being, if our work was to progress, I had no choice but to be the sole interviewer.

"Noᶜam" called me at my Tel Aviv apartment and offered to talk to me on the condition that he be allowed to withhold identifying details. I readily agreed, and we arranged to meet in Jerusalem, on Thursday morning of the following week. The only problem was where to go—he certainly wasn't in a position to invite me to his house, and I didn't think it wise to go anywhere too deserted with a man about whom, after all, I knew nothing. Following an extended discussion, we agreed upon Mt. Herzl—the official Israeli military cemetery and the serene, wooded burial site of Theodor Herzl, the founder of the Zionist movement.

I was waiting for No^cam when he appeared, at the designated time, on the
chosen summer morning. He is difficult to describe—the fact is that he doesn't
look like much of anything. No^cam would be a great secret agent, because there
never was a more inconspicuous-looking man. Maybe a little short, maybe a lit-
tle overweight, maybe a little blond, No^cam looks just like a hundred thousand
other Jerusalemite men-on-the-street—right down to the saucer-sized knitted
kipah on his head, which identified him as "religious." In Israel, "religious"
means Orthodox, and only about one out of every eight Jewish Israelis comes
from an identifiably religious background. The rest of the population spans the
spectrum from the semi-observant "traditional" to the defiantly and militantly
atheist. Amir and I had wanted to make sure that we spoke to someone reli-
gious—and, well, here he was.

Pleased to meet my interviewee, I greeted him enthusiastically, and we found
ourselves a comfortably shady bench, free of bird droppings. The tape rolled,
and the avian defecators sang gaily throughout our talk.

∾

I WAS BORN IN JERUSALEM. On my mother's side I'm the seventh generation here. My ancestors lived in Jerusalem, Hebron, and Tiberias. A very
long-established family here. My father immigrated from Russia in the 1910s,
alone. He was in his twenties then. They were going to draft him into the
Russian army, so he dodged. That's what everyone did. But he was also a
Zionist—he belonged to Hapo^cel Hamizraḥi, the religious Zionist workers'
movement. He is no longer living. I don't know anything about his family.
They didn't immigrate in this last wave. Or if they did, then I don't know
about it.

My mother and my father were both from religious families. But until
their generation, all Jews were religious. My father came to Jerusalem, he was
introduced to my mother, and that was that. They married. That's the way
things were done then. I have two sisters and a brother, I'm the youngest.

It was a very modest home. We didn't have an abundance of anything. My
father was a hardware salesman. He would even earn some money at it now
and then. My mother was very dominant, a good woman. At a certain point,
in the 1950s, my mother decided to open her own business. I don't want to
say what it was, I've already given away far too many identifying details. But
she stayed in business until the 1970s, and this business raised our standard
of living quite a bit. I was very close to my mother. I was the youngest, and

she was already in her forties when I was born. My relationship with my father wasn't as good. He was over fifty when I was born. I would go to him if I needed something—"Dad, give me money," "Dad, give me this." Beyond that, I don't remember that I ever really talked to him.

When my father died and I was going through his papers, I found two or three pictures of naked men with erect penises among his things. That was very strange for me. I never noticed anything about him—it never would have even occurred to me. It might be that if I had found the pictures while he was living, ten years earlier, I would have looked at him differently, maybe I would have seen some hints. But when I found them, it was too late. Of course, I didn't tell anyone about it. I think I tore the pictures up. I've never spoken with anyone in the family on this subject. It isn't anyone else's business.

As a little boy, I would sit for hours and try to masturbate, sometimes even openly. Up to when I was six, when I stopped. I remember it. I needed that stimulation. I don't know why I just remembered that—I haven't thought about it in years. When I began school, I was in a mixed class, and I was always friendly with the girls. I wasn't aware that this was something unusual. I knew that I didn't like soccer. But that was the only thing. Otherwise, I was very social, I was very much a ringleader. I was popular.

Now, when I think about it, I remember that when I was in seventh or eighth grade there was this boy who was one or two years older than me, and we would kind of fool around together. He lived close by, and sometimes he would be home alone. I remember that the first time I saw what semen looks like, it was from him—he was next to me and he came. I don't remember what I thought about it. I think I liked it. I wonder whatever happened to him. I know he's married with children now. I had completely forgotten about that whole thing. Whenever he sees me he's got a very big smile. But I don't know any more than that.

Afterwards I went to a yeshiyah high school, a religious boarding school. At thirteen. It wasn't unusual then. All of my education has been in the state-run religious schools. At home, my parents were concerned with their business, and I was the youngest, my brother and sisters weren't at home any more, everyone was already married. So I really didn't have a place. I felt that. So I went away to yeshiyah.

There, I became very, very close friends with another boy. We would hug one another and so on, but I don't remember that we did anything more than that. We were just very close. He left the school at the end of the year, and we lost touch. Then I had a relationship with another boy in my class. I remember that at first, he had a thing for someone else—when he saw him he would just swoon. Today I look at it this way. Then, I didn't understand it all like this. Anyway, I really fell for him. I really wanted him, and in the end I got him. We would hug each other, and jerk off together. When we wanted to do something, we would run through the names of all the others first, making sure we knew where they were, they were all accounted for, so they wouldn't catch us. But in spite of that, someone once spread the rumor that we were sleeping together, or something like that. But no one really took it seriously. Afterwards, we went together to the higher yeshiyah.

I had two girlfriends at this time. I liked to go out with girls. I had no sense of having an identity different from anyone else. I got along well with the other boys, and no one ever called me names. Today, when I think about it, I see that I should have felt it already at thirteen, at ten, but I can't really tell you from what age I felt it, felt different. I just don't know. All I can say is, at the time, I felt like I was exactly like every other boy. Just like everyone else. When we were in the showers we measured who was bigger and who was smaller, and I joined in. And besides this one boy, I didn't feel anything for the others. I don't remember if I knew the word "homosexual." It may be. But it didn't have anything to do with me. I was not very aware.

So we went together to the higher yeshiyah, and we continued our relationship. And then someone found out, one of the rabbis found out. I really don't remember how. As I talk, all sorts of pictures are coming back to me, that I had forgotten. Things are coming out of my subconscious. But I really don't remember how he found out. Anyway, I felt very close to this rabbi, I really respected him as a person. And he cut off all contact between me and my friend. He called me in for a conference. I don't remember exactly what we talked about, I don't know whether he said that he knew that we had slept together. But he had enough authority to make sure that we wouldn't live together, and we would have no opportunities to talk, that we wouldn't even see each other. I thought he did the right thing. This way, there wouldn't be the guilt of the whole thing anymore, the sinfulness of masturbation, and so on. You have to remember that, at this point, I still believed that if you masturbate then your thing will fall off. It was only later, when I read some books, that I found out that nothing happens. In any case, we weren't allowed to have anything to do with each other, and I didn't talk to this guy for years. This certainly helped me to realize that I was doing things that were forbidden. The whole thing was such a shock that for many years afterward I didn't have any physical relationships with men.

Later on, after we left the yeshivah, we would sometimes get together, talk about things in general, but it didn't go beyond that. I'm curious whether he's still doing it, or whether he got over it. I think he's still doing it. We did run into each other on Hayarqon Street in Tel Aviv once, near one of the cruising spots. I said to him, "What are you doing here?" And he said to me, "What are you doing here?" But both of us evaded the question. I didn't have the courage then for that kind of thing, exposing myself that way. I haven't seen him for years. I invite him to my family occasions, but he doesn't come. When I have seen him, he's been with his wife, and I've been with my wife. So it's not really possible to bring the subject up. But yes, it may be that he is still important to me, somehow. I would be happy to do it all over again—I really liked being with him, doing what we did. Maybe someday I'll run into him in the park. I don't have the courage to just go talk to him today, even though I'm more open, and I can talk about a lot of things now that I never could before.

Of course, I did have my girlfriends the whole time, and I would write them love letters, we would go dancing, we would grope each other, do whatever it is that teenage religious couples would do. I didn't sleep with them. I met them through Bney ʿAkiva, the religious youth movement. Or they were neighbors of mine. We would go to movies, we went out, just like everyone else. I wanted to go with a girl. It wasn't because of pressure or anything. To this day there is that duality in me. I'm aware that I've got this thing, but I'm not willing to give up the other thing.

So we all graduated, left the yeshivah, and everyone went in a different direction. I went to a city in the south for four years through the Frontier Force, an army program. At the time they needed teachers in outlying areas and border settlements. There was a severe shortage of teachers. So I did my army service by working in a school for four years. During the vacations between terms I would do basic training, communications equipment training courses, things like that.

Now that you mention it, in the army, in basic training, I did have a very close relationship with someone, but we didn't do anything. We just liked being with each other. We roomed together—he looked out for me, and I looked out for him. We had a real friendship, we were always together. I went to visit him a few times afterwards, and hoped that something would happen, but nothing did. I don't know where he is today. We had a very deep relationship. We lost touch, I think because I saw that nothing would come of it, there was no chance we were going to sleep with each other. Apparently, I wanted it.

I was there for years, and I don't remember a single contact with a man. I taught in a high school, and lived in an apartment with other teachers. I taught history, education, everything. I had a few relationships with women, and I eventually met my wife there. I do remember that if I went to a public bathroom I would try to take a peek at other men's penises, or something like that. But I didn't have the courage to do anything. What's surprising is that my real burst of courage came only after I was married.

I was twenty-seven when I got married, which was very old, especially in religious circles. My parents married at twenty-one. But I didn't feel like I was ready for responsibility yet. I was still young. To this day I'm young at heart. But what can you do, time does its work. I was under a lot of pressure from my parents to get married already, everyone was trying to set me up with girls they knew. But I couldn't find anyone I liked. And that was the truth.

It was clear to me that I would get married, that I wouldn't go in a different direction. It was clear to me that I would have a family. But it was also clear to me that I would have these other things, that I would fool around on the side. Still, I don't remember if I talked to anyone in a forthright manner about it all before I was over thirty. What's interesting is that, up to twenty-seven, I could have lived a wild life. If I were twenty-seven today, I can only dream of what I would do. But I knew that I would get married, and I wanted to, I looked for it. I went out with a lot of women, until I met my wife. And I fell in love with her.

We worked in the same school. But we had known each other for six years before we got married. We were friends first. She always said that she wouldn't marry a teacher. But, like I always say, she'll never be able to claim that she could have done any better than me. And I know I couldn't have done any better than her. We didn't have sex before we married. We fooled around a lot, but we managed to keep from getting to that point. I had slept with a woman before that. It was good. I guess it was good. It's difficult to remember what I was feeling. In any case, we've been married for twenty-three years now. Our ceremony was in Jerusalem, and we moved here, to Jerusalem, immediately afterwards. We've been here ever since. Within a year we had our first child. My wife was already twenty-five, I was twenty-seven—we wanted to make sure that all the equipment was in working order. And we settled down. We had four children, all during those first ten years. I had a good life, I worked, we had children to raise. I was satisfied.

You know, I'm dying to ask you a few questions. Never mind.

Things are a little mixed up in my head. I don't think that I cruised during the first years of our marriage, but I really don't remember—sorry. At some point, though, I did begin going out and actively looking for sex. I don't remember a first time or anything like that. Only during maybe the last ten years have I been really active. Before then, when I wanted sex, I was with my wife. And when that didn't do it for me, I jerked off. I masturbate to this day. I have no problem with that.

But I always felt that I was missing something. I would walk around, and I just can't stand in front of a man without looking at what he's got between his legs—or if he's good-looking, I'll look at his face. If I go to the beach, and I stand there, the cute guys grab my attention more than the cute girls.

So I wanted to experiment more, to go to Independence Park, to look for it. I felt like I was missing something. That I needed more things for my sexual stimulation. I felt that I needed to hold a penis in my hands, I needed to be blown, I needed to blow. Of course, I didn't want to be penetrated, and I didn't want to penetrate others. I didn't feel like that was what I wanted. But I loved it when they would lie on top of me. Even today, with my wife, she's on top, and it's good for both of us. I tried, at times, with my wife, that she would go down on me, or I would do it for her, or things like that. But, you know, she comes from a very religious home. At some point I saw that oral sex was just very difficult for her, she was having a very hard time with it, and I gave it up. I decided not to bring it up anymore, because of my sensitivity to her, as a woman. But I'm sure that if it would happen, if she would do it, I would look elsewhere a lot less.

So I found the only place there was fifteen years ago, which was the Tel Aviv Central Bus Station. And I would go there periodically. But then I began going to Independence Park, here in Jerusalem, and to public toilets, and then I discovered the bathrooms in the Central Bus Station here in Jerusalem. And I would find someone there from time to time.

I didn't define myself as gay—I knew that almost 90 percent of the other people in these places were married also. I actually preferred them. I still do, because of AIDS.

There was never a problem with finding someone, but naturally there were certain times of day that were better than others. They hadn't yet cut all the bushes in the park, like they have in the past two years, so there was no problem finding mutual masturbation and so on. I met one guy in the park who I was with for a number of years. I would call him up and we would get together, sometimes in the park, sometimes in other places. There were a few other people also, people I was with for years, we would stay in touch. I would also see other men during that time. I wasn't faithful or anything. But we would meet every two or three weeks. And if I wanted more, then I would look for it elsewhere. If I didn't, then I would wait.

I couldn't go to the park in the evenings, because I couldn't get out of the house. So I would go to the park in the mornings mostly, or in the afternoons, when I could. I couldn't do that very much. And there were usually people—a few people with the same problem I had. I remember that I once went to the public toilet around 8:30 in the morning, and I found someone. If someone's there, great, if not, OK. It was always just mutual masturbation.

I've gotten bashed two or three times. Once someone came up to me and said he was a policeman. I flew out of there. Just recently someone tried to pick my pocket. He took my money, but I managed to save the rest of my wallet. I try to keep an eye out for suspicious people.

Cruising itself is very pleasant, but afterwards you always feel like crap. It happens very rarely that I have the opportunity to get into bed with someone. So I have to do it in the stalls of a public bathroom, or in the bushes. It isn't very nice. I'm always disgusted with myself afterwards. Maybe it's this feeling of revulsion that doesn't let me decide to go in this direction all the way. But I'm often angry with myself afterwards—I say to myself, it's a shame I didn't just jerk off. To this day that's the way it is. After years and years. If I can actually get into bed with someone, that's very good, that's a different story.

It also happens sometimes that I go to the park, and I can't get it up with certain people. You go up to someone, start something, and all of a sudden you feel revolted, and you can't get it up, and you regret the whole thing. I have a hard time with people who only want to masturbate, without even a little groping, without hardly any touching at all. I don't want to kiss them— I mean, I don't even know them. But still, that doesn't mean that it should be just sex—the point isn't just to come and that's it. If that was what I wanted, I could do it better alone.

I have someone I've been in contact with for three years now, maybe four. I call him from time to time. He doesn't have anyplace, I don't have anyplace, so it's kind of a problem. But I was in touch with a student at the university for a while—a young guy, who just got married, actually. I had a very nice period of time with him, and through him I discovered the toilets at the Hebrew University, on Mount Scopus. Very large stalls, for the handicapped, where there's room to undress. So I've been going there a lot lately, with the guy I'm with now. And it's very good with him—at least with him, I don't feel like I'm doing something revolting. I call him once every two or three weeks, or he calls me, and I come to pick him up from work. And we both have a quarter of an hour to be together, in this certain stall at the university, which is very clean. A little crowded maybe. But it's good. I like to put my arms around him, to kiss him. I'm not afraid to go down on him, I know he's not seeing anyone else. And I drop him off at the bus stop afterwards.

AIDS is driving everyone crazy. I don't use a condom myself, because I never do penetration. Last week, actually, I was with someone, at his house. An old flame of mine—I ended it with him, because he was fat and he got on my nerves. But I don't know, suddenly he found me, and I went back to him, and it wasn't bad at all. And when I was there, a young guy called him, and came over also, and so it was a fabulous threesome—this young guy, you don't even get guys like this in your dreams. And I saw that he really wanted me to put it in him. Now, it's been years since I last did it, but I put a condom on and gave it to him. I wanted to be sure it didn't hurt him, but it didn't. He was used to it. Personally, it hurts me too much, I can't take it up the ass.

In the course of time I've also been to the sauna. Not a lot. I go maybe twice a year. Usually it's a disappointment. I don't find anyone. During the busy hours, in the afternoons, I can't get there. I went there in the evening once and I was almost the only one there. And even when there are young people there, my body doesn't exactly turn them on.

My sexual demands aren't that great—maybe I'll sleep with my wife once a week. And if I'm seeing a man at the time, maybe I won't sleep with her at all for a while. If I know that I'll want to sleep with her, then I won't go cruising beforehand. So I'll be in shape.

I believe in marriage. But you know what they say—when your cock is hard, your brain is in your ass. There's nothing to be done. I can't do anything about it. I'm aware of the problem, and I've learned to live with it. It's difficult. I don't know. I don't fool around with other women. I'm not looking for that. I only go with other men. Religiously speaking, that doesn't make it any better, but I can't help it. It's very serious, but I can't help it.

You should see how many religious men come to the meeting places. A lot. I can't remember that I've actually talked to someone about the religious question. Usually you just disappear after you've come. It isn't a very dignified situation, you know. All of us, we feel guilty, to a greater or lesser degree. If you meet someone in the park, you don't ask him his views on religious law. The law has already fallen by the wayside. There is no law. Once you've gotten all the way to the park, the law doesn't exist. Everyone has a problem with it. But they've also got another, more immediate problem—between their legs.

Look, I don't know what the real story with my son is. I don't have any reason to suspect anything, though. I know he has girlfriends, he's in eleventh grade now, and it makes me very happy. I hope that he won't have to go through everything I've been through. I don't want to say that I've suffered, because, you know, there is enjoyment in it. But it's a painful process. It's a very painful process. I've never slept the entire night with a man. And I'm sure that it would be delightful. Just to be able to come and then to be able to stay in bed afterwards. The few times when I've been able to be in bed with a guy, what happens afterwards is much more important to me than what happens beforehand. But it's worked out with very few people that I have time afterwards. This guy that I told you about, who I've been seeing, what's nice about him is that we do always try to make some time afterwards—we always talk a little, you know, was it good, not good, how much we need it, how much we miss each other. It makes you feel nice. It keeps the whole thing from becoming degrading, dirty.

I've never brought the subject up with my wife. She's a very puritanical woman. Lately, with the whole thing in the newspapers so much, I try to listen to what she says. I don't react, I'm not for or against. I just listen, I don't say anything. There's talk about Yaᶜel Dayan, this and that, I say, yeah, sure, to each his own.

I'm sure that there's no way I could tell her. But I'm also sure that even if I cheated on her with another woman she would throw me out of the house too. And I'm not willing to take the risk. If we weren't getting along, and I wanted to leave her, maybe then I would bring it up. I've heard about cases like this, where the man just couldn't go on any longer, so he told his wife. But it's not like that with us. We have a good relationship. We care about each other very much, we still enjoy ourselves in bed. We have sex. And she enjoys herself, of that I'm sure. And I like being with her. And there are things she gives me that no man can give me.

I don't feel any great need to expose everything to my wife. This particular subject isn't different from a lot of others in that respect. There are things you just can't say to your wife, you save them for your friends. In spite of everything, even though she's a good friend of mine too. That's just the way it is. I tell her all about work and so on, but there are things that, well, they're just locked in the closet. The saying is really very appropriate.

Look, we've been married for twenty-three years. We have our good times and our bad times. I always say, I'm happy I can still get it up, that I want to sleep with her, that everything works the way it should, and she still wants me, and she's responsive just like she was when she was younger. She's forty-eight already, and there are some women who have problems at that age. My wife also doesn't need a lot of sex. We've always had the problem that she has never initiated sex, I always have to be the first one. But she doesn't fake orgasms for me, and I don't fake any for her.

There's another problem, you're not married so you don't know. Sometimes, when I want to sleep with her, the kids are marching around until very late at night. And all the plans go down the drain. Who has the strength to wait? I joke with my friends, I say, as long as you're young, get your act together, because afterwards you're going to have to do a general survey of the territory before you begin an operation. There's no spontaneity. It's a problem. If we had a big house, with a separate bathroom of our own, and so on, it's clear that we would do it more. But you should know that the amount of sex I have with her, and my cruising, have nothing to do with each other—I must, like a biological clock, cruise at least once a month. I have to do it. It's something about me.

I don't think she suspects anything. When I have time, I run to cruise. When I don't have time, I don't cruise. This past month I've been very busy, and that made me happy, because I cruised less. I think I went to the park maybe once. I have a post office box downtown. I used to work near there, but I don't anymore, so it's difficult for me to get there now. I answered four personal ads this week, but I haven't even been able to check my box to see if I've gotten responses. Once, I called the new gay phone-sex line from our home phone. I didn't know it would be billed so clearly. I told my wife that I just called for the hell of it. I read about it in *Maga῾im*, which I have a subscription to. It goes to my post office box, but I have two copies hidden at home right now. I really should rip them up—my wife is going to find them. That would be the end.

I would have a lot to lose by coming out. It would be very destructive for the people who are closest to me. It's clear to me that my children would be the ones to suffer, especially in our religious environment. So I try not to think about it. I would love to live in Tel Aviv. It's more comfortable, secure there. Do you know that when there was the Turkish bath in Jerusalem, I never even went once? Because I knew that people who went there get known as being like that. It was the kind of place where people could see you, and I knew a lot of people who lived near there. I've been meaning to go to the sauna for a month already, but I haven't been able to find an excuse to get to Tel Aviv. Maybe it hasn't been pressing enough.

There was a certain guy who was important to me for a while, I haven't seen him lately. The funny story with him is that he suddenly found out that his wife was a lesbian. He was very hurt and they got divorced. I said to him, "How can you be hurt?" Now he's living with another woman, who knows about him, and he has a boyfriend.

One time I answered an ad, and arranged to meet with a guy. We sat in a cafe, talked a little, and he said that this wasn't what he was looking for. And that was that. No big deal. A few months later, I walked into a meeting at work, and suddenly there he was, sitting there. But I wasn't totally sure it was him. I knew he looked familiar, but I wasn't a hundred percent sure. At the next meeting, I made sure to get him alone, and I said to him, "Have we met?" And he said yes. And after that we were very friendly. I would call him up, I would go up to his office, he had his own office, and we did it there once or twice. And we talked about the whole situation a lot.

I once had a thing with a psychologist. This was about seven or eight years ago. And I would talk to him about the whole thing. He was one of the first people who, besides having sex, we would sit and talk, and we would call each other, get to know each other. I have become much more aware of the whole thing during the last ten years. It happens, when you get older, that sometimes you can't find someone who wants you. And you don't always want the one that wants you. Talking with him, I all of a sudden understood that I was missing out, that time was running out. And suddenly I was more conscious—I learned to talk about it. And that's what happened. I'm in a support group for married men now, and I'm more aware of a lot of issues. But I don't think I'm ready to pay the price. I told you, I need something more. And that something is a penis. What can I do? Today, I don't think about what's forbidden and what isn't. Today I just think that I've got to do what I've got to do. I'm fifty years old, and who knows what will happen tomorrow? Even now I have trouble finding people. What will be in a few more years?

At a certain point I could have decided to take off my *kipah* and not be religious any more. But I'm religious. Not ultra-Orthodox, not fanatic. But religious. I pray once a day, sometimes I say the grace after meals, I observe Shabbat. There are some things I do all the way. I will not profane Shabbat, and I won't eat nonkosher food. I don't usually wear *tzitzit*.[§] But when I need to, I do. I'm not fanatic, but I observe the commandments. It's important to me. It's also important to me that my children do the same. I'm not sure that

[§] tzitzit: Literally, "fringe"; four-fringed undershirt worn by men who strictly observe traditional religious law.

they will, but I hope so. You need to compromise with your children about a lot of things. You need to let them live their own lives. What can I do if they don't turn out religious? I don't know. But, on principle, I would have a problem with it. And they know it's important to me. That's the message they get. If they'll pay any attention to it, I don't know.

I have pretty ambivalent political views. I'm aware that it can't be that all the settlements in Judea and Samaria will stay there, with all of the settlers living together with the Arabs.[§] I think it will be very difficult, that whole thing. On the other hand, I don't want the settlers to leave. And I don't think we should come down from the Golan Heights—absolutely not. There's no issue of mixed population there. And certainly you can never give back Jerusalem.[†] I have a hard time with what is going on in the Galilee, which the Arabs are just filling up.[*] And I worry about the Lebanese border. We can't have people firing on the northern towns.

I vote for the Mafdal.[‡]

All of my friends went to live in settlements in the territories. Today, I could be living in a beautiful private home very cheaply if I had done the same thing. But I also didn't want that kind of communal life that they have there. Maybe because of who I am—I couldn't live in a closed cooperative group, cut off like that. I'd rather live in the city, be freer to do what I want. And I thought it would be nicer to raise my children someplace where they could be independent, and I wouldn't have to worry about them, chauffeuring them around. This was more important to me. Even though the children who grow up in settlements turn out fine, of course. They're good kids.

I vote for the religious parties mostly because of education. I think they need to be the guardians of education in this country. It's extremely important. That's why I vote for them, and not because of their other views, on set-

[§] Judea and Samaria: Biblical names for the territory making up the mountains of the central West Bank of the Jordan River, seized by Israel from Jordanian control during the Six-Day War in 1967. For many years, the Israeli government encouraged Jewish settlement in these areas, which include most of the lands settled by the ancient Israelites, and long-established present-day Jewish communities such as that in Hebron.

[†] Israel was in control of only the western half of Jerusalem until 1967, when the Israeli army gained control of the entirety of the city during the course of the Six-Day War.

[*] Galilee: Fertile, hilly northern countryside of Israel, where the Arab population nearly equals the Jewish population.

[‡] Mafdal: Hebrew abbreviation for National Religious Workers Party; established by merger in 1956; original platform of promotion of religious culture was complemented in the 1970s by strong advocacy of Jewish settlement in all parts of the ancient Land of Israel, including the West Bank.

tlements, gays, and so on. I don't think that Jewish law needs to be the law for the whole country. But I am a religious Zionist. I think that the Land of Israel is the place of the Jews. For better or worse, this is where we need to be.

I vote for the religious parties in spite of their views on gays. They're only doing what they have to do. That's what's written in the Torah, and that's what they've got to do. And, look, this whole subject of homosexual rights has only become a big thing in the past few years. I think there are more important things going on, with national policy.

You should know that in the Jewish religion, family life is a very important thing. It's not like with the Catholics. It's very important. A man is required to have a wife and to sleep with her, to satisfy her desires. And the proper times have been set, and how many times a month, and when, and how. The rabbis explain exactly how—you must have foreplay beforehand, and afterplay afterwards, there are precise descriptions that give you all the details. It's just amazing to read that "pornographic" literature. Very precise descriptions of everything—what to do, where to touch, where not to touch. It's treated as a very sanctified act, a religious obligation. You can't be a saint and decide not to do it. No way. This world exists. The law deals with everything, the woman's monthly ritual impurity, everything. Ten, eleven days out of the month, you don't sleep with your wife, while she is impure. You don't have any contact.

With my wife, we don't observe the eleven days any more, and after our last child was born, my wife stopped going to the monthly ritual bath. Sure, sometimes we don't sleep with each other for two weeks, but it has nothing to do with that.

I had an affair with an Arab once. Some of the Arab men are so beautiful! A painter came, to do some work inside the house. My wife was at work and I was on vacation. He spoke Hebrew well, and he began talking about the women he's screwed, and what his wife does, and so on. And for some reason or other, I got the message that I could do it with him. One day he went into the bathroom, and I just went in after him, I touched him, and he touched me. It was fabulous. He was very well endowed. But he's one of those men who only want you to service them, to blow them, to do this, to do that. He didn't really want to give me anything. He didn't want to stroke me or put his arms around me. And it's very important to me that it be mutual. We met a few times afterwards, and it was always like that. And then the intifadah began, so he could never be sure if he would be able to come to Jerusalem. And then I got worried, that this Arab could also just call up my wife and tell her everything, so I stopped seeing him. I was frightened. He had a marvelous penis. And marvelous skin.

My sexual experiences with Arabs have absolutely not changed my political views. Someone can have a nice body and cock, but that has nothing to do with anything. When I meet someone, I'm not looking to get to know him. It has happened very rarely that things have developed into friendship, or even conversation.

I wouldn't say that I'm comfortable with my situation. But this is the way it is. I've got to live with it. At this moment, I feel comfortable with it. Tomorrow, I won't feel comfortable. It depends how I'm feeling. Sometimes, it's very difficult for me. Sometimes I imagine very strange things. If my wife were to pass away today, I don't think I would remarry. I might try to find myself a boyfriend. Maybe not openly, but I would look for someone. There was just a whole thing with my wife, she had a growth in her ovary, and we were worried that it might be malignant. And suddenly I started thinking, if, God forbid, something were to happen, I'm not sure I would remarry or even look for other women. Today, I couldn't see myself being attracted to another woman. Today, my direction is more and more toward men. In this respect, I think I've changed over the years. I'm more secure. The mere fact that I can talk about this says something.

RAFI NIẎ

Rafi Niẏ was the first person we interviewed; he was an obvious choice. As the author of a weekly column on gay issues for Qol Ḥeifah, one of the Haifa city newspapers, he was one of the most visible gay men in the country. And he was using his column—in a "family" paper, no less—to broadcast more strident views on gay identity and politics than those held even by most Israeli activists. And was it really true that his current marriagelike gay relationship had been preceded by a marriage to a woman?

On top of all these very compelling reasons to seek Rafi out, it was easy to do so. Amir had worked as the news editor of Qol Ḥeifah, and although Amir was playing the role of the enlightened straight man at the time, he had been influential in getting Rafi's column started. Rafi expressed great enthusiasm upon hearing of our project. It remained only to set a date.

Getting to Haifa to perform the interview posed no great inconvenience. Amir's Haifan parents were not quite thrilled about our freshly uncloseted relationship, but to their credit, they were still unwilling to forego weekly visits from their beloved son, no matter whom he brought along. So, on a lazy Shabbat morning, Amir and I drove the short distance from his parents' apartment to Rafi's. It was a pleasant trip through the winding streets of residential Haifa's bourgeois knolls, where apartment buildings cluster like mushrooms at unlikely angles on the thickly vegetated hills.

Rafi greeted us at the door to his apartment, which was every bit as respectable as his neighborhood, what with the formal dining-room furniture, the large color television, and the dark leather couches. This was a real home. Rafi *himself could best be described as "Romanian-looking"—unfortunately, in English, this fails to conjure up the big-boned, large-faced, light-skinned Israeli stereotype. He was carefully groomed, although it seemed that he must be struggling with his waistline. We were instantly treated to the requisite instant coffee—sugared and milked to taste—with the help of Asaf, Rafi's lover. Asaf was on his way to run some errands, and upon his exit we began recording.*

∾

I WAS BORN IN QIRYAT MOTZQIN, on the outskirts of Haifa, and when I was two years old we moved to Qiryat Bialik, a different neighborhood in the same area. In sixth grade we made another short move, back to Qiryat Motzqin. That last move was, you know, really tough, because I already was a boy who didn't fit in very easily.

I come from a typical Romanian family. My father was born in Transylvania, in a city by the name of Timisoara. My mother is also Romanian-born. She's from a town called Suceva, in the north.

My father was very dominating, something of a tyrant. He kept tight reigns on the household. My brother was more daddy's boy, and I was more momma's boy—my mother would defend me from my father's beatings. Every time I did something wrong and my father would want to give me a strapping with his belt, my mother would shout at him not to hit me. She usually succeeded. My older brother got most of the beatings. There were never physical signs of affection between my parents—I never saw them kiss, never.

I never had any friends until adolescence. No friends at all. I was a very lonely boy. But I knew how to keep myself busy. And even when I finally did make some friends, it was only because I was the best in my class at math, so everyone wanted me to give them private lessons. I remember wanting a girlfriend because, you know, I wanted to fit in. There was one boy in my class, I think he was gay, but it's a mystery to me to this day. I was attracted to him, but I never did a thing to let him know. So it was a hidden attraction. I thought I was strange, a failure of a kid. An empty nothing who interests no one. And that was why no one wanted me. That's what I thought about myself. Then.

When my brother was sixteen, he brought a girl home for the first time. They went into his room, he locked the door, and they, you know, slept together. I understood that something out of ordinary was going on, but I could also tell that it was a thing you had to ignore. It didn't take long for my parents to get used to it, and he kept on bringing his girlfriends to spend the night.

I'm sure that he knew that it wasn't OK, that first time—but he wanted to bring her home, so he did it. He had already had confrontations with my father about all kinds of things, but maybe because it was forbidden to talk about sex, he knew he could almost do whatever he wanted. I can't explain it. But it happens a lot in Israel, even at a younger age. It wasn't like he got the message from them that this was allowed. Overall, it was a conservative house.

We never talked about sex at home. Never. It was a very repressed atmosphere. I remember that at seventeen I would watch television with my parents, and there were some pretty vulgar skits, and even at that age I felt that I was supposed to be embarrassed. So of course there was never any conversation with my father about "it," or anything like that. When it came to the point when I needed to begin shaving, my father kind of said to me, "It's about time you shaved." But it was sort of a casual comment, tossed off. It was sort of understood that I was supposed to begin shaving, but the details weren't totally clear to me—I mean, what was I supposed to do? I was almost eighteen. So I just went and shaved—but I locked the bathroom door. I understood it as a sexual act I should be ashamed of.

When I was a teenager, I was one of the most faithful readers in the country of a film magazine called *Lahiton*. And this is proof that I knew I was gay, even back then. Because I would cut out pictures of men, and I would keep them in a very secret drawer. I was certain that no one would go through my things. But one day, shortly after I had been drafted into the army, I came home on leave and I saw that the drawer was empty—all the pictures and cuttings had been thrown out. I was shocked. All my life, I had taken care of my room alone—I cleaned it, organized it. It was my territory. And my mother knew it. So I asked my mother who had been in my room, and she said that my sister-in-law had cleaned it up. I've never mentioned this incident to her—I don't think she would want to talk about it.

I think that I did know about myself in high school—I just didn't know what it was called. I mean, I had all these pictures of men, but I didn't know that there was a name for my behavior, that I was a "homosexual." Boys in school wouldn't even use the word as an insult.

So we're up to the army now, right? I was afraid of the army. I didn't have any idea what was going on. My brother had been a paratrooper—he had volunteered for it, he really wanted to be a combat soldier. But it was clear that I was no paratrooper—I wasn't in shape, I had the body of a boy, not a man. But according to the army, I was prime soldier material, and they required that I be trained for combat. So I asked my downstairs neighbor what he thought I should do. He had been in the artillery corps, and suggested that. So that's what I did.

I was kind of a zombie in the army. My goal was just, you know, to survive through the week, knowing that on Friday, I could, like, come home to my cozy little corner, to my parents, to the television, to sleep. After basic training, I wasn't sent to a battalion—I was sent to an artillery brigade, where life is a little better. You have, you know, better sleeping quarters, better conditions.

I've never talked about this since then with anyone—I don't even remember if I had a particular favorite soldier who I thought was good-looking. I mean, there was no connection between my fantasy life and the world around me. I couldn't say to myself, you know, this is a cute soldier. It may be that I wanted to do something, but I wasn't in a condition where I could even imagine actually acting on my desires. I don't know how to explain it. It's difficult to explain, I don't know. I wasn't conscious of my sexuality, the fact that I was a sexual being. I had erections, I would, like, masturbate, but I didn't imagine that it was possible to do something sexual with men besides fantasize about them. I really thought I was an exceptional mutation. I didn't think there were, you know, any other people like me in the world.

Most of the guys would shower in the evening. But I would either shower in the morning or the early evening, when I was sure that there wouldn't be anyone else in the shower room. I didn't indulge myself.

When the other soldiers talked about girls, I think I may have tried to toss something out about a girlfriend that I had. Certainly, when they joked about queers, I didn't feel that they were joking about me. Actually, I remember now that there was one soldier who always addressed me in the feminine form—yes, they would laugh at me sometimes. But I didn't really attach any importance to it. The other soldiers didn't really join in. This guy was just, you know, a very brutal type. I didn't answer him. I just totally disappeared. I didn't exactly understand what I was supposed to do.

During my last year in the army, a new soldier arrived on the base. He was younger than me. Kind of, like, arty, sophisticated, more intellectual. He was from north Tel Aviv. I had a reputation on the base for being a somewhat problematic soldier—I would doze off while on guard duty, all sorts of things like that. I was in trouble all the time. And he was like that also.

So we began hanging out together. We talked a lot, about how miserable we were in the army. I remember one night, it was summer, and it was so stuffy inside, no one could breathe, no one could sleep. So he decided that he was going to take a bunk bed out into the fields, which were really only a few meters from the sleeping quarters, and sleep there. The air was wonderful outside, and I went with him and we slept outside—I was on the top bunk, he was on the bottom. It was very cozy.

We would get together on Shabbat sometimes also. We would go hiking in the area around the base, which is beautiful, especially in the spring. I enjoyed myself with him. But eventually it came time for me to be discharged, I had finished my third year of service. To a certain extent it was very sad to have to say goodbye. He was my first friend. I was a lonely person. I've kept in touch with him—he isn't gay. It wasn't a sexual thing.

So I left the army. My parents wanted me to study economics at the Technion, which is also in Haifa. I wasn't a very independent person. I was very dependent on my parents. And in the army everyone had said that economics was a good thing to study. So when my sister-in-law offered to take me to the campus to help me register, I didn't really object.

I don't know if that's what I wanted to study. I didn't really have any desires of my own. That's what I tried to explain to you earlier. I felt that I was nothing. It was like I was being controlled by social forces stronger than I was, that I was a sort of puppet that my family and environment was pushing around.

But actually, it was very nice to be going to school again. I got to know a few people, and we would study together. The whole homosexual thing was very, very repressed. I was living at home for a while, but at some point, I moved out of my parents' house. But even then, it wasn't for the reasons you would think.

It was right after the Lebanon War.[§] I, of course, had been called back into the army for the war. My battalion was stationed in Lebanon, near Tyre, on the shore. But we had nothing to do there, so all the soldiers, we would just, you know, go to the beach every day, and lay out in the sun, in the nude. Almost every day, all day long, day after day. That was the Lebanon War for me. But right around this time, my father was diagnosed as having cancer, and he began having all sorts of horrible operations. He had melanoma—a skin cancer that grows out of a beauty mark. He died from it.

[§] In June 1982, the Israeli army invaded Lebanon and advanced as far as Beirut, with the intention of ending guerilla attacks on the towns of northern Israel.

I went to visit my father after one of his first operations. And when I came, the doctor took me aside, and said to me, "I want to examine you." So I went to his room, undressed, and he saw that I had a beauty mark that looked suspicious. He said, "I want to remove this." And after a day or two I went in for the operation, and he removed it. It was cancerous. I needed a larger operation. It turned out that exposing my skin to the sun was absolutely the most dangerous thing I could have done. And then, for some reason that I don't remember, I had a huge argument with my father, I don't remember about what. But I moved out, and I went to live with my brother and sister-in-law for a week or two, and then I decided that I needed to live alone.

I had periodic check-ups for the next three years, and when three years was up and nothing developed, they said it was OK. But I'm not allowed to go to the beach anymore, ever. Later, when the intifadah began, in 1987, I used this medical condition to get out of doing annual reserve duty.

I got married in September 1983. This was after the war, after I had moved out. I was still on reserve duty, stationed up in Lebanon, and my father was already pretty sick. I met Riyqah, my wife, through someone I knew from the army, a girl. This girl knew that I didn't have a girlfriend, and she was always trying to fix me up with all sorts of friends of hers. It's interesting that she didn't try to come on to me herself.

I went out with one friend of hers a few times, but it didn't work out. I didn't know what I was doing. I think she wanted something physical, but I didn't know what to do, and she didn't do enough to make things happen. We both agreed that it didn't click. I did kind of try to, you know, grope her. I said to myself, let's give it a try. Yes, I wanted to try, I wanted to try. But it was so foreign to me. I managed to kiss her, but it was very, very strange. This was at, like, twenty-one, twenty-two. I had never been out with a girl before.

So it didn't work out, but my matchmaker friend went back to work. And she said to me that with Riyqah, everything would be OK, because we were a good match. Riyqah had been in the army entertainment troupe, she was a very warm, beautiful girl. She played the guitar, her brother was a playwright—well, he wrote a few plays, I don't know if that makes him a playwright.

Our first meeting was together with this friend. The three of us went out to a movie or something. Afterwards, we went to a bar, we talked, it was very nice. In short, things took their course. We went out a few more times, and I told her that I had never slept with anyone before. And she told me that she wasn't sure if she wanted to, you know, take the responsibility on herself, of being the first. And that's it, we stopped talking to each other. But after a few months she sought me out and renewed contact. My first time happened in my apartment.

She took the first step. She said that it was about time that we did it already. It didn't really work at first, because of me, and she said don't worry about it, it often happens that the first time with someone it's difficult. The second time it really happened.

Now, I know this is going to sound really strange, but at this time I was planning a backpacking trip to Europe, and I was looking for a traveling companion. So I asked Rivqah. And her mother said, "If you want to travel with her in Europe, marry her." So we got engaged. And we didn't even go to Europe in the end! We had known each other for eight months.

During most of that time, we had basically been living together in my apartment. We had good sex. I thought that maybe I would, you know, grow out of the gay thing. And I was happy that I had finally found a person to be my friend. It was Rivqah who finally introduced me to a group of people who became real friends, friends that I have to this day. And my self-image improved a lot, because all of a sudden I was getting positive feedback from my environment, about how I looked, and so on. I felt more secure, socially.

I didn't tell her anything about feelings I had had in the past. I did feel that there was something I should have told her, but I didn't say anything. I remember one period when I was very much concerned. It was only a few weeks before the wedding, and I was back in Lebanon on reserve duty. We had already arranged the reception and everything, and I remember wondering whether I was making a mistake. I already knew what it was like with a woman, and I think I already knew then, deep inside, that this was not what I wanted.

But somehow or other I repressed the thought. I pondered it for a few days while I was in Lebanon, but when I came home, I was so swept up in it all, I didn't have the courage to do anything. It wasn't even in the realm of possibility.

I don't think I did anything dishonorable. I don't think that I'm guilty of not revealing to her this great secret—I really thought it would work when I married her. I thought I should give it a chance, that things will work out, that I can control myself. I think that even then, I still believed that I was the only gay man in the world. I mean, I had never met anyone else. I might have heard the word "homosexual," but I didn't know that there were other homosexuals who were people like me, and not men wearing dresses that cruise the park. I didn't know. So I don't think you can, you know, judge me. Riyqah, of course, thinks that I ruined her life. To this day she blames me.

We never had children, but it wasn't for lack of trying. It didn't work. To this day I don't know if it was because of me or because of her. Thankfully, we got divorced before the doctors could really get to work, trying to figure things out.

I hardly remember anything of my married life, only spots. I remember that each year, as our anniversary approached, I would plan out in my mind, I would imagine, you know, taking Riyqah to a restaurant, buying her an anniversary present, and telling her that our marriage wasn't working, that I was gay. But I never did it. I didn't have the courage. Even though it was clear to me that I didn't want to keep on living like this. I was trapped. I didn't know what to do.

When did I begin to know that there was such a thing as gay men? When they began to talk about AIDS on television and in the newspapers—that was in 1983. Then, all of a sudden, they began to talk about gays.

It wasn't like there was a moment of revelation or anything like that. Things don't work that way. You don't wake up in the morning and say, "Hey, I'm gay." But at some point, I realized that there were personals in Ḥadashot twice a week, on Mondays and Wednesdays—and every time, there were some two ads out of twenty that were from men looking for men. I don't know what it was that made me even look at the personals at all, at first. But I know that after I discovered them I began buying that paper regularly, on Mondays and Wednesdays, specifically so that I could read the gay personals. I knew what I was doing. I knew why I was buying the paper. If my wife was home, I would go into the bathroom and read the personals.

It took me a long time before I responded to one of the ads. Maybe it was a year after I first discovered them, something like that. It's difficult to say precisely.

I didn't know about the park scene. How was I supposed to know that you could cruise in the park? Today, maybe, everyone knows, because it gets written about. But back then, how was I supposed to know you could go to the park? There were also gay bars in Tel Aviv, but I had no idea. They didn't report on these things in the newspapers back then.

The ad I answered was very simple—"Young man, student, twenty-five, looking for same." It seemed to me somehow more innocent than a lot of others, maybe more closeted also. So I wrote him a letter. I didn't say that I was married. I didn't say a lot—I hardly described myself, and I didn't touch on anything sexual at all.

By this time I already had my degree from the Technion, and I was working at Elbiṭ, a very big high-tech firm, and I was very successful there. I was named Outstanding Employee of the Year.

So in the letter, I gave this guy my work number, with a name other than Rafi. I said my name was Miḥah. Now, a lot of different people answered the phone at this number I gave this guy. And of course, if he called and someone else answered, and he asked them for Miḥah, they would say they didn't know anyone by that name. But if I answered, and someone asked for Miḥah, I would immediately know what was going on. That was my intention. I found out later that he had to call quite a few times before I answered the phone. But he didn't get discouraged—he had figured out what was going on. Apparently I hadn't, you know, invented the wheel. As it turned out, he was calling from a branch office of the same firm, where he worked part-time. So he had even recognized the number I gave him as being an Elbiṭ office!

Now, at this time, my wife was very interested in painting. And it was very convenient. Once a week, she would have a painting class in the evening, and she wouldn't come home until ten at night. So that was when I invited him. Our first meeting was in my apartment. I went to the neighborhood shopping center to pick him up, and we drove back to my place in my car.

He immediately understood that he had come to a married man's apartment. I remember that I was really into Tom Waits at the time, so I put on one of his tapes, and we talked a little. At first, we went into the study, where there was a couch. We sat on the couch, and I said to him, "I don't know what to do—you do it." Afterwards, we went into the double bed. All of my fantasies were realized. I wasn't disappointed. My head was in the clouds. I didn't know yet what safe sex was, but as it turned out, we had safe sex.

After it was over, we talked some more, and we had some coffee. He said to me that he had never been with a married man, and that it seemed like this was a very complicated situation. He asked when we would be able to meet again, and I said to him, "Only in another week." He left about ten minutes before my wife was supposed to come back. I fixed up the bed, cleaned, you know, made sure there were no signs, did the dishes. We talked a few more times on the phone that week.

To a certain extent, I had already fallen in love with him. It took a week until we met again, and not a day passed when I didn't think about him. This wasn't just a matter of getting laid.

I didn't feel like I was cheating on my wife. I didn't feel like I was doing something illegitimate. I felt good. It's difficult for me to reconstruct how I felt then. I didn't feel like my entire life had been changed. I didn't see that. I think the only thing I really thought was that I was going to have to enroll my wife in more intensive painting classes. That's what I thought.

So it was once a week for three months. And then he said to me that he couldn't go on, that I had to choose, that once a week wasn't enough. I didn't yet have the courage to pack my bags and leave the house. Apparently I wasn't convinced that he was the love of my life—but I did love him, to a certain extent. I didn't see it as a one-night stand or anything, even though the fact was that every one of our meetings consisted of a cup of coffee, sex, and another cup of coffee. That's the way it was. So we split up. But before we split up, we had a serious conversation, and he said to me, "Just so you know, there's no turning back." And I said, "OK." And I meant it. I knew that what I wanted most in the world was, not to be with my wife, but to be with a man, and I knew that I was taking steps that would bring this about.

Meeting him brought home to me the fact that I was not the only one in the world. Before that, you know, I thought I was the only one. And now I knew that there were others, we talked about it. He told me that I wasn't his first.

So I answered another ad—the ad that changed my life. I decided, I don't know why, to answer a more steamy one. "I'm beautiful, hot, very sexy," and so on. Apparently I got a little carried away—I met him, and it turned out that there was no link at all between the description in the ad and real life. We talked for five minutes, and I said to him that there had been some mistake. But I had already given him my home phone number.

When I came back from the meeting with him, my wife hadn't come home yet, so I took the opportunity to write a letter to this guy, saying that I wanted it to be clear to him that I didn't want him calling me. Unfortunately, I didn't have an envelope or a stamp, so I said, OK, tomorrow morning I'll go to the post office. To make a long story short, I put off going to the post office for a few days, and the letter stayed in my wallet. In the meantime, apparently, he had been calling the house, asking to talk to me, and that made Riyqah suspicious. She knew everyone who would call me at home, but this was a strange man. I said he was someone from work. As I later found out, though, Riyqah's suspicions had been raised earlier—she had suspected that I was cheating on her with another woman.

So in the end, she found the letter. And I admitted everything. I remember conversations upon conversations upon conversations. She said she couldn't believe this was happening to her. She asked me what I wanted, and I said that I didn't know. It was totally clear to me that I wanted a man—but I didn't have enough courage to say that to her. So I said that I didn't know. She suggested that I go into therapy. There was one point where she came up with this theory that maybe because I had no social or sexual experience before we met, that suddenly I had reached my belated adolescence, and maybe, you know, I would just grow out of all this. At twenty-seven!

Riyqah told all her girlfriends, and one friend of hers said to her that, you know, it wasn't so awful, and that she should try to live with it. That if she were in her place, she would prefer to try to work something out. But at some point the situation became simply unbearable in the apartment. I moved into the study, and she kept on sleeping in the bedroom. I think I was the one who decided to move into the study—the moment she knew about me, I felt that I could drop all the pretenses. I wanted to be in the other room. And then I moved out.

She felt betrayed. She was in shock at first, and didn't believe that this was happening. She tried to deny it. We argued over money and property—but most of her anger was about her feeling betrayed. She said I had ruined her life. And more or less since then we haven't spoken to one another. We were married for three and a half years, all together. I don't miss her.

After we separated, I left Elbiṭ, in spite of the whole story with "Outstanding Worker" and so on. I went back to the Technion, to get my masters degree in social science and management. Because my undergraduate degree wasn't in psychology I couldn't study industrial psychology, which was what really interested me. So I specialized in organizational behavior, from a more sociological perspective. While I was studying I got a very cushy scholarship—more than I'm earning now, that's for sure. And after I got my degree, I worked for a year as a teaching assistant, for a salary. That was a great time in my life.

There were a few months when I got kind of wild, but not to an extreme. I know a lot of gays who were more promiscuous than me. I mean, I didn't have three men every night—but I had a few every week. I didn't really know what I was looking for. It wasn't clear to me that I wanted a boyfriend. I wanted to fool around. I would meet them either cruising the park or through personal ads. I would go to Binyamin Park in Haifa. In Haifa, it's Beni or Ziki—Binyamin Park or Memorial [Hazikaron] Park.

Yes, I had finally discovered cruising. I don't remember when I heard exactly, but I knew that you could go to the park, and that there weren't men in dresses there. I knew that you could find men there who were, I don't know, real. I still didn't really know that there were gay bars in Tel Aviv—I think that if I had known that, I would have gone. But I knew about personal ads and the park. When I got fed up with the ads I went to the park.

I don't remember the first time I was in the park. It wasn't pleasant. I didn't particularly enjoy going there. I would go into the park, you know, wander around. Any time between sundown and midnight—I would choose an hour. And I would usually find someone. I mean, it wasn't crowded, like Independence Park in Tel Aviv—usually, a busy night would mean that there would be about ten men there at any given moment. Men of all types—old, young, Arabs, soldiers, teenagers, university students, smart and not so smart. You see all levels of society. I would usually find someone, and we would either go to my place or his.

The problem is, of course, that you can't really see very well in the dark. You walk around, and if you see someone who seems attractive, you try to go past him a few times, until somehow or other you make some sort of contact. If he shows signs of being interested in meeting you, you get closer, and strike up a conversation. I think I was usually very direct—"Hello, how are you, what's up," things like that, and then I would get to the point very quickly. I never suggested that we, you know, do it in the park, even though I know that some people who have no place else to go do it there.

Eventually, I met Asaf. We met through an ad—we both had published ads, and we answered each other's ads! He sent me a letter with his telephone number, and I called him. We made a date, at my place. I remember that I sat on the rocking chair, and he sat on the couch—very far away. And we talked for about half an hour, and at some point I said that I wouldn't object to getting into bed. Something like that. And Asaf agreed. It was the middle of the afternoon when we turned the lights out, and when we turned them on again, it was already eight at night. We said, "What should we do now?" So we went to a movie. That was our first date.

Asaf is kind of dark-skinned, and when I met him he was also a little chubby—and I, wouldn't you know it, liked them skinny and blond! His father is Polish and his mother is Greek. I remember being impressed by how friendly and warm he was, and warmth is something that I need very much. He's a student at heart. He's going to be a student all his life—he was studying when I met him, and he still is. We've been together for six years now.

Asaf said that he was looking for a long-term partner. He had had a boyfriend before this, and one of the first things he said was that he wanted someone to really love him. I think he was ready to move in with me after half an hour. For my part, I didn't really know what I wanted. But after we had been together for a few days, I knew that this was something more serious—before this, I hadn't had anybody for more than a day.

It wasn't that I made a decision to stop sleeping around and start a serious relationship. But I think that my natural tendency is to be a homebody. I don't like to sleep around. So we kept on seeing each other regularly, and little by little Asaf moved his things into my apartment, and he began staying the night a few times a week, and we would go on day trips together, on Shabbat.

At first, I didn't really understand that Asaf was, you know, my partner, and not just another guy. We didn't have any framework at all, at first. In the course of events there were some rough times, and we established some ground rules. The most important rule was that if either of us was going to have a one-night stand, then he was coming home afterwards. You didn't sleep away from home.

Little by little, we began making other gay friends, here and there. There was somebody I met at the Technion, and a lesbian friend of his, and Itziq, the accountant, and his boyfriend, Shmuliq, the hairdresser. We began going to the bars in Tel Aviv, and we always would run into people from Haifa there. And so we gradually made some contacts. We went to the Tel Aviv pubs because we wanted to go out as a couple. But Asaf always felt very, very uncomfortable there. I, on the other hand, immediately fit right in. I liked the freedom in the bars. People came to dance, you know, to let loose. It was nice.

We would all talk about how there was no place for gays in Haifa. So I found my way, through a mutual friend, to the owner of Fever, the most popular straight bar in Haifa, and suggested to him that he begin having a gay night once a week. He told me that he had already been thinking about it for a long time, but he wasn't sure it would be a good idea. So we talked about it, and he asked me all sorts of things—like would he have to wash the glasses extra well at the end of the night. I told him that, you know, that would not be necessary. He got a lot of flak from his other patrons about the idea. There was a lot of homophobia, but he didn't care. He was a good guy. Sure, he was ignorant, but back then everyone was ignorant, no one knew what we were talking about. I was still working at the university, so this must have been 1987.

Asaf and me went through a lot of ups and downs as a couple. We had a

few little, like, separations. At one point we actually went for marriage counseling at the Family Care Center, which is run by the Ministry of Employ-
ment and Commerce, the Haifa municipality, and Haifa University. They
were wonderful there. Even though it was a totally government-funded
agency, they gave us no problems at all. It was very impressive. They also give
counseling to straight couples who aren't officially married. I thought it was
something that people should know, that they were so open-minded there,
but the director asked me not to publicize it. She said that she didn't want to
bring the center's policy to the attention of their supervisory bodies!

One of our biggest crises was when I decided that I was going to fall in
love with a guy named ʿAmi, who I had met in Tel Aviv. But he was no idiot,
and he saw what was happening, that I wanted to, you know, prove something to Asaf. In the end he sent me home. After me and Asaf were back together we had a party marking our fifth anniversary—we had about two
hundred people there.

This relationship is forever. There was a time when I was really pushing
for us to pay the two, three hundred dollars, whatever it costs, and have a
legally binding contract of partnership drawn up. Even though we didn't really have that much property—that was before Asaf bought an apartment.
And Asaf didn't really want to, somehow or other. And then Asaf got some
money from his father, and decided to buy an apartment. For legal reasons
having to do with the mortgage, it had to be listed under his name only. We
argued about that—I mean, we could have, you know, drawn up a contract
or something. At first, we planned to buy the apartment, two rooms in the
center of town, renovate it, and move in there. It would belong to both of
us—somehow or other, I would also pay part of the mortgage. So there were
all sorts of arguments about how exactly we would divide the mortgage pay-
ments between us. I don't think these were financial arguments. In the end,
Asaf just bought the apartment himself, as an investment, and we kept on
renting the place where we're living.

My guiding principle was always that we were together, so everything we
do should be together. We still don't have a joint bank account. I wanted us
to have one, but, you know, that didn't work out either, because, well, maybe
if we had any money in our accounts then we would do it, but in the meantime, it doesn't really make sense, technically. I'm drawn more in the direction of making more links, and Asaf, even though he wants to be with me,
wants all the technical matters to be separate. And it gets a little on my
nerves. But I think that time will take care of this, that things will work out.

Our neighbors know about us, but it really doesn't interest me—I don't like that species of human being called the "neighbor." I try to have as little contact with them as possible. Asaf is more of a warmhearted type—he's always exchanging milk, eggs, sugar with them. They know about us, not because we hung any posters or anything, but because we've been living here for five years already. So they know. We don't try to hide it.

One day not long ago, Asaf went to take out the garbage, and some woman who lives in the building came up to him and said, out of the blue, "We're circulating a petition to get you two evicted from the building. I'm worried about my children." He just laughed and walked away. But we talked about it afterwards, and we got very worried. We began planning to move. It got to the point where we went to the head of the Tenants' Association, and notified him that we were leaving. He asked why, and we told him that we had heard that people wanted us out. And he said, "Don't be ridiculous." There was no petition.

After we were together for about three years, I told my mother about us. I don't know how she didn't see it earlier. There were so many hints. Asaf was already, you know, part of the family. I mean, it was understood that when I came to visit the family, I came with Asaf. But we didn't talk about it. It was like we were just regular friends. And my brother and sister-in-law, they also, they just repressed it. There was Asaf, with Rafi, and they knew him, and liked him, but it was like they really didn't know that we were gay.

With my mother there were a few turning points. After me and Asaf moved in together, like after about six months, I went to visit her, some evening, without Asaf. And she said to me, "Asaf loves you, doesn't he?" And I gave her a somewhat stunned look, and she said, "Yes, of course, how could anyone not love my son?" something like that. So it seemed to me that she knew—but she didn't.

There were, of course, a lot of things that I had to hide from my mother as long as she didn't know—I couldn't tell her where we hung out, what we did, and I always had to say "I, I, I" and never "we" whenever I did tell her anything. Very unpleasant.

So I decided to invite her to my apartment one morning for, you know, a talk. And she came over, and it took me about two hours before I got to the point. We talked about all sorts of things. And then I remember what I said to her. We were talking about Asaf, what he was up to, and I asked her if she knew what kind of relationship I had with Asaf. And then she began to cry, and she told me that only a few days earlier, she had been in our apartment, and she had seen a flier from ʿOtzmah, with the phrase written on top: "Equal Rights for Gay Men, Lesbians, and Bisexuals." That was at the time when I was very involved with the gay night at Fever, and the Agudah had given me the fliers to take there.[§] So she had seen it, and didn't say anything. And she hadn't slept for a few nights. It was a lucky coincidence that I had decided to tell her then. Shortly after our conversation I helped organize a Haifa-area support group for the parents of lesbians and gays, and my mother became one of its most active members.

She likes Asaf a lot. I don't think she relates to us as gays. She relates to us as me and Asaf. She loves us and accepts us as a couple. And her attitudes towards gays have changed as a result of the fact that I'm her son, and Asaf her son-in-law. She absolutely relates to Asaf as her son-in-law.

The first time that I found out that there was such a thing as the Agudah was in a conversation with some friends in a bar in Tel Aviv called Divine. Anyway, someone there told us that there was a place on Alenbi Street where people did political things, and there was a library there. So I knew there was such a thing, but I didn't know what it was.

Then, one night when I was running Fever, suddenly there appeared a certain guy from the Agudah. He had heard about the evening, asked who had organized it, and they directed him to me. He introduced himself, and began to talk to me about the Agudah. And then all of a sudden he began making all sorts of suggestions about how to make what we were doing more successful, for instance, to combine it with lectures and some other things. The truth is that, you know, the whole Fever thing wasn't a great success, in general. The high point, though, was definitely a really wonderful Ḥanukah party.[†] There were about two hundred people there. I remember that at some point they stopped the music, said something over the microphone, and suddenly they were giving me a round of applause, as the person responsible. I didn't know what to do with myself.

So to make a long story short, this certain guy said to me that elections in the Agudah were coming up, and he suggested that I come and put myself up for the board of directors. I hardly knew what the Agudah was, I didn't

[§] ʿOtzmah: Political action committee of the "Agudah," the Society for the Protection of Personal Rights for Gay Men, Lesbians, and Bisexuals in Israel. ʿOtzmah was especially active in the late eighties and early nineties; Israeli gay activists now tend to work directly within the Labor Party and Meretz.

[†] Ḥanukah: Eight-day winter holiday commemorating Judah Maccabee's rededication of the Temple in Jerusalem in 165 B.C.E.

know a, b, c, I didn't know anything. But I had a masters degree in organizational management by this time, so I felt confident that, you know, if it was an organization, then I was OK.

So on the day of the general meeting of the Agudah, I went down to Tel Aviv. Asaf didn't come. Now, at this time, I was still basically in the closet, and I was terribly afraid. So this guy said, "Look, you don't have to go out there using your own name, you can chose an alias." So, without giving it much thought, I decided upon the name "Doron Śagi." I spoke very well at the meeting, and they were very impressed with my credentials, and I was elected. But I was Doron Śagi, and not Rafi! And it terribly frustrated me. I was Doron Śagi! And I began to get phone calls at home, for Doron. They would, you know, ask if Doron was at home. The first time, Asaf told them they had a wrong number! It shortly became clear that I had made a terrible mistake.

Little by little I got to know the Agudah, at the same time that I gradually became more aware of myself. And I gradually reached the conclusion that the Agudah's approach is totally ineffectual, which is what I believe now. I remember, right from the very start I had the feeling that there were serious problems there. I saw this real antagonism between the members of the board and the rest of the organization. Well, I don't really know if you can put it this way—I mean, besides the members of the board, there was no organization. We were the Agudah, more or less. And we would busy ourselves most of the time with internal matters, always, you know, looking inward. We would discuss things from the early morning until late at night, and nothing would come of it. And this continued for a long time.

One thing I did manage to do was to organize a number of people in Haifa, and a sort of group was born, with the goal of doing all sorts of things for gays in Haifa. By this time Fever had closed. We mostly organized lectures, speakers on different topics. I was responsible for the lectures, and we had more people coming to our lectures than there were who came to the meetings of the Agudah in Tel Aviv. But for some reason the Haifa group wasn't allowed to be an official branch of the Agudah. Today, the Haifa group is an official branch—but they waited until I had left the Agudah.

I was elected to a second term on the board, which was more of the same old frustrations, and then the real trouble began. I decided that I'd like to organize a putsch in the next elections. And it became clear to me that I wasn't the only one who thought that way. Very quickly, a rumor broke out in Tel Aviv that some guy from Haifa was organizing a brainstorming group to discuss new directions for the Agudah. So I had a meeting in Haifa, and some people came all the way from Tel Aviv, just to be there. To make a long story short, we prepared very well for the elections. A lot of people from this group were elected to the board—the putsch was successful.

The beginning was wonderful. We had the sense that a real transformation in the Agudah was about to take place. We did accomplish things, we felt that something had changed. I didn't have anything negative to say. But I think that by the end of this term I had already developed my thinking to the point where, you know, I no longer was convinced that the only salvation of gays in Israel was this one organization. Because the fact is that there's a huge chasm between this voluntary organization and the majority of the gays in Israel.

And people were very frustrated, very burnt out. We felt like we were taking on a lot more than we were capable of doing, and most of us felt that we didn't want to run for another term. I was one of them. We felt like we were putting tons and tons and tons of energy into things that were really unimportant, and we were always mired in bullshit—that Liꜛora Moriꜛel has a big mouth, that someone is insulted—all sorts of garbage like that. But even though I didn't want to run again, I was convinced in the end to run. I wound up resigning pretty soon after the elections. I was already working at the newspaper *Qol Ḥeifah*—I think that this was when you were there, Amir. I wanted to do other things, I had had it.

I think that the Agudah is really only rebuilding the closet in different forms. It more or less affirms the closet—it doesn't try to break out of it. Just now, I was reading a really typical letter that Liꜛora Moriꜛel, the new chairperson there, wrote to the editors of *Haꜛaretz*. She attacks people like me, who, you know, want to do everything fast—"to tilt at windmills." So she says, come on, let's try first to do things in a nonconfrontational way, and afterwards, if that doesn't work, then we can get nasty. I don't think I'm being nasty. I'm attacking the values that preserve the closet—is that being nasty? I don't think so.

You know, when I was elected to the board of the Agudah, I was in the closet! I didn't even use my own name! And today, I just kept asking myself, how could they do that to me? How could that guy who recruited me actually say to me—come on, be an activist in the Agudah, but choose an alias for yourself, stay in the closet. How could he say that to me? In essence, in a certain sense, he played me for a fool—he cheated me. He didn't tell me what I really had to do in order to be an activist. The Agudah is the only gay organization in Israel and it is too conservative. It's a closeted organization.

After I finally left the university, I found out that there was no work in the field in which I had specialized. So I was on unemployment for, like, six months. I never liked economics anyway. While I was on unemployment, I began to work at *Qol Ḥeifah* as a freelance writer. And after my six months ran out, I needed a real job, so I went to work in the Haifa harbor, once again with a big firm. But I hated every moment of it. It was a fourteen-month nightmare. In the end, they fired me—I made them do it. And then, at about the same time, *Qol Ḥeifah* agreed to hire me on salary. That was about the time that my column began.

Now, I had about had it by this time with being Doron Sági. But I still couldn't bring myself to go all the way and use my real name, Rafi Eppler, as a gay reporter. So I went part of the way, and began to write articles for *Qol Ḥeifah* under the name of Rafi Niy.

I liked this new situation very much, because the name Eppler, the name I was born with, carries a lot of negative connotations for me. It's connected to my past, like when I felt that I had to do what everyone else does, when I felt that I was a zero, a nothing, a puppet. The name Eppler belonged to all of that past. So I was very happy to shed that name, and to take on a new name, of my choosing, in my own way. Now everyone knows me by the name of Rafi Niy, but I don't hide the fact that, technically, my name is Rafi Eppler. I may change it officially someday.

I had never really thought seriously about journalism before, but I first came into contact with *Qol Ḥeifah* through my work at the Agudah. There was a really interesting story with a gay couple, new immigrants from Kazakhstan in the old Soviet Union. One of them was Jewish and the other wasn't. The Jew came to Israel as an official new immigrant, and got all the benefits of a new immigrant—but his non-Jewish partner came as a tourist. And when his tourist visa expired, he couldn't get it renewed. They wanted to stay here together, as a couple, and they went to the Agudah to get help. But for its own stupid reasons, the Agudah refused to do anything to help them. In the end, this couple emigrated to Denmark, where they are today.

I decided that I wanted to publicize their case on my own, to make their story a subject of public debate. So I decided to write an article about them, and I went to them and interviewed them—not that I knew how you interview someone. But I wrote an article, and sent it to *Qol Ḥeifah*. They liked it, and published it. I didn't have the journalistic sense then to realize that I could have brought the story to *Yediᶜot Aḥaronot*, or another national newspaper.

So I began doing just general news reporting and feature writing at *Qol*

Ḥeifah for a while. But then the editor suggested to me that I begin a weekly column on gay issues. He had just come back from a trip to New York where he saw a Broadway show called _Falsettos_. He loved it, it apparently made a great impression on him. So he decided to give me a regular column. I was very surprised. It was only afterwards that Amir told me that he was involved in the decision as well.

At first, I had some misgivings. I was worried about kind of being boxed in, ghettoized, on a designated page. I mean, I was already reporting gay stories, and my articles were appearing along with the other articles. I was worried about being segregated, like people are in the gay ghettos of the larger cities in the U.S. But in the end, I realized that the column would give me a lot of freedom, so I agreed to do it. A week later I already had a long list of subjects I wanted to write about. I wanted to call the column "Mitromemim."[§] I think that even back then, I was already a little more militant than a lot of other people. Maybe not militant, maybe radical is the right word.

I chose the name because I was thinking about the organization named Queer Nation in the U.S. They took the word "queer," and, you know, changed it into a word that they use about themselves. And that way they've removed the stigma from it. The same thing with the pink triangle that all the organizations use today—it's also something that had a terrible meaning in the past. I tried to explain all of this to my editor, I even wrote it all out for him. A kind of manifesto. He didn't go for it. He said, "What in the world are the garage mechanics going to think about this?" He was a little suspicious. He wanted to call it "Inside the Closet."

And then the whole thing opened up, and all of a sudden everyone on the staff was putting in their own two cents' worth. In the end I told him he could do what he wanted. I held out for a few days, but I saw that it was causing such a commotion, it wasn't worth it. So I said to him, chose whatever name you want. We settled on "Gay Veys" in the end.[†] The fact is that the name has caught on, people remember it. The column has been running for forty-seven weeks now, almost a year.

At first, I thought that the most important thing about my writing would be that it would educate straights about gay life. After all, this is a regular city newspaper—90 percent of my readers are straight. I said to myself, prejudice is fed by ignorance, so let's dispel this ignorance. That's the principle that stood behind the column, at the beginning. The problem with that approach

[§] Mitromemim: a mild slang perjorative for gay men; "poofters."
[†] "Gay Veys": A pun on _Gei veis_—the Yiddish expression commonly translated as "Go figure."

was that it limited me, because I had to agonize over publishing items that might reinforce stereotypes. In the course of time, I've freed myself from those inhibitions. For instance, I began writing about the park and the sauna. Why shouldn't I write about them? They have a place in the life of gays in Israel. As part of this new attitude, I created a regular feature—I had a corner of my column that was called "My place or yours?" And in that corner, I wrote about a different meeting place each week. This week, you know, a certain park, the next week a new bar, then some advice about answering personal ads, or what to do about people you work with and have a crush on, and so on. All sorts of spicy little items.

Pretty quickly, I got a letter from a gay guy who attacked me for revealing too much about the gay world to straights. He argued that the goal of my column is to advance the struggle for gay and lesbian rights in Israel, and that I was, you know, perpetuating stereotypes by implying that gay life was only about sex. I responded to him in the column. I argued that, when it comes down to it, "Gay Veys" has no goal beyond the journalistic. But the journalistic goal in this case fits very nicely with my own political goal, which is basically to smash the closet, and reveal what's inside.

I've also gotten flak for interviewing effeminate, stereotypical gays, hairdressers and so on. This is an issue pretty similar to the one in the U.S., about who to put in the gay pride parades. Now, as far as I know, there are no drag queens in Israel. At least not well-known ones.[§] And we have no lesbians who, like, run around with their shirts off. But if there were, I wouldn't hide them. I would put them in my column. We've got to stop running around saying "Oy, oy, oy, what if they know there are also effeminate gays?" So what! If we print a picture of, you know, bare-breasted lesbians in the newspaper, are all of our readers going to think that lesbians walk around with their shirts off all the time? Our readers are not so stupid.

Lately, I've been having some misgivings about the interviewing style that I've developed. I'm worrying about this openness thing again. Because I've come to the conclusion that there is an inequity here—you aren't going to see a feature article on someone with the fact that they're straight being mentioned as of special interest. But you find so many very invasive interviews with gays—questions about their sex lives and so on. So I've been asking myself lately, if I was interviewing someone who wasn't gay, would I be asking such personal questions? Of course not. And in some sense, I think that this is discriminatory. But on the other hand, I'm a journalist, and I

[§] See the Introduction for the remarkable recent developments in this regard.

know that this is what sells, this is what's interesting. This kind of excessive public interest in the sex lives of gay men is the consequence of the inequality created by the closet, where gay sex is supposed to be precisely the thing you don't talk about. So explicit reporting is part of the battle against the hold of the closet—you just keep reporting on all the intimate details of homosexual life until they're sick and tired of reading about it, until it is totally cliche. We may be getting close to that point already.

Most of the reactions I've gotten have been very, very positive and supportive. People have told me that I've changed their lives, especially young people. I got a letter not long ago, from a seventeen-year-old who wanted to thank me for what I had done for him, that it was thanks to me that he had the courage to come out of the closet.

Recently, some kids in Haifa got together and started a group for lesbian and gay youth. I publicized them in my column and helped them get started, but the initiative was their own. They wanted to affiliate with the Agudah, and there was a very messy struggle—because these kids are all underage, you know, they're in high school, they're minors. The Agudah was worried about potential legal and public relations problems, so they cut all ties with them. I had a lot of problems with that decision—it was based on fear. I wrote about the whole thing in my column. I would say that at the moment, I'm a pretty unpopular guy at the Agudah.

I think they don't like me because I represent something, like, more radical, more open. I guess you could say that my views are probably the most "advanced" in Israel—the closest to the most progressive views of gays in the U.S. I don't define myself as radical, because there are other words that are connected to that, like fanaticism—I'm just an open person. But, you know, I'm free of a lot of straight values and prejudices that a lot of other gays are mired in. I've managed to liberate myself from that. I take heart from the example of Michelangelo Signorile, in the U.S. In the beginning, there were a lot of attacks on him for being too radical. But now he's somehow more accepted. He's less controversial today than he was two years ago. His approach has vindicated itself. It may be that in another two years that will happen to me. I don't know.

There are two major streams in the worldwide gay movement—there are the more moderate ones, who want only to be accepted into the straight world, and don't really want to change it in a basic way. And then there are the ones who reject all straight values, like I do. I have the desire to lead a revolution, but I don't have the strength. I have no money, I can't create a political party, I can't influence the masses. My bank account is six thousand shekels overdrawn. In the meantime, I have a certain means at my disposal, in this column, and I'm using it as best I can. But, sure, I could see myself saying those words, "I have a dream." I do have a dream. But, like, everybody fantasizes about being in an influential position, where you can take a stand. I do too. I don't deny it.

I've been thinking lately, I haven't really talked about this with anyone, but I've been thinking that, you know, in the parliamentary electoral system the way it is in Israel at the moment, it seems very reasonable that there should be a gay political party in Israel. For every group that wants to have influence, the best way to achieve that is through the Knesset. In other countries, other systems, it doesn't work the way it works here. I mean, what Ya'el Dayan is doing is wonderful, but there needs to be someone who will, you know, serve exclusively the needs of gay men and lesbians. I think it has a chance. I'm sure it does. You just need the right candidate. I don't think I'm that candidate—I'm much too controversial right now. But it might be that Professor 'Uzi Even would be elected to the Knesset, if he ran. I'm sure that he would get the votes of a lot of gays who are in the closet, but who would be willing to cast ballots for the advancement of their own interests. No one can see what ballot you put in. I mean, I just heard that Meretz, the left-wing coalition party, is looking for an openly gay candidate for their Tel Aviv city council slate. They think they need a gay of their own, so that, like, people won't say that Meretz doesn't care about the gays.[5]

I think that the most damaging thing for Israeli gays is the fact that we're so deeply closeted. That's our biggest problem. Gay and lesbian liberation movements around the world are built on coming out of the closet—and you just can't run a liberation movement from the closet. It's that simple. So I'm at war with the closet.

One of the things you need to do in order to explode the closet is to bring public figures out of the closet. I've outed people before, and I'll do it again. My editor at *Qol Ḥeifah* won't let me do it directly in my column, but there's a small magazine, called *Maga'im*, read by gays and a few of their straight friends, where I've also been writing lately. In my column there this week I have a list of popular Israeli singers and I write that they "aren't exactly totally straight." That's outing.

[5] Meretz placed 'Uzi Even on its slate of candidates for election to the Knesset in 1996 and 1999. Lesbian community activist Miḥal 'Eden was elected to the Tel Aviv city council on the Meretz slate in 1998.

They're all public figures who make their money through their images. They invite all kinds of publicity about themselves, their private lives—but only the kind of publicity that will help them sell their recordings. I'm totally convinced that, for instance, in one case a singer is being advised to stay in the closet by his agents, his publicity people. And that's not fair. I don't agree with the consensus that it's an awful thing to be gay or lesbian— so why should it be an awful thing to write that someone is gay or lesbian? Mistakenly, it's called "outing." But it isn't outing—it's an attempt to equalize the status of gays and lesbians and straights in the media. To break the taboo.

In spite of Ya‘el Dayan and ‘Uzi Even and the law preventing discrimination in the workplace, and all of that, from a social perspective, it's difficult for me to believe that anything is going to really move here unless people like me get up and begin to dismantle the closet. Gays will feel good here, and teenagers will feel comfortable here, only if and when they can come out of the closet. When I visited the U.S., people were, you know, very impressed by our law against discrimination on the basis of sexual orientation in the workplace. There's nothing similar on the federal level in the U.S. But they forget that here, it's very easy to pass laws—I call them passive laws—laws that prevent discrimination. It's comparatively easy to pass laws like that, because even religious people say, "OK, they're sick people, but people who have epilepsy shouldn't be discriminated against either." But generally speaking, you know, you can still say that the U.S., in certain places of course, is a real paradise for gays. It's much easier in the U.S.

I'm pessimistic about the situation in Israel, at least for the coming five years. It's hard for me believe that things are going to change dramatically. So there will be an Agudah Pride Day "Happening" on Sheinqin Street in Tel Aviv, and twenty or thirty people will be there—does that mean that it will be easier for a gay in Dimonah or Qiryat Shemonah to come out of the closet?

For me, it wasn't a sudden transition from being a married man in the closet to being the most radical gay in Israel—it took me years to get to this point. Six years. But I can't explain why there are so few others who have taken my path, who reject the closet. Is my personality so rare? I don't think I'm much smarter than a lot of other people I know. I can't explain it. Maybe it's a matter of taking risks. I don't have a lot to lose in life, after what I've given up. I could have, you know, stayed in the closet, and I could have stayed on in management at Elbit, and today I could, like, own a car and a half, and be making a salary four times what I make today. I could have done that.

I think it's true that gays tend to vote more for the parties on the left, because a minority is more sympathetic to the needs of other minorities. There's something to that. I oppose the occupation. I'm in favor of a Palestinian state. But I remember reading in a poll that large numbers of gays also voted for parties on the right.

I don't know if I'm a Zionist. It isn't really clear to me why I live here. I mean, it's clear to me that this is my language, and that it would be very difficult for me to live in a different language, a different mentality. And I guess that sometimes I do feel what you could call, like, the rootedness of the native Israeli—even though there are lots of alienating things around as well. There's certainly nothing ideological keeping me in Israel. But I guess you could say that I have a certain kind of cultural loyalty. Besides, there's something that's called "home," and yes, I miss home when I leave. And "home" means both this apartment and also something larger, someplace where I feel at home. But beyond that, I have no loyalties.

I've tried to check if there is a correlation between homosexuality and emigration from Israel. I think there is. When I was in New York, I heard about a group called "Israelis and Friends"—its purpose is to help gay Israelis who come to New York to acclimate themselves. I talked to a guy there, and he told me about a real phenomenon, of gays who leave Israel in order to come out of the closet. They mostly go to New York or San Francisco. Maybe if I had money, I'd do it too.

I don't really see myself as Jewish. I'm a humanist, an atheist. I don't feel very connected to the tradition. I used to fast on Yom Kippur—but it was only because my mother fasted, and I felt the need to identify with my mother. On Passover we have a family seder, but it doesn't really mean anything to me.

I'm acquainted with gay approaches to Judaism, and I've been in gay synagogues in the U.S.—Beth Simchat Torah in New York, and Bet Mishpachah in Washington. I remember, like, the first time I went into a Reform synagogue, it just seemed really foreign to me. I mean, I don't know their prayers. The whole Reform movement seems to me, you know, just a product of the desire on the part of American Jews to keep hold of some kind of tradition, while being religious in the sense of American religious people, and not Jewish religious people. To me, as an Israeli, it's very foreign. For them, it's the most natural thing in the world to sit around singing "Hineh mah ṭoy umah naʿim" on a Friday night. But for me, "Hineh mah ṭoy umah naʿim" is a song we sang in music class in first grade. So it's really strange for me to go there and, you know, sit and sing songs from elementary school. I don't see any commonalities between gay and Jewish identity. One thing has nothing to do with the other.

Asaf would like to have children. How we'll manage it, you could kill me, I haven't a clue. In the meantime, we aren't exactly, like, in a financial situation where we can take responsibility for a child. In practical terms, one possibility would be to enter into some kind of relationship of obligation with a woman. But that's a problem—I'm a believer in partnership, and I wouldn't want to bring a third party into our lives, as things stand now. If we had the money, we could just try to rent a womb, I guess. But in the meantime it isn't on the agenda.

Asaf has had two offers so far—one from a lesbian couple, and one from a single lesbian. But there are all sorts of conditions attached. Suddenly there are, like, a million issues. What does this mean—is he going to be the father or not? What will be the degree of his involvement in the child's life? All sorts of questions come up, you know, which you have to think about. It isn't so simple. And he needs my consent. I mean, it's out of the question that if Asaf decided tomorrow morning that he wanted a baby, that he could just, like, take some lesbian and make a baby. The two of us need to talk about it, because, you know, this concerns me too.

At the moment, I'm kind of worried about my future. I'm already thirty-three, and I have no pension plan. It may be that I'll grow old and poor and destitute. I'm kind of preoccupied with this matter. I guess what I'm trying to say is that, you know, if you take a look at things, I've paid a pretty heavy price for the way I've chosen to live. I could have been a lot more upstanding today, much more socially acceptable. But I don't want that.

ʿAMIT

At an early stage in the process of planning this book, Amir and I made ourselves a joint list of the different "types" we wanted to interview. Even in this preliminary list, there appeared—the male prostitute. Beyond pure prurience, we agreed that an interview of this sort would provide us with a distinctive angle of entry into the closets of a large number of men. In spite of our concurrence on the desirability of such an interview, however, we kept putting off its performance. Unfortunately, neither one of us had a personal acquaintance with any sex workers, and, when it came down to it, Amir was as shy as I was about taking the obvious steps to get to know one. So we kept putting it off, until this interview was actually the very last one that we needed to perform. And then— our time ran out. The summer was over, and I was leaving. I had no choice but to endow Amir with the solemn mission of performing this last interview on his own. He would have to send the recorded text to me in the U.S.

Amir fulfilled his task most admirably—by opening up the newspaper, calling up one of the very clearly advertised "agencies," and explaining himself and his project. I am sure he did this in his gorgeously formal Hebrew. Amir was put in touch with a willing volunteer, "ʿAmit," and arranged to make the trip to his Tel Aviv apartment. According to my sources, ʿAmit's appearance would seem to warrant his standing at the top of his profession. But personally, I think Amir has got questionable taste in men.

∾

My father immigrated from Chile when he was twenty. My mother was born in Israel. They met in the army, and they were some of the first people to settle in the small community where they live to this day. Most people are farmers, or work in the factory.

I'm the oldest in my family. I always got everything I wanted. I had a fucking amazing childhood—everything a kid needs, I got, I had. A big house, my own room. Really, we never were lacking anything. We had very good relationships within the family, we all felt very close.

My parents had incidents now and then, but I think that's pretty natural. I don't remember, like, shouting matches or beatings or anything like that. When I got to be a little older, it was clear that I was, you know, more distant from my father, and closer with my mother. My father was just, at least this is the way I felt, he was just very distant, and he wasn't that interested in all of the things that were going on in our lives, things that did interest my mother, who would ask, and would kind of draw things out of us. And my mother was always kind of more in control at home. She was the one we went to about everything. My father was busy with his own stuff, his hobbies, technical equipment, computers. He would work very long hours in the factory, and he would always be playing around with electronic equipment, he would repair it for all kinds of people. So he was busy with his own things. Less involved in what was going on at home.

My earliest memory is just of friends from the neighborhood. We were always very close, we were together all the time. We all grew up together, and I remember that the parents would always be getting together at one of their houses, and they would bring all the kids, and all hell would break loose. Because we were very close—we were very unified. You could go freely into any house you wanted to, there weren't any problems. You were totally at ease with all of the neighbors. And everyone was always over at everyone else's house, we would all walk around hugging one another. It was like, everyone knew everyone else's aunts and uncles, their friends. It was fun—we were all together all the time, all of us were friends, and all of our parents were friends. We would watch television, or play outside, or just talk. We would swim in the community pool.

I was always popular. I always got along with the other kids. There was a time when, like, I wouldn't exactly say I was in charge, but there was a group of friends, and I felt like I was the one who everyone assumed would, you know, take care of things, organize things. If anything was done, it was done through me.

When my grandmother would come to visit, my parents would speak Spanish. My mother knows Ladino.[§] They would talk, but I only understand very few words, and I can't speak at all. I'm sorry they didn't teach me. Sometimes my mother talks a sort of Spanish to me on the street, or someplace where she doesn't want the people around to understand, and I get the drift of what she's saying. But I can't talk.

They made sure we had things to do besides school—I had piano lessons, and guitar lessons, and flute lessons, all kinds of stuff like that. I don't remember how to do any of that stuff any more. You've got to practice. Some people had horses, and I really like horses, and I would spend most of my time in the stables. I would always be finding something to keep me busy. The kids had a kind of clubhouse, we were always setting things up there, hanging pictures and all that.

We never talked about sex at home. My parents never explained anything to me. I don't know why. I think they should have at least had a talk with me or something. But my friends at school made up for it, you know? I got by without my parents, but I think it would have been better if it had come from them. Because they're, like, a little more experienced than the other kids who you hear things from. I think it was different with my sisters. Because my little sister is very open about these things, and she was always asking my mother about it. One day my sister brought home a book from the library about sex, and they read it together, my mother and my sister. But that's because she was always asking, asking. I never asked. I didn't know what to ask, and I was embarrassed. I certainly wouldn't ask my mother. And my father, I wasn't exactly so close with him. So I learned what I could from friends, movies, books, newspapers. I got over it.

Sometime around sixth grade I had a girlfriend. It was the regular process—we would go to parties, get to know each other, talk, this and that, and one day we just, like, began to be boyfriend and girlfriend. I don't know, it was natural, I can't really explain it. I liked her, I was attracted to her. And we got along very well. We would only kiss and hug each other, nothing more. And all the rest was just regular friendship, talking, playing around. I would hang out with her just like I hung out with my other friends.

She was in my class. She was, in my opinion, pretty, of course. And very popular. We were together for a long time, maybe six months. I don't know how it ended, I just remember that one day I wrote her a letter saying I had

[§] Ladino: A dialect of medieval Spanish with an admixture of Hebrew vocabulary; spoken by the Jews of Spain before the expulsion in 1492, and preserved by many of their descendants.

had it with the whole thing, and that the time has come for us to cut it out. Because it was, like, there wasn't really any point any more. We were both looking for new friends, and we were beginning to bore each other. So it just ended like that. After her, I would have a crush on one girl for three days, then another girl, and so on. But with her it was more serious, I remember.

I knew that a "homosexual" was someone effeminate, someone who dressed like a woman. A sissy. It was an insult. Maybe I first heard the word around first grade. I would use it myself, as an insult, sometimes. But I guess I still use the word as an insult today.

In seventh grade we began smoking, when no one could see us. We moved up into a new school at this time, so there were different people, everything was different. We left our elementary school behind—it was really like a hothouse there, everyone had known everyone for six years already, everyone was everyone else's friend and neighbor. But now we got to a school where we didn't know all the other students, with a lot more people. And your whole style changes, you know, externally. So I would have a cigarette during every break. Some of my friends began to smoke also. Life was different.

I began smoking because it sort of attracted me. A lot of my good friends didn't do it. You could say that most of them didn't smoke. But it really attracted me. I think it made me feel, like, more grown up. I stayed with my old friends who didn't smoke, but we also did, kind of, form a group of smokers, who got to know each other because of this. You understand? All the girls said it was smelly, that I smelled like cigarettes when I came back from break. It didn't really make much of a difference to me. I liked it. It was the girls' problem. It just made me feel good. And it gave me a little high also. The first cigarettes of your life. I would come back to class with my head aching, kind of dizzy all through the lesson.

So then two girls from my class, very good friends of mine, asked me please to stop smoking, they said that it was bad for me, and all that bullshit. And of course I didn't pay any attention to them, I kept on smoking. And they, out of the goodness of their hearts, went and told the teacher! So the teacher called my mother to school for a conference, and told my mother, and sent her to talk to the guidance counselor, and the guidance counselor explained to her that it was very dangerous, that this was my adolescence, that I was developing very quickly now, that it would cause heart problems, blah blah blah.

So my mother came back home, teary and bitchy. And she said she wanted to talk to me. She called my father also. She cried nonstop through the whole thing. She begged me to stop. She said she was in shock, she couldn't believe that her son was smoking at such a young age. And I promised her that I would stop. Because she was just totally hysterical. Crying like that. In my entire life I've never seen her like that. Unfortunately, it wasn't like my grades were so good, that this might make up for it or anything—they also took the opportunity to tell her at school that my grades were the pits. So that's it. She took it very hard, and I promised her that I would stop, even though I didn't. During the whole conversation, my father kind of just sat on the side and watched. And when it was over he just walked away.

If I had told her that I wouldn't stop, it would have just made her feel bad. And I really didn't want that. So I just said yes. I said, I'll try to stop. I didn't really think about it. And I just kept on smoking. I didn't really take that promise very seriously. I've never lied to her, at least I try very hard not to. Because we were always very close, and I never saw any need to lie. But about this, she was just so hysterical, and she frightened me so badly, I just said yes, I'll stop, and that was it. I think she knew that I didn't stop, even though I would never smoke at home.

Around this time, I had a friend, a neighbor of mine, and we would watch porn together. Videotapes. I don't remember being especially interested in either the men or the women in the movies—I just watched the whole thing, the experience, as a picture. The sex itself. And we would kind of jerk one another off while we watched. Just for the fun of it. We were doing this pretty regularly before either of us actually came for the first time. We didn't even know what it was we were doing—we were just trying to make each other feel good. One of us would, like, play with the other one, and then the other way around. This was around seventh, eighth, ninth grade. We would either do it at his house or at mine, or in the clubhouse. I think the whole thing was his idea.

I remember that it began one day when we were sleeping over, a bunch of us, in sleeping bags and all that, and we decided that we were going to, like, measure the length of everyone's penis. And little by little it became touches, and kind of mutual masturbation. That was how it began. Afterwards, everyone continued, in pairs.

At the same time I had another neighbor, and I remember I would sometimes do the same thing with him. We would also, like, masturbate together, although less often. The two of them are the only ones I remember myself doing it with. It was just fun, you know, nothing more than that.

Later on, I would take the first step more often. In ninth and tenth grades, I remember that I would be the one to suggest that we do it more, I remember that I was more into it than he was. But sometimes my friend would be the one to suggest it too. He wanted it also, he had fun also. I wanted us to do blow jobs, but he was against it. That was a letdown, but I lived with it. We would really do it all the time. And I would jerk off a lot, besides. I would come maybe twice a day. But he was the only one I felt comfortable enough with to do it. I didn't have a girlfriend, and I wouldn't do it with my other friends. I think I was, you know, attracted to him. But I only realized that much later.

I didn't feel like there was any problem with what we were doing. I didn't feel like there was any need to explain it to myself or something. It was obvious to me. I had read in all sorts of places, like in the newspaper, or in *Ma'ariv Lano'ar*, the children's magazine, about things like this. They wrote a lot about mutual masturbation, and they said that it was natural, that everyone did it. They had a column there by a psychologist, a sociologist, I don't know what. So I knew there was nothing wrong with it. Of course I knew I was supposed to, you know, keep it quiet, but it wasn't something unusual. It never once occurred to me to think that I was, like, gay or something. I remember that I had a very big crush on a girl, who wasn't really interested in me. I would think about her a lot. But I just needed that sexual release from time to time. And he was there.

At some point, he began watching movies with someone else. He would find excuses. And he would just spend more time with girls than with me. There were a lot of girls who were after him. He was very good-looking. And that's it, I just went on. I would jack off by myself, watch porn movies, fantasize, look at magazines.

When I was in eleventh grade I fell in love with a guy from my class. But in spite of that I didn't call myself gay. He was in my class, we spent a lot of time together. And it was just that all of a sudden I kind of noticed that I was thinking about him a lot when I was at home, that I always wanted to be with him. I was always thinking about him. It was very simple—I was just in love with him.

I remember that when it would happen that I wouldn't see him for a long time, I would really go crazy. I would begin to cry. I just wanted to be with him, to hug him. Sex with him really wasn't important, I didn't think about that—what I wanted was his attention, his closeness, more than just sex. He didn't know. I never told him. He was a very good friend of mine, we would sometimes walk with our arms around each other. But it was all within the boundaries, things that any pair of friends would do—you know, pats on the back, putting your arm around the other's neck.

But I remember that, for instance, sometimes he would kind of hold my hand for a long time. Sometimes I felt a sort of closeness that just isn't there with men usually. I wouldn't see other people doing that. I knew it was different, because I could see that I was the only one who was doing it, wanting it. I was the one who pushed for that kind of thing. I never thought about the definition "gay" or anything like that. I was just a person who loved a person, you understand? I was very naive, very insulated from the whole thing. I mean, I didn't know anything about it. I didn't even know what it really was. Except what we said before, sissy, and all that.

I wanted more than he was willing to give. And it was clear to me that it would be impossible. I didn't think about telling him anything like this—I didn't even know what to tell him. He might tell the others. It was like, what did I want from him? What? He was a guy, and I was a guy, and we needed girls, and not any of this. It was clear to me that I couldn't say anything to him. You understand? It was out of the question. I just wanted to be hugged by him, to have him pay attention to me, more than to the others. And that's the way things continued, for two years, I think. I was in love with him, you know. I didn't think about anyone else.

At the same time, I had some things going with some girls. If I saw a girl who I thought was pretty, I would try to come on to her. I knew that I should have a girlfriend, a female partner, and not a male partner. It was clear to me that I needed to find a girl. Not that I had much luck. But then again, I don't remember that I tried very hard. I didn't really find a girl I liked, who I felt like pursuing. There just weren't any girls I felt like putting any time or effort into. It was like, I didn't have any shortage of friends who were girls, but not more than regular friends.

I remember that in tenth grade there was a girl I really liked, but she left to go to a different school, and after her there wasn't really anyone. There were some girls I tried to get to know better, but the moment we got to know each other better, I would find something wrong with them, I would be turned off by something about them. But there were always girls I was attracted to, from the other classes. I didn't get to know them, they went with different crowds. I was attracted to girls' faces. But I would also think about sex with them. To this day I think that I'm bisexual, you could say. I enjoy sleeping with women.

I was sure that it was my fault that I wasn't having much luck with girls. I thought I wasn't, like, smooth enough, not pushy enough, not brave enough. I wasn't trying hard enough. I would get discouraged very quickly. If my friends didn't push me, I would just give up.

I was an OK student, average. I didn't work very hard. I really didn't see the point. There wasn't any need—why study? What would it do for me? School was, like, just something you did—you go to school, and then after twelfth grade it's done. I didn't really see the point.

We really didn't get too excited when our draft notices came. We had a few conversations, here and there, if we wanted to be a combat soldier, or something else, but the whole subject was very marginal. I was sure I didn't want to be a combat soldier. I'm not exactly the type who gets into running up and down mountains. I would always cut gym class. I would never do the long runs we were supposed to do. So I knew that I would just get some kind of an office job—because if you're not combat, what's left? That's it, that's what I was thinking, and that's what I requested when I was drafted. Most of the people in my class felt the same way as I did. I don't think anyone was particularly drawn to be in combat.

So I was drafted, and they gave me a course, which had to do with my subject of specialization in high school, electricity. I was stationed on a base where you went home once every three weeks. I was there for three years. In most places, if you're not a combat soldier, then you get to go home every night, leave the base—but not here. I had to stay on the base. I would wake up in the morning, go to work, finish work, and maybe I would have to do guard duty or something after work, or I would just go back to my room. We would have to stay there in what they liked to call "preparedness."

At first it was very difficult for me, I was very depressed. Because it was, after all, a very boring, routine life. Work, guard duty, kitchen duty, all that bullshit. I never liked the army, but I knew I didn't have any choice. So I just did it, and tried to pass the time as well as I could. Towards the end, when I already had a better position, like, more administrative, a higher professional level, with a lot more friends, it was a lot better. I could go home at better times. Towards the end I remember that I really was having fun there. After all, at this time, when I was in the army, I had some girlfriends, and I was with each of them for a pretty long time.

The first one was a secretary in the place where I worked. She was also a soldier. We were, you know, together all day at work. And we would talk a lot, and then she began coming to visit me in my room, and that's the way things got started. It was a very good relationship. Towards the end it really became, like, love, which included everything, including sex.

Our first time was really funny. Because we didn't really know what to do—it was the first time for both of us. It was in my room, on the base. We tried all sorts of positions that we had seen in movies, and it was very funny, we were both laughing the whole time we were having sex. I didn't really enjoy it. I mean, I said to myself after we did it, what, that's what the big deal is about? That's it? That's what everyone talks about all the time? I wasn't very impressed. But it was nice. And I enjoyed the release that it gave me. That's it. So it was pretty ordinary, you know, but I kept doing it.

I was attracted to her. We would talk a lot, we were together all the time, deep conversations in the middle of the night. We really had fun together. We would also get together when we were off the base—if one of us was on leave, sometimes the other would sneak out of the base in the evening. We were very good friends. It ended the way I ended it with the first one—we just lost interest in each other. It was like, little by little, I was less interested in her. And she began to bore me. She felt that way also. It sort of faded away. Little by little we would see each other less often, and one day we talked about it, and we said, well, maybe we should just split up. And that's the way it was. I wasn't very sad about it.

I remember that after her, I fell in love with a guy, my roommate. We were very good friends, and I was very attracted to him, I thought about him all the time. I really wanted physical contact with him also. But he was totally straight, and he wasn't interested. All of my little attempts totally failed. One day I tried, I, like, put my arm in his shirt, and I began to kind of stroke him, kind of. But he just moved my arm away really irritably, and left the room. I would try to touch him, you know, to hug him, and he would walk away. He didn't want any physical contact.

I loved him more than I loved my girlfriend. And maybe it was because I could tell that it wasn't working, and all that, so that made me want him more. I thought about him much more. And there was nothing I could do, what could I do? I never said anything to him. I thought it over, but I realized that there wasn't any point. I figured that he would just give me a funny look, and I thought that he might not talk to me any more because of it. And I was afraid of it, that he might, like, tell someone. I didn't think he would tell the commanders or anything. I just didn't want anyone to know. They might decide not to hang out with me or something.

I think there must have been gays on the base, but I didn't know about any. I still didn't really know what this whole game was about. I didn't really know what a gay was. I was very naive. I knew that I was attracted to him, but I didn't know what it meant. I knew that it was strange, but I didn't know how to, like, define it, I didn't know what it implied. So I just kept on going, I said time will tell, and we'll see what happens.

And then I remember that at the same time exactly, I met my second girlfriend, who also worked at the same place, and we spent a lot of time together. Really, a very similar story to the first one. But this one just couldn't get enough. We, like, had sex constantly. Maybe three times a day. In her room, in my room. Today, when I think about it, I think she was, you know, a nymphomaniac. She was the one who initiated the sex—every time. I can't remember a single time when I said to her that I wanted her to come to my room for sex or something. Because at the same time, I was thinking about my roommate all the time, even when I was with her. You understand? I just wanted to get it over with and leave. I didn't love her. But she did make me feel a lot better, and other people also treated me better.

I felt like, since I had become her boyfriend, and began telling my roommate about what sex with her was like, he was a lot more interested in me. He got closer to me, we had a lot more to talk about. And I wanted him to see that I did have a girlfriend, that I was, like, successful with girls. It made me feel very good. When I was with her, I would, like, only think about him, and about how to get rid of her as soon as possible. But I felt obligated to be with her, because, well, I don't know why. I did enjoy the sex, but I would enjoy it a hundred times more if he touched me, or put his arm around me, or if we would just lay down with our beds next to each other in the same room and talk. I would enjoy that a lot more than being in bed with her and doing everything.

At some point, I made another friend on the base, basically because this guy really liked my girlfriend. So he got closer to me. And I remember that I really cut things off with my roommate, who I had been in love with, and I got closer with this other one. And I fell in love with him. And I wouldn't think about my roommate anymore, I would think about my new friend—who was actually only interested in my girlfriend. And me, you know, I didn't care what he was interested in, I was interested in being with him. I didn't care if he really cared about me or something. He liked for me to tell him about her all the time, to talk about her all the time. And I liked to be with him. And of course, when I would go to her, it was just to be able to come back and tell him about it for hours and hours afterwards. I would do it with her as quickly as I possibly could. Because she didn't interest me at all.

This guy was more interested in physical contact with me than my roommate had been. He would, like, ask me to give him a massage sometimes. He was more romantically inclined, more sensitive. But nothing more than that. And at this point, I finished my service, and was discharged from the army.

At first, I kept in touch with my girlfriend, and with this guy, of course. She put a lot of pressure on me to stay with her. So I did. I mean, like, that's what there was. It wasn't like I had anything better. I had her, and I was getting from her what every man wants from a woman. She also finished her service around the same time. And we both went back to our parents. We lived pretty far away, so, you know, we could get together only once or twice a week. I went back home. And I remember that I didn't keep in touch with my other friend for very long, because I could see that there wasn't really any point. We didn't have anything to talk about any more. Nothing. He had lost all interest for me.

At this time, when I got out of the army, I began to really understand that I'm attracted to men. At that point, I really figured it out. But the sexual release, which I didn't have any way to get with a man, I would do with her. After all, it wasn't so bad with her, you know. Looking back on it, I think I even enjoyed it. But in spite of that, I would think about men every time I was with her.

I wanted to meet men, but I didn't know how. I didn't know what you did, nothing, I didn't know anything. I tried to meet someone through the personal ads in the paper. Once I took a trip to Tel Aviv especially to buy *Maga'im*, the gay magazine. But I was very frightened that someone would find out, that my parents would find out. I had no idea how the whole thing was done. I wanted to answer an ad, but I didn't do it, because I was afraid.

So I went back home after I got out of the army, and I was there for a week trying to figure out what I wanted to do now. And then I went down to Eilat, to work. I worked there for six months in a hotel, as a waiter. Because what kind of work can I do, besides be a waiter, or do odd jobs? And of course she followed me down there. Because she was in love with me, and she couldn't bear to split up. And besides her, I didn't have a lot of friends. I mean, I didn't know a lot of people. It was kind of like, well, there's no choice. It wasn't like it was so bad with her, but I wasn't really interested in her. I was with her all the time, and I would just look around at everyone else.

We went down to Eilat together, and I found a job, and she didn't. So she had no choice but to go home, in tears and hysterics. She went home, but she kept on calling me and crying that she wanted to be near me. I wasn't particularly sad to see her go. I really didn't care one way or another. Really. I mean, I felt terrible about how hard she was taking it. She would really cry and, like, the two days from the moment she realized that she would have to go home until the moment she actually left, these days were like from a movie, she did nothing but cry and make me feel bad. She asked me over and over again to go back with her. But I told her that, you know, there wasn't anything for me to do in the north. So she just went back, and I stayed down there for the next six months.

I would go up to my parents' maybe once a month. Because every day of work I missed meant I wouldn't make money, and that was a shame. And bus trips back and forth from Eilat are no joke—they're expensive, and they're such nightmares. And besides, I liked it there. I met new people. For the hotel workers, it's like a kibbutz. All of the workers live together, and we have our own disco, and we would all go to the beach together. I didn't miss her at all. Even though we were in touch at the time.

I remember that one day I saw an ad in the women's magazine, La'ishah, for a magazine called Neptune, which had personal ads for gays and lesbians. So I sent them money and a letter, asking them to send me that magazine. Because that seemed to me the only way I had of meeting a man. And I really wanted to meet someone. I really wanted to be with someone. So I sent it—with my ex-girlfriend's name on the return address. All of the other workers met her when she was here, and I let them know that, like, she might be getting a letter, and that they should save it for me. Because I said to myself, if it comes in a clear envelope, or if someone opens it, it's better that they should think that it was hers. I was very embarrassed and afraid.

In the end, it came in a closed envelope. It wasn't a big deal. And there wasn't a single thing in that magazine that did me any good. I had put an ad in there with my telephone number, and I got some calls from Jerusalem and some from Tel Aviv which didn't do me any good at all, in Eilat. So I threw it out, and that was that.

I was very frightened of the whole thing. So even though I really did want to find someone, I just kept on thinking, one of these days I'll find someone, it won't be a problem. Like all those stories about how people meet on the beach, or in discos. Today I know that they say that the park across from the Neptune Hotel in Eilat is a meeting place, but I didn't know it then. It's probably not very serious anyway, not like Independence Park or the Hilton beach in Tel Aviv. But then I didn't know about it. I think that if I had known I would have gone. But I didn't even know there was such a thing as meeting places for gays, I had never heard of such a thing. So nothing happened the whole time I was in Eilat.

I remember that I had a roommate, and I would always be, you know, going into the bathroom when he was in the shower. And I would spend a lot of time hanging out by the pool, like, looking around. I was always looking around, but nothing more than that. And that's it.

One day I just got fed up with my job, and with Eilat. I think it had something to do with homosexuality. But it wasn't only that. I mean, how long can you be a waiter? It made me want to throw up. I was so fed up with the people, I felt like I was just going to explode at any moment. I just saw that nothing at all was happening. It was another day, another day, another day. Everything was so routine and pointless. So I quit.

I quit, knowing that I wanted to move to Tel Aviv and rent an apartment. It was clear to me that I was not going to go home. There's nothing for me to do there, and there isn't any work in my area. I don't have any friends there. I have no desire to go back and live with my parents, there would be no point in that. So the only choice I saw I had was just to go to Tel Aviv, and, you know, find some sort of work, and live.

My old girlfriend wanted me to come with her on a trip to the Far East, but I really didn't want to do that. I was much more interested in being gay, in finding someone. That concerned me more than the Far East. And if I went, then I would have to go with her, and I didn't want that either. So I said to myself, I'll go to Tel Aviv. We'll see what happens. And that's it.

It took me about a month to find an apartment. During this time I lived at home, calling all sorts of places, going in to Tel Aviv to look at places. It isn't easy, you know, to find an apartment here. But eventually I found this apartment where I am today. That was six months ago, that I first came to Tel Aviv—May of '93. I found work pretty quickly, in a hotel, again as a waiter.

Around this time, I called 056, the gay party line, and I talked to someone there, and we decided to, like, get together. He was the first gay I'd ever spoken to, that I knew he was gay. And that I knew that I was going to get together with him to sleep with him. It didn't, you know, really make a difference to me who he would be, what he would look like. I mean, I had hoped that he would be someone I was attracted to. But that wasn't really what interested me. I was more interested in just getting into the scene, just seeing what it all meant. To see if I'm really like that. I mean, I had never slept with a guy. It might be that I was just fantasizing, and that it was a temporary thing or something.

So we met, and I was really disappointed. It took me just a few seconds to see that he wasn't my type. He was older than me, twenty-nine or thirty or something like that. And that wasn't what I was looking for. I was looking for someone about my own age, good-looking—just what everyone else wants. So I was a little disappointed. But in spite of that I went to his place, and we talked for hours, and then we met a second time, and a third time.

We slept with each other the first time, but without, like, penetration or anything like that. It was my first time with a man. I didn't enjoy myself very much. I wasn't attracted to him. But I liked the way he touched me, and I liked it that he told me about this whole new world. He told me about his friends, and, you know, we watched gay porn, and he showed me gay magazines, and gay, gay, gay, we only talked about gays. He was really the first person I had ever told I was "like that," and the first one I could really open up to and tell what I really was, tell things that I had kept bottled up inside up to that point. I was used to hiding everything. I'm still in touch with him, and we really laugh when we remember those conversations. He told me that during our first conversation I barely did anything besides stare at the ground, and answer questions with yes or no. Not more than that. But I kept on meeting with him because I hoped that he would introduce me to someone else.

He described the gay world as a dark, very negative place. He told me that people have sex with you only once, and then you never see them again. He told me about all kinds of places for dark meetings, where people, you know, do it in the bushes. He told me what it meant to be a "top" or a "bottom," active or passive. He told me about KY lubricant and condoms. I had never used condoms with my girlfriend, she was on the pill. This was the first time I had ever touched a condom, that I even understood what it was. I saw this world in a not very positive light. But I knew that I was like that. So I said, well, I've got no choice. This is what it's like, this is the gay world. This is the way I am.

I never felt like I had a problem with the fact that I was gay. But I was very lonely. I suffered because I didn't have a boyfriend or a friend. But I wasn't saying to myself, oh no, oh no, I'm gay. What am I going to do? I took it pretty well. It only hurt that I was alone, that I didn't know anyone. This was the only thing that bothered me. Nothing more than that.

So that's it. He told me about the parks, he told me really about this entire world—all the places, how people meet, how they get to know one another. Everything I knew I learned from his stories. It was a very dark world, but I wanted some of the things he told me about to happen to me also. He met with people for one-night stands, and he had had a boyfriend for a while, that he loved, and then they split up. I didn't really like the way it sounded, you know, but I wanted some of it to happen to me. I was so lonely, and I didn't have anything. So I was very jealous of him. He told me he had slept with, like, forty people in his life. So I was very jealous of him, I wanted that to happen to me, that I should begin to meet people. And after all, he was the only one I had ever met.

So one day I went to Independence Park and I met someone there. I was terrified, very frightened. The first time I tried to go, I just saw all sorts of people and then ran away. The second time, I went in, and someone came up to me. He said to me, "Good evening." I said, "Good evening." He said to me, "Nice weather today," and all sorts of bullshit that was beside the point, and then he asked me if I wanted to go to his apartment, and I said yes. He was maybe twenty-seven years old. He was a lot better-looking than this first one. We got together twice. I had a pretty good time with him. I already knew, like, everything about penetration, and I had already done everything. The first guy, we had already slept together like six or seven times before I went to the park. And he had already taught me everything, and we had done everything, blow jobs, fucking. I liked it all, but I really didn't want to do it with that first guy. I would rather have done it with someone else. So I had a much better time with this one I had met in the park. He was better looking, more to my taste.

When I told the first guy about what I had done, he told me that he was very jealous, that he was in love with me. He called me up one night in the middle of the night, and said he couldn't sleep, he was, you know, thinking about me all the time. And he wanted to know if I was serious about this other guy, if I meant to cheat on him. So I told him that what was going on between him and me was not what I was looking for. And he was very hurt. But he understood. He accepted the way things were. He had said from the very beginning that he was getting himself into a situation where in the end he would be hurt. I think that he had a feeling from the very start that I wasn't particularly attracted to him, because I would talk to him about how I wanted someone my own age. But he fell in love with me anyway. From that time when I met this guy in the park, we never slept together again. So there were a few weeks when I didn't have anyone.

I knew that there were other gays out there, but I just didn't know any of them. I saw tons of people there when I went to the park. So I knew there were people. I knew there was a gay magazine. So I said to myself, well, if they publish a magazine, obviously there's some group of people out there buying it. So I always knew there were people, but I didn't know how to find them. It seemed to me that they were, you know, hiding from me. I had never met anyone, I had no contacts.

I met the guy from the park after I had been here in Tel Aviv maybe six weeks, something like that. He wanted to keep on seeing me, but I lost interest in him. He gave me his telephone number, and asked me to keep in touch. I had told him that I was still in the army. Because this first guy told me that usually people, like, lie to one another. So I lied also. He told me, "No one ever tells the truth about himself," so I gave a fake name, and said I was a soldier, I said I was from Kfar Saba. I made up all sorts of bullshit like that. It isn't like I enjoyed making all that up, but it's part of the game, really. That's what I thought then. I thought that's the way you've got to do it, that's what you do. I didn't know. So that's what I did.

We got together once or maybe twice more, I don't remember. And I lost interest in him, I stopped calling him. I had never given him my telephone number, of course. And a lot of time passed between our meetings. I told him that I couldn't get leave from the army. I told him all sorts of stories.

I was still in touch with this first guy. I told him absolutely everything, what I did, where, for how long. He really, you know, became my best friend. To this day I tell him everything. He's the only one.

But I didn't want to sleep with him, I wasn't sexually attracted to him. And I was very afraid to go to the clubs that he told me about, I didn't want to expose myself in that way. Although eventually he did convince me to go. And it just didn't seem to make sense to me to try to meet someone through the personals. So I went to the park again, and again I met someone. This time I had a little more courage. I mean, this was already my third time in the park, and I knew exactly what went on there. So I saw someone who looked nice, and I just followed him. And at some point he stopped, and we began talking. "Good evening," "How old are you," all sorts of questions like that. I don't really remember what we talked about. I asked him if he wanted to come to my apartment. And he said he would, and we went to his car. He lived with his parents. So we came back to my place, and the sex was really nothing, I mean, like, nothing besides blow jobs, and very fast. He just wanted to come and get out of there. And when he left, we didn't exchange telephone numbers, nothing.

I remember that at that time, I began to say to the first guy that I felt like I had done it with my two girlfriends, and with the guys I had done it with also, that I had sex, not to enjoy myself, but out of curiosity, interest, the need to get to know, to check things out, to see what the world is like. And I was already, like, pretty fed up with my job. And I said to him, you know, I would be willing to have sex with people for money. I just mentioned it in the course of conversation. But it was true. I mean, the last few times I slept with this first one, I, like, didn't enjoy it at all. But I would just close my eyes, and imagine that it was someone else. I just began to be disgusted by him. But I did it because I really liked him, you know, as a person, as a friend, as someone who was looking after me, and who I talked to about everything. And he would always lead me into bed. That was kind of my way of, like, re-paying him for his friendship. So I said to myself, well, if I could do it with him, when I don't enjoy it at all, and I'm not attracted to him, and I just can't wait until it's over, I can do it with anyone. And if I know that it's for money, and good money, why the hell not.

So one day I remember I opened up the city newspaper, ʿIton Haʿir, and they had written there "Wanted: Guys for Work as Call Boys"—that's a nice way of putting it, "call boys." They had a number there, so I called, made an appointment to meet the manager, the guy in charge. I just called him and said to him, "I'm calling about the help-wanted ad." And he asked me how old I was, if I had experience with men, whether I had ever done it for money, if I was a bottom or a top. All sorts of questions about my measure-ments. And he said, "Look, there's no point in drawing out this conversation on the phone, I've got to see you. Because if you aren't appropriate, it's just going to be a waste of time." So we arranged to meet.

We met at a certain public phone. Near the place where the work takes place. I wouldn't exactly call it an office—it's more of, you know, an apart-ment. So we arranged to meet, and of course I got dressed very nicely, and put on cologne, and slicked my hair back, and all sorts of bullshit. I wanted to look as nice as I could, because, like, I really wanted to get the job.

He took me for a walk around the neighborhood. He asked to see my identity card, of course. Because he doesn't hire minors, and he wanted to know exactly who I was—after all, he was going to bring me back to the apartment where he lives, where he works, and he was giving me a key. He wanted to know my real name. Because he's hiring you, after all. It's not like, "Nice to meet you, come up to my apartment."

So we walked around for about ten minutes. He asked what I knew how to do, what I liked to do. I said that I was a top. Up to that point, I had never imagined that I would ever let anyone penetrate me. It really frightened me.

I couldn't conceive of it. And it didn't interest me at all, I didn't see how anyone could, like, enjoy it. When I was with that first guy, I was active and he was passive, every time we slept together.

So we went back to the apartment, and he asked, you know, to see my body, so I undressed, and he took a look. He asked me to turn around, to see from the back, the front. To see me naked. And he said, "OK, no problem. So far as I'm concerned, you can begin working." He was, like, a pretty nerdy guy, he didn't make me feel uncomfortable. I didn't expect someone like that. He was just a regular guy. Only twenty-three years old. Not at all threatening.

I saw it as an opportunity to meet people. After all, if they were putting an ad in the paper, that probably meant that there were other workers. And they chose them carefully, so the other workers were probably good-looking. So I really liked the idea, that I would meet people. After all, you know, I had only met three gay men in my entire life. Now I would certainly meet some people who were better looking than the ones I had been with.

It was clear that what we were talking about was prostitution, but I didn't really have a moral problem with it. I mean, I don't stand out in the street, but that's what it is, when you come down to it. But I don't have any problem with that. None at all.

I got involved out of naivete, really. All I wanted to do was meet people. So I just said to myself, what will be, will be—we'll see how this thing works. I could back out any time I wanted to. And it was also very good money. And I'm a naturally lazy person. I really didn't have the patience to, you know, be a waiter any more.

The whole operation is run out of an apartment. A very roomy apartment in north Tel Aviv, in a ritzy neighborhood. There are a lot of rooms, two telephone lines, a television. The rooms are set up especially for this. Every room has a bed and a closet, and every closet has condoms and KY and all the things you need for sex. There are a few rooms like that. And there's a living room, where the guys sit, and where the phones are.

That first night I just sat there, in the living room. When we're not working we just watch television, or cable, or a video. That night there was only one other worker there, because it was pretty late at night—we were introduced to each other, but I didn't think he was so attractive. I sat there for a few hours, I saw how the thing was run, listened to the guy talking to clients on the phone, calling workers who weren't at the apartment and sending them to all sorts of hotels. I sat there for two hours. And I asked him not to get anyone for me that night. I just wanted to see what went on there, how things were run. And after two hours I felt like I needed to leave, to go home and think about it, to work things out. I mean, it was a new place, a change, I was thinking about working in something, you know, not particularly moral, something I had never done before. So I just got up and said to him that I was going home.

I opened the door, said, "See you later," and the manager said to me, "Hang on a second, close the door." And he began to, like, kiss me, and, to make a long story short, he came on to me. And he asked me to stay the night—he basically invited me to have sex. I wasn't at all attracted to him, and I just wanted to get the hell out of there. So I said that I didn't feel like it, maybe some other time. Although I was sure, like, there wouldn't be another time when I would feel any differently. You could see disappointment on his face, but we parted on good terms. I went home, and didn't really think about it too much. I mean, I intended to go there the next day and see how things went out in the field.

So the next day I went back. Now, two weeks before all of this, I had changed jobs, I began working as a bartender. I took a course and got work as a bartender. I really liked it, but it's very hard work. A shitload of hours. I was working twelve-hour shifts, on my feet. I thought it was pretty satisfying, but it was very hard. I would go home absolutely dead tired, you know, all sweaty, smelly, irritable. I knew that I needed to do something else. I knew that I couldn't keep that up very much longer. Even though I liked it. It was too hard.

So I went back there the next day, and they set me up a first appointment. He was about forty years old, fat. I was sent down to the public phone to bring him up to the apartment. We didn't talk about anything—we didn't have anything to talk about. We went into the room, you know, undressed, got into bed. We did what he wanted, which is what most of them want actually—some hugging and some head. Some of them want to fuck, some of them don't. Looking back on it, it was the most, like, disgusting time I ever had, out of all the times. Because it was the first, and he was kind of violent, and I didn't really know what to do, how to act. I mean, we had a whole hour—and I had to just kind of play around with him for three-quarters of an hour. I had to make sure that he enjoyed that three-quarters of an hour, I had to be busy that whole time, to make sure that he had a good time, that he would want to come back again. So I got through it. It was, like, one big nightmare, and he paid, and left. The second time we were together, I found out that he was married. That time we did it in his house.

I remember that, a half-hour later, after I finished with him, I went to my job as a bartender. And for the whole time that I worked tending bar that day, I was, you know, thinking about how, in three-quarters of an hour, I had made double the amount of money that I was making over the course of ten hours in that bar, wasting the entire day. And it wasn't even interesting. So even though being with this guy wasn't, like, the most fun I ever had in my life, I decided to quit the bar, and I put all the time that I had spent bartending into, you know, prostitution. I went to the apartment more and more often, and began making more and more money. I would make, like, six, seven hundred shekels a day.

Let's start from the beginning. Let's say you saw one of our ads in *Ha°ir*. We also sometimes put ads in the national papers, in *Yedi°ot* and *Ma°ariv*. But we always have an ad in *Ha°ir*. There's also an agency where they, like, deal with girls. There's a woman in charge there, she advertises herself in a lot of different places, particularly in hotels and guidebooks, all sorts of tourist publications. And she says in her ads that she also provides services for gays and lesbians and things like that. So when they call her looking for men, she directs them to us. And of course she takes a percentage on every referral that she makes. She used to have her own men working for her, but it didn't really work out. Now she only has girls. So when tourists call her looking for men, she, you know, refers them to us and takes a cut. So people find us either from the newspaper, or through her.

So let's say you call. He says to you, "We have a number of guys, eighteen and older. For a hundred eighty shekels an hour, you will be able to meet with one of them, in a discreet apartment in Tel Aviv, with air conditioning, a shower, everything. Or in your house, or in a hotel." And then he asks you what kind of a guy you're interested in—most important, top or bottom, but also dark-skinned, light-skinned, tall, short, muscley, boyish, hairy, hairless, all sorts of things like that, to get someone who fits your fantasy. So the client basically says what he's looking for, and we try to find someone for him, from among the selection of guys that are available, the closest fit. There's a kind of a bulletin board in the apartment, where we have listed your name, age, if you're a top or a botom, your general appearance, your height, all the data about you, if you're boyish, or macho, or muscley, or hairy, as many details as possible. There are about fifteen names on that list. For me, it says, "°Amit, top, five foot nine, muscley, slightly hairy chest, hairless behind, light-skinned." Something like that.

The client chooses who he wants, and chooses a place. If you're a client, and you want to come to the apartment, you have to go to that public phone that's in the area, and call from there, and say you've arrived. Then the guy you've chosen goes downstairs to meet you, and takes you back to the apartment. Because we won't tell you the address on the phone. If you want someone to come to a hotel or to your house, you just give us your room number, or your address, and the guy goes there. You pay cab fare, besides the basic price. We also take your telephone number and name, and we call right back to make sure that it's right—there are a lot of jokers who call out of curiosity or something, or to play a joke on someone. And a lot of people make appointments to come to the apartment but never show up. What kind of kick they get out of this I'll never understand. They keep you on the phone for, you know, ten minutes, explaining what they're looking for, deciding on the right guy, making a time, everything. And they don't show up. It happens a lot.

And that's it. It's never happened to me that someone decided he didn't like me. There are some guys who prefer to come here and choose, you know, to see a few guys and then say who they want. But they're usually pretty embarrassed. No one has ever, like, pointed or anything like that. The manager just takes him into the other room and asks him who he wants, and then he comes out and calls the guy. It's just a matter of taste. But most people don't want to see anyone but you. Because most of the patrons are married, and they, you know, prefer as much discretion as possible.

I take home two-thirds of my fee, a hundred twenty shekels. That's my minimum. But a lot of them leave more than that. Almost everyone leaves two hundred. The extra twenty shekels is, like, a tip, I don't know what you would call it. And all of the tourists who come by way of the call girl service, we take a ton of money from them. I once took two hundred dollars from someone for half an hour. There are a lot of examples of huge fees. For the average Israeli, we cost a hundred eighty, but, like, there are a lot of them who want two guys at the same time, which costs three sixty. And then there are people who want to do, you know, all sorts of strange things, which cost more—things like, I don't know, having sex with a woman while looking at you, putting his finger up your ass, drinking a cup of coffee in the nude, putting a dress on you. All sorts of things like that. And there are some of them who only want to watch while we do it with each other. That's easier for us. Because when you do it with each other, it's more fun, it's easier, than with some random stranger who you don't feel anything about. There aren't a lot of people who want this, but it happens enough. I do what they want. I don't care.

When I meet someone, of course, we, like, get undressed right away, and get into the bed. I put on a sort of mask, and think about something else. After I leave I have trouble even remembering who it was. I forget that it happened, and that's that. The whole time I'm with him I, you know, do my best to close my eyes and think about something else, to imagine that I'm not there. Not that I suffer so much. I mean, after all, they also try to make you feel something. They'll also give you head, and jack you off. And you come with them at the end. And they cuddle you. So it's not all bad. Actually, with some clients I enjoyed myself as much as they enjoyed themselves, you could say. And they paid me for it and left.

Of course, you don't have to keep to any sort of set hours there. Nothing like that. You come and go whenever you want. You only see the clients you want to see. And if you don't want someone, if you've already been with someone and you know who he is and you don't want him again, no one's going to force you, that would be out of the question. And you can choose the things that you want to do with them—there are some guys who are bottoms with their boyfriends, but won't be bottoms with a client, you understand?

The clients determine what our hours of operation are. It works out to be from around ten in the morning, although some people do call earlier, but the first ones get there at ten in the morning, and the last ones leave at two or three in the morning. After that hour, there usually isn't anyone to answer the phone.

I don't have to ejaculate every time—I usually try to do it only with the last one of the day. By that time you also begin to feel the need. It usually doesn't bother them if I don't do it—I mean, there are some of them who couldn't care less. There are some who do want you to come with them, but after they've already done it, they don't care what you do. They just get up and get dressed. Also, if I get off with the first or the second ones, which I try not to do, then it's a problem to get it up for the others. Because I'm not, like, attracted to them. And some of them really disgust me. So it's perfectly natural that it's hard to get it up.

The whole time I've worked there, there have been maybe, like, two attractive guys. They weren't absolutely gorgeous or anything. They were married after all. But I'm very discreet. The clients are all scared to death, they have families, children, so they can't go to bars or anything. And their whole way of life is, like, the life of a straight, with a family. It's very difficult for them to come to terms with it, but they just need to get it. So they come to us.

The average client is around thirty-five or forty, not at all attractive. Most of them are fat or bald. I don't find that attractive. Most of them are married. It's happened to me a lot of times that I would, you know, go to their apartments and they wanted to do it in their son's room, for instance. This has happened a lot. Or in the bed where they, like, sleep with their wife.

The tourists are very pale—very, very white. Hairless. Fat. Almost all of them are fat. Most of them are old, but not all of them. I once was with a twenty-seven-year-old tourist, for instance. I went all the way to Jerusalem for him. He paid enough, believe me. He, of course, wasn't attractive—he had never had sex with anyone before, man or woman. I've got all sorts of stories. One tourist paid me a thousand dollars for two hours. I'm serious. I've got all sorts of stories like this. So you see, the business is, you know, very seductive.

I'm making more money than I've ever made in my life, more than my mother and father together. And I really enjoy this situation, having money. Especially since today I no longer have any problem, like, doing it with just anybody. No problem at all.

After a day or two in this job, my life totally changed. I've begun to throw money around all over the place. I only travel in taxis—I never walk anywhere. I buy all kinds of bullshit, eat in restaurants all the time, order food delivered to the apartment. I'm a member of a health club. I buy expensive cologne, all sorts of kitchen appliances, coffeemakers. I really enjoy wasting money.

And at the same time, I've begun going out to clubs, to Brothers, to Works. Without any fear at all. And this I never would have dreamed of, I never would have even considered it before I began this work. And I've met a lot of young guys who work with me. And all of sudden I've begun to talk about this whole thing very freely, without any fear, suspicions, like I used to have. Really, my life has changed—from a life of loneliness to the life of, well, a call boy. And I like it. I have a friend who calls me Alice in Wonderland— because Alice sounds like ᶜaliz, and because, like, right now, I'm living just like Alice, who stepped into an imaginary world, filled with things she had never seen before.§ The same thing with me—I'd like to try everything in this new world.

I've begun smoking drugs. Things that I never even knew what they were, all of sudden I'm in the middle of them, living them. Some of the guys offered me some, and of course I didn't particularly object. After all, you know, I want to try everything. And I liked it. We put on some music, and we, like,

§ ᶜaliz: literally, "gay," in the sense of "happy, joyful."

went into a kind of trance. And it makes you very horny. Especially me. But I think that lately just about everything makes me horny. A lot of us have slept with each other at one point or another.

There are a lot of different kinds of call boys. There are some of them who work independently. They put an ad in the paper, with their beeper number, and they run, like, the whole thing alone. People call, leave messages, they call them back, meet, everything. They're totally independent. Then there's us, like a sort of matchmaking office, where the manager takes a cut, and all that. Organized. And then there are the ones who hang around across from Independence Park, waiting for cars to stop. There are a few, you know, transvestites there, or whatever you want to call them. I can't even figure out what they are, they come in all sizes and shapes. Like the whores in Tel Baruḥ. And then there are the ones at Electricity Park, who are doing pretty much the same thing, working the street. You just drive up in your car, stop, and they, you know, either get into the car or not. There are, of course, big differences in price.

I'm still looking for a boyfriend, but I haven't found one. I mean, it's not like I'm looking for sex, I've got enough of that, but a boyfriend, to talk to, to wake up with in the morning, that's real fun, and I'd like that, I feel like that's missing. I'm looking for that. I've begun going to the gay bars, and I answered a few personal ads in *Ha°ir*. I met a few people, and I'm still meeting people. I haven't really found anyone I liked yet. There was one guy, and I thought things were going really well, he stayed at my place for, like, a week when he was having a hard time. And we were really interested in each other. But the moment I told him I was working in this, because I just couldn't hide it any more, and also because I didn't want to hide it, he, you know, stopped calling me. If I really fell in love with someone, and if I was faced with a decision, I think I would stop it. But, like, if he isn't ready to accept me the way I am, doing what I've chosen to do, then he doesn't have a place in my life.

I never would have dreamed that I would be doing this today. Because when it comes down to it, the definition of call boy is a whore. And that isn't, like, a very pretty word. That word kind of says all there is to say. I never thought I would be doing this. In the meantime, I think I'll keep doing it.

It does make some problems for me—I mean, all of a sudden I've got a lot of money, and I'm not working in anything else. And my mother is, you know, asking me how I'm supporting myself, how I'm paying rent. I mean, I'm not working, she knows that I'm not working. But I could never tell her what I'm doing, in my entire life. It would really hurt her, and that's the last thing I would want. I did, like, have some money saved from my last jobs, and I told her that I was living on that savings, and that I was going to register for unemployment. So that's how she thinks I'm getting by. But I can't keep this up much longer, because she knows how much money I've got in the bank—in my old bank account, that is. My new one, that I opened here, she has no idea about. And I have no intention of telling her about it. So she thinks that at some point, I'm, like, going to run out of money.

I'm thinking a lot now about what I can do. If I register for unemployment, then I'll be able to keep this going for another six months, if I get money. But she probably thinks that I'm struggling to get by, living in poverty, when that is certainly not what's going on. So let's say I do manage to work things out for another six months, eventually I'm going to have to think of something, you know, find some kind of other job. I'm taking classes now, so I tell everyone, I tell her that I'm, like, taking a class, and that it's difficult to study and work at the same time.

I'm trying to improve my scores on my high school matriculation exams. I'd like to go to college. I'm not really sure what I'd like to study—I've thought about economics, or architecture. But I don't know what I'll do. In the meantime, I'm trying very hard to bring up my scores. I'm taking five courses at a very fancy, expensive private school, and I'm taking private lessons on top of that. Everything. I really want to get ahead. I know that I won't be able to do this for my entire life. And I do want to make something out of myself. I really want to go to college.

Another problem is that my first friend in Tel Aviv, you know who I'm talking about? He's always having these, like, serious talks with me about how much this is going to hurt me in the future, emotionally. He says that after a few more years of this I'm going to have to go to a mental institution. He says that in a little while longer I just won't ever agree to work in anything else, because it will just seem like pennies, all of a sudden to work for fifteen shekels an hour—I'll be telling myself, why should I work so hard for fifteen shekels an hour, when I can make that ten times over in the same amount of time, while enjoying myself, and with a lot of conditions you just don't get in other work? That what he says. He's right. He's talked to me a lot about it, and he's trying to convince me. Today he left a message on my answering machine, that he had an offer for me, some sort of job he found me. He's trying very hard to get me out of this. But I don't really listen to him.

He's not the only one. Besides him there's another one, who was once a client. Now we've become friends. He had me to his apartment. He's much older—well, he's thirty-eight, but that's almost a twenty-year difference. I'm only twenty-two. What is there for me in someone older than my own father? But we've become good friends, really, and I spend a lot of time with him, and he also is trying to get me out of this work all the time.

He's not married. He lives alone in a very big apartment. And he has a lot of money. At first, he would pay me for everything—you know, every time I went to see him, he would pay me, like, the regular rate, just for talking. But now it's become friendship. I mean, I go to see him because I want to. I don't take his money. He said to me a week ago that I'm very dear to him, and that if he had enough money, he would be ready to pay me not to do this kind of work. And he told me that this was going to do me emotional damage, that, in a little while longer, it will be very difficult for me to get out of this. He said to me, "You don't even belong there, you come from a different background, you're from a good background." And he said to me that the others, this is their life, they'll never make anything of themselves, they'll never learn anything, do something serious, they'll never live the right way. But I'm the kind of person who will be hurt by this. That's what he told me. He introduced me to a good friend of his who worked in this once. He did it for a year, and got out of it, and he told me that even today, years later, it's difficult for him to get used to any other life.

I'm really beginning to think that they're right after all. But right now I'm too young, and too innocent to understand that it will happen to me. I push it to one side, and keep on telling myself that they're talking bullshit, that it isn't true. But look, if two people are telling you the same thing, it might be that, you know, there's something to what they're saying. In the meantime, I feel pretty good about it. And after all, I haven't been doing it for long.

Not long ago I left a message with someone who put a personal ad in *Haʿir*, just to meet someone, and he called me back, and we talked for a long time, and in the end we figured out that he knows just about everybody from my hometown—their names, last names, he knew everything. And it turned out that he's, like, from the next town over. We went to the same high school, I was in his sister's class, he has a very good friend from my neighborhood. Can you imagine what that's like, to talk on the telephone, and all of a sudden to find out that he knows who your neighbors are? We both got very frightened. But we decided to get together in spite of that. So I went to his place, and, you know, he really did look familiar, I recognized his face. In the end, it was nice. Now we've got each other's telephone number, we're still seeing each other. Of course, we're keeping this all discreet. And that's it. I'm very worried about getting into a fight with him or something, what he might do. But in this world you can never know what will happen, that someone won't tell someone else. And even if he did decide to tell about me, then he would be, like, exposing himself. He promised not to do it. He said he wouldn't mention anything.

I think it's more accurate to say I'm bisexual than gay. Because I do look at women, I am attracted to them. And I'm sure I'll get married some day. I wouldn't have any problem with that. I'd enjoy being with a girl very much. It's just that, like, right now, I feel like I'm in a thing, it's very new for me, and it's pretty much filling up my whole life right now. So you could say that right now I'm putting a lot more into my homosexuality than the other side. I mean, I'm not doing anything to meet a girl.

I'm not especially crazy about being a family man with children, going to work every day and coming home, supporting them. That life seems very boring to me. But I do want a kid, to get married, you know, to be like everyone else. So I think I'll do it. I would do it all just so I could raise a kid, like, one or two kids, not more than that. To leave something behind me in this world. I mean, I can never get rid of my gay side. I'll always, like, have something of this in me. Maybe it's even my stronger side. Because you always want what you don't have. And the moment I'm settled, I'm sure I'll miss this.

I'd like to be with a woman who knows. I'd rather she knew. I'd rather tell her everything, like, not hide anything. Because, like they say, when it comes down to it, lies are always found out. How can you lie to someone, when you share a bed, you have a kid together, you have a whole life together? But if I see that I'm losing people because of this, I'll be forced just not to tell. You understand? I won't have a choice.

I'd rather that my parents never found out about me. Every time I imagine telling them, I see my mother's condition when she found out about the cigarettes, that I was smoking. How she looked. And to tell her something like this, when I'm the only son, after all, I think she would take it very hard. It would really hurt her. And I love her too much to do that to her. Too much. But my parents are asking me, "So, do you have girlfriend, are you going out with someone?" So I make things up here and there, I say it's not very serious, you understand? I try to avoid the questions. But there are neighbors, friends, all of them are in and out of our house, just like they live there. My sisters' friends. And anyone could find out and tell them.

At home, the jokes about gays just flow. And I have no choice but to laugh. Because, just like I used to think that all gays were sissies, that's what they still think, you understand? So I don't think they suspect anything about me, right now. Maybe my mother knows—because they say that it's difficult to hide things from your mother, your mother always understands what's going on. I'm sure she, like, suspects something. My father is too indifferent. I think he would just turn his back on me, and that's it. He's too indifferent. He doesn't really show any signs of caring one way or another. He lives in his own world. He's very quiet, dry.

One of my sisters is in tenth grade, she's still a kid. There's no point in telling her. And the other tells me jokes about queers. She's in the army. So, what, I'll go and tell her? In the meantime it doesn't bother me. You just, like, push it aside, another day goes by, another month, another year. In the meantime I have no desire to tell them. But it won't be pleasant if they find out through the grapevine.

I've slept with a lot of men—a lot. Figure it out—over two months, an average of three a day. I know that what I do is very, very dangerous, with AIDS. Very dangerous. But I do use as many preventatives as possible. Condoms. I won't go with someone who looks sick. Condoms are the main thing. Lately, among other things, I've also become a bottom—there's a lot of demand. That's something else this work has, like, changed about me. At first, I said to myself, I would never do that in my life. It seemed very painful, and beside the point. But today I really enjoy it. Today, let's say I meet someone as, like, a serious boyfriend and all that, in a case like that, this is going to be very important to me. I mean, I would definitely feel like something was lacking without it. I would feel like something was missing in sex. It just wouldn't be ideal. So that's very dangerous.

But, look, I try to use as many preventatives as possible, and to pay attention to the guidelines of the AIDS Task Force, and all that bullshit—how to be careful, what not to do, what to do, all sorts of things like that. Like, they say that it's very dangerous to lick someone's anus. So you don't do that. And you don't have sex without a condom. And the moment there's precum, you stop giving head. You're as careful as possible. But it's never careful enough. I'm aware of that—like, there's a danger. But, I mean, the same thing goes with someone who's your boyfriend. You can't do this, you can't do that, you can't do this, so if you can't do anything at all, then what's the point of life? There is no point, if you take the spice of life away, the enjoyment. So you've got to take some chances. Because you can't stop doing it altogether. And everyone is putting himself at risk. So, OK, I'm putting myself at risk, like, a lot more. But I do my best to be as careful as possible.

I don't know anyone who has AIDS. I can only imagine, you know, all the suffering, physically, emotionally—not to mention the parents who are suffering, and all the guilt. Very painful. I've never seen it myself. I don't really want to know.

There are other dangers, too. I mean, you go into a strange house, and you meet someone there. You might never leave. It's a danger. You don't know what kind of person you're with. You don't know anything about him. There are some dangers. Every time someone new comes in the door you don't know who it is, and what he is capable of doing, and who he knows. And if the police got on our case, I think they would close us down. What would happen to me then? There's always the fear that something could happen.

I'm not a Zionist. For me, a Zionist is someone who loves Israel, loves his country, who would do a lot for it, would give of himself for it, would sacrifice for it. Would express some interest in what's going on, would care. He would, you know, be involved in politics, it would be important to him to keep control of national territory. I think that it goes together with being traditional, religiously. But I'm not interested in politics. I don't keep kosher. I don't fast on Yom Kippur or anything like that. I'm Jewish because that's the way I was born. I was circumcised. I live in a country like this one, celebrate its holidays, among others. The Jewish holidays. There are civil holidays, and there are Jewish holidays. I used to fast and all that. And I would go to synagogue. But not any more.

I've thought about living somewhere else. I would do it. If I could leave, I would. I'd go to the United States. I've been there—I once lived there with some relatives for about a month. And I didn't want to come back to Israel. Because it's different. In lots of ways. They live well there. The atmosphere is different, like, life is different. You've got, you know, a lot more choices there. For instance, this book—the fact is that you're planning on publishing it there, not here. I would absolutely not rule out living there for a few years.

I mean, I'm not ruling out living in Israel either. I love this country. I know that I'm better off staying here. The language I speak is here, the same mentality is here. That great sentence, "There's no place like home," is a big factor. I don't think that you can say, in general, that life is better there. It is better for some people, and not for others.

My political views tend toward the right wing. But I'm not very involved, not very interested. I know exactly what's going on, what the situation is, and exactly what kind of people are running this country. But it doesn't really interest me at the moment, or attract me. It's not important to me. Where I come from, everyone votes for Likud. They identify more with the right wing. And I think that their views make more sense to me.

I've learned a shitload about people, and about what this scene is about, through this work. I've met all kinds of people. It's really made me look at things in a new way. All of a sudden I feel like I live in a kind of never-never land, where you can't know what will happen to you, and what's waiting for you, and what will happen tomorrow.

I'm pretty close with the other guys I work with. We just laugh about all kinds of clients that we see. And every one tells about what he's been through, and what he did with this one or that one. We just live it up, and we don't settle any accounts with anyone else. It's a very unique life. You don't have to wake up in the morning for anyone, you do what you want to do, whenever you want to do it.

I've been told that I've gotten into this very quickly. Because, after all, after three people, to begin working in this, is very unusual. But that's the way things have worked out. I haven't wasted a minute since I began this life. That's it. I use every moment. To make more money, to learn something else, to enjoy something else.

When it comes down to it, I feel like I've missed out on so much, until I got started with all of this. It was just like I was frozen, for five or six years— what a waste. I was just living the life of a vegetable. I ate, drank, did whatever I was told to do, and that's it. I didn't enjoy anything, I didn't do anything with my life. I really regret those years. And I feel like I need to make up for them. And that's what I'm doing.

ANDREI

One of the most easily recognizable figures on the Israeli scene is the Russian-speaking immigrant. Pale, wild-haired, and bewildered, these newcomers seem to be everywhere. This is unsurprising, as Israel has absorbed over eight hundred thousand immigrants from the former Soviet Union during the past ten years—proportionately, this is the equivalent of the United States absorbing the entire population of France. Amir and I were convinced that there had to be some stories among these statistics.

Rafi Niv came to our aid—his journalistic duties had taken him to the public parks of Haifa, where he had met just the fellow for us. He put Amir in touch with "Andrei," and on yet another bright Shabbat morning, we set out with our tape recorder and plenty of batteries.

Andrei's apartment was difficult to find—located in one of the flat districts just outside of Haifa, the neighborhood seemed an infinite expanse of five-story stucco apartment buildings, the unmistakable products of the 1950s, preternaturally aged into seemingly ancient decrepitude. When we found the right street, we emerged from the car into the atmosphere of a wholesome slum. Every doorway, every window, every balcony broadcast its own cacophony of voices, adult and child, Hebrew-speaking and alien. The echoing sounds seemed to defy the dilapidated architecture, suggesting the protective bosom of a vibrant community. Such community was embodied in a group of astoundingly buxom Russian-speaking matriarchs stationed on lawn chairs. As we approached, the women met our disoriented gazes with interrogating glances of their own. Our question—"Andrei? Andrei?"—was met with an enthusiastically appropriate response—"Andrei! Andrei!"—and general gesticulation directed us to enter a nearby building and ascend its stairwell.

Andrei answered our knock. Upon seeing the delicate nature of his boyish, glowing features, I had no doubt that we had arrived at the right apartment. His pale skin and brown hair reminded me that most American Jews were also of Russian stock. He invited us into his cramped living room, overfurnished with overstuffed, oversized couches. Andrei's mother shyly served us up some ice-cold water with a smiling and presumably polite flourish of Russian. A grandmotherly figure peered at us from behind the kitchen door.

This domesticity, far from disarming me, made me slightly uneasy. I was unsure what exactly Amir had said to Andrei during their telephone conversation, but this hardly seemed a setting conducive to the kind of uninhibited conversation we had in mind. Amir diplomatically conveyed this sentiment to Andrei, who, smiling sweetly, explained that there was no chance that his mother or grandmother would understand the Hebrew in which we were speaking. We had no need to be concerned.

Andrei himself spoke Hebrew with a thick accent. Clichés and slang came easily to him, but he was frustrated by the limitations of his vocabulary when he wanted to express himself more precisely. "Oh, the stories I could tell," he said with a wistful grin, "if only we could talk in Russian."

∿

I WAS BORN IN BYELORUSSIA, in Vitebsk. Near Moscow. Eight hours by train. That's thought of as near. Russia is pretty big.

I come from a very humble family. My mother is a worker—she used to work in a shoe factory. I have no father. My parents were divorced twenty years ago, and I don't remember him. I don't know where he is now, I'm not in touch with him. I've just got a picture of him. My grandmother and my mother, that's my whole family.

Vitebsk is a very small city. There are some factories, and most of the people in town worked in them. Factories, workshops, things like that. The city was very small, and there weren't a lot of possibilities. But, of course, everyone worked, there was no such a thing as unemployment. Now the situation has changed, and a lot of people there are unemployed, a lot of people can't find work.

The city was very old. We had our own house, with a yard and all that. And I lived there ever since I was born. We had three rooms, everyone had their own room. And that's it. Later on we sold the house and came here.

I went to nursery school. I had a lot of friends then. I always had friends. In every period of my life that I can remember, I always had lots of friends. In nursery school, in school, in the army. I got along well with people, I never had any problem. I was popular. I don't know why. I knew how to talk to people, how to get by, I got along with everyone. And people liked me, I just felt that.

I always felt attracted to boys. I always played with them, even in nursery school, I remember. But it wasn't just playing with them, it was a deeper feeling than that. It was more than playing, I don't know what it was. I can't describe it exactly. But at this very young age, it didn't make me feel different from the other kids. Afterwards, when I matured a little more, I began to feel that I began to be different from the others, to feel something different, to be attracted to something else. And I thought, what am I doing wrong? I'm trying to lead my life like the others are doing.

It was in elementary school that things began to change. Fifth grade, something like that. I was ten or eleven. My friend, who was in my class at school, his parents were workers from Poland, and they brought some erotic magazines. The moment his parents weren't home, we looked at those magazines, and my friend said, "Come on, let's try that." And for me, it didn't even occur to me, that someone might have something to say about the fact that we were two boys doing it, and not a boy and a girl. It was totally natural to me that I should try it with him, and not with a girl. So we tried it, and we liked it. I remember that first feeling. He had fun, and so did I. And so we kept on doing it afterwards, for years.

When his parents weren't at home we met, after school or during vacations, to study together. We sometimes got together every day. There was no problem. We used to go to the theater, to the movies, we both liked to read books, we always told each other the stories. We were real friends. We had other friends during this time, but the sexual relationship was only between us. No one asked any questions. I don't think the other kids knew what was going on, that such a thing could happen.

All I knew was that I liked it. I didn't think about it, is this a good thing or a bad thing, is it right to feel this way or not. I knew that I liked it. It wasn't like today, when I say I want one person who will be with me all the time, I'll love him, and he'll love me. I wasn't in love, you understand? It was just simple, physical attraction. We liked having sex, and that was that. And that didn't stop me from thinking about others either.

But I did know enough to hide it, because I knew that if I tell someone, I will probably get shouted at or cursed or something like that. I just had the sense that this will happen. We never talked about the fact that we needed to hide it. It was totally obvious to both of us. We never talked about it. We didn't need to talk about it. We were just having fun.

I don't really remember how I felt about him exactly. It was such a young age, you just can't compare what I think about today when I think about a boyfriend, and what I thought of him then. I was a kid. It continued until tenth grade, because at that point he left the school, he went to study something else, I don't even remember what. This was at fifteen, sixteen, something like that.

We never talked about sex at home. Never. And there was never any sex education in school. But I had heard the word "homosexual." I thought, maybe, maybe I'm one of those. But I didn't really know. Because at such an early age you can't know. It didn't really bother me very much. Kids didn't call each other "queer" or anything like that, I never heard that. In the army I heard it sometimes, not directed at someone specific, but just kind of kidding around, they said it.

I don't remember the first time I heard the word. It doesn't appear in books. It's in the encyclopedia—or maybe I saw it in a scientific dictionary. But in literature or in school, or just in conversation, never. Not even in newspapers. I never remember seeing it. I really couldn't tell you how I learned the word.

All of my friends in Russia were Russians, real Russians. There were Jews in my city, but I didn't hang out with them. I always knew that my mother was Jewish. I don't know her family's history. I just know they were from Vitebsk. My father was a Russian, so everyplace I ever was, I was registered as Russian, in school and also in the army. And that helped a lot. If you have mixed parents, you can choose your nationality. So when I was old enough to get my passport I chose to be Russian. Life is easier that way, because of antisemitism. Wherever you go, it's easier. You don't have to worry about being called names, you get treated better. If you have "Jew" written there, it's as if you're worthless.

I'm not circumcised. We don't do that in Russia. You had to go to the larger cities, they do it there, if you really want to do it right.

My mother's being Jewish never affected the way people treated me. No one ever asked me if I was Jewish. I danced in a Russian folkdance troupe for ten years, and a lot of people knew my mother, and they knew that she was

Jewish. But they never said a word to me, not any insulting jokes, never called me names, nothing that hurt my feelings. I never heard anything.

I danced from the time I was in second grade. My grandfather was a clarinetist and saxophonist, and he wanted me to learn something cultural as well, he wanted me to be a dancer. So he put me into this troupe. And I stayed there. I loved it. I danced for ten years. And after I got out of the army I went back to my troupe.

In the big cities, they say that dancers, especially ballet dancers, are all gay. But in my city they didn't even talk about it. I remember one case, where a guy who danced with us, he was married and he had a daughter, but his wife once caught him with another man. And she came running to the troupe, and began to tell everyone about it, about how she caught him—she told the manager, everyone. And afterwards they kicked him out, he couldn't dance with us anymore. It was awful. Really disgusting to see, the way people treated him, I can't even describe it. It was so horrible. And I remember thinking to myself, maybe someone thinks the same thing about me, maybe something like that will happen to me someday. I was very afraid of that. I made sure not to give anybody any reason to think that I was like that. I tried not to attract attention.

After my friend left, at fifteen or sixteen, it was around this time that I began to feel that I was really different from the other kids. I was always looking at the boys in my class, I was always hung up on someone different I thought was good-looking, dreaming about him. It was only thoughts, because I couldn't go up to him and just tell him that I want him, or something like that.

I felt like I was different. In my class, I didn't find any other people like that. I made some tries, to invite people home. Everyone knew that I had a lot of books. I had books, romance novels, which I read, and which I gave to others to read. But I always wanted to be sure that someone was really like that before I said anything. I didn't want to get involved with someone who was just kind of confused, who didn't know what he really wanted. Because there were a lot like that, they were confused at that age, and they didn't know exactly what they wanted. But I wanted to avoid trouble.

So I had two more years of school like this after my friend left. I was a good student. Not the very best, but I was one of the outstanding students. I did my lessons well.

I kept on dancing in the troupe, and eventually I met a guy there. He just came back from the army. He danced before he was drafted, but I never saw him, because I was in the children's troupe, and later on I danced with the adults. Dancing was just his hobby. He was—I don't know how you say it, a man who sews clothing. A tailor. He was six years older than me. And this guy, whenever we danced or did exercises lined up along the wall, he always looked at me. Staring, staring. What in the world could he want? I wanted to believe that this was what he meant, but I was very scared to say anything. One day, when he was looking at me all the time, just looking, looking, all of sudden he began talking to me, but not about sex or homosexuality directly. He said he wanted to walk me home. I said OK. So he was the one who made the first move.

Nothing happened on that walk, he just gave me his telephone number, and we began seeing each other. One day, he invited me over to his house, and I went, and we talked about all sorts of things, and drank a lot of alcohol also, and little by little, we began having sex. And that's it. Things continued that way. He lived close by, I didn't need to make up any excuses. There was no problem. We met once a week at his house, when his mother wasn't at home—she went to visit her sister in some village once a week.

I knew that, besides me, he had a girlfriend. And he was also meeting with her. I felt very jealous. I didn't want him to go with her. I told him this. He told me that he was also attracted to women. I believe him. But I don't think he loved her—he was just with her for sex. I felt that I loved him, and I wanted him to stay with me for a long time. I thought about my dream future a lot. But I waited. I thought that at some point he will give up on her, and stay only with me. He won't have another woman.

We talked about it, but I was afraid to tell him that I wanted to live with him. I never saw two men living together as a family in Russia, like you see here. I never heard of that. But I thought about it. I didn't say anything because I just didn't know how he could react. I wanted to see him more than once a week, but I couldn't, because his mother was at home all the time.

Except for my old friend, who left, no one else knew about me. I never felt the need to tell my mother. I felt like there was no point, that the time will come.

The law in Russia says that everyone has to go to the army, and everybody goes, unless you have some kind of connections so that you can work something out. But everybody has to go, Jews also. If I remember right, if you are going to study in a university, you serve only one year in the army, instead of two years. But I never wanted to study in a university. I had no patience for that. I never really thought about what I wanted to do with my life.

You can't choose what you do in the army. You go where you're sent. They choose. They send you for examinations, tests, interviews, and then they choose for you. We didn't talk about it in school, we weren't prepared or anything. We just had a few lessons about guns, they explained how guns work, a few things like that. But you can't learn anything from one lesson a week. We didn't talk about what we wanted to do in the army, because we all knew from the very start that what we wanted didn't make a difference. You didn't go where you wanted.

They didn't ask about sexual orientation. And if they asked, what do you think I would answer? That I'm "like that"? They would probably put me in jail or something. I think that was the law then. Now the situation is different, they changed the law. But then, if they knew that you had sex with another man, they had no problem sending you to jail. Everyone knew that. There were a lot of cases like that. Nobody I knew personally. I just heard about it.

So I finished high school, and one day I got a letter, a draft notice. I had to go on a specific day. So I went to get my hair cut, a crew cut. And that's it. I didn't even know where I was going, what I will do. I knew that I was going in the direction of Moscow, but I didn't know exactly where. No one knew anything. We asked, but they didn't answer. "You'll find out. Just come on, you can write letters to your family, it will be OK." They put us all in the train, and that was that. Very simple.

I didn't take a single thing from home with me—well, all right, I brought my shaving kit. But you don't need anything. They give you everything there. What to take? Sheets, clothes? Everything is there.

I didn't want to go to the army at all, but I knew that I had to go, that there was nothing to do about it. Most of all, I really did not want to go to Afghanistan. Because at that time, they were sending a lot of guys to serve there. I didn't want that. And I also didn't want to go to the navy. Because you serve for three years there. I wanted to stay as little as possible—two years and that's that. But I had no control.

This was from '85 to '87. Gorbachev was in power at this time. I really wasn't interested in politics. I didn't think that what was happening at the time was very interesting—I wasn't interested in such distant things. I don't really remember if I felt any difference between the different regimes. The only thing I remember about perestroika is how we laughed at it—because it's meaningless, in my opinion. Because nothing changed. Everyone had their own new little plan, and in the end, nothing at all changed. Everything stayed exactly the way it was.

I knew I was not going to be able to have sex in the army, and I just thought that will kill me. So I said to myself, patience, everything will be OK in a little while. At the induction center, as soon as we got there, they told us where we were, and all that. It was a base specializing in, I don't know how you say it in Hebrew, missiles against missiles, big missiles. It was near Moscow. Not far from home.

We all showered, got our uniforms, boots. Then we began basic training, which took a month. You learn all sorts of things. They explain to you all sorts of nonsense, all the army rules. And then you go in like a regular soldier.

They treat you very badly during your first year. Someone who is already in their second year has more of a right to do nothing, you could say. But someone who has just come has to do all the dirty work, and all that. That's the way it is for everyone. So I knew that I will work very hard during my first year, and afterwards I will be older, and I will sit on the side.

It was physical work. We carried all sorts of things. We worked very hard. We built all sorts of buildings, all sorts of nonsense like that. For the generals. You could say that we were construction workers. We fixed up their houses, their gardens. All sorts of things like that. That was our job. Everyone knew that.

My whole first year I didn't have any sex. My second year, I was transferred, I was a clerk. I wrote exit forms for drivers. How did I get that job? By way of sex.

I had an encounter with, I don't know what to call him, he was the officer, the manager of all the low-ranking soldiers. He was in a very important position. He was about forty years old. One day he came to me and said that he had something to talk to me about. And he brought me to his room, and closed the door, and began to tell me that he liked me, all that nonsense, and he began to move closer to me, and he began touching me, sort of stroking me. And I was afraid to tell him to stop, to get out of there, because I knew that he was more important than me, and was able to assign me to do a lot of things that I didn't want to do. I was afraid that he will do something to me, if I said no or something. So I just went along. I didn't want to. But I saw that he wanted it, and that he was very important, and I was very scared. I knew that I had no choice. But you could not say that it was rape, because I agreed to do it. I didn't say no. It wasn't what I wanted to do, but I felt that I had to do it.

It was only once. But I had no way of knowing whether he wanted to continue meeting me. Maybe he will want to do it every day. The way it worked out was that it only happened once. I certainly didn't want it to happen again. But I said to myself, if it happens again, I won't have a choice, I've got to give him what he wants. I never noticed whether he did the same thing with other soldiers.

It all ended well. Afterwards, he arranged for me to be moved to a better position. I began to be a transportation clerk. I didn't ask him to put me there. He did it himself. I didn't even plan to ask anything from him afterwards. But he did it by himself.

It was very good work, very clean. I sat in an office all day, organizing lots of papers, keeping track of the gasoline, nonsense like that. I never told anyone about what happened—I really wanted to be able to stay in this job. Everybody asked me, "How did you get that job, what did you do?" I said, "I have no idea, I'm also asking myself the same question."

So I became the transportation clerk, I had a clean office. I dealt with all the drivers, they had to come to me all the time. And they were really nice guys. They brought me all sorts of presents—fruit, candy. Everyone liked me. They said things like, "It's a shame you're not a girl," "If you was a girl I would go for you," all that nonsense, I heard that a lot. They all treated me very well, and I liked that. Everybody treated me well. I really enjoyed it.

Later on, I began to have a sexual relationship with two of the drivers. Besides them there was no one. These two drivers were very good friends. They came from the same city, and knew each other from nursery school. I had a relationship with both of them—and I think that to this day they don't know about the other, that he was having a relationship with me.

With one, it happened on New Year's Eve. They let us watch television until very late—they let everyone lie in bed and watch television from their beds. We had a very big room for the soldiers, and from my bed, where I slept, I couldn't see the television. It was too far away. So I went to his bed. I wasn't the only one who moved closer, there were a lot of people who were lying in bed together and watching television. I wasn't afraid.

So I went to his bed. And it was a very small bed, and we were lying there very close to each other. And I made the first move, I put my arm around him, and I saw that he didn't do anything. But I could tell that he also wanted something, to do something. I felt that his body was moving closer to mine, and I could feel his arm, his leg. I was able to tell that he also really wanted something.

When the television program ended, they told everybody to go back to their own beds, and he said to me, "Stay here, no one will see. We have a blanket, we'll go underneath, no one will see that you're here. It will be dark." And I stayed. We didn't do anything that was a big deal, it was very simple—we did what we could do in the middle of that room with all those people around.

We slept together the whole night, until the morning, and in the morning, before everyone woke up, I went back to my bed. That's that. To this day, I can't be sure that no one saw what was happening. But it all went off very quietly.

We met in his truck afterwards. He was a truck driver, he had a very big truck, so we began to meet there, and we had sex there.

And then I also had his friend. I didn't want to start anything with him, he made the first move. He became close with me little by little, all sorts of nonsense, he began to tell me all kinds of jokes. And I had no idea what he was after. Later on, he also had a truck, and he invited me, "Come on, let's go out together." And I agreed. I sat with him in the truck, and I saw that he wanted to have sex, and that's how it happened.

I was very frightened to tell them that I was meeting both of them. But that's the way it continued, all through my second year.

For the whole two years I was in the army I didn't go home once. They hardly ever let people out on leave. Less than one-third of the soldiers get to go. The very best. I didn't think I was such a good soldier that I deserved it. So for two years I didn't see my grandmother. Only my mother, when she came to visit me. She visited four times. And my work was nothing. Those two years were a complete waste of time. I didn't learn a thing, I didn't come away with anything that will help me in the future. Meaningless. And that's not just my opinion, everybody said the same thing.

I was twenty when I got out of the army. I went straight to see my old boyfriend, the dancer. My relationship with him didn't really end until this point. My first year, I didn't get any letters at all from him, in the army. Afterwards, a few girls from my troupe came to visit me, and they told me that he was married. Afterwards, he wrote to me, and told me himself that he found a new girlfriend and got married. I really didn't want that to happen. But I understood why he didn't write to me.

When I came back home after the army, I went to see him, and I felt that it wasn't the way it used to be. He was very scared to have sex with me again, because he thought that if he began doing something with me, then he won't be able to live with his wife. So he said to me directly, "We need to stop this, because I also have a wife and a normal life, and I want children. And it's difficult for me." So I gave up on it, and that's the way our relationship ended.

I moved back home after the army. That's what everyone does. I didn't make any plans at all, because all of a sudden my uncle and my mother began to talk about Israel, going to live in Israel. This was already '89, the time when a lot of people began to leave Russia. So we also began thinking about it.

I don't know why they began talking about it all of a sudden. Before I left for the army, I never heard anyone talking that way, from our family. I, for instance, I wanted to leave Russia, to live better, but I never thought about Israel. I thought I wanted to live somewhere in Europe, I didn't care where.

I already knew that I was gay, there was no question about that. I saw that I won't be able to find what I wanted in Russia. I didn't know of any gay organizations, bars, nothing. In the large cities, people met in the public bathrooms, or in the parks. There were no clubs or bars, like here. It's probably different now. Now there are a lot of things. But there was nothing then.

My old boyfriend, he had a friend that he knew from the army who was also gay, they had also had some kind of sexual relationship, and I met him. He lived in Leningrad, and I went to visit him. I was with him a lot of times in Leningrad. He knew another few people who were gay, and I felt that life in Leningrad was better than the life I had in Vitebsk, which was a very small city.

Leningrad was a big city and there were a lot of possibilities, and a lot of gays, and there was a time when I thought, maybe I'll leave my city and I'll move there. It will be relatively easier for me to live there, because I know more people there who are gay. I never met anyone else from my city, as long as I was there. Maybe there were others, but I didn't find them.

The people I met in Leningrad were good people, of all ages. Very intelligent, smart. I liked to talk to them about all kinds of subjects. But I didn't have a lot of opportunities to go there—maybe I went there once a month. We went out. There weren't any gay places to go, so we went to all kinds of theaters, there are so many, all sorts of performances. We went to a ballet, or a movie, or something like that. We all liked that, those kinds of things. It wasn't expensive there.

When I first heard the discussions about Israel, I didn't want to come. But I felt like I didn't have a choice. Because everyone was already set on going, my mother, my aunt, everyone wanted to go. I could stay behind in the house, and continue my life. But I didn't want to separate from my family. So I didn't have a choice, I came with them.

They felt like the situation was very unstable in Russia, it was getting worse and worse all the time. Economically. And Israel was the only country that was taking everybody. If there was another country, we would have gone there. But there just wasn't any choice. That's everybody's reason. A person wants a better life, he leaves his country, and goes somewhere else. If things work out in the new place, he'll stay, if not, he'll look for someplace else. So that's it.

There were a lot of problems with food, getting food. I mean, there was food, but the lines were so long, and on one line they're giving one thing, on another line they're giving something else, a third line, something else. But you have to go after a full day at work, and you just don't have the strength to stand there. You have to work tomorrow also. It drives you crazy all the time, lines, lines, lines. All that nonsense. And you can't get clothes at all. So we got fed up by all that. None of us felt like political changes will make any-thing better. I just wanted things to stop getting worse. No one had the sense that things will be different in the future.

I didn't know anything about Israel. I didn't have any information. I once saw a sort of publicity movie about Israel, a half-hour movie, with all sorts of panoramas of Haifa, Jerusalem, Tel Aviv, factories, what people in Israel do, all sorts of things. So I saw the movie, and I said, nice. But it was in He-brew and I didn't understand what they were talking about. From the movie, I thought that Israel was very beautiful. I didn't know what to think. I de-cided that I will go. I didn't think that it will be worse than the way things were there. I thought it will be better. I was sure that gay life in Israel had to be different than in Russia—better. I knew that this wasn't Russia, that this was a another world. Different people, everything different, so I thought that my life will be different.

It was very difficult for me to leave. All sorts of Russian friends that I write to now, I know that they'll never leave Russia and come to live here. Maybe they'll come and visit at most. So it was very difficult for me to leave them. That was the most difficult thing. But everything about it was difficult. You have to experience it. But I did it. And by now I've gotten used to Israel, you could say.

Some of my mother's relatives got here a little earlier, they lived in Haifa, and they sent us what's called an "invitation." So we took this letter to the Jewish Agency, and we worked out all the details of our emigration. The whole thing took about three months, which was pretty quick. We flew from Moscow to Budapest, and from Budapest to Tel Aviv.

I personally didn't know anyone who was in Israel. When I got here, we took a bus from Tel Aviv to Haifa, and all of the surroundings were so strange for me, everything was totally different. I really didn't think I will ever get used to it. Everything was different—different people, different surroundings, different houses. I really didn't like it. Those small apartment buildings where people lived, with tiny windows, everything shut up, I couldn't understand how people live like that. Like a warehouse. In my town, the houses were older, bigger, everything was more open, you understand? Also, people here were so free, open. In their speech. I didn't understand what they were saying, but I felt how they were talking, the way they spoke. And how people dressed. That was also different. All sorts of small things. I didn't think I will ever get used to it. I was very unhappy during that first period, when I just got here. I didn't see myself fitting in here.

So we went to my mother's relatives in Haifa. We lived with them for our first week, and afterwards we rented an apartment. This was 1990. I had no idea what I wanted to do—I didn't even know where I was. I planned to get into contact with the gay scene, but I said, in a little while, first I need to calm down, to settle down. Because it's very difficult to go through that, the road from Russia to here.

My first day in Israel, I remember, I went to the big supermarket, in downtown Haifa. I went in there, and it was a tremendous experience, I had never seen such abundance of things. You could just buy anything, whatever you wanted, all of it. It was so new to me, to see all of that, so many things in one place. I never saw anything like it in my life. So I said to myself, with so many things, with such beautiful stores, life here must be pretty good after all. No lines, nothing. You come, you take what you want. Unbelievable.

At first, I began eating more. I wanted to taste everything, to choose exactly what I wanted. And I began to buy nice clothes, which I missed in Russia. I could only dream of it back then, and suddenly I saw things here, and I was able to buy them.

At first, the Jewish Agency helped a little, and we had money. And we got a government stipend during the time when we were studying Hebrew, for six months.

There were about twenty people in our class, something like that, including my mother, my aunt, and me. My whole family studied together, in the same class. I was the worst student. I just was not able to figure out this language. Back in Russia, I opened up a book of the Hebrew alphabet, and closed it immediately. I saw those scribbles that were supposed to be letters, and I said, no, this is not for me. So I didn't know anything besides "Shalom." I couldn't talk at all in class. I couldn't open my mouth. It was so difficult to say all that nonsense, and it was so boring. The teacher said one sentence, and we repeated it. Like that. We had the same teacher for the whole six months, every day. After six months, I still was not able to make a sentence.

I had a friend who I studied with for class, also a new immigrant from Russia. He was a neighbor of mine. One time he told me that he heard that there was a park in downtown Haifa, Memorial Park, where, at night, gays meet. And I said, "No kidding. That's awful." And that same night, I went there.

I really wanted to meet some people. So I went there, and I saw a lot of people, everybody wandering around. And I was not able to speak Hebrew at all, maybe a few words. If someone came up to me, what could I say— what my name is, and how long I've been in the country. Because those are the questions people usually ask—how long you've been here, how you feel, where it's better, here or there, the standard questions. After a while it began to get on my nerves, I felt like saying, can't you ask anything different? But it was always, where is the food better, there or here? All sorts of nonsense. And that's it. I began going to the park almost every day. In the morning I went to Hebrew class, in the afternoon I studied, and in the evening I went to the park. You could say that that was my daily schedule. It continued that way for a long time, the same thing.

And I learned the language there, you could say. Someone said something, and it stuck in my mind, and when I got home, I looked it up in the dictionary. I found the word, and I wrote it down. And that way, word by word, over time, I had a list of words that was enough for basic Hebrew. There were, of course, some words I heard there that I couldn't find in the dictionary.

I was the first Russian to go to the park regularly. Before me, there were never any there. So I was an attraction. They never saw one before. They said, "What, there are gay Russians also?" And I said, "Yes, there are." I really wanted to find another one.

The first time I went there, I saw a lot of people, and I felt so low and dirty, I can't tell you. Maybe it was because the way most of the people behaved there. I never saw anything like that. Maybe that's the way it has to be, I don't know. They acted like women, talked like women, they did all kinds of nonsense. And, I don't know, I thought it was funny, but at the same time, I thought it was gross. In Russia, for instance, I never saw anything like that. Such effeminate men. The men I knew in Russia were men, they were all men. It didn't make a difference what they did in bed, they looked like men, they acted like men. Very cultured people. And here, it was totally different. Maybe that's the way it has to be, I don't know. I really didn't like it, to this day I can't get used to it.

It wasn't that they dressed up like women, it was their behavior, the way they talked. They only used the feminine forms. One guy addresses the other in the feminine form, and he answers also using the feminine form, you understand? I said to myself, maybe they're only kidding, it's only a game. But they continued talking that way. That's the way they talk. I don't think that's acceptable, things like that.

I didn't meet anyone. I wandered around, I just wanted to see exactly what was happening, who the gays were, what they do. Just to see. I went every day, because I felt very comfortable when I was with gays. No one came on to me. Or maybe they did, but, again, I was not able to understand anything. I don't have any problems picking someone up—if I knew the language, I didn't have any problem. But sometimes people said something to me, and I just had to answer, "I don't understand." So what exactly people wanted, I can't tell you for sure. With time, the situation improved.

I went back every day because I wanted to meet a Russian. But I didn't see anyone for a long time. I wanted to talk freely, you understand? A lot of time went by, I couldn't even tell you exactly, but it was a long time. Months. What I remember is that a few times, Israeli gays invited me to go out with them. One time I went with some of them to Tel Aviv, to a club, the Metro. The first time I went in there, I was just amazed. I felt really out of place—so many people, so crowded. I couldn't believe it, what, everybody here is gay? And I was really happy to see this, that such a thing existed in Israel. It made me feel good.

After the Metro, I also went to other places. I wanted to find someone, to have a relationship. And I didn't. Maybe because of the mentality, because the mentality here is totally different. It isn't only me. Now I have enough Russian friends here, and we get together and talk about it a lot. And everybody has the same problem. People here are totally different. We can't understand one another. For instance, let's say I go to a bar. I go in, I see all the people, I check out who I think is good-looking. And let's say I see a handsome person—attractive, European-looking, seems intelligent. I haven't spoken to him—I'm looking from far away. But he looks at me, really staring, and I stare back. We're looking at each other. And I get the message that he's interested, but he's afraid to come up to me and make the first move. Maybe he has a problem with that. But I have no problem with that.

So I make a move, I go up to him, begin talking to him, how's it going, anything, just begin talking. And what happens—and it isn't just once—what happens is that he says "I'm sorry, I have boyfriend," or he just doesn't answer. And he gives me a look like, you might think that I had cursed him or I don't know what. People don't want to talk! OK, so fine, nothing will happen, I'm not going to force you to do something, but just for the hell of it, to make a friend, it's very simple. You don't need to make a big deal out of it.

And I tell these stories to my Russian friends, and you know, the same thing happens to them. So everyone is asking, why, why? Why does it have to be that way? We decided that it's the Israeli mentality, and we should not take it personally—if they look at you, it doesn't mean anything. Don't get your hopes up. So I'm used to it. Now if I go somewhere, and someone looks at me and I look at him, I don't even think about doing anything. We just look. I'm experienced with these situations. Nothing ever happens.

I'll tell you, no offense, but I think it's very difficult to meet, to get to know Israelis. Maybe I'm confused. But I just can't do it. It's very difficult to communicate with them. We can't understand each other, who wants what. And in the park it happened a few times that I met Israelis and they ask such primitive questions, I can't believe it. I can't believe what I'm hearing. Maybe it's acceptable in Israel, I don't know. For instance, "Are you a man or a woman, what do you do?" How can you divide gays between masculine and feminine? I don't think you can do that. Maybe it's just the way things are done in the park. Because I hear it a lot, and I think that people are just used to asking it. Or you meet someone, and it's like, "Let's have sex," and in five minutes it's over. Like dogs. That's sex?

I've had a few things with Israelis. But they were in the park, and they weren't very worth remembering. People meet, and want to have sex, and, OK, there's no place in my house, and there's no place in your house, so let's do it here, in the bushes, one two three, we go into the bushes, like dogs. And that's it. That's the way it ends. And the next day you see that guy, and he acts like he doesn't know you. I can't begin to tell you! It's like he never met you, he turns his head away, like he doesn't see you, and keeps on walking. He doesn't want to say hello, nothing. I can't explain that, to this day. And it happens a lot. I don't understand it.

One day another Russian came to the park, and I met him. A very nice guy. I was able to tell from far away that he was Russian. I practically ran up to him and hugged him, after so many months! I was so happy to meet him. At least now I had some kind of a relationship, someone to talk to, to tell my problems to, he'll tell me his problems, and we'll understand each other. We had sex a few times, but now we're just friends. We're still in touch, we talk on the telephone. He found an Israeli boyfriend, they're together now for a year and a half, something like that.

I learned Hebrew very well in the park. I once met my Hebrew teacher on the street, and began talking, and her mouth dropped open. "Where did you learn to speak so well all of a sudden?" This was maybe a month after the end of the course. And I began to talk and tell her all sorts of things in correct Hebrew, she was shocked. "Why didn't you participate when we were in class? You knew all along, didn't you, you were just afraid."

Once my Hebrew class ended, I began working. I worked as a janitor in a computer company. I was there for a year and a half. I knew from the very start that I will have to do that kind of work. Because I didn't have a choice. That first period in Israel was so difficult—you have to do all sorts of things. We wanted to buy an apartment. And we had to buy everything, we didn't bring anything. All the furniture. And so I went to work to earn some money and get things organized here. My mother wasn't working yet. Now she works in a bakery, she bakes bread. She was unemployed for a year.

At first the work was difficult, but I got used to it. It was OK. When I was in Russia, I never imagined that I will work someday as a janitor. Never. I remember the kind of people who did that kind of work in Russia, the type of person. And I felt like people treated me very badly all of sudden, in that job. Because, if I, for instance, am working as a janitor, it's clear to everyone that I'm doing it because I have no choice. I can't do anything besides that kind of work. So people think that I'm worthless, that I'm incompetent. If I'm doing that kind of work, that says everything there is to say about me.

My boss was actually OK at first, but afterwards I began to get into arguments with him all the time. I did very good work, that's what people said. I wanted to be the best one. We worked there on call, they requested that specific workers come to specific rooms. And people called and said that they only wanted me, because they knew how well I worked. So I felt like I deserved a raise, and I asked my boss. And he didn't give me anything. In the end I stopped working, and he gave me a pink slip, and I went on unemployment.

All this time I didn't have any other relationships, besides with this Russian guy. We got together sometimes, but I didn't have very much time. I was working most of the time. I stopped going to the park. It was a time when it really disgusted me to go there, to see the same people, because it's usually the same people who come, and they talk about the same things and it's always the same. I decided that I'd rather not go there, rather not have anything at all than live that way.

I never got angry with Israeli society. I wasn't angry, asking, why are you this way and that way, not like I am? And I knew that there were people I was able to have a relationship with, but I just couldn't find them. And I wasn't angry that I had to work as a janitor. It was what I wanted to do—no one was forcing me, go, be a janitor, with a pail and a mop. It was my idea, my will. I went and worked, no one made me. And when I was working I did manage to save money. I bought a lot of things for the house.

I was also studying at that time. I took a course in bookkeeping. I finished it, and I got licensed. I tried to find work doing this, but I was not able. Because in most places they want workers with a lot of experience, years of experience. And I had no experience. I even, as a way of getting started, when I was on unemployment, I offered to work for free. I figured I was getting unemployment, and I could also get experience. But no one agreed. No one wanted to hire me, even for free! So I gave it up. To this day, I'm a bookkeeper without experience.

While I was unemployed I was at home a lot. I read books, I went to Tel Aviv. I met another Russian in the park. I began to talk to him, and I found out that he lives here, close by, not far away. I was very happy that I met him, and we saw each other a lot, we went out together. Afterwards he moved to Tel Aviv. He's married. He's about my age, but he immigrated with his wife. We're just friends, not more than that.

Once, in the park, I was attacked. It's a very complicated story. At one point, a whole group of Russian teenage boys began coming to the park and doing it for money. They were letting someone blow them for twenty shekels. They were really young, they were in high school, maybe sixteen, seventeen. I talked to them once, I asked them what they were doing in the park, and they told me, "We're making money."

I met Rafi Niy, the gay journalist, in the park a while before then, and I mentioned to him what was going on. He said that he wanted to talk to these kids. So we went to the park, and walked around a little. We were with an Arab friend of ours also. And all of sudden we saw that no one was there. It was Friday night, and this was strange. So we began to leave. But then these three big Russians were walking towards us. And one of them came up to us and asked, "Are any of you Russian?" I said, "I'm Russian." So he was very happy, began to talk to me, very nice at first. But pretty soon it was clear to me that I was going to get beaten up. He said he heard that gays come to this park, and that lately a lot of Russians were coming also. And he just couldn't believe that it was true. So he wanted to check it out.

I turned to Rafi and the other guy, and said we should leave. But Rafi wanted to talk, so he stayed, while we went to get the car. We went out to the street, and then we saw that Rafi was coming after us, and these Russians were running after him. So I said, "Come on, let's call the police." I said that loud enough so that they heard me also. I went to the public telephone, but it wasn't working. And one of these guys caught me and hit me. He kicked me in the balls, and I felt dizzy, and passed out.

When I woke up, I saw Rafi fighting with them. And I saw a man I know leaving the park, and I went to him, and asked him to help. He gave me a telephone token and said to me, "Here, close by, there's another telephone, call the police." So I began going to the telephone, and I saw that Rafi was coming after me, and from the corner I saw a car turning, and Rafi saw that it was our friend driving the car. We got into the car, I closed the door. I was sitting next to the driver, and Rafi behind me. But those guys came after us, and I didn't have a chance to close the window, when one of these guys put his hand through the window and tried to pull me out. And I was kicking him in his face. I don't know how we managed to leave. He had my foot out the window, and he was trying to take my shoe, and Rafi was trying to defend me. And all of sudden he turned to Rafi and punched him in the face—he gave him a black eye. Finally, I closed the window, the car began to move, and that guy, out of anger, punched the car so hard that it left a mark.

Afterwards I got very depressed—I was afraid to leave the house, to see friends, to walk on the street, because I might see these guys again. Because these people were capable of doing anything. I was very frightened. Without Rafi, they would have killed me. Really. They had no problem with that. They came to the park to beat up Russian gays. They were looking for those kids who were working there, but they found me. If they didn't see me, it was another Russian. They didn't want there to be gay Russians.

Nothing else like this ever happened to me. They say that it happens to everyone once, at one point or other. So it already happened to me. That means that it won't happen again. If it happened in Russia, I wouldn't have been surprised. But I didn't know that something like that was able to happen here.

I was unhappy a lot. I felt that something was missing—no, not something, I felt that a lot was missing. I had no job and no boyfriend. It was very difficult. So of course I was dissatisfied. I wanted to make a family—a family of two men. I thought about it in Russia, and when I came here, I said to myself, here in Israel, you can do that. You can do that here. And I thought about it all the time, and I wanted to do it. To live with someone. I read a lot of personal ads, but I don't believe in that. Once I did do it, I read some ads, and I wrote three letters, but I didn't get an answer from anyone. I said, that's it, I'm not sending any more, I've had it with this.

I didn't write long letters, just some basic information. I wrote that I was Russian, maybe that influenced something. But why should I hide it? If I hide it, and someone will want to meet me, and what, he won't be able to tell where I'm from, who I am? He needs to know from the start. There are sometimes gay personal ads in the Russian newspapers, but that's not for me. "Man looking for another man, has large video collection," all that nonsense. I won't answer an ad.

I don't know why everything has to be just once. That's it. I've thought about it a lot, and also my friends tell me the same thing. Why does it always have to be just once with Israeli men? Why can't you build something together? I don't know why, I can't explain it to myself to this day.

After my six months on unemployment was up, I began looking for work again. My friend moved to Tel Aviv, took a course to be a waiter, and found work as a waiter. So he was always telling me, "Come here, you'll find work here." So I went to Tel Aviv and took a course, which was run by the owner of a catering company, who put me to work right away.

At first, I moved in with my friend and his wife. We all lived together. He had, by that time, stopped having sex with his wife altogether. Later on, she caught him with another guy. He brought someone home, and she caught them in bed, and began to shout and throw dishes, everything. That night he called me up at work and told me the whole story, and he said "Call her up, talk to her, you can explain everything that's going on better than I can." So I called her, and she started right in, "Oh, Andrei, you have no idea what I saw." I said to her, "Everything's OK, come over to my place, I'll explain it all to you, don't worry." She came to my house the next morning and we talked for four hours.

She said she never had any idea that such a thing could happen. In the end, she took it pretty well, considering. The biggest shock for her was when she found out that all of his friends were also like that. She wasn't able to believe it. And she said, "Andrei, you're also like that?" Now the situation between them has totally changed. She left him. They're going to get divorced. She moved in with her mother.

I began working in all sorts of places in Tel Aviv, in catering halls, at weddings, hotels, the Moriah Plaza, the Ramada. It was always in a different place. And besides work, I went to Independence Park, and to clubs. I met a lot of people, but I didn't find what I wanted.

Independence Park is different from the park in Haifa, because every day there are different people there. That's good. Every day you see different people. It's bigger, there are more people who come, and a lot of tourists. It's nicer. I like Tel Aviv. It's a very big city, and there are more possibilities, you can do more. You can find more.

I was there for six months, and during that last period, I didn't get a lot of work. There wasn't a lot of work, so I didn't make very much money. I wasn't able to pay my rent or my bills. So I left everything and came back to Haifa, I moved back in with my family, and I found work in the Dan Carmel Hotel, which is where I work now. I'm a waiter. It's harder than what I did there.

Here, all of the other waiters are Arab. I'm the only Russian. But I get along with them fine. Everybody is satisfied with my work and I have no problem. I'm not learning Arabic—they're learning Russian! They're always asking me how to say things in Russian. One of them is actually going out with a Russian girl, and I translate everything for them. Some of them asked me, "Do you have a boyfriend?" They suspect something. I said to them, "Why a boyfriend, what are you talking about?"

My mother still does not know about me, but I want to tell her. Right now I feel like that moment is getting closer all the time. In the end, it will happen. It is a process. I am sure it will happen at some point, but I do not know when exactly. Something will happen and I won't have a choice. I think that it will happen when I have a stable relationship—then I will tell her. When I am sure that my relationship is good. In the meantime, my mother knows that I have never had a girlfriend in my life. At any point. I have never brought a girl home, and she has never asked me why.

I've been in Israel for three years now. I'm satisfied, but I don't know if I'll stay. The thing with people is that whatever they've got is never enough, they are always thinking about something better. To succeed in life, to change their lives. So in Israel, I'm happy, sure, why not be happy? But in the long term, I don't think I can fit in here, and find what I'm looking for. For instance, a relationship. I always dreamed of living in Europe. If I have the chance to move there, I will do it. But I will only go there together with someone, not alone. I will need my boyfriend's support.

I'm not a Zionist. I don't feel Jewish. And no one says I'm Jewish here—

here, everyone says I'm Russian. Here, we're Russians, and in Russia we were Jews. It may be that Zionism is right, that only in Israel I can be free from worrying about being Jewish. If it turns out that way, I will have learned something. But I have no way of knowing, now, if that's true. Maybe I'll make a mistake, I don't know. But, for instance, I went to Tel Aviv, and when things didn't work out, I came back to Haifa—and now at least I know what goes on in Tel Aviv. You don't learn by talking.

In general, I do not waste my time with politics. I did not vote in these last elections and I would not ever vote in any elections. It doesn't interest me. It has nothing to do with me. It doesn't seem to me that I would get anything good out of it. I have nothing against the left, against socialism. I personally haven't been hurt by them. I like the kibbutz movement, and I guess that's Israeli communism, right? I think it's nice. I don't really know what life is like there, on a kibbutz, because I've never lived like that, but I think it looks good. They always said in Russia that they were building communism, but I don't think they even began. There, it's impossible.

I will only go back to Russia to visit, not to live there. I'm used to all sorts of good things here. And I already know that I won't have them there. So it will be difficult for me. I don't think things are any better there now. By what I see on the Russian television, they're getting worse all the time. People are really suffering.

I recently met a guy from Leningrad in Tel Aviv. He knows my friends from there. And now I'm seeing him. I think that it has a lot of promise. Because I think we understand each other, and I think that this is what I was looking for all along. And, at least for right now, I found it. I don't know if it will last, but up to now it's fine.

ELI

Once we had completed half of our interviews, I had the sudden realization that we were in danger of replicating a rather old-fashioned bias on the part of the Israeli establishment in favor of Ashkenazim—*Jews of Central and Eastern European origins. Although* Ashkenazim *still compose a majority of the economic and academic elite of Israel, the last twenty years have seen a gradually increasing consciousness of the ethnic diversity of the country's Jewish population.* Sefardim—*the descendants of communities that are heir to the culture of medieval Spain—have roots in the Mediterranean; the partially overlapping groups known as* ᶜadot hamizraḥ, *or simply as* mizraḥiyim—*"Easterners"— come from other North African, Middle Eastern, Persian, or Central Asian countries. Together, they make up about half the Jewish population of Israel. To me, it seemed obvious that these ethnic variables would influence people's experiences of their sexuality. Shouldn't we make sure to talk to a more diverse group of people?*

Amir—his own family hailing originally from Romania and the Ukraine— objected to my tokenism, and argued that my assumptions were nothing short of presumptions. He pointed out that he had no idea where many of his friends' grandparents had come from and he pointed to statistics indicating that large numbers of young Israelis marry Jews of different backgrounds. He saw my late-1980s American-style ethnic determinism as inappropriate to the modern melting pot of the Israeli gay scene, yet he agreed that, if merely for appearance's sake, we would do well to protect ourselves on the Eastern flank. When it came to finding an interviewee, however, Amir too had to admit that national origins still have significance in contemporary Israel. The fact was that, in our circles of acquaintance, mizraḥi Israelis were few and far between.

Ultimately, "Eli" came to mind. Amir and I both recalled him as one of the highlights of a dinner party we had recently attended. Eli's charming smile, rich brown eyes, and jet-black hair had made his innocent, self-effacing demeanor all the more ... memorable. And though we had no way of knowing for sure, it seemed a good guess that his dark features had not come to Israel by way of Lithuania.

Amir took care of the formalities, and another clear Shabbat morning found us with Eli in his boyfriend Moṭi's exquisitely decorated Tel Aviv apartment. Wall-sized windows splashed warm light onto the plush carpet, and Eli served us cola in heavy crystal as we settled into the cushy sofa. Although Moṭi had seemed to be on his way out to the gym when we arrived, he somehow wound up hovering around the living room throughout much of the interview. He later explained that he had just been curious—he had never before heard Eli talk so much about himself.

⌒

I GREW UP IN A NORMAL HOME in Bat Yam, near Tel Aviv. There were always a lot of people around—I have two brothers and one sister. So there was always a lot of action at home, a lot going on. And the fact that I was the oldest, the first-born son, this, of course, definitely, like, influenced my childhood.

My mother is from Iran. She came to Israel when she was four years old, something like that. Her father was pretty traditional. He wasn't a fanatic, but he was religious. He was a scribe. In Israel, he worked as a technician, something like that. So my mother's family wasn't very well off. They weren't, like, poor either. They were sort of middle class, I guess. Lower middle class.

My father is from Lebanon, but his parents came there from different places—his mother is from Spain, and his father is from Egypt. My father's family moved from Lebanon to Israel when he was ten years old. This was after the state was established, shortly after. His family was pretty much like my mother's—they didn't have a lot of money. My grandfather was a civilian employee of the army here. Also, like, lower middle class.

My parents have achieved a lot very quickly. They have a big apartment now, and they just bought another one. But we're not rich. I mean, they live well, but not, you know.... My mother is a secretary in a hospital. My father is a policeman. He works very hard. They've come a long way, through hard work and loans and mortgages, and they get by.

We lived in a ground-floor apartment until I was three years old, and then we moved to a sort of housing development, with lots of apartments. We lived there until I began second grade, at seven, and then we moved to the city, to a pretty prestigious neighborhood. But the people were kind of, you know, snobby there, and my parents didn't like it, they wanted to go back home. So we lived there for only a year and a half. Then my parents decided that they wanted to be near their family and friends, so they found a house back in Bat Yam that they bought and renovated. So after a year and a half, we went back to Bat Yam, to a rented apartment, while the renovations were being completed. It's a real house, two floors. And that's where they live to this day.

My earliest memory is of right before I began school. I would always roam around with a pack of other kids, and I remember that, one time, I fell, and that's when I got this little scar on my face. See it? I was around four, something like that. It hurt a lot. I remember it very vaguely. I remember only that there was this candy bar, I had it in my hand. And I think that what happened was that someone grabbed it from me, and I began running after him, and then I tripped over something, fell, and cut myself. And that's it.

There weren't, like, a lot of hugs and kisses in my family. I think there were when I was little, even though I don't really remember. When you're little they always look after you, and they pick you up, and hug you. But as I got older, there were no hugs and kisses. It wasn't, you know, a very warm house or anything. And with my parents, little by little, we've become more and more, I guess you could say, distant. I guess, apparently, we've never really communicated well.

My parents threw all the responsibility and work around the house onto me. I was the oldest. My mother—she's very, well, let's say she's a very dominating mother. This is really the key word here. My mother is very controlling, and she gets annoyed very easily, and she gets, like, a little hysterical sometimes. For instance, she would come home, let's say, when I was in second or third grade, and the house was a mess, and she would shout, and sometimes even curse. I didn't like that. And that apparently distanced me. My father was sort of dragged along behind her. My father is a nice guy, his heart is in the right place, but it's my mother who makes the decisions. He does whatever she wants.

It's apparently because of this that I also put everything into my schoolwork. I studied a lot, and as time went on I spent more and more time studying. And that was how I kept my distance, how I ran away. It wasn't like we stopped talking or anything. I would come home from school, and I would tell them everything that was going on. I think that they're very proud of me, my studies, that I'm doing well. It wasn't a very cold atmosphere, that's not what I'm trying to tell you. It was an OK atmosphere. Just not very warm. We were very direct with each other.

I got along pretty well with the other kids my age. I wasn't the most popular or anything, but I had friends. Everyone finds his own kind of friends. My friends were pretty quiet, we didn't make trouble.

In my high school, there were a lot of troublemakers. Actually, in Bat Yam in general there are a lot of troublemakers. A lot of kids didn't want to be in school, and they caused a lot of problems. As far back as high school, you could have guessed what they were headed for. They would, you know, get on the teachers' nerves, disrupt classes, walk out of class, all sorts of things. They would argue with other people all the time, get into fistfights, you would see them in the principal's office every day. Especially in junior high, it all got worse. It was hard to learn anything in this school. I mean, there weren't knives or guns or anything like that—although, now that I think about it, some people probably did have knives. But not everyone. These kids who made trouble, some of them became more violent with time, and I guess a few of them turned out to be criminals. Not everyone was like that, but that was the atmosphere. I chose the quieter people for my friends.

My father never spoke to me about sex. Maybe it was because of my parents' background, they're shy about these things. They don't talk about these things, although my father is a little more open about it than my mother. And besides, like I told you, we were kind of distant. We weren't really communicating well enough for them to feel comfortable talking to me about this.

I never felt any different from any of the other kids I knew. Not at all. I would think about girls, and I would draw pictures—sometimes I would make sketches of girls on paper. Naked girls. And I was also in love with a certain girl. She knew I loved her, but she was in love with this other guy, one of the troublemakers. I loved her right up to high school, until I left the local school, and went to school in Tel Aviv. I went to high school in Tel Aviv.

I think that I love her to this day. I mean, I ran into her not so long ago on the bus, and a lot of my old feelings for her came back. It's difficult to explain what I like about her. She's a sort of very mischievous, risque kind of girl, bouncy and enthusiastic, vivacious. She speaks beautifully, and very quickly, she's funny, and she's also smart. I was always too shy to try to ask her out or anything. And besides, I could tell that she was always running after guys who were, you know, strong, heroes. She wanted a troublemaker.

So up to fifteen years old, I never once felt any different from anyone else, and I never had any thoughts that could be considered homosexual. I was absolutely like everyone else. It wasn't until I was in high school that this, like, changed. I don't know exactly how this came about, how this switch happened. But already when I was in high school, at sixteen or seventeen, I began to think about it. And at seventeen I did something about it.

I found myself wanting to see guys naked. I would think about it at night, when I would lie in bed. Sort of picture it to myself. It didn't really disturb me. I liked it—it excited me, I guess that would be better to say. It just came to me, I don't know how, I can't really single anything out. I remember that I was very curious to see semen on the penis of a man. It was very interesting, exciting. Because I had never really looked at it on someone else. I wanted to see it, to compare it, see if it was like mine, or something, I don't know. I think this was right before I turned sixteen. I mean, I wasn't physically attracted by it, but I was curious. I think, at least, this is what I remember.

Sometimes I would go to public showers, on the beach, for instance. I just wanted to take a look, see what other guys looked like—was it like mine or something. I hadn't seen a naked guy very many times. All of my memories were of little boys, not very developed. So all of a sudden I, you know, wanted to see it. And that's it. I would go in, shower, and leave. I didn't feel uncomfortable. Everyone was taking a shower. I didn't draw any attention to myself. It wasn't something I would do all the time. I was also very afraid to do it. I felt like I was doing something wrong.

The first time I heard the word "homo" was when I was eleven years old, maybe twelve, something like that. By the time I got to middle school, I think I knew what it was. I knew it primarily as an insult. Especially in Bat Yam, it's a very powerful insult. Sometimes people would say it jokingly, saying about someone, "What a homo" or something like that. And they would laugh about it a lot. It seemed like something so bizarre, so demented. I thought just like everyone else. Just like them. It seemed pretty revolting to me—I was pretty disgusted by gays. It never occurred to me that what I was thinking and doing had anything to do with this word, or with the kids who were picked on. They all seemed like, you know, misfits, freaks. They revolted me. I was having all kinds of fantasies about men, but I didn't make the connection to homosexuality.

I didn't know that two men could love each other. I thought that homosexuality was just sex. It was a pretty squalid picture. But I didn't see myself as being like that, so I didn't see any problem. I wasn't really thinking that I wanted to sleep with another guy—at this age I was only trying to imagine what men looked like. But it was only out of curiosity, not out of attraction. It was all very wholesome.

There was one girl who was in love with me, Ronit. But I didn't want to be her boyfriend. I didn't like her. By this time, at sixteen or seventeen, some other guys had girlfriends, but not many. I didn't feel any pressure. But things were developing. This sense of curiosity changed into a real attraction for other men. And at seventeen, I answered a personal ad in the women's magazine, *La'ishah*, where there were personals in the back. The ad said: "Good-looking, athletic guy, twenty-two, wants to meet other guys," something like that.

I really can't explain what gave me the guts to go ahead and do something so bold. But I wrote this guy a letter—I don't remember whether I gave him my home phone number or not, I think so, but I'm not sure, because I think that I was the one who finally called him. I don't really remember. Anyway, I answered the ad because I wanted to give it a try, to do something about the attraction I felt. To meet someone.

So we arranged to meet, and he came in his car to pick me up. He had a big American car. We drove around for a pretty long time, talking. I remember that I was, like, very, very worked up. I was really tense. I was, you know, fiddling with this thing in his car, a button, I nervously played with it the whole time. I really don't remember at all what we talked about. I told him the truth about myself, I didn't make anything up. I was naive. It didn't occur to me to think about it. And that's it. He parked the car near the beach, and we sat there for a long time, for more than an hour, and we talked. And that's it. We had sex, my first time, and that was that. It all happened very quickly.

He was experienced. I had told him that this was my first time. I think he liked that—he got into my being a virgin. I think he was pretty considerate. I don't really remember it very well. It happened very fast.

I felt awful afterwards. Really terrible. As soon as it was over I couldn't stop thinking about my father. I was afraid to go home. I don't know why— I was just afraid of what my father would think if he knew that I had done something like this. I just had this feeling like, what, I just had sex with a man—I don't believe I did that, you know? I couldn't believe that I had been with a man. And I kept thinking about my father, what he would say if he knew. And it was a terrible feeling. Very serious guilt feelings.

The feeling I had right after we finished was a terrible feeling, but after a day or so, it just disappeared. And I wanted to do it again. I don't know, I liked it. And I remember noticing this change, which happened really suddenly. It was really strange.

So that's it. I liked it, and I wanted to do it again. So I called him, and we got together again. The same story. And afterwards, I called him a third time, and then, you know, every time I called, they told me that he was sleeping, and couldn't come to the phone. So that was pretty strange, but I figured out eventually that he wasn't interested anymore, and I stopped calling. I don't think I was really hurt. I really hadn't felt anything in particular for him. It was my first time, and it was really fun, and that's it.

I ran into this guy a little while ago in a bar in Tel Aviv. He's living in America now. I think he's got some rich, older guy that he's living with. He's found himself a rich American guy.

I remember that there was a time when I thought I was the only one in the world. That was the feeling I had. The people that I told you about, that would get pointed at and laughed at, they got on my nerves, and frightened me. They were the very people I wanted to avoid. I didn't want to meet them. Because people laughed at them. And besides, it's not for certain that they're even gay. It was just rumors. But I did want to find out if there were other people like me.

Even after my first time, I didn't really let myself make the connection between homosexuality and my own feelings. I just repressed it, denied it. I never thought I was gay. I mean, sometimes I did make the connection, but then I said to myself, what, me, a faggot, get out of here, it can't be, I'll grow out of this, I'm not a homo, it can't be. To me, it was a terrible insult, this word, like a curse. So I just let things happen, without, like, thinking about it very much, you know? Without making any connections. I just let things flow, without calling myself a homo. You just live with it, you know, you just live.

Afterwards, there was a very long period when I didn't do anything at all. It was maybe a year, where I never got together with anyone. I didn't want a girlfriend, and I really didn't feel any pressure to have one. And then I was eighteen, and high school was over.

I was drafted, of course, and I chose to enter the officer candidate academic studies program. I was in a technological track in high school, and I wanted to go to college. So I chose to put off my regular army service until after I got my B.A., which you can do on the condition that you study something the army is interested in, and you commit to six years of full-time service, instead of the usual three, after graduation. Being in the army for six years doesn't really bother me, because they guarantee you that you'll be doing professional work there. It's just like a job.

So I began basic training and the squad commanders' training course. It was hard. It was really hard. But I got through it, somehow. It wasn't a problem being gay. The showers didn't excite me. It was just natural. I didn't even look around. There just wasn't time to think about sex. We were under so much pressure. You didn't have time for nonsense. We were all worn out all the time, tired all the time. Maybe I felt a little uncomfortable sometimes because of it, socially. But I still didn't call it by name, and I don't think that other people felt anything about me.

Afterwards, I would look back and think about exciting things that had happened—for instance, someone undressing in front of me, or being in the showers. I would look back and think, this is exciting, the whole situation. And I would say to myself, too bad I didn't take a look around. There were some real hunks there. But in general, you know, I didn't like the other people in the officer candidate academic program. They're smart-alecks, you know? And they're very self-absorbed, selfish. They look out for number one. That's the way it was during basic training. There wasn't any sense of cooperation or friendship. Everyone just tried to use everyone else. I can't stand that.

After I finished my army preparation, I began taking courses at Tel Aviv University. At first, I chose to study physics. That was my top preference, followed by business administration. Beforehand, I had been thinking about medicine, and I changed my mind twice back and forth. But I was accepted into economics, and I'm glad about that, because, after the fact, I know now that I don't like physics, even though I studied it in high school. And I'm happy with my classes, with my field.

I didn't move away from home when I began going to college. I would go to the university in the morning and come home in the evening. But I liked being in school a lot. It wasn't like high school, there wasn't a lot of pressure. It was totally different. It was more fun to study, and more comfortable. In high school, everyone is always looking over your shoulder, checking homework, and so on, but that doesn't happen in the university. You're free to do what you want—if you want, you can study, if not, you don't. Usually, the people who go to college do want to study. So it's very free, and you choose your own schedule, and you have a lot of services to help you out. I liked it a lot.

Once I began school, I answered another ad. I think it was in *Ha^cir*. So I met this guy, we got together downtown. He was pretty good-looking, pretty cute. He was twenty-six, his name was Yehudah. We walked around for a while, but we didn't have anyplace to go—neither of us had an apartment or even a car. So he gave me his phone number and asked me to call him. I called, and we met again, but again, neither of us had anyplace where we could go, so we would, like, meet in places where there was no one around and we would do it. Dark alleyways, where no one ever passed, or places like that. He knew where all the places were. He knew them very well. In schools at night when no one was there, all sorts of places like that.

And he took me to Independence Park also. He apparently knew it pretty well. He told me all about it. We went, and we sat on a bench, and he told me about it. The men who were there were really gross. But you could always find, like, one guy who was a little better-looking than the others, and a little nicer. And if someone there knew Yehudah, then he would come over to us. And that's it.

Afterwards, all of a sudden, Yehudah decided that we were boyfriends. He sort of tossed this off. So, OK. I really didn't want a boyfriend, but that's what I got. I didn't want any sort of obligation, this was not what I was looking for. But I was willing to live with it. OK, he wants us to be boyfriends, OK, we're boyfriends. But I got fed up with him pretty quickly, because he wanted to get together every day, and I didn't have time. I was studying very hard. So he was always angry that I wasn't seeing him enough, why don't I have time, why am I always studying PASCAL and math and calculus? And it got to the point where he really began bothering me, so I said to him that I didn't want to be his boyfriend, but I would be glad to be his friend, that we should stay friends. But no sex, no love. I never loved him. I didn't hate him, but I never loved him. We weren't even very affectionate with each other, we never really kissed except during sex.

So this went on for a month or two. But we really saw each other very little, maybe every two weeks. He would take me to the park or some empty school, places like that. This was one of the reasons that I stopped seeing him, these meetings in these abandoned places.

I still didn't conceive of myself as gay. It's very difficult to explain. The word had never passed my lips. It's very difficult to call myself gay. Even now, it's difficult for me. Sure, he had been around, he was experienced, and he had gone through a lot of guys. But it's like that t-shirt: "I'm not gay but my boyfriend is." I mean, I knew I was gay, but wouldn't admit it to myself. I would even correct other people—"What's your problem, I'm not gay." I would say, "I'll get over it, this will pass, it's temporary."

I was attracted to women, but only very beautiful ones. I only like a very particular kind of woman, not your average woman. But sometimes I would see a woman on the street who would attract me.

I did want Yehudah as a friend. I figured he would be a good sort of opening to that world. He had a lot of connections, he knew a lot of guys. And he, really, introduced me to this world, for better or for worse. He taught me all about the parks. It was new, and seductive. I was naive, and I didn't see the bad sides. The whole park thing was really bad. Sometimes we would get together, and he would say, "Come on, let's go to the park." And he would always, I mean, he would kind of trick me, give me promises, he would say, "There're going to be cute guys there today, I met some cute guys there the other day." He would always seduce me, very sly, like a snake. But he really put me into this state of mind where I knew that, like, the park was where you went to meet someone. That it was the only place you can find guys. Only there. And he made all sorts of promises. He's very clever with words, he knows how to play with words very well. And that's what happened. So we stayed friends, because I thought that he would help me find someone new. But little by little, I saw that it wasn't really working, and that nothing was happening, that only old, gross men came to the park.

Yehudah did introduce me to some guys, eventually. I went out with two of them, and slept with them. One was awful, really, but the other one was a little better, and he had an apartment also. This was my first time having sex in a bed. And I liked this a lot better. But it wasn't like we had any kind of relationship or obligation to one another.

Now that I think about it, with all of the people I slept with up to this point, they were the ones who really pushed for sex. I didn't stop them, but I was pretty scared. Sometimes I was frightened of what they might do, and I was afraid to say no—I was afraid to say no. If they knew who I was, they could do something, they could tell someone. I was really afraid of that. I also just didn't know how to say no, aside from fear. I mean, I really didn't want to hurt people's feelings, or reject them. It was really difficult for me. With this guy, the last one, we went to his apartment, and talked, and I didn't find him really attractive, but he pushed for sex, and he put me into the bed, and it happened. Even though I didn't really want it to. I didn't want it.

It was Yehudah who put it into my head that I should have a boyfriend. He talked about it all the time, boyfriend, boyfriend, boyfriend, and at a certain point I began looking for this also. So I put a personal ad in the paper. I wrote: "Eighteen-year-old guy in search of true, honest friend," something like that. You can see his influence. I was looking for a boyfriend, not for sex. This is what I wanted, a real relationship.

And that's it, so I put the ad in the paper, and I met some guys. I got a ton of letters—maybe thirty. And I got together with some of them. I decided according to the letter. There are some letters that are all of two sentences long, and you can just tell by the way they write, by what they say about themselves. I met, for instance, this one guy, a boy really, he was sixteen. And he was a punk rocker. His letter was very touching. He told about how people were taking advantage of him, and using him, just because they wanted to have sex with someone young, and he was also looking for someone who wanted more than this. I really liked what he wrote. So we got together, and I saw that he was really a very, very messed-up person—no, not messed up, but it was just that his life was very complicated. He liked industrial rock, he dressed like a punk, with black makeup on his eyes and everything—it was really something. At first he really frightened me. I thought he was interesting, but things didn't work out.

Even though I got so many letters, I didn't find a boyfriend. There wasn't anybody I liked. I was looking for someone attractive, someone I could love, I don't know, it's difficult to define. Someone warm, someone I could talk to, a good person. That's it.

I did find someone eventually. OK, it's a very complicated story. In this case, I wasn't even looking for it, but I could see it was meant to be. I had already given up looking for a boyfriend. But one night I was going home from a friend's house. It was about eight at night, at the beginning of the spring semester of my first year at the university. And I was waiting at a bus stop, which happened to be near the park. Now, after a few minutes, someone passed by, pretty pleasant-looking, tall, very well-dressed, with a very shiny white coat. And I looked at him. And he also, all of sudden, looked back at me. So we exchanged glances, and then, I don't know, I suddenly summoned up a lot of courage, and took a chance that he was on his way to the park, and began following him. Now, the very fact that he had looked at me, this already lit up a little light bulb, and so I already thought that he might be "like that," but I wasn't sure. There's always a certain percentage of doubt. So I crossed the street. I wanted to check if I was right. My guess was that he was going to the park. And it turned out that I was right. And so I followed him from a distance. I just tailed him, like in the movies. I would go a few meters, stop, look into the store display windows, and then continue. There was a pretty big distance between us. But I kept on going, and as I got closer to the corner, I could see he was waiting for me there. I kept on walking, up to where he was, and I stopped at some display window close to him, and then he came up to me, and said to me, "Hi, my name is Yaniv."

And then he kind of chuckled a little. And I was really laughing, because it really surprised me, because it really was a very funny situation. I mean, I went and followed him! I mean, it really took some guts, a lot of courage, to do something like that. So we introduced ourselves, and then we just kind of walked around for a while, strolling. We got something to eat. He was very considerate, he asked me if I was hungry, he wanted to pay for everything, he was really nice, and it was fun talking to him. He's a good guy. And that's it.

After eating, we didn't have anywhere to sit down, I mean, we walked and walked, so in the end, we went into the park, not because of what goes on in the park, but just because we were looking for a bench. All the other benches were taken by old people. We really couldn't find anywhere to sit and talk, to get to know each other. So we went into the park, sat on a bench, and talked. And after a few minutes, who should come by but Yehudah! Afterwards, "Yaniv" explained to me that he had met Yehudah in the park before, and that they had slept together. And Yehudah said to this guy, "Hey, Yosef, what's up?" And that's how I found out that he hadn't told me his real name.

We became boyfriends. I loved him a lot. But it took time. He wasn't attractive. Not that he's ugly, but I wasn't really that attracted to him. He was six years older than me. Sure, I followed him in the street—but it was dark, and he was dressed very well. I mean, he looks OK, but it took time to fall in love with him. He really fell in love with me, very quickly, and he did everything for me. And I suddenly felt like, wow, someone is giving to me, is doing things for me. I mean, he was also very warm, a really warm kind of guy, and he would say things that were just fun to hear, and I was so touched by this love that he was giving me, this courtship, the way he pursued me. I just loved his warmth so much. So we would get together downtown, and we would sit for hours in the cafes, and I went to his place a few times. He was also living with his parents. It was a problem finding someplace to have sex. Twice we did it at his house, when his parents weren't home.

I was very much in love, but at a certain point, it all came to an end. It ended because all of a sudden, I felt like he had changed direction. He got mean, and I felt like everything was different. That he wasn't interested in me at all. So I ended it. He was always saying that I was imagining things, that he loved me very much. But I didn't feel like that was true anymore. So I didn't call him anymore, and he didn't try to call me.

He was pretty comfortable with being gay. I was also, although I still couldn't talk about myself as a "homo." It isn't until really recently that I'm able to say that word. Seriously, it's very difficult. I can't say that word. I really didn't want to define things. When I imagined what my future would look like, I still saw a family, children. All of this was temporary, I would get over it. That's what I thought.

So that's it. I saw that he wasn't calling me anymore, so it ended. Meanwhile, Yehudah had had a boyfriend, Roni, who he met from an ad he put in the paper, but then they broke up, and he suggested that I might like to meet him. Now, this Roni was very good-looking, I remember that I was very attracted to him. So I met him, and we began going out together. We would get together, but not a lot. Maybe once a week.

He wasn't a very educated person. He didn't get a real high school diploma, and he really didn't know how to make conversation. He was a pretty shallow person. So I didn't have very much in common with him. And besides this, he was a very cold person, in contrast to my old boyfriend, who was so loving. We were together for a very short time—a month, a month and a half, something like that.

I felt that I was not falling in love with him. That I wasn't feeling anything at all. In fact, what was happening was that my love for Yosef, my old boyfriend, was becoming greater and greater. I was talking about him all the time, and this was really getting on Roni's nerves.

Yosef was from a background like mine. His family was *mizrahi*. But Roni was Romanian. I'm sure this had something to do with it. Roni's house was very cold, Romanian, stiff, chilly. I think it had an impact. But the *mizrahi* house that Yosef came from, it had an influence on him, this was where that warmth came from. A warm house, I really liked being there. There is a very close and clear connection between their backgrounds and how I felt about them.

Now, I saw that I was not falling in love with Roni, and he was putting pressure on me. And again the complaints began, that I never see him, that I never visit him, that I never have time. So I decided to end it. I didn't think he loved me. I mean, he never demonstrated any affection, caring, warmth. So I called him up, and I told him that, like, I thought that we weren't compatible. I talked to him in the nicest, gentlest way that I possibly could. I was very, very nice—really, I practically made myself nauseous, I was so sweet. But he began crying. On the telephone.

That really shocked me. Really. Because I didn't even think he cared about me. I told him that, like, I still wanted to be his friend, but he wasn't interested in that, and he stopped talking to me. I would call him up and he would hang up on me. That happened a few times, until in the end I stopped trying.

Afterwards, I got up the courage to call Yosef again, and he was very happy to hear from me, and we picked up where we had left off. But not for long. It only lasted a short time, maybe a month. And again he disappeared. He stopped calling, and I didn't call either. He had gotten gross again during the end of this period of time, and I realized that it had been a mistake to try to get back together. I had wanted to move in with him, we talked about it. He wanted to buy an apartment, renovate it. We talked about it a lot, how we would renovate this apartment, redecorate it, it would be all bright and shiny, and we would move in and live together. But it didn't happen that way.

After the end of my second try with Yosef, I went through a pretty difficult time. Not very difficult, but difficult. I got over it. I was pretty depressed, moody. And I put a lot of my energy into my classes. I, like, tried to run away to my classes. I had a lot of exams, and I worked very hard. And I did very well—it was my best semester.

Then I met Moṭi. It was right around my twentieth birthday. I had driven down to the beach by myself, and I was just sort of sunbathing, lying there, looking at the sky. And I saw Moṭi at the other end of the beach. He looked very sexy, very handsome. I really liked his body. I mean, I still do. So I lay down, like, not really right next to him, but at a short distance. There were other people on the beach also. He was wearing dark sunglasses, and lying on his towel sunbathing. And I was lying maybe a hundred meters away.

And then I noticed that he was looking at me. So I looked back at him. And then he smiled. A real, broad, ear-to-ear smile. And I couldn't figure out why in the world he was smiling. I looked around to see if he was looking at someone else. I was, like, pretty confused. So I looked back at him. And this happened a few times. I would look at him and he would smile—so broadly you could see his teeth, his white teeth.

So I got up and went into the water, and so did he. Little by little, he got closer to me, and I got closer to him. You can never be absolutely sure that someone is gay, there's always a certain percentage of error. But by this time it was pretty clear. And I said to him, "Do you always swim with your sunglasses on?" Because he was still wearing them. And he just kept on smiling, and he laughed. He said yes, he always swam with his sunglasses. And we began talking.

We swam back to the beach, and I brought my things over, and sat down next to him. And we talked. Each of us, like, told his life story. He seemed really sad. He told me about his old boyfriend, and how much he loved him. He was going through a difficult time. And I also told him about Yosef, and everything that had happened with him. He gave me his telephone number at home, and he asked me to call him.

Now, there were a lot of things that I didn't like very much about him. He was pretty distant, and I also thought that he was pretty arrogant. Let's just say that he wasn't very nice. I figured that it must have been because he was sad, but I still didn't call him. Two or three weeks went by—I had to go to the army to do reserve duty at that time. But I called him when I got back. I don't know why. I liked the way he looked, and I had kind of forgotten the way he had acted. So I called. I said, what have I got to lose? And I really didn't have anything to lose.

So we got together, and we slept with each other. That was a lot of fun. And I discovered that he was, like, a very smart guy, and very interesting, and he speaks beautifully, intelligently. But all he wanted to talk about was his old boyfriend, and he was very sad. And you could just hear it in his voice, the way he talked. I drew him out. I asked him to tell me about how he was feeling. I was really interested. I don't know why, it was very touching. I liked to hear his stories, they were very interesting. I mean, I had never really had any encounters with long-term relationships before. Especially not like this. So I was very curious about it. They had been together for five or six years.

At first it was like we were just friends, but we were also sleeping together. We didn't really think in terms of "let's build a relationship" or anything. I mean, I would listen to his stories, and we would talk. We didn't think about the possibility of becoming boyfriends. I even told him that I really hoped that he would get back together with his boyfriend. I really did want that, that there would be a happy ending to his story. Like a fairy tale—they should live happily ever after. But little by little I felt that I wanted him to be my boyfriend, that I was beginning to fall in love with him. And that's it. That was about thirteen months ago, something like that. We're still together.

I like the way he looks. But that's not everything. Roni, for instance, was a very good-looking guy, but I didn't love him. Moti is very smart, very bright. And he's actually pretty warm. I was wrong when I decided on the beach that he was cold. He knows how to be loving, but in his own way—you can see it in the things he does, and not the things he says.

There was a certain amount of time when we took some time out for a month and a half. I don't know if I can really talk about this, I've got to ask him. Because it had to do with some other people. Let's just say that I had a bad feeling. I was pretty down and depressed, but I really loved him, and we got to the point where we were, like, arguing a lot. He asked me what I thought we should do, and I said that I didn't know. So he suggested that we take some time out, and I said OK. So that's what happened.

Now, I thought that this time out meant that we had split up. And I developed this real anger about it, and at some point it really became hate. But I got over it. At some point he called, and I was very cold, maybe a little nasty. But we decided to meet. I was convinced that he didn't care about me, that he never had, that he was only in love with his old boyfriend the whole time. So when we got together he told me that he loved me very much, that he thought about me a lot. And we didn't really plan on getting back together, but that's what happened. And it really helped, having this time apart. It really healed a lot of problems in our relationship.

We love each other. And that's what holds our relationship together. Sometimes he gets on my nerves, and sometimes I get on his nerves. But when it comes right down to it, we love each other, and that's the glue that, in spite of everything, keeps us together. Lately, I've kind of moved in with him. I've been here maybe two, three months. We never really talked about it, or said, OK, now you're going to move in with me. I guess technically, I still live with my parents. But I always tell them that I'm going out. It began, like, at the end of the semester, when I had all of my exams. I told them that I was studying for my exams, and that I was staying with friends. And little by little I would spend more and more time here. Until now I really live here. I visit my parents pretty often. They don't know that I'm here.

Moṭi is fourteen years older than me. In a certain way this is an issue, but it isn't really very much of a problem. The thing is that he has already been through a serious relationship—more than one. He has this whole history. And sometimes that really bothers me. I'd like it if he had no history. I'd like to be the first man he met, that he loved. It still bothers me that he talks about his old boyfriend. I'd just like to erase everything that happened before me. I mean, it fills a really big portion of his world. And sometimes it really bothers me. But it's not really meaningful. I've learned to live with it, with all of his past boyfriends. And he had serious relationships, it's not like me, a month and a half here and there. He had long relationships, and it's a whole world for him, almost a whole life.

The fact that he's more experienced has a big influence on our relationship. He knows what it is to live with a partner. And he taught this to me. It means sharing everything with someone else. Sleeping together in the same bed, every night, eating together. Like my parents. The same thing. Faithfulness. The fact that he's a professional, that he makes a large salary, and I don't, this interferes with our being equal. But then again, his bank account is always overdrawn anyway. I try to help as much as I can. I've also overdrawn my account. I do my best. And now I've found a part-time job, because I want to help out. He understands. And besides, it doesn't really matter. I can't do any more than I already do.

I think it's wonderful, the things that have happened in gay politics in the past year. It's really exceptional, especially in comparison to even the most advanced nations. Our country is, like, very progressive from that point of view. I mean, the Knesset passed that law for equality in the workplace, and that's really something. And then there was that hearing in the Knesset on gay, lesbian, and bisexual rights. There's a whole wave of change, and this atmosphere has really made the public aware that homosexuality is not a perversion, that it's a normal thing, with its own stories of partnership, commitment, and love. It's a very gradual process, what's happening, but the change is going to come. I think that what has happened in the past year has really advanced the process to where the public will eventually come to accept homosexuality as a normal thing. It's a long process, but I feel the change. The new generation doesn't think about these things the way my parents do.

I haven't told my parents. I haven't wanted to. I may tell them at some point, I don't know. I don't really feel the need to tell most people I know from the university, either. Only if I feel, like, very close to someone. There's only one friend I'd really like to tell, but I don't know if I'll do it, because I have a feeling that he won't know how to deal with it. I've heard what he's had to say about other people.

It's not hard to know what my parents think about the subject. My father can't stand gays. He's really repulsed. You can hear him, like, talking about it at home. My mother also. Actually, I don't really know what she thinks, but I have a feeling that she wouldn't accept it. But my father, for instance, if he sees gays on television or something, he laughs at them. I remember once they showed an interview with a gay man talking about his life with his boyfriend. I was sitting and watching this, and my father came into the living room, and sat down and began watching also. And at the end he said, "Disgusting." Just like that. I had to try pretty hard to keep from bursting out laughing. I guess I did laugh. It was pretty funny—I mean, it just didn't occur to him that maybe he was sitting there in the same room with a homosexual. And he said it out of such ridiculous prejudice, that it really just makes you laugh. I might tell my mother someday, but only her.

I know they don't know. But I think that my mother might suspect something. I think she's more sensitive. It's not that she's said anything, but I just figure. But actually, yes, she has been a little sad lately. When she talks to me I can hear a little sadness in her voice. It might be because I've kind of disappeared, that she doesn't know where I'm living. I mean, they know that I'm living with a friend. I try to go home a lot, to stop by for an hour or so, to be there every Shabbat for a little while. And soon I'll be moving into the dorms, so there won't be a problem anymore. I've told them that I want to move out. So I think that right now, they just think that I can't wait to move out. And actually, I have really had it with living at home. My brothers and sister are growing up, and they're always there, and they've taken the place over. It's difficult to live there, to have privacy.

I feel like I'm leading a double life. I feel very uncomfortable about hiding my whole life from my parents. But one of the reasons I don't want to tell them is that I know that it will cause them a lot of suffering. And I want to try to spare them. I don't want to hurt them. If they found out that Moṭi was my boyfriend, they would certainly throw me out of the house. My father would, like, disinherit me. I would be an untouchable. There's no doubt about it. I don't even want to imagine it, I don't even want to think about it.

Sure, my mother is in control, but only in, like, practical matters, not about emotional things like this. She's more sensitive than my father—I think that she could understand this a little better. If either of them were to understand, it would be her, even though I think that it will be very difficult even for her to come to terms with it also, and that she would go through all seven levels of hell before she finally came to terms with it.

I'm very close to the oldest of my brothers. I love him a lot. We grew up like two friends. He's the closest to me. But I know that he also has really negative ideas about gays. Even though he's very liberal about other things. That's the way he's been educated. He went to a military boarding school, where they talk about it as something deviant. In general, people in Bat Yam aren't, like, very enlightened. They're not very educated or cultured. They are simple, working people, struggling to make ends meet, and they've got lots of prejudices. And that's where I come from, and that's where my family lives. And this atmosphere, these surroundings, they influence my family. And that's the way it is with my brother. They have strong prejudices about gays.

The status of the people there explains a lot about this. Wealthy, upper-class, educated people do not live in Bat Yam. Maybe they would be able to understand. But the people in Bat Yam are middle class, lower class, and, I'm not saying that no one there would accept it, but when it comes right down to it, the atmosphere there is hostile. People have very strong objections to homosexuality.

Right now, the problem is that I'm very dependent on my parents. I may be living with Moṭi, but I'm very dependent on them. If I left Moṭi now, where could I go? I only have them. And I'm financially dependent on them, even though I have a scholarship that's paying my tuition, and I work too. So I want to be independent first of all, and then maybe I'll begin to come out of the closet a little. Maybe then I'll tell some other people, and maybe even them.

The fact that my family is *mizraḥi* has certainly influenced their views. If you compare, for instance, someone who comes from Iran with someone who comes from Europe, I think that you will find that the Iranian is inferior in both education and social status. And my family also comes from a more religious background. My grandfather's family in Iran was very religious. And very prejudiced, you could say. I mean, it could be that they are also hostile in Hungary—but I think it would be easier than in Iran. So there is a connection. In spite of that, they say that a *mizraḥi* family is a warmer one. That's what they say. And it may be that the mother's warmth in the end softens her heart, and she can eventually come to terms with it better. But I don't know about that. It might be the reverse, that the mother loves her son so very much, and is so concerned about him, that in the end it will be much more difficult for her to come to terms with her son being gay.

Today, I'm much more aware of AIDS. Moṭi has really made me realize how important it is to be careful. I never realized, like, how widespread the problem is. I used to just size people up, and based on how they looked, I would decide that there was no chance they could be sick. But then I would get very frightened afterwards, after I had been with someone. At a certain point I would become very frightened; I would say to myself, what if this person actually was infected? I think most people are aware, but it doesn't really influence their behavior. I've been tested a bunch of times. I got tested when I met Moṭi, and that really helped. I could kind of draw a line under everything that had happened in the past, and be more secure. Since then

Moṭi has asked me to be checked a few more times—which is irrational on his part, because he knows that I haven't slept with anyone else since we met. But he is very scared. He had a friend who died of AIDS.

I'm not really a Zionist. I'm not a patriot. If I wanted to leave Israel, I wouldn't think twice. It may be that I will leave. If I felt like I had a chance at a better life in the United States, then I would go.

I do think life is easier there. But I would have a problem supporting myself, finding work. Also, my family is here. And besides, I really like it here. I think I would really miss it. I like Israeli music, I like the atmosphere here. But there are a lot of bad things here. The army, unemployment, national issues—I mean, until there is real peace, war can break out at any moment.

I don't think Jews have to live in Israel. Everybody has the right to live wherever he wants. Wherever is most convenient, wherever you feel the most comfortable. If Jews feel more comfortable in a Jewish state, they should come. If someone wouldn't feel comfortable here, no one says he has to come. In the meantime, I like it here. I don't feel like I have to leave.

I voted for Meretz, the left-wing party, in the last elections. My father is very right-wing. I always argue with him about politics. He thinks I'm a bleeding-heart liberal. He took it very hard that I voted for the left. When I was in high school, I had right-wing views, but my views began to change when I was around eighteen, something like that.

There is no doubt that I've been influenced by my own experiences to be more sensitive to issues of individual rights, of minority rights, also with respect to the Arabs. I'm opposed to exploitation, oppression, and humiliation in all cases. Of course, the case of the Arabs is very complicated. I mean, there's no doubt that the Arab population in the territories is hurting, although I don't know if they deserve an independent state. But I think that they are suffering, and we've got to stop that. It is oppression, it is a kind of oppression, the military government in the territories. It's terrible. And I think that what just happened in Lebanon, in "Operation Accountability," is also unacceptable. To drive an entire population out of their homes, even temporarily, just to put some pressure on some terrorists. The very idea, it's a terribly inhumane thing to do, and totally unjustified.

I think it's a different story with the Israeli Arabs. I think that most of them are very pleased to live in the Jewish state, to live in a democratic country, and with such material abundance. I think they're pretty pleased with the situation. I don't think they're oppressed at all—they're free to leave if they're unhappy. But I think they feel Israeli.

Most of the people in Bat Yam are very right-wing. The Likud has a lot of support there. And many of the people in Bat Yam are *mizraḥiyim*. I think there's a connection between ethnic background and political views. They're also more Zionist. The fact that people may have come from Arab countries, or spoken Arabic at home, has definitely not made them more sensitive to the Arabs. People who came from Arab countries were persecuted there, and they remember that. If you look at my own family, they were persecuted by the Arabs. They'll even talk sometimes about revenge for what the Arabs used to do to them.

We celebrated all the holidays in the traditional ways in my family. We would fast on Yom Kippur, and go to synagogue. We would go to my grandfather's for every holiday, and we did everything the right way, with prayers and a festive meal. It wasn't an ultra-Orthodox home or anything, but there was, like, a religious atmosphere. I went to a religious high school for about two years. I think it's a good thing that they taught us about our heritage. I'm glad that my family was traditional. It's important to be in touch with your roots, the tradition, the atmosphere of the holidays. It's something very special.

I feel like I've been become more distant from religion lately. I don't keep any commandments. I don't fast anymore on Yom Kippur. I eat unkosher meat now, and sometimes I eat milk and meat together. This was really forbidden in our house, it was a very serious offense. On Yom Kippur, we weren't allowed to turn the lights on, and if someone broke their fast they would hear about it. But I don't have the patience for it anymore. I mean, I don't want to fast on Yom Kippur. It's a matter of convenience. It's more fun to be able to eat any kind of meat you want. Apparently, my parents didn't manage to sink it all into me deep enough for me to continue doing it.

Homosexuality does not contradict Judaism. Even though it's written that it is forbidden, that it's punishable by stoning—that's the punishment for homosexuality, death by stoning, which is a very serious death penalty, one of the most cruel ones. But I don't think there's a contradiction. It's a matter of faith and God. Like, you can be gay and believe in God. Besides, the laws in the Tanaḥ are very ancient. I mean, there are laws about slavery, but we don't do that anymore. All of the norms that are written in the Tanaḥ are very different, you just can't relate to all of them in the same way. I have a positive view of Judaism. And I'm glad about that, because I don't have to feel totally without foundation, without any support.

I think it's great that there are gay synagogues in the United States, for instance. If they had one in Israel, I would go. I think it's nice that they connected homosexuality with Judaism, even though I don't think they have anything to do with one another. I guess they, like, wanted to go out openly, so that no one from the Jewish community would reject them. At least that's what I understand. But obviously these synagogues are only for people who have come out of the closet. I'm trying to imagine what would happen if people in my family's synagogue knew about me, if I came out of the closet there. It might be that they would reject me. But it wouldn't be because of the connection between religion and homosexuality—it would be because of their own prejudices. I'm not even sure most of them know about the law in the Torah.

I still don't really have a picture of what my future will look like. I don't know if Moṭi and me will stay together. I mean, I'd like for that to happen, but I don't know if it'll happen. I have a lot of fears about the future. That we'll split up. I really don't know what will happen. He's taught me that you can never know. Anything can happen.

I'd like to live with a partner. I don't know if it necessarily has to be a man. I sometimes think about how much I'd like children. I know, it doesn't fit together, it doesn't make sense, I know, I know. It's impossible. These two tracks just don't intersect.

I'm not thinking right now about men in general, I'm thinking about Moṭi. I mean, if I'm going to live with a man, it's going to be Moṭi. But, on the other hand, I always imagine myself in the future as a married man. I imagine myself a married man, with children, a family I care about. That's why I say that I really don't know what I'll do, I don't know what will happen. I just can't, like, see the future. At the moment, I'm gay. But I'm only twenty-one. Sometimes I imagine that it's just a temporary thing with me.

Sure, I know that there are all sorts of ways for gay couples to get children, to raise children. But that's not the same thing. You understand? I sometimes imagine myself with a wife and children, living in a house with a family. To raise a child with Moṭi would be something totally different. All of my thoughts about family and children are, like, thoughts about going back to the so-called straight and narrow path, thoughts about leaving this world behind, and beginning heterosexual life. Now, if Moṭi and me raised a child, that would be great, terrific. But it's not the same thing as family life. It's that simple. And I'm not saying that it's worse or anything, I mean, it could be even better. But from the point of view of returning to heterosexual life and building bridges with my parents, it's not the same thing.

DAN

"Dan" was a friend of a friend, and his story sounded so intriguing that we dared not pass it up: we were told that he immigrated to Israel from the United States as a teenager, became religious, got married, fathered children, discovered his gay identity, and stayed married in spite of that. To us, he seemed a very enticing subject—he could provide a look at gay life in Israel from an American's perspective, from a religious perspective, and from the perspective of a married man and a young father.

Amir called Dan and explained our project, and Dan said that while he felt it would be indiscreet to tell his story, he would be glad to meet with us to hear more about the project. Coming up with a sufficiently private location for our meeting was, once again, not easy. In the end, we agreed upon a conference room near the main library at the Hebrew University on Mt. Scopus, overlooking the walled Old City of Jerusalem and the Temple Mount. Confident of our powers of persuasion, we brought our tape recorder along.

Dan was prompt, and, true to our intuition, so amiable that he was talking "on the record" in no time at all. Although he tried at first to be guarded, the effort was so clearly contrary to his nature that he quickly abandoned it. More recently, however, he has reviewed the text of his interview with a censor's pen. "I expect that my kids will read this," he explains.

Dan appeared to be in his late thirties, and his slim figure was clothed with the masculine carelessness favored by Israeli men of all stations—the kind of men who make a daily uniform out of brown slacks and short-sleeved, button-down shirts made of easy-to-care-for materials. Dan's Hebrew was completely fluent, yet no one who heard him could fail to note that English was his first language. We agreed that Amir would ask his questions in Hebrew (which was easier for him), I would ask my questions in English (which would be easier for me), and Dan would answer in English (which would save us the trouble of translation). It took Dan some time to adjust to this—he kept slipping back into Hebrew. But as time went on, he became more at ease with his native tongue, and I was left with the mistaken impression that this interview would need no translating. How wrong I was. As a fellow bilingual resident of Israel, I had been completely unaware of the huge amount of Hebrew vocabulary that was seeping back into Dan's English. Although it was painful to sacrifice this potentially invaluable opportunity to document the Hebrish dialect, equivalent English vocabulary has been substituted where necessary.

∾

I COME FROM A MIDDLE-CLASS Jewish background. My mother was a Holocaust survivor from Poland. She was seventeen when the Holocaust started. She lost her whole family. They were all killed, she's the only survivor. She met my father after the war in a displaced persons camp in Germany—my father was with the American army. She had wanted to join the illegal immigration to Israel that was being organized. But the organizers turned her down because her family had owned some property in Israel, and they felt she could make her own way there. So she returned to the displaced persons camp and married my father and came back to the U.S.

So I was brought up almost, like, preprogrammed to move to Israel at some point. All the artworks in my house were Israeli paintings. When my father would ask, "What's new, what's on the news?" he didn't care about what was going on in Chicago, or, you know, what was going on in Washington—he wanted to know about Israel. That was the way I was brought up. That was news. Other things were irrelevant. My parents, every Shabbat afternoon, would sit together and read ʿAgnon's Hebrew short stories and novels.[§] They went through all of his collected writings over the years. You know, with a lot of people from the States who have moved to Israel, when you scratch, you find that they're actually first-generation Americans— maybe they never felt completely at home in America, maybe they were brought up with different ideas, I don't know, but it's interesting.

[§] Sh. Y. ʿAgnon (1888–1970): Modernist writer of Hebrew fiction. Awarded Nobel Prize for Literature in 1966.

My mother's experiences in the Holocaust had a very definite influence on me. I came to Israel, by myself, at seventeen. And people say, by yourself? How could you do that? But my mother, she left her whole family, her whole culture, never to see them again, at seventeen. And with a lot of guilt—you know, she has her own stories. But the end result was that there was no room for any emotions in my house—basically because my mother couldn't handle the emotions that she had. Perhaps if she had been more open to the emotions that she felt, she would have committed suicide or something, or gone crazy. She had to go through a lot. So the final result was that there was no room for emotion, emotion was taboo, I mean, dangerous. When I was in high school, my mother was, I guess, an on-and-off psychotic. You know, looking back on it I can give it a name. She had episodes where, well, it was really very difficult for her. In retrospect, maybe she should have been admitted to a hospital. Except that my father was taking care of her, pretty much.

Overall, I guess I see a pattern in my life, like a lot of people who are gay—even if you come out to yourself at a later date, even if you're not aware of your own tendencies when you're a child or when you're an adolescent even. Well, I shouldn't speak for other people, I should speak for myself. And, you know, when you look back at things, certainly there was a pattern that, you know, afterwards comes together and makes sense. And I think that until I came out to myself I was to some extent very alienated. I felt like I was outside. Without knowing quite why. That's why I think that coming out is like a process of reconnecting to the human race, because all of sudden you realize that you're not one person that is on the outside, looking in, but you're part of a group. And as a group, you're, well, wherever the group is, but you're certainly not—I'm certainly not—where I was.

It's an almost stereotypical story. I wasn't good at sports, I didn't enjoy a lot of the things that boys were supposed to enjoy, I enjoyed some of the things that girls were supposed to enjoy. I was more interested in arts and crafts than in sports when I was in kindergarten.

When they had to pick teams to play baseball or soccer, or whatever they did, I would always feel very sorry for the team that had to pick me. Because they were, you know, sure to lose. Well, maybe not sure to lose, but I understood that they didn't want me. But what could you do, I was the last one left, and they got me. Sorry! I know it's a hard pill to swallow! It wasn't a great feeling, but you learn to live with it, you know. I was very good in other areas, so it wasn't like I was a total reject. But, again, looking back, it fits, you know, it's not a tremendous shock that I turned out like this. It makes sense.

We didn't really talk about sex at home. My parents' idea of sex education was to leave a book, a sex manual, somewhere where me and my older brother could read it on the sly. That was the extent of it. I seem to remember some kind of antigay remarks that my father made at some point—not that he was a prejudiced person, he was actually very liberal politically, but I think that he was, well, maybe that was just the prevailing atmosphere. It didn't make any impression on me then, it's just looking backwards now that I remember it—I mean, at that point I didn't think of myself in that way.

I was a very good student. That was maybe what balanced everything else. But it was almost like a distortion, it seemed like everything was pushed in one direction. My family was only interested in my intellectual life, there was no room for emotional growth, or recognition of needs. I mean, it wasn't like my father quizzed me at the dinner table, or anything. But maybe, if things had been like that, very obvious and clear-cut, then it would have been much easier for me. Then I would have said, this is crazy, I mean, what, you sit me down every week and ask me a, b, c—what kind of family is this, this is ridiculous. And it would have been easier for me to say no, or inside to say, "I don't accept that." But it really wasn't stated, it was very subtle, in a way, which made it all the more difficult to recognize what was going on, or what was not going on—you know, what was lacking.

I don't remember the first time I heard the word "gay" or "homosexual." It wasn't like some kind of an earth-shaking, dramatic event. I don't remember. I suppose I could dig back and think of something, but it's just not a significant memory. Not something that sticks in my mind at all. I think the general tone was negative. It certainly wasn't positive. I think it was kind of like, you know, I have a memory of my father saying something about how gay men have a tough time because they don't have the right equipment to do it. You know, where are you going to put it? I guess he didn't use his imagination—it doesn't seem to be a problem these days!

I think maybe I had a tendency to bond to some extent to other boys— like, I remember sometimes having best friends. I remember maybe in third grade, or second grade even, thinking about a certain boy that I was kind of, I guess, attracted to. I mean it makes sense now. There's another memory that just came back to me now, maybe it fits, I don't know in what way. I must have been in seventh or eighth grade, and I had a friend, and we were talking about electronics, you know, hobbies, radios or something, and he said something about the "male" plug and the "female" plug, and I couldn't figure out which one was which. And he said, you know, it's obvious. And I couldn't figure it out. I mean, the female is the one with the boobs, *she's* the one that sticks out, right? Looking back, I can't understand how I didn't understand. But at that moment I was just like, that's the male one? How could that be? It looks more like a female to me. Maybe the whole subject was repressed, I don't know.

I don't remember sex being an issue. I think at that time, when I was around thirteen, my fantasy was some kind of a very elaborate, sophisticated game of "playing doctor" with a woman. My fantasy when I was an adolescent was always with a woman, a girl. I don't know when I began thinking about boys, men. Except that I know that it was always there also, in the back of my mind.

I went to summer camp, and I had a girlfriend. We used to kiss under the apple trees. This was at fourteen, fifteen. It was kind of like a status thing. You know, everyone was amazed that Dan was also doing it, doing something under the apple trees, no one really knew what it was—could it be . . . ? I think other people were doing more things under the apple trees. I was really always kind of on the outskirts of things, so you know, when I acted just like everyone else, it was cause for amazement. What, he's conforming? How unconventional!

In religious terms, my family was sort of right-wing Conservative when I was growing up. Almost Orthodox, very close to being Orthodox, but I went to public high school. I accepted my family's religious orientation very much. In fact, I even became more religious when I first came to Israel. When I came here, like a lot of other people who come from similar backgrounds, I sort of felt like you had to choose—you're either going to be religious or nonreligious in Israel. And growing up, we observed Shabbat, we kept kosher, we went to synagogue. But you know, Shabbat was not strictly according to the law—no car, no cooking, but lights, yes. And my parents had this idea that you mustn't watch T.V. on Shabbat unless it's opera. Or educational T.V. Or some sort of classical music. It made perfect sense to them.

I don't think my idea was that I would be cured by religion. But I think I did conceive of it as kind of—how can I put it—an obstacle. It was good that religion was there, you know—it would save me from myself. I remember thinking, maybe I am homosexual, and then thinking, well, it's good that I'm Orthodox, because this way, you know, I won't be tempted. I won't have those opportunities to succumb to temptation, I won't have so much freedom. Because socially you're more circumscribed, there are a lot more do's and don't's, and what's accepted in the community is very clear, there are very clear ideas of what's allowed and not allowed. I thought that would be good, it would give me an extra little obstacle, you know, and it would make it a little more difficult. And that's good. For a while, that was the way my head went.

After the kisses under the apple tree, I didn't have any other girlfriends. I suppose it was unusual, but I was so much out of things, I was so much in my own world, I didn't notice. I was very involved in a Zionist youth movement, and I certainly didn't fit in, in any way, with my high school crowd. I didn't socialize with people in my high school. And I was more religious than everyone, so it made perfect sense that I wasn't carrying on, and I was more academic. I was a little more Jewish than everyone else, and obviously Jews don't have sex. Not good Jews.

Everyone was doing their own thing at this time—it was the late sixties. And my counterculture movement was Zionism. Everyone in my high school knew, "Dan is crazy, he's doing his thing." To some extent, the whole idea of the Zionist youth movement somehow fit together with the whole counterculture business. It dovetailed very nicely, actually. I felt like it fit right in. I went to demonstrations—for Soviet Jewry. We were involved in our demonstrations and our activism, and I have this memory of, you know, doing some educational work on Jewish values and poverty or something, and going to find out about a new welfare rights organization in the ghetto.

I remember, once a month we had some kind of organized meeting, the people who were more committed, from the Zionist youth movement, and we would go to see films in the city that were "counterculture." It made perfect sense to us that we should be doing this, I don't know why. I remember one film of this guy who was naked, and the image was that he was fucking mother earth. Anyway, that was supposed to be very Zionist.

I did have longish hair. And I remember coming to Israel with a kind of hippie-ish pair of jeans, on which a friend of mine had embroidered a couple of flowers. My Israeli relatives were absolutely horrified. I said, "It's just a flower." But they had this idea of the ultimate in, I don't know, hippie license or something. But I didn't smoke pot. I was almost Orthodox—I wasn't sure whether that was appropriate.

So I graduated high school, and most of the people in my class went off to college, but I went off to Israel. I was seventeen.

I don't think it was a revolutionary step or anything. It seems like it looking back, but at the time it didn't seem at all exceptional. It was like, in the youth movement I was in, everyone else was talking about emigrating also. But I had the guts to actually do it. So it wasn't like I was doing something that wasn't expected. And at this time, after '67, there were a lot of foreign students in Israel.

Why did I do it? I mean, that's already a subject for years of therapy. On the surface I was a Zionist, and always planned on it, dreamed about it, and I was kind of brainwashed in the youth movement and everything else. But it goes beyond that, because lots of people were brainwashed—and then came here and they looked around and left, with misgivings or not. Not a lot of people with my background came to Israel and stayed. I think that, on the personal level, I was running away from my family. Coming to Israel was kind of like having my cake and eating it too, on a personal level, because I was able to fulfill my parents' wishes—you know, on the list of priorities, going to Israel was certainly very acceptable—but at the same time I could separate from them. So when I moved to Israel, I escaped with their blessing.

As difficult as it was for me to leave, it was much better than staying in the States to take care of them. It was painful to be on my own, but at least I was on my own. Subsequently, you know, my family moved here also. But what can you do—where can I move now, India, Australia? But that was years later. By that time I had already become independent.

My brother also came to Israel, a little while after I did. He was a draft dodger. He got his first induction notice, left the country, and immediately got himself drafted into the Israeli army. That was his plan. And when they sent him his second notice he told them, "Sorry, I'm already in an army— they won't let me out of the country. I'd love to come, I'm dying to go to Vietnam, really, but sorry, you know, they won't let me out of this little hell-hole of a country here in the Middle East."

I turned eighteen when I was in Israel, so I had to register for the American draft from here. And they had a loophole, typical of all the monkey business that went on. Anyone who turned eighteen abroad had to register with a special draft board that sat in Washington—and no one was ever called from this draft board. Ever. It was set up for the sons of diplomats. And so no one was ever called.

I basically became a citizen as soon as I got here. And I got into the army's officer candidate academic studies program, which, for me, meant first getting my B.A. at the Hebrew University in Jerusalem, and then going into the army for five years afterwards, in some kind of professional capacity. So it was like I was on reserve duty during the whole time I was studying for my degree, and then, only afterwards, I was drafted into full-time service.

Although I was suddenly a citizen, I had never been to Israel before. And the country was most peculiar on first sight, I must say. It was really very different from anything that you could conceive of. Back then, Israel was much more provincial. People traveled less, spoke English less. Things were different. Very different. And it was very difficult.

Israel was, basically, backward. The Ministry of the Interior, where they took care of all the immigration bureaucracy, was one big hall where everyone pushed. If you had to go there, you used to have to begin preparing yourself twenty-four hours in advance, psyching yourself up, you know, kind of spoiling yourself, getting yourself some ice cream, and you went to bed early, of course, so you could be there by 7:30 in the morning, ready to start pushing—you sharpened your elbows. And at the bank, you would have to wait on one line for one clerk to give you a slip of paper so you could wait on another line for a cashier so you could get the money from your account. And it wasn't a "line"—you pushed to get to the clerk, and you pushed to get to the cashier. And I remember how they used to prepare dinner by leaving the eggplants out on the roof to "sweat," with the flies on them, you know—that was supposedly good for the process. I don't think they do that anymore. And you never left the house without a wad of toilet paper, because you knew that none of the public toilets would have toilet paper. This was a well-known fact.

For the first year I was in the country, I was in a sort of "absorption" program, run by the government for foreign students, and only afterwards did I officially enroll in the university. So I had the summer free, for a trip back to the States. But I wasn't let out of the country. I had to get an exit permit from the army. And when I appeared at the draft office, they said that I couldn't leave—because I had already been out of the country once within the past year! And I said that I hadn't *left* the country within the past year, I had come *into* the country within the past year. And they said, "No. It hasn't been a year, and you were already abroad once—how many times do you want to go abroad?"

And so I appealed it. They gave me an appointment, and when the time came, they connected me by phone to someone who said, "I am the representative of the committee that was appointed by Moshe Dayan to decide on your case—and the answer is no."[§] And I said, "But if I were an Israeli, I would be allowed out of the country—I know Israelis who have left the country four weeks before being drafted. And if I were an American, then I

[§] Moshe Dayan (1915–81): chief of staff (1953–58); defense minister (1967–74); foreign minister (1977–79).

wouldn't have a problem either, because then I would just be classified as a tourist." And he said, "But you're not either of these—the answer is no."

So I had no choice, I went back to Jerusalem, resigned to hanging around the university alone all summer, kind of depressed. But after two weeks, an administrator noticed me, and said, "What are you doing here?" And I said to him, "Well, they wouldn't let me out of the country." And he says, "Oh, you have to talk to my friend the general." And so I went to talk to his friend the ex-general from the reserves, and he called up someone, and the next day, I went to the draft office, and I got the exit permit. That's a good example of the kind of problem I had at first—I didn't know how things were done. Everyone needs their own network of connections, but I didn't know it—and I didn't have anyone to go to, in any case. So the bureaucracy was bad news for me.

Around that time, I remember going for therapy, or trying to go for therapy, to a social worker—maybe this was a year or so later. I was depressed and I was having problems separating from my parents, dealing with Israel, you know, finding my place at the university. And I remember coming to the social worker, and she said, "Your problem is that you're not sleeping with anyone. You're a healthy young man, and you don't have any sex life." And I remember at that point being absolutely aghast at the idea. I said to myself, "I'm religious, I don't believe in this—how does she as a social worker come and tell me what values to have? I don't think it's appropriate, I don't think it's an option at this point. When I get married, I will have sex. Until then, I'm not going to have sex." There was no question in my mind. It wasn't something that I was even looking into at that point.

Homosexuality did not come up in my conversations with the social worker at all. I didn't go into therapy because of the gay issue—it wasn't an issue for me. Maybe it was too repressed, but it was not something I consciously thought of as a problem one way or the other. It just didn't come up. At that point my entire approach toward sex was, you know, I will wait until I get married. At that point I wasn't consciously aware of another option, I wasn't considering anything else. It was perfectly obvious to me that at some stage you get married and you live with a woman and you have a family. This is what you're supposed to do and that's what I was going to do.

The thoughts I had about men were, you know, restricted to going to the beach and looking at the men, not at the women. And I always thought to myself that I was doing it because I felt inadequate, that I was comparing myself. Once I would get married and "prove myself," that would obviously change. That was how my mind went in those years.

When I was about twenty, and I was already very serious about my future wife, I went to visit my family in the States by myself, and I remember going to a gay cinema in New York. Kind of to try it out, to see what it was like. I mean, obviously I had some inclination in that direction, otherwise I wouldn't have done it. I saw an ad in the paper, and I went to the cinema on the second day of Passover. I didn't feel right about going to a gay cinema with my *kipah* on, but I didn't feel right about taking off my *kipah* especially in order to go to a gay cinema. But on the second day of Passover, I would have to take my *kipah* off anyway, because of *mar'it 'ayin.*§ So I remember thinking, well, if I've already got my *kipah* off, I might as well go. Something like that. I don't remember thinking in terms of "sin" or anything like that. My idea of being religious at that point was opening yourself up to other options—I felt that being religious meant adding things to my life, not giving them up. So the fact that I wanted to try something else was maybe, technically, a little bit complicated, but this was no more than a practical obstacle. So I went to this gay cinema, I remember the film—and I didn't get it up. It didn't turn me on at all. Maybe because I was so repressed or whatever, but I had no overt reaction. I said, well, I guess that's not me. And I kind of put the subject on the back burner for three years or something. After I came back from that trip I proposed to my wife.

I had first met her at summer camp in the States—I'd known her since age twelve, thirteen. She was also in the youth movement. And at some point, when we were already in Israel, I began, you know, getting very serious about her. She came to Israel about the same time as I did. We started going together at about twenty, and got married when I was just twenty-two. We had been engaged for about eight months before that.

§ *mar'it 'ayin*: Literally, "what is seen by the eye." The Talmudic principle that the creation of the spectacle of the violation of traditional religious law is as grave as the fact of violation.

Dan's situation was complex. According to traditional religious law, Jews who live outside the Land of Israel are obligated to observe extensive restrictions, similar to those observed on Shabbat, during the first two days of the Passover holiday. But Jews who live in the Land of Israel are obligated to observe these restrictions only on the first day of Passover. Dan, as an Israeli, was therefore free of these restrictions on the second day of the festival, even though he found himself temporarily outside of Israel on the day in question. But if Dan were to publicly engage in activities that would normally be forbidden to New York Jews—like traveling or handling money, for instance—while wearing his *kipah*, he would create the spectacle of flagrant violation of the law, even though this would not, in fact, be the case. Therefore, in accordance with the principle of *mar'it 'ayin*, Dan removes his *kipah* on this day: without his *kipah*, he cannot be identified as a Jew, and so cannot create the spectacle of the violation of Jewish law.

I think it was because I, basically, had no family. My parents were in the States, my brother was married, and I think I had a need to set up a family to feel comfortable. At least that's how I explain it. Neither of us actually thought, is it wise to get married at such a young age? Maybe it was because we were in these religious circles where no one questioned such a thing. It was very accepted, a lot of people were getting married. It isn't like secular society, where even people who are family-oriented will put it off until they're twenty-five, twenty-six, and then they'll wait even longer before they start having kids. It wasn't like that. And interestingly enough, my parents also didn't seem to question it at all. Looking back, I don't know if it's good to get married so young—I think a lot of people have problems with that, choosing someone for such a serious relationship at such an age.

She was a very special person. I felt very much that she understood me. I felt very connected, and I, kind of, earlier than she did, I decided I wanted to make it into a serious relationship, and, you know, proceeded. I kind of led, in all the different stages. I was definitely attracted to her. We had a sort of unwritten agreement that I would agree to have sex before marriage if she would agree to become religious. She didn't really come from a religious background. I don't know if that was a fair agreement, but that was the way it worked, for a couple of years at any rate.

There was definitely a sexual element. Definitely. That was part and parcel of the whole process. I don't think that we would have progressed unless that was also involved. It wasn't like some platonic relationship. Not by any means. There was no indication at that point that I was gay. I've heard stories from married men who said that their biggest worry was that on the wedding night would they be able to do it or not. And they were terribly worried and anxious about it, would they be able to pull it off, how were they going to get through it. But that wasn't my story at all. I was different. That's just the way it was.

When my three years of college were up, I was drafted. I got married six months after I was drafted. I knew my draft date, but we had to plan the marriage pretty far ahead, because we had to take into account when parents and relatives could come from the States. So we timed it for an appropriate vacation. We moved to a "development town," and that's where we lived for our first couple of years together.[§]

[§] development town: A new Jewish settlement within the internationally recognized borders of Israel. The government provides economic incentives for internal migration to such towns.

In terms of the army, I kind of felt that I always managed to get by, but with difficulty. I was amazed that I managed as well as I did. Maybe I underestimate myself in terms of that. I was pretty physically fit, that wasn't too bad, but I certainly was not an outstanding soldier. The thing that really helped me was that, you know, I had good friends who went with me through basic training and the officers' training course, and we helped each other out.

Our particular unit was drafted a few weeks after the cease-fire of the Yom Kippur War. If you remember, it was months and months before things got back to normal. Half the country was still doing reserve duty for five or six months—they were out there in the Sinai somewhere until the agreements were negotiated and whatnot. Originally, my draft date was during the war, but of course it had been postponed.

The reason that we were drafted so soon after the war was that we were all in the officer candidate academic studies program. And a lot of the people in my unit were in professions which were in high demand—engineering, science, Arab studies. So the army decided after the war was finished that it needed to draft these people quickly and put them to use. We were to be drafted and sent to an "accelerated and abridged" officers' training course. And basically the order from on high was to pass everybody—unless there was a problem of honesty, in other words, people who were caught lying. Or unless you fell asleep during guard duty, which was considered to be very bad. If you managed to stay up all night and you didn't tell any lies, you were through. We were lectured at our graduation ceremony by the commander of the base on how we were the worst group in the history of the officers' training camp, and if it hadn't been that he had been given an order to pass us, we could rest assured that most of us would not have gotten through. So I got through—I can't say it was a high point in my life. Subsequently I feel like I've been a very spoiled soldier. I keep on getting kicked upstairs—now, when I get called for reserve duty, I'm a captain. The whole thing is kind of funny.

You know, I once met someone who said that all during his army service he couldn't take showers when other people were taking showers because he was scared that he would get an erection. So he would only take showers after everyone was done, or before, or something. He didn't want to risk it— he was so turned on, and he was in such close quarters with all these guys. But it wasn't an issue with me, at that point. It wasn't a problem, for one reason or another. I was still in my religious phase at that point, I was about to get married. I was very much oriented toward women, or toward *a* woman, in any case. It wasn't a problem.

What I do remember are some very, very good friends, good buddies. We stuck together throughout several courses, and, you know, helped each other out. In particular, I remember one person that I bunked with, he was up and I was down or something, and we were really together all the time. It was kind of a male bonding that we had. I wonder now whether it wasn't an expression of something on my part. I don't think on his part. But we were really very close.

So much so, I remember that, after we had been drafted, there were six weeks when we weren't allowed home. And I was engaged at that point, and, you know, my future wife had no family here, it was difficult for her to be cut off like that, and it was certainly difficult for me. But my buddy had gotten married a few months before, he was about the same age as me, and he had moved to a kibbutz—he was a gung-ho kibbutz type, he had fulfilled his Zionist dream and moved to a kibbutz—and his wife had been installed on the kibbutz and then he had left. And she, from the beginning, wasn't so keen on the idea of living on a kibbutz, and here she was with these people that she didn't know, left alone, newly married. At some point, I think in week number five, I was told I could go home for the weekend. And I gave him my pass. I said, "You go. I'm not married yet, my wife isn't my wife yet, you know, she misses me, but she's not living off by herself on a kibbutz with no one around." And I gave him my pass, and he left for the weekend.

After I finished my training, the army put me to work in my profession, and my wife and I made a home for ourselves. So I was married, drafted, and we moved, all about the same time, as planned. I'd rather not say exactly where we lived. Let's just say this—the Jewish Agency once put out a film about development towns, where they contrasted a successful one with one that was unsuccessful. In that film, our town was the one that was unsuccessful. I was a social worker there—I worked with juvenile delinquents, basically. Kids that were not working, not in school, not in any framework. At that point, the army was committed to this, and that was my military service, most of it. It worked out that it was also what I wanted to do. And by that time I'd also learned to pull some strings, and this was really a super manipulation of everyone. From my point of view at least, it worked out.

It's hard to understand this town from the outside. It was pretty far from the major cities in Israel, and entirely made up of new immigrants from North Africa—Morocco and Tunisia—who had been settled there by the Jewish Agency. All the immigrants from North Africa came from a traditional kind of Jewish society. But already, before they came to Israel, there were lots of signs of disintegration of the traditions. And, in general, when they immigrated, there was an even more rapid disintegration. So what happened was that families, you know, just fell apart—not all of the kids who went to school stayed in school, girls were known as prostitutes, and so on. Certainly there were a lot of boys who did manage to stay in high school, but once they graduated, they had no profession to find a job in.

For us, living there was very difficult, socially. Not just because we were a young couple just starting out, but because we were Ashkenazi Americans. There were, I think, four other English-speakers in the whole town. And we didn't have a car, so our social life had to be there—we couldn't jump into the car and run off to the nearest city. We made an attempt at fitting in with the local intelligentsia, the children of the immigrants, who were about our age, who had been educated, you know—the teachers, the bureaucrats. We made an attempt like that, but it didn't work out. So socially it was difficult. At one point, we actually succeeded in convincing some other young couples to come to this town. Unfortunately, they were French speakers, and no sooner did they get there than they excluded us from their little group. We had put a lot of effort into getting them to come, and we were hoping that this would be our social grouping. And it didn't work. So at some point, we were left high and dry socially. After about three and a half years we left.

After a certain amount of time working as a social worker there, the army suddenly pulled me out and sent me to work as a clerk at military headquarters, in Tel Aviv. This was still during my first few years after getting my degree, and they had violated the terms of my contract. In other words, my agreement with the army was that I would be employed for a total of five years in my profession, and they reneged on that, and sent me off to work at this job in Tel Aviv. And that formed the basis for my leaving the army at the end of three years, because they hadn't kept up their part of the bargain.

But for a while, I had to commute every day to Tel Aviv, which was, like, two and half hours both ways, hitchhiking in the early hours of the morning. I was the assistant to the Israeli army's liaison officer with the International Red Cross. The liaison officer was an elderly lieutenant colonel, a stuffy German-speaking type, who was a specialist in international law. He was the national expert on the Red Cross. He had been out of the army and then subsequently redrafted, because after the war in 1973 everyone was holding a lot of prisoners of war, and there were a lot of goings-on between the army and the Red Cross at that point.

By the time I got there, though, there was nothing going on at all. There were no prisoners of war being held by either side—everything had been completely negotiated, and I had nothing to do. So I was told to take all the names of all the Arab prisoners of war that Israel had held since 1948, and file them alphabetically, according to their Hebrew spellings. Now, you have to realize how ridiculous this was—because, you know, there's "Maḥmud" and there's "Muḥamed," and then there's "Maḥmid," but there was no standard way of differentiating between these names in Hebrew—you could write them seven different ways, or all the same way. And of course I didn't know Arabic. So I was trying to make order out of something that was by definition ridiculous.

The whole point was that when the Red Cross would send an inquiry to the army, saying, "We have a request for information about Maḥmud Muḥamed Maḥmidi, missing since the war in 1956. He was last seen on the eastern front on this day, and so on. Do you know anything about him?" we should be able to answer them. And, of course, the Red Cross wrote to us in English. But how do you spell "Muhammed" in English, and then connect that with "Maḥmoud" or "Muḥammad" or whatever in Hebrew? And the relation of all of this to Arabic, who knows!

At any rate, the point is that, of course, we didn't have information, because by then everything was clear. We weren't holding anyone. So we were supposed to answer them, "No, we have no information, but we would like to point out that you made the same inquiry on January 31, 1958, and on January 2, 1962. And on January 15, you asked for Muḥamed Maḥmud Maḥmidi, last seen on the eastern front, etc. etc."

This was supposed to be my life's work—I was supposed to be doing this very assiduously. And when I finished, who knows what I would have to do next—the bottom line is that there was nothing to do. So I had my own office, and I had all the information cards spread out all over my desk, and in the drawer of my desk, I kept a science fiction book. The drawer was constantly being opened and closed as my commanding officer would walk by. After about three months he asked me, "How come there's no progress?" I said, "It's slow work."

I think that my attraction to men was always in the back of my mind. Well, not always. Sometimes more, sometimes less. But it was something that kind of cropped up every once in a while. I remember another bout of depression, and another couple of sessions of therapy that I went to, around this time. During my last session, I was terribly upset, and I said, "I think maybe I'm homosexual." And the therapist's reaction was, "It isn't so awful." He was very calming. And basically I left it at that. It wasn't like I'd done anything about it, but obviously it had occurred to me, because I remember very clearly bringing it up. And I left it at that. It was like, "By the way, you know, I also have some problems sleeping." This was at twenty-four. I was already a father.

I was twenty-three when my first daughter was born. It was a very positive experience. I was very happy to have a kid. A lot of work, very difficult, but I think my wife suffered much more than I did. I was still in the army, and I was eight hours at headquarters in Tel Aviv, and four or five hours daily hitchhiking back and forth, so I wasn't much help at all. But when I could, I certainly took care of our daughter.

I knew at that point that I was attracted to men. But I had always thought that, if I stayed in a religious framework, then I was less likely to do something about it. Which I perceived as something good. You know, I wanted to be married, I wanted to be comfortable with that framework. But I think that my going for therapy was part of a general loosening-up process, getting over a lot of my being obsessive about religion, being uptight. It contributed a lot to my being able to let go of the values I'd brought with me from my parents, from my upbringing. And eventually, my values changed in terms of sexuality also. But that was a process which was just beginning.

My wife knew all about the therapy, and she knew that I thought I might be gay. I didn't say I was bisexual at that point, because I guess I wasn't so up-to-date with the different possibilities or terms. I don't know if I knew there was such a thing as bisexuality.

People ask me, on occasion, "When did you tell your wife?" And the answer is, I never did. I mean, there was no moment where I said, you know, "I have a secret to tell you." I've heard stories like this—of married men who, after twenty years, sat their wives down and "told" them. But it wasn't like that with me. I never told my wife, there was no point where I told her something that was shocking.

I'll explain what I mean. I got married very young. I certainly wasn't "out" to myself at that point, by any means. But slowly, over time, I did come out, and I decided where my preferences lay—but it was a whole long series of little steps, and every time I made a little step, she knew about it, I told her. It wasn't something that I kept hidden, it was not like a big revelation after twenty years. It was little revelations, and little steps all along the way. And so even at that point, if I went to my therapist and said, "What if I'm homosexual?" I'm almost positive I told her. I don't have any memory of not telling her, and we talked about everything.

I don't remember any particular reaction, on her part. I think the reaction was one of understanding. At that point, it was just some kind of very hypothetical thing, it wasn't anything to deal with on a real basis. It was something sort of crawling around in my head, and as far as I know, I told her, and the reaction was something like, "Well, probably you aren't," or "Maybe you have some tendencies, but what difference does it make." She didn't pack her bags and move out. Maybe the most significant thing is that there was no reaction that was memorable, at that point.

I'd also written to my wife about the trip I'd made to the gay cinema in the States before we were married. And I think I even sent her a photocopy of the cinema's ad from the newspaper. I mean, we were kind of into having lots of different experiences and trying out things, and here I did a bizarre thing—maybe she even thought I was really cool, that I had the guts to try it out. I mean, after all, I was this religious boy, with a beard. Outwardly, I was this very conventional type of person, about to get married.

At some point my wife and I took a mini-vacation in Tel Aviv, and left the kids with my in-laws. My wife's family had moved to Israel also, and we'd had another daughter by this time. The kids must have been very young then. So we went to spend a weekend in Tel Aviv—we went to a hotel, to the beach, the movies, and whatnot. And I remember lying on the beach in Tel Aviv and reading in *Ha'ir* that they were about to begin shooting a film about Tel Aviv gay life, in Independence Park. And all of sudden I said, "Independence Park, we passed that, that's right around here, you know." And she said, "Well, you feel like trying it out? You know, it's right here after all— we're in Tel Aviv."

And on Friday night, after my wife went to sleep—no, that doesn't sound the way I mean it to sound. It's not like after my wife went to sleep, I tiptoed out, careful not to wake her. But she was very tired from running around, and I was very horny, and she went to sleep. And I decided that I still had lots of energy and interest, and I walked down three blocks, and I was in Independence Park. I had taken off my *kipah* again, because I didn't feel right walking around Independence Park with a *kipah* on—especially since it was Friday night. And I sat down on a bench, and someone tried to pick me up. Some older guy, who kind of made nice to me. He was a little bit chubby, a little bit older—he must have been at least my age now—at any rate he was interested in me. I remember him asking me all these questions about where I was from and this and that. I said I was from Haifa, and he said, "What's the scene like up there?" And I said, "Well, I'm really not so involved in the scene." We talked for while, but I wasn't about to go anywhere with him, so after a while he moved on.

After this experience in Independence Park, that door was kind of closed for a couple of years—I didn't do anything nearly so adventuresome until, I think, '82 maybe, or '83, which was about three years afterwards. I was working as a social worker. I was about thirty-one years old at the time. And I began going to Jerusalem's famous Turkish bath. Actually, I had been there before, once or twice, but I think that what changed at this point was that I'd gotten contact lenses—and I could see what was going on. For years I had glasses, and when I went, I couldn't see anything. Thank God for modern technology, yes.

You don't remember the baths? Oh, you've really missed out. The Turkish baths were located in the center of Jerusalem, in the old Bukharan neighborhood, which was becoming more and more religious. It was open on alternate days, only men one day, and then only women the next. The building must have been more than a hundred years old. It was huge, you know, there were three stories, and they had lots of showers, lots of different pools—they had a very hot pool, about the size of a huge jacuzzi, and they had a very cold pool, where you could swim laps almost, it was that big, and they had a medium pool. And they had a roof where you could sun yourself, and another room where they had someone giving massages, and they had two steam rooms—dry steam and wet steam, I think. It was quite an establishment.

Married men who weren't gay would go to the baths to relax, to get a massage, to do whatever you do in the baths, but for many years it was also the kind of place where gay people could go and do what they wanted. And that was the way it was for many years, that was its calling card, that was what was attractive about it—you could go to the baths without necessarily defining yourself as being gay. Because lots of people go to the baths. I mean, it wasn't like going to the gay sauna in Tel Aviv. In Tel Aviv, it's perfectly obvious—you can't claim that you're not gay, or that you're not interested. I mean, that's what people go there for, that's what they advertise, that's what they are. But the Turkish bath really let you have your cake and eat it too, in that way, for many years.

I think that by the time I started getting interested, in '82, '83, the baths were getting more and more gay—I mean, it was getting a reputation. I know that once a week a whole crowd of people would come from Tel Aviv specifically to go there—there was one night that was Turkish baths night. And in terms of Israeli gay life, this was pretty revolutionary, that people would come from Tel Aviv to Jerusalem for gay experiences. Maybe it was going on for years before then, and I just don't know about it. The baths were run by this Sefardic family that had been running it for ages and ages and ages, and I guess they probably closed one eye. They couldn't have not known what was going on—one night a week lots of people came from Tel Aviv and did whatever they did.

There were all of these dark corridors off somewhere in this huge maze-like building, and people would go off into these corridors, I think, sometimes. Or they would meet and go somewhere else. I have the memory at that point of going to the baths, and lying on the roof naked, and bringing a book to read, and someone said to me, "That's it? All you're doing is reading a book? I mean, you're not . . . That's it?" It was like he was saying, "Really, I mean, who are you kidding? You didn't really come to read a book here, did you?" And I guess I was kind of looking at what was going on, but I wasn't, you know, taking an active part.

The roof was for naked sunbathing. On the roof people took off their towels. Inside, you wore a towel, but you took it off when you went into the pools and when you took a shower, obviously. There were also places where people would lie down on these stone slabs that were heated from underneath, and give each other massages and whatnot. I don't remember if that was with or without towels. It was a cruisy atmosphere. If I had gone into the corridors I think I would have seen a lot more—I think there was a lot going on there. But I was kind of naive. I didn't see that much going on.

You couldn't be sure that someone was gay there. You were never sure. So, you know, I remember times when—it was a cruisy business, you know—you're in this hot bath where everyone is crowded together and all of a sudden you feel someone touching you, or moving up against you. And you can either move away, or you can move closer. If you move away, OK—obviously you're not interested, and the other person could say, "Sorry, well, I just got pushed up against you by mistake, didn't mean anything by that." But if you responded, or if you stayed put, well then. . . .

At some point my wife had been enthusiastic about being religious, but I think that it kind of wore off with time. She was certainly positively inclined toward the idea, it wasn't like I forced it on her or anything. She was willing to look at it as a kind of experience, maybe, so she was willing to try it out, and she even did some things that I never would have asked her to do— when we were living in the development town, for instance, she started keeping her hair covered in public. She felt comfortable doing that.

At that time, we had gone on a visit to the States together, to see relatives. And my wife was pregnant, and she was also in the habit of wearing a head covering. When we got to New York, we wanted to feel like we were in the big city—so we went to see *Deep Throat* together. And she was the only lady with a belly and a head covering in the whole movie theater! Some guy said, "Hey, lady, could you move, your hat's blocking my view."

But by this time we were less religious. It was a long, downhill road. Maybe uphill, I don't know. But it was a very gradual thing with us, that we gradually became less and less religious. I was no longer wearing a *kipah*, but I think I was still observing Shabbat, still keeping kosher. This was a process we went through together, fortunately, because some couples have a lot of problems with that, where, you know, one is and one isn't religious, or perhaps they got married on a certain basis and subsequently one of them changed. But we kind of reinforced one another, very slowly, over a long period of time.

I had contemplated taking off my *kipah* for a long time before I actually did it. But then I was starting a new job, and I said to myself, this is an opportunity, when I walk into my new job, people will know me without a *kipah*, and without having to go through all these complicated explanations about how, when, and why—for them, Dan doesn't wear a *kipah*, never did, for all they know, and that's that. I went through a period where I kept it in my pocket for meals and whatnot, and eventually that kind of stopped as well. It was a gradual business.

Taking off your *kipah* is really a very strong statement, and some of our friends dropped us at that point. I remember that it was during Sukot, and my sister-in-law said, "Come quick to our *sukah*, I have to talk to you, and convince you how horrible this is, what you've done," something like that.[§] But most of our friends accepted it.

I remember a period where I stopped going to synagogue on Friday night, and one of our religious friends said, "Why did you stop?" and I said, "I found something better to do." He said, "What could be better?" and I said, "Well, I go running during the sunset—it's really very nice, running in the street with the sun setting on a quiet Friday night. It really makes me feel much more spiritual than going to synagogue." I remember my wife getting

---

[§] Sukot: Eight-day late-autumn festival marking the fall harvest and the aftermath of the exodus from Egypt, during which period, according to the Torah, the Israelites lived a nomadic desert existence in temporary dwellings for forty years. *Sukah*: Literally, "booth" or temporary dwelling; a gaily decorated roofless shack in which Jewish men are traditionally required to reside and dine during the eight days of Sukot.

involved in a Conservative congregation during those years. She felt more at home there. There was a group of ex-hippies, very "sixties" people who had come to live in Israel, and they wanted something very Jewish but not Orthodox. So she was involved in that, more so than me, at that point.

Our older daughter started out in the religious stream of the public schools, with an ultra-Orthodox teacher—they often had ultra-Orthodox teachers in the government religious schools. I remember her coming home one afternoon, and deciding that she was going to do what her teacher Sarah told her to do, and she put a pail of water under her bed, so that when she got up in the morning, before she did anything else, she could wash away her ritual impurity.

But our kids went through a metamorphosis over the years—this particular daughter just finished high school in a secular high school. It wasn't like one day we woke up and said, everything is thrown out the window, nevermore—which I've heard some people do. With us it was a very gradual process. We still keep kosher. But my younger daughter has announced that the day she turns eighteen, she's going to have a shrimp party and videotape it. She thinks we're terribly hypocritical. I said, "When you're eighteen you can do what you want, until then. . . . "

We're fairly traditional about holidays. This past Passover, my oldest daughter said, "For secular Jews, we do an awful lot of cleaning for Passover. Really, this is not necessary." But we're very traditional, even though it's an untenable position to be in. At a certain point, we were Sabbath-observant to the point of not turning on the TV and not using electrical appliances— but I would never go to synagogue. And that was very difficult, because that meant we weren't part of the religious community, on the one hand, but on the other hand, all of our secular friends were off hiking or on car trips on Shabbat, and we were sitting at home, because we didn't ride on Shabbat. That was absurd, it was the worst of both worlds.

It finally just got, you know, too schizophrenic, and we had a heart-to-heart conversation, the kids were away, and we had this conversation that lasted twelve hours. And one of the things that we decided was that it was impossible to continue like this. In the States, it's different—OK, Saturday you don't do anything, but you've got Sunday to go on family trips or do whatever, so it's possible. But in Israel at that point you only had Shabbat, and to stay home on Shabbat but not to have religious friends was awful. So we decided that we would be secular, and eventually we started traveling on Shabbat and everything.

For a long time, I felt that my relationship with the gay community was, like, "there but for the grace of God go I"—if I weren't married and weren't this and that and the other, then maybe I would have turned out this way. We had these friends who had a gay couple visiting them, and I met them, and, particularly with these friends, the subject came up very frequently for one reason or another. And I was certainly sympathetic, but not involved. I didn't say to myself, I am gay—I said I have tendencies, or I'm interested, or maybe I would have been, if I hadn't. . . . But I didn't identify myself as gay.

I remember a stage where I was into buying magazines. I'd go to used bookstores and buy old copies of *Playboy* and *Playgirl*—the *Playboy* was just to give me a "cover." I didn't want to make my interest too obvious to the cashier, so I got a little of each, you know, for him and for her, sort of. And at that point, someone at Steimatsky's, the major chain of Israeli bookstores, was going over the copies of *Playgirl* with a black magic marker, and inking out all the essential parts on the male models. I still have those old magazines. The women were certainly fully exposed, in *Playboy*, but the men in *Playgirl*, this was apparently too much. So someone at Steimatsky's had the job—I don't know why I didn't apply for it—of going over every single copy of *Playgirl* sold in Israel and inking out the essential parts. This was in the early '80s.

The first time I saw a gay film I was kind of disturbed. It was, like, I was so unused to seeing things like that. It took getting used to. We had no gay friends, we didn't know anyone. There were no role models, no one to say, well, you know, this is an option, or that's an option, or people do it like this. Now, it looks almost absurd, looking back, but it took a conscious effort to cultivate friends and to look for connections. It wasn't at all obvious. We were living this suburban existence—two kids, three bedrooms. And no one around is gay. Even to this day, it's like a subculture that's transparent—if you're not looking for it, if you're not cultivating it, it just goes right past you. You don't see it anywhere. And lots of people, even if they see it they don't see it, you know. Like my father-in-law, he said at one point, when the topic came up, as it does very frequently in that family for some reason or other, and I don't initiate it—he said, "I don't know anyone who's gay. Never met anyone." So my wife said, "But your nephew, your own nephew was gay, he died of AIDS last year." "Oh, but I don't really know anyone who's gay." It's like, he knows, it's just that he prefers not to know, so in effect he really doesn't know. So for him, the only people in the world who are gay are the ones who hang out in Independence Park in the wee hours and do who-knows-what in the bushes. But he doesn't know anyone like that, so obviously he can't sympathize with them.

Around this time, my father moved to Israel. My mother had already passed away. My father retired, sold his house in America, moved here, bought an apartment, started renovations—and two months later, he died. And that really threw me for a loop, in all kinds of ways. I was in a real crisis for several months. Somehow, you know, everything came to a head. It's like, maybe the experience of losing a parent is like all of a sudden growing up, even though it's at a later age. But all of a sudden, it's like, you have no one you can turn to, even theoretically. I don't know, but for one reason or another, everything got shaken up.

It was, like, a time of reevaluating everything, from A to Z. And of course, my being gay, which had been cooking and cooking and cooking on that back burner, was also mixed up in things. So after my father died I went back into therapy. And this time I really wanted to talk about being gay. And I remember going to the therapist I was working with, after my friend came out to me, and saying to him, "You know, there are people out there, you just have to open your eyes." And he said, "Yes, it's true." And I realized at that point that he himself was gay. He was living with another man—he had introduced him as his "partner," and I had assumed that he was his business partner. Subsequently at some point he told me directly that he was gay—I was the first of his patients that he had ever come out to, and it actually was very helpful to me. I remember saying to him that he was a role model, not meaning that I wanted to live my life the way he did, but that he taught me that you can be gay and still live after that. I mean, you have your ups and your downs, but it's not the end. It was, like, significant to me that here, you could be gay, and it wasn't the end of the story—he was still alive, still around to tell of it, you know.

For a while it seemed like everything was spinning, like everything was going around, and there was nothing stable, there was nothing to hold on to. Like you're in a whirlpool. You know, I had this identity of being religious and being a social worker and being heterosexual. I was married and a father—that was my identity. But all of a sudden I needed to reevaluate who I was. And I remember saying to my wife that I had found a new identity—"I'm gay. That's who I am. I'm attracted to men. It's a very important part of me. That's who I am." And she said to me, "You can't have an identity based on sex. That's not an identity. You can have an identity based on work, you can have an identity based on where you come from, your background, your nationality—you're Israeli, you're American. But sex?" And I remember saying to her, "I'll have an identity any way I want. You're not going to tell me what to put into my identity. If that's important to me, that's what I am. That's what I'm going to be. You have an identity based on your work, I have an identity based on something else." It was a crisis. It took a while for her to accept that.

I wouldn't say that being gay means being exclusively attracted to men. Because I'm attracted to my wife. We have sex. I enjoy it and she seems to enjoy it too. You know, we've had ups and downs in our sex life. And I think that, ironically, this helped. I always used to say, "You don't fulfill me"—not in so many words, but there was always something missing, it wasn't enough, it wasn't right. And that kind of made her feel horrible, kind of like giving up in advance. But now, all of sudden there wasn't that pressure on her, or on us. All of sudden I could put a label on it and say why, and it made it much easier. I said, "Look, I'm attracted to men, I don't expect you to fulfill that. It'll be nice together, but, you know, it's not what I dream about in my head."

There's a difference between saying and accepting something. It's a process of internalization. I've come across other people who say "My wife knows." But it's really not the same thing, because their wives say, "OK, you've told me, now do what you have to do and I don't want it ever talked about again. If you have to, go to the sauna, or if you have to, go to the park. But do it on your own time. I don't want to know about it, don't want to hear about it, don't want to see." And she "knows." But it's so different—it's not internalized, it's not accepted. But I went through a very long process with my wife to make sure we could talk about it.

You know, I feel a little funny. I mean, I feel like I'm telling you all these things about myself, and it's a very funny feeling—it's kind of exposing. It kind of feels, well, it feels like kind of a false sense of intimacy or something. I mean here I am telling you all these things, and you're listening—I mean, obviously, otherwise I wouldn't continue talking, you're good listeners. But I feel like, I know so little about you. I'd really like to ask you some questions.

I think the same is true even with a regular reporter. If someone has a very personal story, and tells it to a reporter, the person might feel that the reporter really understands him, and because of this understanding, that they have somehow become close, and sympathetic to one another. Or like in therapy, where one side tells everything, and the other side listens very sympathetically. And you walk away saying, "We're friends." But it's not that way at all. I mean, the reporter or the therapist might walk away and say, "Gee, I'm glad that's done, one hour a week is plenty. This guy's nuts." But that's the situation. So let's start from the beginning—tell me about your childhood. No, I'm just kidding. But let's do this. I would really like to, at some point, get together with you both for a friendly conversation, without all this equipment. Because I'm getting a certain perspective on myself from this conversation, which may be what you're trying to get as well, in a more general sense. And it would make me feel better. Deal?

So after my father died, there was a period of a great crisis in my relationship with my wife. I think that we were close to being divorced at that point. I felt very claustrophobic, for a while, very suffocated in this suburban, yuppie family existence. I was really going crazy, I really couldn't live like that, and something had to change. And this was really very difficult for my wife, because I think she, even more than I did, she had internalized this Hollywood myth about getting married, being faithful to each other and living happily ever after—you know, this perfect monogamous couple, that fulfills each other's needs and loves each other without any problems, without any questions, and goes off into the sunset or something. My wife had to give up finally, totally, and completely on this myth that maybe if we would just work on our marriage more, we would be able to live happily ever after, and we wouldn't need to look outside for anything.

I think that it's also very common among wives of gay men that they feel guilty—as if they caused it, as if because of their own inadequacy or something or other that they did wrong, they pushed their husbands into looking outside. And, you know, it's a struggle to reframe things and explain that it isn't like that at all—after all, I would be looking outside in different directions if that were the only problem. If that were the case, I wouldn't necessarily look outside to be with men, I'd look outside to be with women. Lots of people do that. So this constant direction outside to look for a man is clearly not because of her.

She felt very threatened, but she came to terms with it. It was a process of, sort of, renegotiating the terms of our relationship to make enough space, well, for both of us. Sometimes we laugh and we say that to get married at age twenty-one or twenty-two and to keep it going for so long is really kind of crazy. And I say, "Well, you know, we don't actually have a marriage that lasted twenty years—we kind of started all over again about ten years down the road." Things changed so radically between us—I mean, it's like I'm not the same person—we both grew, we both changed. We're different people.

Except for the fact that I am attracted to men, I'm very happy with my situation. We're great partners, we get along very well, we understand each other, we support each other. Just yesterday, my daughter said something that kind of blew me away—she said, "You and Mom are so close. A lot of parents of kids that I know aren't like that." And she had a little insight there, I think. It's true.

But we had to go through a period of a lot of difficulties, and a lot of negotiations also—about how to fit in my needs and her needs, in a way that, well, minimized people getting hurt. We renegotiated things. And the decision that we made, and that we've lived with since, is that we should be open about everything to each other. Because, you know, while there are no guarantees about what the future will bring, at least we'll go into it with our eyes wide open and our heads clear. My wife's worst nightmare was that all of sudden I would come to her and say, "Well, I've been having this hot and heavy affair for the last year and a half every day, and I've decided to move out." *Fait accompli.* So we decided that it's much better that, if something develops, she can see it coming. And if it happens it happens. I mean, even with heterosexual couples, who can guarantee the future? All I can say is that at the moment I'm certainly not looking for a different relationship, and I don't think I will in the future.

For a while I was reading newspapers obsessively and looking for items about people who were gay. But the things that were in the newspapers were all negative. That was when they had lots of articles about Zalman Shoshi, the transsexual prostitute. There was a big scandal with him, and he was put in prison for extortion. And I remember an article in *Yediᶜot Aharonot* called something like, "The Night Life of Tel Aviv." It was divided into two parts— one part was about Tel Baruḥ and all the prostitution there, and the other part was about Independence Park and the gays, you know. And these two, together, were supposed to represent the smutty, dirty underside of Tel Aviv, you know—as if to say that what goes on in Independence Park is the equivalent of the prostitution, drug addiction, and exploitation that goes on in Tel Baruḥ, you know, with those pitiful women there. And that was what they were printing in the newspapers.

But at that point, Ilan Schoenfeld wrote a book of Hebrew poetry about gay subjects, and it was published. And the newspapers made a big fuss over it. It was called *Lines to a Friend in Parting*—he wrote it around the time that his lover died. And I remember writing him a letter. I just said how impressed I was that two men could be in love like that, in this country. It just seemed so novel to me, you know, I didn't know there were any relationships like that. This, maybe, is indicative of how isolated I was, or how naive I was.

But just how do you connect yourself to a community when there's no publicity, no nothing? It was very difficult, very difficult to meet people. I wasn't able to go to a gay bar at night or something, not that there were any anywhere outside of Tel Aviv. At that point, even in Jerusalem, the only thing to do was to go to the park. So I found it difficult to make my way into this community.

We did have this cousin, in the States, and it was common knowledge in the family that he was gay, but it was not public knowledge—I mean, he wouldn't admit it. When we would visit the States, it was very strained, because I was trying to be open, trying to be sympathetic, trying to kind of open up a door, and he was completely closed. I mean, it's like, any hint I made, any comment I made, fell flat, instead of getting a response. I finally wrote him a letter, I kind of sat on the fence and said something like, "You know, I've had enough doubts and thoughts of my own to really understand that you're not interested in getting married—that's OK." And he finally picked up on the hint, and said, "Oh, you're gay."

From then on, we kept up this relationship by letter, we kept writing. We were very open, and my wife was writing also, and we got closer to him as a result, and this glass wall he had around him, where you couldn't touch him, kind of fell down. Subsequently, it turned out that his lover got sick and fairly quickly died of AIDS, and my cousin himself was HIV-positive. But after he found this out he met someone new, and they were together for several years. He died recently.

I guess it was part of my process of coming out to, you know, try to reach out and make a connection with someone like this. And it was also part of the process that this was talked about freely with my kids, even before I came out to them—you know, this person is gay, and we're writing to him, and he's living with so-and-so, and we got a letter from him, and he said such-and-such. It was part of the whole process of introducing being gay into the family, instead of its being something foreign and distasteful.

My kids know that I'm gay now. They feel like Dad's got this thing going on in his head—his craziness. And my wife says, "Well, we have to humor him. If he thinks he's gay, well then, let him be gay." It's that kind of thing. I don't think that in growing up, as teenagers, they need to know the details of what their parents do. They ask us questions all the time, "Were you a virgin when you got married?" "Did you ever have sex with someone else?" and we don't answer. We say, "That's something we don't talk about." You know, we'll talk on the general subject, but we don't want to talk about what we do.

I wanted to be out of the closet at home. I wanted to feel comfortable with myself as much as possible. Some married men don't even tell their wives—they lead double lives. But I couldn't live like that. And, you know, I'm close to my children, and I want them to feel close to me. I want them to know who their father is. I've heard of stories of children finding out at a later age that their parents were gay, and feeling terribly betrayed. Because this is something very important about their father that he hid from them. Why? He didn't trust them? Suddenly the person they loved, you know, seems like a different person. "How could he?" You know, it's a shock. And I didn't want that to happen.

With the first one, it didn't work out exactly as I would have hoped. At some point in this whole process of dealing with my being gay and dealing with my own particular problems besides, I went to see someone who was supposed to be the best therapist in Jerusalem. He happened to be a psychiatrist. And he said that he couldn't see me, he didn't have an opening, but he would do an "intake," and then he would recommend someone to me. And if he's the best therapist in Jerusalem he must know what he's doing, right? So I went to him, and he asked me lots of questions, very intimate questions. Am I passive or am I active? What position do I like to do it in? And so on.

He told me that being gay is like having a stomachache—we won't know what the causes are until you go into therapy, whether it's very serious, or whether it's kind of a light case! And I remember coming back from talking to him, and—I didn't react so much when I was there, but afterwards I was just up the wall. I said, "I don't buy that—a stomachache is not good, even if it's a light case." You know, it's not something that's normative. At some point, I remember, I felt like being gay was like being short. You know, something inconvenient to live with, but certainly within the norm. At a later stage I felt like it was like having brown eyes or something—it's just different, and lots of people are like that. But even at that stage, I couldn't accept that it was a stomachache.

So I remember telling my wife how upset I was about this, and my daughter overheard us, through the partly open door. And she put two and two together, and said to my wife, "Is Dad gay?" She was very upset for a few hours. You know, "What else are you hiding from me? What else don't I know?" that kind of thing. She was thirteen, I think. And we calmed her down, basically, and she didn't have any problems with the actual fact.

You have to remember, I had over the years made an effort to bring friends home who were gay, and to maintain contact with this cousin who was gay, and I read about the subject a lot and went to see movies and talked about it. So, you know, it wasn't like the idea of being gay itself was a shock or a problem. It was just that all of a sudden, you know, "What have you been hiding from me? What dark deep secrets are there that I don't know about?" But it wasn't a big issue. It was a few hours where she was upset, and she got over it.

And two years later my younger daughter found out—the way it worked out was much more to my liking. We were kind of doing a day's vacation trip in Tel Aviv, and we were at the beach, and we had to decide what film to see in the evening. At that point *Torch Song Trilogy* was playing in Tel Aviv, for a short period. And I'd read the review, and I said I'd really like to see the movie. I was in the waves with my daughter, and she said, "How come, Dad, you always want to see gay movies, and all you read is gay books, and all your friends are gay?" And I said, "Well, I guess I have some tendencies in that direction myself." And she said, "Oh, that makes sense."

I feel very comfortable in my family, and they're very protective of me, in a way. Once we brought the dog with us to visit my in-laws, and my daughter was kissing the dog. And my father-in-law says, "Yuck! Don't kiss him!" And my daughter says, "It's not a him, it's a her!" And he says, "That's worse!" And she says, "What difference does it make!" Another time, they were showing *Maurice* on TV, and my father-in-law and mother-in-law were at our house for dinner, and we sat down to watch the movie. And my father-in-law was going, "Yuck, feh, ick," and so on. So my daughter turned off the TV and said, "Grandpa, either you shut up, or you go home." So it's almost like, in a way, they're in the closet too, with me, to some extent.

I don't think that I've had any influence on their sexuality. If someone is gay, lesbian, or straight, I think it's something that's very deep down inside—nothing that I do is going to change it. And I think that it's very healthy for them to know about their father, because they're growing up with a feeling that things are not like Hollywood. You know, we're close, my wife and I, but we're not this ideal couple where everything is just Leave-It-To-Beaver wonderful. And I think, you know, growing up, they're going to have their own problems, I don't know what kind. But they'll need to confront reality and whatever life is going to dish out to them, and this way at least they have an example of, OK, there are other people that deal with problems, and difficult situations, and you know, life is not just a rose garden and a lot of Hollywood platitudes. I think that's good.

I get the sense that, in both the general community and the gay community, people like to pretend we don't exist, gay married men. But I have a feeling that there are a lot of people out there. Because Israel has been a very conservative society, very family-oriented, very child-oriented. And people got married young in the past, not just the religious element, but everyone, compared to the States. People eat dinner with their parents every Friday night, and everyone is physically close together. There's a lot of pressure to get married and have children. This is a very, kind of, enmeshed society. So I think there are a lot of people out there.

I think that most of the people who go to the sauna are married. I mean, it's almost funny—it's busy from three in the afternoon until about seven at night, and then it empties out completely. Because everyone stops over on their way home from work. You know, they could "work late" until seven o'clock or something, but then they have to go home. It's very obvious. Otherwise, why would everyone go at three, four in the afternoon?

There are certainly a lot of gay religious men who are married. And that's an even more difficult situation to be in. You know, sometimes you come across someone who's so deep in the closet it hurts. People saying that if someone found out, "I'd lose my family, I'd have to get divorced, I'd lose my job." And what hurts even more is to hear people saying that their children make homophobic statements—you know, the kids make funny comments about fags or whatnot, and the father doesn't want to say anything because he doesn't want to expose his own tendencies. So he just has to kind of live with it. I don't know what the way out is. A lot of people are very closeted, leading double lives, very scared of being found out.

What's interesting about Israeli society is that on the one hand, you've got the religious, and all their crazy reactions. And on the other hand, in a lot of ways, this is a very liberal society. You don't really have phenomena like gay bashing. Not at all like the States. True, it might be that the hatred, the violence is directed toward other channels. But you have examples of couples who are even more open with each other than we are, who got married knowing in advance that one or both of them was gay. I've heard of one story where a woman was, I guess, in her midthirties, she wanted a family, she wanted children. And she was very friendly with a certain gay man, who had a lover. He was fairly well-to-do, and she married him. They have a family, and she has a house and financial security, and he's a very good father. And once or twice a week he spends the night with his lover. I've also heard of gays marrying lesbians, two or three stories like that. There's one couple I know personally.

But if we're talking about more conventional gay men who are married to women, it's a difficult situation to be in. I think that very few people are as comfortable with it as we are. I'm very fortunate. It was a lot of hard work on our part, but I'm very comfortable with my wife and with my kids, my family. You know, I come home and I don't feel like I'm in the closet. They know that I'm being interviewed for this book.

There was an antigay article in the *Jerusalem Post* not long ago by Rabbi Riskin, who is a pretty well-known Orthodox leader here. His main argument was that the Jewish tradition says you must have children and multiply, and you're cutting yourself off from the possibility of having children by being gay. So it's against Judaism and this, that, and the other. This whole line of argument seems to me really screwy—I mean, why didn't he attack spinsters too, on the same basis? For what it's worth, I did a little figuring in my head—among the gay men in my support group in Tel Aviv, we had nineteen children between us—and we were only five people. I felt like writing Riskin a letter and saying, this is a myth, that if you're gay you don't have children. It's not necessarily so. So does that mean now that being gay is OK? Does he now accept my lifestyle, because I have children? Am I not cutting myself off from the Jewish tradition this way? I mean, the whole thing is ridiculous on his part.

I prefer to think of myself as "homosexual." I think to say "gay" sounds appropriate at times, but also seems like kind of a euphemism—you're kind of skirting the issue. About a year ago, my wife was going for therapy—we're big believers in therapy, or have you noticed—and her therapist apparently said something to her like, "How come your husband says he's homosexual? He cuts you out, by saying he's homosexual. Why doesn't he say he's bisexual? After all, he has relations with you. That's with a woman. That's bisexual, isn't it? Why does he have to define himself as homosexual, because if he's homosexual, what are you doing there in the picture?"

And she came back with that, to try it out as an idea, and I said, "You know, if being bisexual means, anyone who is attracted to women, or has had relations with a woman, then, yes, I'm bisexual, I certainly am. I live my life as a bisexual. I mean, I have sex with women." Well, I have sex with *a* woman. But I said to her that it doesn't fit politically, the way things are. There's a very small minority of homosexual men who have actually never looked at a woman, never touched a woman, never thought of a woman, never considered getting married. So, yes, if things were divided up so that only those men were homosexual, and bisexual was everyone else, who's ever considered, looked at, thought of, or had relations with a woman, I certainly belong to the bisexual category. But it isn't divided up that way. And you know, by my going out and saying, "I'm bisexual," I'm cutting myself off from the homosexual community. I'm saying that I don't belong, I'm something else. And it's more than that. By saying that I'm bisexual, I'm saying that I'm equally attracted in both directions, and I'm not. I'm not! Also, it's perceived as sitting on the fence. "Oh, so you don't accept yourself, you're 'bisexual.' We know what that means." But that's not me.

There was a TV show that I saw a few months ago that was really kind of interesting, it sticks in my mind. It was a *Donahue* show that was on cable TV—finally we have cable, instead of seeing one channel. Progress has come to the Middle East! Anyway, he had these three women on his show, and they were Americans, and each one had one black parent. And the question was, how do they define themselves? Are they white or are they black? And the three women said, "Without any question I am black."

And Donahue was trying to interview them, saying, "Why don't you say you're multiracial, why don't you say you're white, I mean you're fifty percent this way or the other way, why do you say you're black?" And I really identify with these women, because they answered, "If I say I'm multiracial, or I'm mixed, then all of black society is going to reject me, saying that I'm, you know, too uppity to consider myself black, that I want to take advantage of the fact that I have only one black parent to make it in white society." So they said they're black. And they said that in order for them to feel comfortable with themselves, they have to accept that part of themselves. Of course, if you dig down, OK, well, yes, they have a white parent, and they have white relatives that they are close to, but when you belong to a minority group which is basically looked down on, then you can't sit on the fence and feel good about it, because it's like saying, "I'm better than you guys," or something, and that's not where I want to be. That's not at all how I feel.

So I'm a homosexual man living with a woman. That's the way it is. Let me try to put it into terms that are more understood by the gay community—I've met couples who've said, you know, they're together, maybe for several years, and one of them says about the other, "But he really wasn't my type—I always used to look for people that were younger, or more muscular, I never used to look at this type of person, but we met, and you know, unbelievably, we're in love, and we've been together for five years and it's a steady thing." And somehow I feel like, you know, this is the way it is with us. She's not my type, if you're going to talk about types. You know, if I were looking now . . . but we're together, and we're very close, and it works.

WALID

Arab citizens of Israel—"Israeli Arabs"—form a group that is often forgotten by the world. Most headlines are grabbed by a different group, the one and a half million Palestinian Arabs of Gaza and the West Bank, all of whom lived without the rights of citizenship under Israeli military control from 1967 to 1996. But few seem to realize that, of the more than six million people resident within Israel's internationally recognized borders, over one million—18 percent of the population—are also Arab. Most of them are Muslim, although a significant minority are Christian or Druze. They are Israeli citizens, carry Israeli passports, and—officially—have civil rights equal to those of Jewish Israelis, although most are not drafted into the Israeli army. Of course, one may well wonder what it can mean to be a non-Jewish-yet-equal citizen of the "Jewish state."

In spite of Amir's rather right-wing take on Zionism, he was fully in agreement with me that an interview with an Israeli Arab would form a necessary component of our book if we were to make any pretense of providing a comprehensive picture of the experience of being Israeli and gay. A friend of ours—an avowed computer junkie—told us that he had met someone "on line" who seemed just right: "Walid" was an Israeli Arab who lived with his parents in Haifa, where he was a college student. We made contact with him, and he was willing to talk to us, although the logistics here were once again a bit complicated. Walid's home was out of the question, and there was no chance of privacy at Amir's parents' Haifa apartment either. In the end, Tomer, Amir's high school buddy, came to the rescue: his parents were traveling, and he said that we were welcome to perform the interview at his place. We arranged to meet Walid and head over together.

At Tomer's parents' apartment we settled into a spare room—one of those frozen-in-time, former-child's bedrooms so characteristic of empty-nest homes— and we began our chat. Seeing Walid on an Israeli street, you would be unlikely to identify his jeans-and-sweatshirt style of dress, his dark, slightly pudgy features, or his slight build as distinctively Arab in any way. There was no denying that Walid's Hebrew was accented: his r's tripped delicately off his tongue, instead of falling harshly into his throat, as with most native speakers. Yet Israel is a nation of immigrants, and in comparison with the cacophony of contortions to which the language is daily subjected by Jews, Walid's language was only subtly distinguished.

~

I HAD A NICE, NORMAL CHILDHOOD, just like other kids my age in Haifa. My parents didn't fight, and we all got along. I went to a Catholic school. It was run by nuns. I was there up through eighth grade, and afterwards, I went to an Eastern Orthodox Christian school. My parents aren't religious, but the good Arab schools in Haifa are all private schools, and who runs private schools besides religious institutions?

I never remember going with my mother and my father on Sunday to church to pray. Not once. In school we did it a few times a year, and that was that. It was not that there was a huge conflict here—don't get the impression that this was a very religious school. Yes, there were the nuns, and there was a church there, and we prayed sometimes, but there were also students of other religions, there were a lot of Muslims and even a few Druse and Baha'is.[§] There were no Jews.

This model exists in the minds of Jews, that, like, there is this separation between Arab Muslims and Christians. But it doesn't really exist among Arabs. I don't know, I never felt it as strongly as it is described in Hebrew books and journalism. It never came up with my friends. Maybe just in jokes. I choose my friends because all of them are enlightened people, not religious at all. It doesn't make a difference if their background is Christian or Muslim.

Both of my parents work in education. They weren't born in Haifa, but they have lived here for a very long time. They are both from the Galilee

[§] Druse: Followers of a small religious sect that split from Islam in the eleventh century; concentrated in northern Israel, southern Syria, and Lebanon. Baha'i: Religious sect of Persian origins, founded in 1844; international headquarters are located in Haifa.

area. Both of the villages, my father's and my mother's, after 1948, ceased to exist. What do you want—it was a war, the villages were destroyed. If you wanted to put it in political terms, you could say that they were refugees in their own country. They went from place to place until they settled down in Haifa, twenty-six years ago.

Growing up in Haifa, I was never conscious of being a minority. It depends, from the start, what there is for you to compare yourself with. And I don't know, I never, in my childhood, compared myself to Jewish kids my age. I never felt different or something, because I never went to a Jewish school, I didn't go to a Jewish school. So, because your environment is basically homogeneously Arab, you don't feel different.

My neighborhood was once the symbol of coexistence. It has changed, in a slow process that began about ten years ago. All of the Jewish young people moved away, and only the old people are left, and they are getting fewer with the years, until now I figure that the population is about 95 percent Arab and 5 percent Jewish. It may be that the Russian immigration has changed that a little, but not a lot.

This kind of difference is a thing you don't talk about at home. A kid lives it, he, like, grows up with it. Someone who is growing up in an all-Arab village in the countryside would have a very different experience. Because, in spite of everything, I did have some contact with Jews, there is cooperation, on the bus, in the street, in the market, in life in general, and you see them. And you always meet Jews, some your own age, and even some of your parents' friends are part of that "other people," if you want to put it that way. So you live it, but you don't talk about it. Things that you live, and you feel all the time, you don't need to talk about. It is a matter for all sorts of psychologists who come from the outside and begin talking about it. But you live it, you don't feel it.

There was practically no sex education in school. I remember discussions on the subject of sex with a priest, or something like that, who explained everything in a very funny scientific manner. I remember that we all laughed at it, because it sounded more like a caricature than sex ed. And of course they did it for boys and girls separately.

There wasn't a total taboo about talking about sex at home, but it wasn't, like, a subject for Friday night dinner conversation. We would talk about it when it came up, if we saw something on television, maybe, or if we heard a joke. My father never took me aside to have a talk or anything like that. He never explained anything. But we talked about it when it came up—it wasn't, "this is how it is done," it wasn't "education," it was just conversations about sex. But I don't remember that homosexuality ever came up at home. Not even in jokes or insults.

It is difficult for me to reconstruct the first time I felt that I am, basically, gay. But I don't think it was at a very young age. It may be that as a boy I felt something and I didn't know how to explain it, that is also possible. But I wouldn't say that I felt different from all the others in this respect. I never remember having any problems socially. When they talked about girls, I can't say that I found it particularly interesting, but I didn't suffer either. There were pornographic magazines that made their way around school, of course. They weren't gay magazines, they were regular ones, with women and men. I would look at them too. It wasn't a matter of playing along, you can't say that at all. It just wasn't an issue. I wasn't aware of anything.

Later on, I remember that I would look for items in the newspaper. I always remember myself reading the newspaper on Fridays, even at sixteen, and I remember that I would read the articles on the subject. I am talking about the Hebrew newspapers. I have yet to see news items on the subject in Arabic.

Let me tell you about the first time I told someone that I am, like, gay. I was almost seventeen. It was after reading an article in the newspaper. I remember that it was in 1986. There was a story in the Friday supplement of *Yediᶜot Aḥaronot*, a very long article, four pages, about an American guy who was found guilty of the manslaughter of his brother's friend. Do you know the story? His father was a lawyer, the family was of high socioeconomic standing. He was "like that," but his parents didn't know about him, of course. He was graduating high school and wanted to throw a party for guys he had met through computer talk-lines. So he had the party in his parents' summer house, while they were in another city altogether. Anyway, his brother and his brother's friend wanted to play a practical joke on him—so they eavesdropped on his conversations when he was inviting his friends, and that is when they found out that he was "like that." And in the middle of the party they came and surprised him, and afterwards, they went to this guy's parents, and told them that they, like, caught him with his pants down with someone, or something—I don't know what exactly. Afterwards, this guy asked them to go back to his parents and tell them that it was all a lie. They didn't exactly agree, so this guy stole his mother's credit card, ran away from home, and bought a gun. And he waited for his brother's friend in a parking lot somewhere, drove up behind him, closed him into his parking space, they argued, and then he took out his gun, fired a round of bullets into him, and ran away. He was a fugitive for two months, and then he turned himself in. That is the story.

Reading this story was the first time I identified with someone "like that" in a very strong way. Really, I think I read it, like, three or four times. It really got to me. It was a very radical story. I really identified with that guy. It was written so beautifully, I don't know. I was very moved. So I brought the subject up in conversation with someone who was then a good friend of mine. It was in the middle of twelfth grade, if I remember correctly. It wasn't like I had made a decision to tell him. It just came naturally in the course of the conversation. I told this friend of mine the story, and I said that I wouldn't want that to happen to me, and then I took the opportunity to say that I am "like that." He was very surprised. At first he didn't really believe me, but afterwards he did. And after a few days he got used to it. We are still friends. It wasn't a sudden, dramatic thing, for me. It was a process, and this was in some way, like, the culmination.

The whole thing was something that developed together with me, and only afterwards did I find a name for it. But I did finally define myself as gay before I had any sexual experience. I was certain about my definition without having to "check" it. My first sexual contact was more than a year after I talked to this friend.

I never tried to change myself. I never felt like this was something forbidden, terrible, and awful. I still don't feel that way. I never felt like this was going to make a mess out of my life or something. I don't know, I just didn't think. I knew that this is what I am, and that's it. You deal with it. Suddenly, as a seventeen-year-old kid, am I supposed to think about what will happen to me when I am sixty-five, old, and without children or something? Everyone has his own way of dealing with things, and it may be that I deliberately avoided thinking about it, but I don't remember myself in, like, week-long crying fits of depression, or anything like that. Not even close.

During this time I was always on the lookout for information on the subject. I read a lot of books. Really, a lot. I felt that I needed to learn a lot more, so that if there was an argument I would win. And that's it. I began to think about it a lot more, also. I remember myself reading the chapter about homosexuality in every book on the subject of sex I could find. They all said basically the same thing, I don't remember a lot of differences between them.

The books were all in Hebrew, except for one in Arabic, a very old Egyptian book. It said ridiculous things, but I didn't let that bother me. It said things so far removed from what I knew, I could just laugh at it. Things like that don't get to me—I know that it is the others who are wrong, and not me. That was always my approach. If I read something that said that homosexuality is a perversion and a terrible act, then it was the book that was wrong, and not me.

I always thought this way. I made a selection. Things that reinforced myself I adopted, and things that opposed me I rejected. Not everyone agrees about everything. Not everyone thinks the same. So I agree with some and not with others. I mean, is someone else going to tell me what I am? That can't be. There is a limit to how much I believe what psychologists say. I can explain why there are some of them who believe that you can change yourself, it is obvious to me—parents will not hesitate to send their children to someone who has a "cure," and every session costs a hundred and fifty shekels. So there will always be psychologists who say they have a "cure."

In Arabic, the word you use is *homo*, like in Hebrew. It is basically a derogatory word. I have yet to find a word for it in Arabic with a positive connotation, I don't know. The pseudo-scientific term for it in Arabic is "sexual perversion"—when you talk about "the sexual perversion," you are talking about homosexuality. That is the most common literary term. "The sexual perversion." Some people also use the word *Luti*, which comes from the story of Lot in the Bible. But on the street, the word people use is *homo*. It may be that there is slang in other Arab countries, I assume that there is Egyptian slang, for instance, but it doesn't reach us, because this is a different society.

At some point, my friend said that he wanted to tell someone else, who was also in the same class and also a friend of ours, and I said I had no problem with this, so we told him together. He was a little shocked, but people deal with it. He couldn't run away, we were in the same class, after all. You can't just put your head in the sand, so you deal. When you lay the cards on the table, people have to deal with it. And they do.

My relationship with my friends never included a lot of physical contact even before I told them, but afterwards, it was clear that they were being careful to avoid it. To avoid any accidental misunderstandings. It wasn't nice—it was really not nice. But I knew that there was nothing I could do. I understood why they did what they did.

It may be that someone who comes from the outside might, like, imagine that Arab boys have sexual relationships among themselves. I can see that. Because you often see friends holding hands in the street, which Jews don't do, for instance. But it doesn't mean anything. It is just natural, it just means they are good friends. I never held hands with my friends or anything like that, but I saw that others did. It is not unusual to see men walking along holding hands or embracing. But it is difficult for me to believe that it reaches a sexual stage beyond that. I remember that once I read somewhere a description of the Arab *debqah* folk dance as a basically homosexual dance. It was very funny, because I see it as a very masculine, macho thing. But the fact is that, in this dance, the men are all embracing one another. But Arab culture is a different culture. You can't look at it with Western eyes, that is what I am trying to say. I don't think that there is any sexual element in it when Arab men embrace.

You are not unusual if you don't date girls in high school. It is not out of the ordinary to hear a mother saying, "I am so proud of my son—he doesn't go out with girls." You can hear that sentence. Sure, among the other boys, you can get known as a kind of nerd, if you are not interested in girls, but nothing awful. Nothing more than that. That was me. A good student, good grades, obedient, a nice boy. I think that there are people who were in my class who still think of me that way. The ones that don't know about me.

I didn't feel any pressure or tension or problems from the people around me. It may be that it was just that I told the right people. They had no choice but to be with me, and they wanted to stay on good terms with me—they needed help in physics and chemistry! When I think about it now, they really needed me, a lot of them. So I told them, and it was a relief.

At this point, I began to look around. This is the point where I had come to terms with myself, and I could step out and begin looking for what I wanted. The first thing I did was to buy a pornographic video. Beginning in tenth grade, I worked on the weekends in a minimarket, and I had money from that. At that time, there was only one store in Haifa where you could buy such videos. I went in, asked for a video "like that," and he gave me one. It was French. I still remember it—it was a good movie. I wasn't disappointed. I had total privacy at home, there was no problem with that. And since then, I have always had one movie or another in my drawer, and no one has ever found it.

I thought about, like, telling my parents at some point, but I decided to postpone it in the end. They still don't know. It may be that they have their suspicions, but nothing more. I have never brought up the subject, and neither have they. I changed my mind because I just said to myself that there would be no turning back, and it may be better to wait. When you tell them, you have to be ready with a backup plan for the worst-case scenario, and I didn't have one.

The worst possible scenario would be that I would have to leave home for a certain period. And you need money for that. At the time, I didn't really have any money. I remember a point, up to when I finished high school, when I was working very hard after school, so that I would have money, so that, like, I would be able to live without taking any money from them, even if I had to pay my own college tuition. I remember the stash that was sitting on the side for three years, so that, if they found something out, and I needed to get out of there quickly, I would be able to get by for a month, a month and a half. I had $1,500 at one point, I remember. It wasn't that I lived in fear of being thrown out, but I just thought that it was a good idea to be prepared. You have got to be ready for anything—and I didn't want to live on the street.

I don't know what my parents would think. There are several possible scenarios, from total disbelief to acceptance. I don't know. I figure that it could also be that it will be difficult for them, but in the end they will accept it. At least that is what I think now. The moment I can support myself, I will tell them. At that point, there won't be any reason to hide it from them. If they figure things out on their own, then I won't deny anything, of course. I always knew that, that if they figured things out, then I wouldn't deny it. But I won't bring it up on my own initiative, not now.

I never intentionally left clues for them or anything, but there were a few times when I made mistakes. I remember that once I left the video in the machine, and it sat there all day. In this case no one had used the machine, so it was OK. Another time, I left *Maga°im* out on my bed. I know that my mother straightened the house that day, but apparently she didn't notice, I don't know. I saw it on the side of the bed later on that day, it had been moved. But I don't know. It could be that she figured it out, and just isn't saying anything. But maybe not, because I had left the magazine open to a page of printed text—there wasn't any picture or anything there that would have jumped out at you. There are a few pages like that in *Maga°im* too.

After I graduated high school I went on to the Technion. I study industrial management there now. I still live at home. The army never even came up as a possibility. Why in the world would I think about going into the army? Why waste three years that I could spend studying? Besides, the army never sent me anything—they don't see fit to draft Arabs, so why should I go out of my way? I can't understand the Arabs who volunteer. They do it for their own reasons.

I began taking classes at the Technion when I was still in high school, so it wasn't really a drastic change for me. There is no social life at the Technion. Everyone knows that. There was a time while I was politically active in the Arab students' organization, but not to any great extent. I came to the conclusion that the organization should be dismantled, because, like, it was doing more harm to coexistence on campus than anything else. My friends on campus are both Jewish and Arab, although I am the only Arab student in my department. There are other departments with greater numbers.

After the video stage, I began to feel that I really had to find someone. That I needed to meet people, flesh and blood people. It was clear to me from the very start that I was not going to try to meet Arabs. It is something that I never really thought about, really, looking for someone Arab. I don't know why. It wasn't that I wasn't attracted to other Arabs. But this was a case of a part of my life that I lived in Hebrew.

We speak Arabic at home, of course, but Arab schools begin to teach Hebrew in third grade. Today, I can think in both Arabic and Hebrew. It depends on the subject. I can't think about engineering in Arabic—I am not used to living with the Arabic technical vocabulary. Likewise, homosexuality is something I live in Hebrew, and not in Arabic. So it was clear that I would meet Jewish men. Even in the face of the difference between Jews and Arabs, I think it is much easier to meet Jews, to be the boyfriend of a Jewish guy than an Arab. Arab gay men are much more difficult to find.

I knew what was going on in the park, but I never went in there, because, I don't know, it frightened me. Everyone knows about the park, even in Arab society. It is known that the park is a meeting place for gays. I always knew, but I never went there at night. It was, I don't know, a fear. I still don't think it is a very pleasant place. Not that I have got something against it, but it is not for me—so dark, you can't see anything, the whole atmosphere is as if you are doing something wrong. And that really bothers me. That is what keeps me from going there, that is all. You just can't go in there with the feeling that you are doing something good. It is just unpleasant to wander around in the dark. I have heard that some Arabs come from the territories to the park, but I have never met them.

At some point, I began to see the personal ads in the local paper, in *Qol Ḥeifah*. I remember that I began to read them, the gay ads. I never answered any of them, but I would always buy the paper, because I knew that there were ads there. When I try to reconstruct events, I can't remember where my first ad was, but in the end I decided to put my own ad in. I think I put it in *Maga°im*.

The wording I chose was extraordinarily inappropriate—very, like, mature, very unsexy, intellectual, intimidating. A caricature really. I wrote "college student"—I knew at this point that I had been accepted to the Technion, so it wasn't a lie—"college student, Arab, good-looking, humanist, likeable, looking for refined and intelligent young man for long-term, lasting relationship." That's what it was. Really frightening, right? I remember that the only one who answered it the first time was a thirty-five-year-old man. I ended our meeting as quickly as I could.

I put "Arab" in because I didn't want any surprises on the first time. I have seen a lot of ads by now, and you rarely see someone saying that they are Arab, so, I don't know, either most other Arabs don't say they are Arab or don't publish personal ads. I have answered a lot of ads, and I have never answered the ad of someone who didn't say anything and turned out to be Arab. I have no idea what other Arab gays do. I really don't know.

I kept running the ad, and I met a few people, but they were awful. Now I understand that the ad was inappropriate, that it didn't even describe what I wanted. I mean, how many eighteen-year-old kids are looking for a "long-term, lasting relationship"? No one under twenty-five is going to answer such an ad, what with my being Arab on top of it all. That was the problem.

I published a post office box number in the ad, and people wrote me, I wrote them back, they wrote me back, and so on, until we got to the point of giving a telephone number. That was back when we would write six or seven letters back and forth until we got to the telephone number. We would meet, it would be clear that this was not it, and then I would leave. This scene repeated itself a number of times. I usually made sure that it was in a public place, but there were a few times when I went to people's houses. It was very difficult for me to tell people that I wasn't interested. If I got to a meeting, and immediately saw that I wasn't interested, I would just try to get it over with as quickly as possible and then cut off all contact. You don't have to answer letters you get in your post office box. It is a little unpleasant, threatening, even frightening, but there's nothing you can do.

I met, like, about twenty people through this ad, before I finally had my first time. It was very discouraging. That is a lot of letters, and lot of meetings. It was terrible. But I kept on meeting with people—you always have hope. As time went on I learned how to make a better process of elimination before meeting someone. These are things you just develop a sense for.

So I got to someone around the twentieth—maybe he was the eighteenth, maybe the twenty-third, I don't know. I was eighteen and a half years old at the time, I think. We met in his apartment. He had written that he was nineteen, good-looking, and so on. And it was there that I had my first sexual contact. We had sat and talked for about an hour. He was in the army—not that I get my kicks from soldiers. No, really, I have met soldiers of every kind, and they don't do anything for me. Besides, he wasn't a combat soldier, just a clerk. But seriously. . . .

We sat across from each other the whole time, and after about an hour, maybe an hour and a half, he came and sat next to me, and then he asked me if it really was my first time, and I said yes. And he asked if I really wanted to give it a try, and I said yes. And it was already, like, happening. He wasn't looking for a "long-term, lasting relationship," that's for sure. But it was good sex. Afterwards, he didn't believe that it was my first time. I knew what to do—it was just like the movies.

Of course, I felt wonderful afterwards. It was like a dream come true. Would you like me to be dramatic about this, can I be? It really was something beautiful, something different from everything else. And I even told him that. This was a mistake, but that is a different story—it gave him a lot of power.

Anyway, I told him how I felt, at our first meeting, even. I felt that this guy, he was the one I really wanted. And time passed, and we met again, and again, and it kept on that way. But it was very spread out. There were a lot of telephone conversations—our schedules didn't exactly fit, and the conversations were basically about setting dates. You couldn't really say that we had a relationship. We met about once every two months over the course of a year and a half. It was basically, like, sexual. No—it was exclusively sexual.

I wanted something more than that. Like, at least to go to a movie or something. But if you have one meeting every two months, you are better off not wasting your time watching a movie. It was such a new world then, I didn't even know what the standards of behavior were, in this new society that I had entered into. It takes a while to learn. He wanted to meet once every few months—so, apparently, I thought, this is what you do. I had hoped for something different, but, OK, if this is what happens, then that is OK too. It was such a new world that I didn't know what exactly to expect, so I just lived with it.

The period when all this began was also the beginning of the intifadah. I was very strongly aware of the political implications of everything. Yes, I did feel the connection between sex, politics, the army—as the expression goes, "fuck the Arabs"—but then again, I was usually a top. No, no, that's just a joke, just a joke. But seriously, I think I just managed to keep everything separate. I don't know.

You are looking for something dramatic, I understand, so OK. I mean, none of this is really important—it is all just things that you live. But since you want drama, I will give you a drama. I remember once, it was 1988 I think, yes, the intifadah was at its peak, of course. And I went to a political demonstration in the morning, at eight in the morning at the gate of the Technion. I stood there for one very long hour, and I spent the whole time, like, thinking about how I had come home only five hours earlier, at three in the morning, after having had sex with a soldier. And there I was, standing and demonstrating against the occupation. And I just thought about how it didn't make any sense, it didn't fit together. But I don't know, I managed to keep things separate, it is something that is part of life. It is just life.

I think it is really sad that politics determines so many of our human relationships. But it is a fact. And it isn't something that we decided. It is just a fact that we have got to live with, not something we need to talk about.

After I stopped seeing this guy, I began to answer ads again, and to put my own ad in again. But I finally changed the wording. I had lots more meetings that didn't work out, until something finally clicked that continued for three or four months, and I even began to feel that it was a little, like, smothering. It was like, suddenly someone has come into my life who I have to talk to every day, who I have to see two or three times a week. That was a very difficult transition. He was twenty-three. He had finished his army service, he was working, living alone, and looking for a relationship.

I always kept my friends up to date on my personal life. I didn't go so far as to introduce them to my boyfriends, but they knew what was going on. It wasn't like two different worlds—they knew when I had someone new, if I split from someone, if something happened. For them, it was all new. They didn't know anything, so anything I said, they accepted. I was their only source of information, so they believed everything I said. I felt the need to explain to them, so I explained. I didn't see myself as an educator or anything. There was no sense of mission. But I felt the need to talk, so I talked.

I also talked about everything with my new boyfriend. We argued sometimes, but nothing serious. It was a fulfilling, good relationship. I wouldn't define it as a "relationship" if it hadn't been worthwhile.

I don't think I loved him. It wasn't love, it was a close relationship, mutual concern, friendship, but not love. That was why it didn't really last. Three or four months, that's all. It ended very slowly, by mutual agreement. After the first two months of very intimate contact, it got weaker and weaker until we were talking on the phone once every two weeks. The relationship continued much longer than that, but I define it as really only lasting three months.

So it was back to the personals. I met all sorts of people, all sorts of people who I was with for varying lengths of time and with varying degrees of closeness. I always went through a lot of people until I found someone who clicked. It just doesn't work that you meet people and things work out one after another. You have to see ten people and say no to each of them. That was the only way I met people.

I grew up knowing about AIDS. I grew up knowing what safe sex is, and, like, what you need to do, and I live according to those rules. The hysteria influences me only in that every six months I have to pay fifty shekels and have a blood test. But besides that, I don't let it get to me. I know what to do.

I always mentioned in my ads that I was Arab. I even felt that it was a matter of misrepresentation if I didn't say it. I felt that I had to say it, so I did. I never tried to hide it. . . . Well, actually . . . this is going to be published in English, right? I hope it won't get translated. No, I'm kidding. But if you are looking for turning points for me, I think this is actually an important question.

At some point I really got discouraged—it doesn't happen to me easily, but it happens. I debated the question a lot, if I should say that I am Arab or not. From a marketing perspective, it was in my interest not to say it, that was clear. Maybe a lot of blacks and whites in the U.S. are attracted to each other, I don't know, but it isn't the same here. We are at war. And I knew that this fact wasn't helping me.

But I was unsure what I could do. So I made a few experiments—postponing the point where I say that I am Arab, to see how far I could go. Statistical exercises. But there was one incident that made me decide that I was through with experiments.

When I think back on it, it was pretty scary. I was twenty then, he was nineteen and a half, in the army. I think I answered his ad, and then he answered my letter, and I wrote him back, and finally there was a telephone call and we talked. And I didn't tell him I was Arab—he was part of the experimental group. We made a date to meet. He was on an army base somewhere, and he suggested that I come to meet him on the base! He was doing guard duty, and I think he, like, wanted to have sex right there. Of course, I refused that offer. There is a limit, after all. I said no, I can't, we are much better off doing it sometime later. So, to make a long story short, we met later on, in a public place, downtown.

We met, we passed each other's final inspection. He was coming back from the army base to his parents' house, in the suburbs of Haifa. His parents weren't at home, and he invited me to go back to his house. Now, I had just come from the Technion, and I didn't have a backpack, only a sort of folder, which had a sticker on it saying, "Abort Abortion Restrictions," right? And he apparently was searching for subjects to talk about, so he said, "What, is that all you do in the Technion all day, throw slogans around?" He wanted to talk about abortion, whether you have got the right to do it or not, and pro and con, and so on. And from there, it was a very short distance to politics. And this is on the way to his house, right—everything was happening very fast.

So we got to politics, and then it turned out that he was very, very, very right wing. I mean very, very. OK—he didn't hide the fact that he was in Kah's youth movement, Kahane's political party.[§] OK. So then I said to myself, OK, it's a good thing that I didn't say anything to him when we first met. And I was debating with myself during the whole trip, whether I should, like, say anything, get out of the car somehow, stop things or continue things. I didn't know. I was scared to death. In any case, it was clear to me that if I was going to go ahead with this then I would really have to hide it.

So we got to his house and we went into his room and, what do you know, there was the yellow flag of the Kah party there, on the wall of his bedroom. I remember that. I remember it as a horrible, horrible thing. Now I can laugh about it, but it was not a simple situation. I was afraid to try to leave once we got there. And he began to tell me about all the demonstrations he had been at. It was actually really interesting to hear his side of things, because I myself had been at some of these demonstrations too. It was very surprising to hear the other side's version. There was even something nice about it. He didn't hide the fact that he would sometimes go out to beat up Arabs, and he told me how he and his friends instigated violence at those demonstrations. It was very interesting. But it did, like, raise my blood pressure at the time.

And then he asked me about myself, where my family was from, what kind of an accent it was that I had. And I said that I was born in South America. And he also asked me who I vote for, and I said that I voted with the left—I said that because my parents had been persecuted where we came

[§] Kah: Israeli political movement founded by Rabbi Meyer Kahane, advocating Jewish theocracy and Israeli territorial expansion, as well as the elimination of all Arabs from Israeli-held territory. Banned by Israeli authorities as a terrorist organization in 1994. Kah is identified with the graffito slogan "Death to the Arabs."

from, I thought that it was wrong to persecute others—something like that. And I tossed in everything I know about South American history. Let's face it—this guy was an idiot. I have never lied so much in my life. I think he could have figured things out very easily.

I was very afraid to have sex with him. Very, very much. For one thing, he would be able to see that I wasn't Jewish. But when it got to that, I made something else up—I said that my mother was Jewish and my father wasn't, and he insisted, I don't know what I said—something totally unbelievable, in any case. But what can you do, he was very stupid. I just wanted to get it over with.

When it was done, he offered me a ride back, and I said no, no, no, that's all right. He asked for my telephone number, which I had never given him before, and I wrote six totally random numbers on a sheet of paper, and gave it to him. And I remember that I left the house, walked calmly to the corner, and then, like, broke out into a sprint. I ran to the nearest bus stop and caught the first bus that came, just to get as far away from that place as I could. I didn't even care where it was going.

There is another part to the story with him, actually. The whole time I was studying at the Technion I kept working in that minimarket as a cashier. I remember one Saturday night, after a big soccer game had let out, a car stopped across from the minimarket, four guys got out, and he was one of them. I remembered that he had said how he liked to go to soccer games. They were walking toward the store, so I quickly called someone to, like, fill in for me, and I ran up to the second floor and hid there until he left. He really did come in. That was the only time I have met him since then. I remember his face, of course. I don't think he would remember me, I don't know. That is the story.

That was the first time I slept with someone who didn't know I was Arab, and I will never do that again. The lesson is that it isn't worth trying to hide it—you should just write it in the ad, and that's that. Since then, actually, I have answered very few ads, and published none.

Recently, in the last year, really, I have become more involved in gay social life. I actually tried to get some sort of gay social life going in the Technion, but failed. It's a long story. What happened was that the student paper published a letter from a student who had been to a meeting of the gay and lesbian student group in Jerusalem. And he wrote asking, in a very ironic tone, why, in the macho Technion, the brotherhood of engineers, builders of Israel, or something like that, there were no meetings like this, why was this topic taboo? He had come to the conclusion that it was a result of the difficulties of exposing oneself in this masculine atmosphere, the difficulty of being first. I wrote a letter in response, basically saying I was taking the initiative, and that gay, lesbian, and bisexual students who were interested in evening meetings should write to my post office box. And I got fifteen letters—all of them from frightened Technion students who didn't want to meet anyone else, and didn't want to come to any public meetings! I don't know why they answered. I don't know what they wanted. A lot of them gave me their post office box addresses, and I wrote to them. And I met with every one of them separately, but no one wanted to meet anyone else, because they were afraid that they might be in the same calculus class some day or something. There's no figuring Technion students. It was a total failure.

Gay life interests me in general. I went to one meeting of the Haifa branch of the Agudah, about a month ago. But if I go back, it certainly won't be every week. It was pretty disappointing. It isn't what I am looking for. Every week, to talk about the same thing with the same people, who you don't really have anything in common with, can be pretty boring. It might be that a group in the Technion, which would be a little more homogeneous, where there would be some more things to talk about, would be more successful. It may be that there will be another attempt, I don't know.

I am interested in gay rights, but it is not an obsession. I think the Agudah is doing very good work, but I don't really feel very much a part of it. I don't know. Maybe it is just because it is in Tel Aviv. It is a little far. I am not going to go to Tel Aviv twice a week or anything—for instance, I wouldn't take a special trip to Tel Aviv to participate in a march, if they had one. If I lived in the area, it might be that I would, like, stop by.

I have met a lot of people through the Internet, on the computer. I have always had a computer account, but I didn't know this existed until a friend showed me. He left me in front of the menu, and I, totally by chance, went into the "gblf" conversation—"gays, bisexuals, lesbians, and friends." Since then I have been hooked on it. Maybe a little too much, I don't know.

It is basically a party line on the computer. Everybody can type whatever they want into their own computer, and it appears on everybody's screen. The subjects are very diverse—it depends on who is there. If you tend to come on line at regular hours, you meet the same people over and over, and you already have a kind of social life. They are people who you, theoretically, can talk to every day. People from universities all over the world, all sorts of countries. It is amazing. Any time that you are in front of the computer, any time you feel the impulse, you are going to find at least ten other people who are interested in talking about a subject that interests you. And it is not always homosexuality—it can be all sorts of crazy things. There are people who come on line in the morning, and there are people who come on line at night, but it works out that, like, you have a group of regulars that changes every few hours. People from Europe are usually on during the same hours I am—England, Holland, France, Italy, Poland. The United States, of course, is always on—there is always someone who comes to talk on the computer at four in the morning. But people are generally free during the same hours, so you always meet the same people. That is what makes it social.

I correspond with some people privately now, through electronic mail, and some even by conventional mail, exchanging pictures of ourselves and so on. Then there is even more of a relationship. And if you find someone who is close by, it may happen that it will develop into, like, an actual meeting. I never fell in love with anyone from the computer, but I did have some one-time meetings, sometimes two or three times. Not really love, because it was never the right person.

When you are on line, sometimes you just make conversation, sometimes you tease one another, because you get to know people very well, after a time, so there are running jokes. They are just like regular friends. There is also computer sex—just like erotic stories, but much stronger, because it is a conversation, it is being written directly to you.

Of course, you are exposing yourself in a very serious way when you participate in these conversations, much more than, like, going to the park or something, because your name and even your identity card number are there, and anyone who is on line can see. Anyone in the Technion who is a little curious can find me logged on there. But it doesn't bother me. I know for a fact that there are a lot of people in Israel who talk regularly on other channels who know who I am. But whenever I am working on the computer I also leave a window open and log on. You could say that I am addicted—when something interesting is going on in that window, I can leave everything that I am doing very quickly. It takes priority in my attention in certain ways.

There are some friends, people who I talk to, who don't know about me. I don't feel the need to tell people any more. Of course, I don't go too far out of my way to hide it either. If someone is close enough to me to know, he knows. I assume that there are some students in the Technion who I have never talked to about the subject, but who know about me from the computer. If the subject came up, I would say what I think. I don't hide my opinions. But no one has ever asked me the question directly.

I am twenty-three now. In the last two or three years I haven't really been in any serious relationships. I haven't been looking for that. There was one guy who I was with for seven months. It was an exclusive relationship, at least on my part. I would like to find someone who I can be with for more than seven months and still find interesting and attractive. Maybe I would be able to move in with him at some stage. But that's a dream, right? I always try to be practical.

One positive thing that came out of that Technion story was a very close friendship with someone who is also a student. He has a steady boyfriend, of course. But through him, you could say that I have found a certain crowd in Haifa that he and his boyfriend are part of. I meet people through them, not that they try to set me up or anything. But they hang out with a group of people that it is really nice to be with.

Most of them are over thirty. There is one other Arab. The first gay Arab I have met. We have never had a private conversation, even though I knew him beforehand, from other contexts. He is also from Haifa, and he is a member of the same church as we are. I never knew he was gay. Now, if we were to meet in the street, I would talk to him. But I don't know how things will develop—it doesn't depend only on me. He has a Jewish boyfriend at the moment.

Everyone chooses his own surroundings. If your surroundings are not suitable to you, you find new ones. You don't have to accept everything you are born into. It is a decision that is totally under your control. You can't force yourself into membership someplace where you have no place. I have no problem leaving behind an environment that makes problems for me— what logical reason would there be to stay in it? For instance, I am not going to join the Islamic movement in order to change it, so that it will be more enlightened. There is nothing for me there, so I am not going to become a member. From the very start I choose for myself a different environment. Right now, I think that Jewish society is more enlightened than Arab society when it comes to homosexuality. So that is where I go, more and more.

I cut out something from the newspaper *A-Sinarah* that was published a year ago, I think. This is the most popular Arabic-language newspaper for Arabs in Israel. It is published in Nazareth. And it has an advice column, called "Dear Marie"—it is written by a doctor, I think she is a gynecologist, who also happens to be the editor's sister. Here it is—May 29, 1992. Here, she is answering a letter from a seventeen-year-old who has written to her that he is gay. Now, remember, this woman is supposed to be secular, democratic, progressive, and she is writing in a newspaper that is supposed to be secular, democratic, and open to everything. I will translate for you what he wrote. "I am in eleventh grade, I am seventeen, and I am attracted to guys, and not girls. And this worries me. I want to tell the story from the beginning. A year and a half ago, someone in my class brought a pornographic magazine to school, and we all looked at it, and I felt that my friends were looking at the women, but I was looking at the men, and that happened a number of times. Afterwards, a friend of mine had a pornographic movie in his house, and there also, I looked at the men and not the women. And then it really began to worry me. And it continued, and it began to bother me all the time. And then I began to feel sexually attracted to one of my friends. I would spend a lot of time with him, and one time I even intended to tell him, but I didn't do it, because I was afraid."

The letter goes on. He writes that he knows about the park, and that he went there—he says that two weeks ago he went there and stood near the park for three whole hours. Wow. During this whole time he just stared in front of him, but he didn't have the courage to go in. He was afraid that someone who knows him would see him. But two days later he went there again, in the early evening, and again he stood "paralyzed by fear" outside. This time, though, a guy came up to him where he was, and began to talk to him, and he answered him, and then he was even more frightened, because the guy was Jewish and he "made him worried." They walked around a little bit there, and apparently there was something—what he writes here is that "I went all the way with him." I figure they changed his wording—I can't imagine a seventeen-year-old writing "I went all the way." It sounds very odd. He ends his letter, "since then I have continued to think, I don't know what to do, I know that this is what I wanted, but I'm afraid."

What does she answer him? This is the interesting part. "You are not gay." That is how it begins. "You are not gay." That's it, she has decided. "And you need treatment." Nice, huh? "All you have to do is to distance yourself from this bad crowd you have fallen in with, your friends with the pornographic magazines and movies, and to stop looking for the meeting places of all kinds of perverts. You need to do the opposite. You need to redouble the energies you are putting into your studies, which you have nearly finished. In the time that is left in school, busy yourself with other positive activities, such as reading constructive books, playing sports, learning a hobby, helping the elderly, or any other good deed." This is painful—you get the idea—do I have to go on? Is this interesting? OK—"These things will keep you busy and strengthen your personality, and won't leave you time to look for all sorts of perverted people."

Now for the prognosis. "If you keep on looking for the meeting places of the perverts, and doing with them these deeds, you will be the Chief of the Perverts, without a doubt, and all of your future will be lost." She continues, "What is called 'the sexual perversion,' or the sexual orientation toward the same sex, is not inborn, but rather is acquired at a certain point in life, if a boy is exposed to certain causing factors, such as you were exposed to, for instance, and there is no one at his side who understands him, who understands the essence of things, and will point him on the right path." And she continues, "The numerous medical studies that have been done and continue to be done throughout the world in order to explain the sexual perversion have not yet found any common biological cause for this sickness. Thus it is that all scientists agree that a biological cause is only the root in very few cases, where it is found in conjunction with numerous other mental and physical problems, and treatment is very difficult, or even impossible. But the cases of acquisition are much more numerous, especially in the Western nations that have inherited a liberty which knows no limits. It is this liberty which has caused these phenomena, together with the collapse of the cultural system"—and so on, I don't have to translate it all, it goes on like this. "This is the reason for the breakup of families, drug addiction, failure, and terrible diseases, in particular the deadly AIDS, which, in essence, all of these liberated people are infected with, as well as everyone who comes into contact with them. Their end will, of course, be death."

But that is not all—she continues, "The sexual perversion begins as a one-time act, out of curiosity and the need to know, that individuals do with a number of perverted people. But then they become a part of these people and then it is difficult for them to leave it." Bullshit! "The treatment for the sexual perversion is very simple, and just as people say, when you have the desire to do something, even the impossible is possible. It is enough for a person, for instance, to notice his perversion and to decide that he wants to distance himself from this, and to distance himself from this particular environment, and to switch to a more natural, normal environment, where there are no family problems." No family problems—I don't know how you are supposed to be able to find *that* environment. "This returns his balance to him, and he finds the natural and correct path that doesn't allow all of those causes to come into contact with him."

Now for her conclusion. "There is one problem that particularly concerns me in this boy's story, and that is, how he got himself onto this path of failure and death, after all. Yes, the perverts are many, and they are to be found everywhere, to our regret, and their exclusive desire is that there should be as many boys like this as possible, for them to collect," and so on and so forth, "and they just want to catch all the boys in their net, as they have done with this boy. But the question which bothers me is this: where are his parents? Where were they all the days when he disappeared from the house to see those movies, and to look for the perverts so that he could do what he has done? Why did his parents not see that he was far from his house, why did they not see that he came home late, why did they believe him every time he said he was at his friends' houses? What were his grades on his exams?" Blah, blah, blah. "Where are his teachers, where is their sense of responsibility, to look after their students, that they don't see that the students are bringing pornography to the school and exchanging it there, instead of reading constructive books, instead of engaging in constructive competition, and studying for exams, at the very least, which is the reason their parents are sending them to school. These are important questions which I leave for every mother and father, and for every educator and responsible party, so that they can find the correct and true answer. And to all the boys and girls, you must beware of all the seductions that appear so attractive, because their end is death and utter loss." Bullshit.

It is clear that a lot of things would be easier for me abroad. Absolutely. It is a fact. I have thought about it seriously in the past, and I still think about it. But I have no specific plans. I want to go on for my masters degree—I will either study in Tel Aviv or in the U.S. There are pros and cons, and I still haven't made a final decision. If I can find a job here then I won't emigrate, at least not at this point. But I am thinking about this subject very seriously. It may be that I will leave in the end.

I don't feel any ideological need to stay. I will live wherever I feel comfortable, wherever I feel that I can live best. It's just life. I don't feel any special connection with Haifa. I could just as easily live in Denmark or the U.S. or any other place. You create your own social life, and you can find that in all sorts of places. That is not a problem.

I don't think my life is any different from lots of Jewish guys who live at home and whose parents don't know about them. I think my life is pretty similar. I can't say if my being gay has influenced how I feel about Arab culture as compared to Jewish culture—the whole thing is very hypothetical. It might be that if I hadn't been gay I would be different. I will never like gefilteh fish, though.[§]

I don't see myself as a victim. If I were to wake up one morning and there would not be any discrimination, I would think I was in a different place. I am not sure I would know what to do. It's part of my life. You finds ways of coping, you deal with it, you live with it, and you even begin to, like, enjoy it. It isn't something so sad. OK, if, for example, you read something that is written with the intention of upsetting you, you can laugh about it, you can't take everything to heart. It isn't healthy to take things seriously. Why get involved thinking about things that you know from the very start will only make problems? Why even get involved with it? Why think? Live the way you want, and that's it. Life is for living, not for thinking about all the time.

I define myself as Israeli. If I had to think up some sort of definition of what I am now, I would say I am a Palestinian-Israeli—an Israeli of Palestinian background. I think this defines me pretty well. I am reluctant to ever use the word "Arab" to describe myself, but there is no choice, you have got to use it. I dislike it, because it suggests connectedness with all sorts of places and people who I don't feel connected with at all. That is why I try to limit it.

I don't feel negatively about Zionism, which I define as the national liberation movement of the Jewish people. But I am not part of the Zionist project—I am part of the State of Israel. You are the ones who need to learn to differentiate between the two things, and you don't know how to do that. I can do that. With the creation of the state, I think that Zionism lost its meaning—at some point, it should have been replaced by "Israelism." But for all sorts of reasons, it wasn't replaced. And it stayed the way it was, and people still define themselves as Zionists or not. But that has nothing to do with me. It is your problem. I have no problem at all in defining myself as Israeli.

People need to think about the future, and not go backwards all the time. Why should I waste my time researching the land where they are building a new Jewish settlement today, to find out to which tiny Arab village which no longer exists it belonged? For instance, I know that there has been an army base on the site of my father's village for many years now. OK—the fact is, after '48, there was no one there anymore. It doesn't really bother me, because I feel no connection to that place. I don't know, I barely feel a part of Haifa.

My feelings are for people—much more than for places, for earth. I get emotional over people—living, breathing, changing things, that you can

---

[§] gefilteh fish: A Jewish delicacy; boiled chopped fish, usually carp.

touch—and not chunks of earth which could just as easily be in France or in Jordan or in Israel. It's pathetic, the way people look for a sense of attachment to a place, of belonging. I don't know why. They look for roots in a particular place, historical roots, but I don't feel any need for that. Old historical sites and tourist attractions are not for me. I live my life here and now, and I think about the future more than the past. I have no problem with that. And if I decide tomorrow that I want to be a Buddhist, then nothing is going to keep me from doing that, so long as it interests me. Afterwards, I can change it, if I want. I choose my connectedness, and I can change it tomorrow if I want to. I belong to the groups that I choose for myself, and not to any homeland.

YOSSI

The week before he met me, Amir answered the personal ad Yossi put in the newspaper. That means that, during the weeks that passed between our first few meetings, when I was trying to decide how attracted I was to this earnest and gentlemanly Israeli, Amir was trying to decide if he preferred Yossi the curly-haired kibbutznik or Jacob the blue-eyed American. Of course, I was not to know Amir's side of this story for some time after we had both made our decisions.

In the meantime, Amir and Yossi had kept in touch (only by telephone, Amir tells me), and more than a year later, Amir arranged an evening for all of us to meet. I enjoyed myself, and Yossi suggested that we come spend a weekend at his kibbutz. We accepted, and even chose a date. We drove to Yossi's kibbutz straight from our first interview, with Rafi Niv. As we drove along the winding, dark, sloping, narrow roads leading up to the Lebanese border, we talked about Rafi's interview. We were excited. I was also scared—it seemed that we were driving a little faster than Amir's '75 Passat (or I) could comfortably handle. And then Amir told me that at one point the road actually crosses into Lebanese territory for about a quarter of a mile—topographical difficulties in construction, he explained.

Rafi's interview had taken a great deal longer than we had expected, and we were late. We called Yossi from the kibbutz gate, and he came and accompanied us to his one-room apartment, part of a series of identical, ivy-covered, shedlike structures. Once inside, Amir and I plumped onto the low couch. Yossi, in ripped jeans and a kibbutz t-shirt, served us the now-cold meal he had taken from the dining hall for us. He hopped back and forth as we ate, grabbing at his *hippielike mop of dark hair and tripping over his electric space heater—which, even in this warm weather, served as his cigarette lighter.*

Yossi's heavy face lit up when we explained the reason for our being tardy. "Great!" he said, "Do you want to interview me? I've got a tape recorder and cassettes if you need them." Amir and I looked at each other. We hadn't actually planned on including Yossi in the book—but we hadn't planned on excluding him either. So we finished eating, Yossi cleared the dishes, lit yet another cigarette, sat down in his easy chair, and began to talk. The couch was at an angle and the pillows were slippery: at periodic intervals we had to call a halt to the conversation, stand, and cooperatively restore order to the upholstery.

∾

MY MOTHER WAS BORN IN TANGIER, which is part of Morocco now. Back then, the region was under Spanish rule, while the city itself was considered "international." Her family lived in the Jewish part of the city. By our standards I guess they were poor, but back then, most people lived like that. After my grandmother had six children, she divorced her Jewish husband and married my grandfather, Carlos Gonzalez, a Catholic Spaniard from the Canary Islands, who had fled to Tangier after the Spanish Civil War. I don't know what the story was, I don't know how they met. But he married my grandmother. Their only child was my mother. My grandfather was, you know, a Marxist, a Communist, an atheist.

So my mother grew up in Tangier, she lived there until she was, like, twenty. In 1960 she left, and began wandering the world. She lived all over Europe. She was in England for a while, she was an *au pair* there, learned English, in addition to the Spanish and French she knew from school. She went to Switzerland, learned German in, like, two years, and worked as a secretary in a city in the French part of Switzerland, Canton de Neuchâtel, in a town called La Chaux-de-Fonds.

In 1964, I think this was two years after Morocco became independent, something like that, Tangier became part of Morocco. So my mother sent for her parents and brought them to Switzerland. Before this, all of my mother's brothers had immigrated to Israel through ⁽Aliyat Hano⁽ar and that whole deal.[§] And in 1966, after my mother, like, almost married a Swiss man, she

[§] ⁽Aliyat Hano⁽ar: Literally, "Youth Immigration." Department of the Jewish Agency responsible for organizing the immigration of unaccompanied minors, often orphans or refugees, to the Land of Israel.

decided that she was Jewish, and decided to emigrate to Israel. Her parents stayed in Switzerland. My mother got to Israel just a few months before the Six-Day War began—she went straight into the pathos of that stupid war. And that's the story. In 1968 she met my father, they got married, and, like, after a year and a half, I was born.

Now my father. My father was born in Romania, in Bucharest. On his side, my grandmother was Romanian, my grandfather Russian, but my grandfather left Russia for Romania as a teenager, after the failed revolution in 1905. This grandfather was a Communist too. So you see, I'm from a good family, on both sides. In Romania, of course, my grandfather became part of the underground, like, fighting the king, and he was forced to leave the country. He fled to Palestine, but then he went back to Romania again for some reason, married my grandmother, they had a daughter, then a year and a half later they had a son, my father. Now the Second World War began. By the end of the war, the Germans and their collaborators were the real ones in control of Romania. Because my grandfather could pass as Slavic, he was sent to a work camp, and not any worse. And that's it. Then the Red Army came and liberated him.

In 1946, my grandparents took all of their portable property, including my father, and got on a train to a port city, where they had arranged places on a boat of illegal immigrants to what was then the British Mandate for Palestine. But on a station on the way, or something like that, they lost their train. And with it, all their property. They had to go back to Bucharest without anything. And it wasn't until 1949 that they could get on another boat to Israel.

They settled in Hadar, Haifa. Here in Israel, as a young boy, my father didn't go to school at all. I guess you could say he was a political activist—he was in Hashomer Hatza‘ir, he would have, like, fistfights with the kids in rival youth movements, and he built all sorts of settlements.§ He's a plumber by profession. That's a good skill for a pioneer. When the time came, my father went into the army, the tank corps. He tried to leave the army once he had finished his service, but he wound up going back. He became an officer, and he made the army his career.

I have memories of living in Upper Nazareth, but I don't think they're my own, I think they're from pictures and stories. We lived in a government housing project for career army families. We were three kids in one room,

§ Hashomer Hatza‘ir: Literally, "the Young Guard." Socialist Zionist pioneering youth movement; aimed at educating Jewish youth for life on kibbutzim; in contemporary Israel, one of the organizations filling a social role similar to that of the American Boy Scouts.

me and my two little sisters, who are twins. Afterwards we lived in Safed, where my brother was born. I went to one nursery school, my sisters went to another. I would take my sisters—they were three and I was four—I would take them to school. It was an apartment building, we lived on the fourth floor, and my mother would, like, look out the window above us and watch us cross the street, she would shout down, "OK, now it's safe to cross the street." Street—it was more like a dirt path. There were six entrances to our building, like, six stairwells: A, B, C, D, E, F. We lived in D. You didn't have your own phone in your apartment—there was one telephone in each stairwell, and everyone had to share it.

We lived in this building during the Yom Kippur War, 1973. The day before the war, my father came to visit. We heard him come in the jeep, and we ran to the window, of course, to wave hello. But the moment he parked and got out of the car, our neighbor, Osnat, put her head out the window next door, and she shouted to him, "Doy, they called, something's going on, everyone's going back, they want you back at the base." I remember the scene only very vaguely. He had to go back.

And then I remember that the air-raid sirens began. At night we would sleep with our shoes on. And I remember cockroaches in the bomb shelters at night—actually, like, one, specific cockroach which was there. He was very friendly.

One of the more traumatic things in the war were the helicopters that brought the injured from the Golan Heights to the hospital, which was very close by. And I remember this as a bad thing, apparently because they explained to me that this was bad, and there were sad faces. The helicopters would land very close by. And we could, you know, see smoke and planes on the Golan Heights.

I also remember the visits of the "city officer." Her job was to come and notify families of injuries. But every time they sent the doctor—it was always this same man who carried a black bag, that was the doctor—every time he came, we would know that somebody had been killed. When the doctor's car would pull up, all the kids would run outside, in front of the building, and all the women would peek their heads out from the windows. I try to imagine how he must have felt—it was awful. And then he would choose a specific stairwell to go into, and all the women in that stairwell would bring their heads back inside. All the others would stay in their windows so they could see where it was that he was going this time. I remember one time there was a loud scream—the sound of a heart being broken—on the second floor of our stairwell. From stairwell D, where we lived, two were killed and four more were wounded. Only my father and one other neighbor didn't have anything happen to them in that war.

It was three and a half months before my father came home. This is my first really vivid memory of him, when he arrived. He drove up in his jeep, and he was wearing his combat helmet, and there was a laurel wreath on it. He came inside carrying a sort of a backpack. And I remember his smell, the smell of a soldier. I remember how my mother cried when he came in. He was at home only, like, a very short time. We ran straight to his bag to nose around and see if he had brought us anything. And that's it, that's the first time I really remember my father.

After Safed we moved to Hertzliya. I was used to the ritual of moving, the boxes and the truck, I remember it well. From Hertzliya we moved to Acre, there I began to go to school, until I was six, and we moved again. I didn't have a problem with our moving all the time. It seemed natural to me. Until Hertzliya we lived in places where everyone was like that. Every time, not a single month would go by without someone moving and someone else coming. Everyone was career army, and everyone moved. I remember how strange it was, I was shocked when people told me that they had been living in the same house for fifteen years.

My father finally came to live at home after he left the army in 1980. We were already in Acre. This was the first apartment that wasn't rented. I remember little arguments between my parents that began at that time, but nothing exceptional. Nothing that didn't happen with the neighbors too. They didn't get us involved.

I was one of the best students in "Homeland" class—by fifth grade they called it "Geography." And I remember that we would go on lots of family day trips, in the car, to all sorts of sites. We would sing. It was wonderful.

My mother, although she had learned all these different languages, has problems with Hebrew to this day. In many ways, she remains, like, a new immigrant. Her accent is strong, she doesn't read the Hebrew papers—she gets news and things like that only from foreign newspapers. So I was brought up, like, speaking Spanish at home. My mother, until I was six or seven, would not answer me if I spoke to her in Hebrew. I would speak to my sisters in Hebrew, but with her only in Spanish. So I know the language well.

I was the first in my class to have a girlfriend, in fifth grade. I had a crush on someone else, but she didn't want me, she wanted my best friend. My girlfriend was very sharp-tongued, cynical, brash. We would go folk-dancing in the school gym after school. And afterwards I had another girlfriend. I got along very well with the other kids. I made friends immediately wherever I went. In Acre our apartment building was like a commune—the doors to the other apartments were always open, we would go into houses freely, there was a sort of a, you know, cooperative atmosphere.

I was never the most popular kid in the class, because there are certain particular qualities of the most popular kid that are difficult for me to define. I wasn't at all threatening. I never used force. I wasn't one of the kids who, like, walked around with a slingshot, I didn't play soccer, I learned to ride a bike late. But I liked team tag, jump rope, or hopscotch, games that both boys and girls played. I was very lazy—I didn't like physical games.

I was more friendly with the kids who were older than me. I didn't find any interest in friends of my own age. Because I was a boy like that, I was one of those little prodigies that, like, they don't send to a special school only because they don't want to ruin their lives. I had an IQ test and all that garbage.

I remember sexual fantasies from when I was about ten. I imagined, like, going from apartment to apartment, floor to floor, checking out all of my friends—downstairs were Tzyiqa and Tzyiqa, next door were Ya‘akov, Beni, and so on. At thirteen, I already had clearly homosexual fantasies. Once, I went to visit a friend, and he had just gotten out of the shower, and he got dressed in front of me. So in the fantasy, instead of getting dressed, we got into bed with each other, and rubbed up against each other, with our underwear on. Once, in one of the fantasies, we took off our underwear, and he said to me, "Do you know what we're doing?" So I was like, "Yes, we're fucking." This was all in the fantasy. But I enjoyed it very much, it was very much what I wanted.

I liked having a girlfriend, but I got fed up with it very quickly. Because, like, there wasn't any point. Really, we were little kids. There wasn't any point. Afterwards I had another girlfriend, the mayor's daughter, Sigal. She must be beautiful now. She had, like, chestnut-colored hair, not vulgar red, not orange, but red-brown. Amazing hair.

We would, like, hold hands, and we would kiss each other behind the ears, and we would tell each other everything. She would lie with her head on my chest, and we would totally relax, and I would play with her hair, her ear. Exciting, yes. I remember it as very exciting. Being tongue-tied, blushing. But it ended very quickly. It was like that for the first one or two weeks, and then that was it.

When we were younger, kids didn't use the word "homosexual," even as an insult. But I understood, like, the deeper meaning of what was going on. By seventh, eighth grade, I knew that the word "homo" had something to do with me.

There were always kids who were more effeminate than I was. It was connected to a system of persecution, where the other kids would always need someone to get hold of to give him a working over. That was never me. I never had a status where someone would dare do that to me. But there were other kids in the class who got beaten up because they were effeminate. They said that one of my friends was queer—he wore wooden clogs, no one else wore them.

This didn't really affect me, it wasn't from this that I understood that homosexuality was bad. I don't think I ever thought about it as a bad thing. I thought it would pass. I had a girlfriend in eighth grade to prove that I would grow out of it, and she suffered for that. She was exceptionally ugly. I would spend time with her, and I would, like, think about the boys in our class.

When I was fourteen, we moved again, from Acre to Qiryat Ḥayim, Haifa, and there I met Mihal, my next girlfriend. With Mihal the relationship was more serious. We would go hiking together with the youth movement, and sleep cuddled up together. We didn't have sex. Hugging and talking, things like that. I think she was waiting for some sort of pressure on my part that never came. If she knew about me today, she would understand a lot of things. But we would hug a lot, and I liked to hold hands, so we would do that.

When I was with Mihal, I still thought that I would grow out of my homosexuality. I wanted to see what I could do to help that process. It was all, like, very calculated, the relationship with her. When I imagined my future, I tried to imagine marrying her.

I felt guilty about cheating her, like, ripping her off in a way. At that time I was very close to one guy, we were very good friends, and I was very attracted to him, I really liked him. We would do our homework together, he would call me up and I would help him, we would go to the beach together, he would sleep over at my house, I would sleep over at his. I didn't tell him how I felt, because I knew that there was a chance that he wouldn't be interested at all, and that it might even drive him away. My attraction wasn't so important to me that it was worth ruining our friendship, because that part wasn't based on physical attraction. It was based on the fact that he was a charming person.

We would watch porn videos together sometimes. But while he was looking at the women, I would look at the men. I was sure that I was the only one who did that—who would rather look at the men than the women. I had no doubt that I was the only one in the world. Maybe there were people like that in books, but I was the only real one. It didn't occur to me that it might actually be possible to do something sexual with a boy until I was much, much older. Until, like, seventeen, eighteen. At this point, something like that was inconceivable.

Afterwards I understood that I was in deep shit. But not in the sense that homosexuality was evil, that it was a sin. Do you know what I mean? In the sense that this was a really complicated thing—that I could fuck up my life, that it wasn't "acceptable." For instance, I remember when the movie *Infected* came out—when was that, 1984–85? It was a short Israeli film about a gay teenager. I remember, from reading the reviews and things like that, that being gay was a big deal, and got the message that this all was referring to me, more or less. I understood that I had a serious problem. Like, a real misfortune. But I made sure I was busy all the time, so that this whole problem would be left only for the nights. And in the course of the day, I wouldn't think about it.

I remember that the Tanah teacher in fifth grade, she talked about this subject, homosexuality, even though it wasn't what we were studying, specifically. And she explained that in the Tanah there was one mention of the subject, in Leviticus, where it was prohibited. But then she compared this prohibition with another place—she gave the passionate friendship of David and Jonathan as an example. She, like, compared the passages, and said, "There are two approaches here, just like today. There are people who see it as a sickness, a sin, but this is a primitive approach," and she used that word, "this is a primitive approach, and it is a fact that there are places in the Tanah where they relate to it as a perfectly natural thing." She was pretty amazing, now that I think about it. This was in 1981.

At fourteen, this was a very encouraging thing to hear. But it didn't help the fact that I still felt that it was a terrible misfortune—and a terrible misfortune needs support of a different kind. The real problem was more practical—you could even say, emotional—rather than moral.

From about sixteen until I was nineteen, the element of loneliness came more and more into play. Again, I was pretty lucky, because, like, while there were a lot of couples around, in my particular crowd, there wasn't a lot of pressure to date. By eighth grade I was already hanging out with people from the socialist youth movement. My clique was mostly boys, about ten of us, and two girls.

I did have some pressure from my father. But I knew how to deal with him. From time to time he would say, "When are you going to ask me for eight hundred shekels?" And, "Well, you haven't asked me for eight hundred shekels yet." Finally I just said to him, like, "What, what, what is eight hundred shekels?" He said, "That's how much an abortion costs." He really wanted me to come and, like, announce to him that I had knocked some girl up! But I put him in his place. I said that for me, it has to be someone special. "I mean, I'm not celibate, but I don't fuck all day long." I tried to, like, speak his language.

My first contacts with the socialist youth movement were very casual. I remember that in Acre I was just a regular member of the Scouts, but when we moved to Qiryat Ḥayim, we asked where the Scouts were, and they said that there were no Scouts, but there was this. They were very organized—everyone was assigned to a group, and each group had a group leader, who was older, sort of a counselor figure. By the time I was fifteen, the serious, ideologically oriented activities began—we learned about politics, coexistence with the Arabs, socialism, cooperation, mutual assistance, communal life, and so on. The movement was the most important thing in my life. We would totally belittle the importance of schoolwork, and we would have long talks about the way in which the movement was more important than anything else.

At some point in eleventh grade I decided that I had to try to do something with a guy. I was seventeen. I knew that girls didn't especially interest me, and that I wanted to try it with a guy. Now, it just didn't occur to me that there could be a serious relationship between men. I thought it had to be just sex. What else could there be? And right about this time, they began to publish personal advertisements in La'ishah. It was the only newspaper in the country that published them at the time, and we had a subscription to it.

So I decided to publish my own ad. I was certain that, at the very least, I was the only one in my region of Israel who had these feelings about men. I was convinced that I was totally alone, that there was no other way to meet people.

I didn't know about the park cruising scene until I was in the army. I remember that in one of the letters I got, a guy asked me if I went to the parks. You know what I answered him? "Yes, sure, sometimes I go to the parks— and I like to hike too." I'm totally serious. I didn't know what he meant. I didn't know about Independence Park until I was in the army. So an ad, like, seemed to me to be the only choice. Besides, writing is my strong side.

There had been theoretical conversations in the movement on the subject of, like, love between men and homosexuality and all that. And we talked about why people have a problem with love between men, and the importance of being open to physical contact, not being afraid. "That a man touches a man doesn't mean he is gay. It's OK." That was the way our discussion went. And the attitude was, like, "It's totally fine for someone to be gay, but of course none of us are, and none of us should be afraid that others are going to think such a thing about him." Those conversations didn't make me feel comfortable enough to say, like, "Hey, you know what, I'm gay."

Deep inside me there was jammed, like, a very basic uncertainty concerning the attitude of society to this whole thing. I couldn't really say where it was coming from, exactly. But I had the sense that I was in dire straits, and that it was far preferable just to bury it, forget about it. And I liked my life the way it was, really, I was enjoying myself, having fun. So I said to myself that I was better off not telling my friends.

So anyway, this guy answered my ad. He was nineteen, a soldier. We talked on the phone, and we agreed to meet on neutral ground, in a public place. We agreed on the old Sheqem department store in Haifa. We met there, and, like, he had a car, so we drove in his car to the old road to Tel Aviv, up to the Beit Oren intersection, and we pulled off the road there. We talked for a while, about his job in the army, about what I would do when I was drafted, about his kibbutz. He wasn't a very interesting person. He seemed like just a regular guy. Very predictable. But meeting him did convince me that I wasn't the only gay in the country. I came to the conclusion that there must be about thirty or so. So it totally made sense to me that he would drive halfway across the country to meet with me, which was basically what he had done.

After we had been talking for a while, I said to him, "What do we do now?" And so we began to sort of fool around, kissing and groping. But at a certain point I stopped him. I told him that I didn't want to do any more than that. He was pretty pissed off. I remember that when I stopped him, I did it because I didn't want to do things that I would be sorry about afterwards. I just wanted to give it a little try, and then think it over. And that's it, I went back home. I was totally swept away, of course.

Now, this is an interesting story about my clique, also. Because, you know, you can't, like, disappear, even for an hour. You can't do something everyone doesn't know about, it just doesn't happen—every moment of your life, someone knows where you are. So when I got back from this rendezvous, I went to a friend's house. Everyone else was there too, and I came in, and everyone was in shock. They were like, "Where have you been?" Because there had been a few hours in that day when I was unaccounted for. I avoided the question at first, but afterwards I just had to give them some sort of an explanation. So I told Yafit, my confidante in everything, at least up to that moment, that I had met a girl. And I told her the whole story of what I had felt with him, but I told it as if, like, he had been a girl. The lies snowballed after this. There was my life, and then there was my hidden life.

At this point, my group decided to do something that was new in the movement back then—we began planning to do a year of community service after high school and before the army. The goal was, like, in the course of this one year, to try to see how we can implement our ideas about socialism, cooperation, and democracy, all of these things that we only talked about all the time. We were going to try, for one year, to live according to our beliefs. Some of us didn't want to, like, waste a year. But we would talk about seeing it as not wasting, but gaining a year of life. I mean, would you gain from it or would you lose from it? It just consumed me, like, all of the excitement of planning this. It swallowed up my entire world.

I didn't tell anybody else in my group about being gay because it seemed totally irrelevant. Because there wasn't any chance that someone else there was gay. I mean, the chances were one in a million. Besides, I felt like I was broadcasting my homosexuality in a direct, live, and color transmission twenty-four hours a day. But no one was receiving my signals—I was surrounded by, like, total idiots. By the end of high school I was dying for them to figure things out.

At one point, I answered a very sexy ad, with a very detailed description of the writer. He wrote very well, and he had a wonderful voice on the telephone, one of those deep voices. So that night, I really wanted to make an impression, I just wanted to knock him dead. So I went around to everybody, all of my friends, and borrowed an article of clothing from each one, which was what everyone did when they were getting dressed up. It was, like, a ritual: a shirt from this one, a belt from that one, shoes from the other one. And so it was totally clear that I had a date. But I said it was with a girl.

So I got dressed to the nines, went to meet him in town, and he was fat and ugly. At that time, I had a real problem explaining to someone I'm not interested. So when it came time for something to happen, I said, like, I had to go, and that's it, I blocked him out. That was my approach, just to, like, cut off contact. I got another letter from him, and I ignored it. And that was that. I was so disappointed. I gave up trying to meet people through the personals.

I finished high school and instead of going straight to the army, I went with the group to do a year of service, as a communal unit. We, as a group, had already decided, in eleventh grade, that we wanted to go through the army in the Naḥal program, as a group, combining military service with "pioneering" service to the kibbutz movement. But first we were going to spend a year doing community service.

So it was like we founded our own little kibbutz, only we had no land. We all were doing, you know, wage labor for the kibbutzim in the area. We did all sorts of jobs, in factories, in the fields, and we would, like, pool our salaries, and decide as a group how to divide the money. We started with thirty-two people, and it slowly got smaller, down to twenty-six. At the end of the year, because there were so few girls, we added another three girls, in order to keep the holy balance of two-thirds guys and one-third girls at least stable.

We lived this year with an incredible intensity. You have to imagine the situation—taking a group of kids who have done nothing but study, and putting them into a situation where they needed to work. We needed to support ourselves, to decide how we were going to spend our money, how to divide it, how much to put into transportation, how much for food. We had to learn by experience, to handle all the problems that came our way, like, unemployment and so on. In short, a ton of work. And we were also serving as counselors for younger groups just starting out.

It was a very difficult year. I have a lot of difficult, unpleasant memories. But for me, it totally changed my life. In Israel, they always say that you grow up, become an adult, in the army. But this gave us a stage before that, a chance to mature through a different kind of experience. So we got to the army with a totally different mentality. Our attitude was that the army was a game—basic training was just something to survive, it was a joke. And it really helped to have this kind of distance.

So this year ended, and I went on a short trip to Eilat with Ran, my best friend, who I, for some reason or another, haven't mentioned yet. In the middle of all this communal intensity, Ran was my best friend from outside of the group. He was very opposed to the whole kibbutz idea in general. He helped me keep things in proportion. I had a totally platonic relationship with him.

This was already a difficult time at home, with my parents. This was right before they got divorced. For three years already, it had been, like, arguments and threats. "The second the children go into the army, I'm divorcing you," my mother would say. My father totally ignored her threats. He couldn't have cared less. "Sure, go, don't go, it doesn't really make a difference to me one way or the other." And then I was drafted.

I believe that socialism is ultimately irreconcilable with the existence of the military. Because the army, to me, is force, and that's something I'm very sorry exists. It saddens me that this is the national consensus, that it's the heart of this nation—if there is one thing that the entire Jewish people in Israel have in common, except the ultra-Orthodox of course, it's the army.[§] Everyone knows everyone from the army. And I think that's sad. It saddens me that on the forty-fifth Independence Day of the state, the main thing we're waving flags about, that we're proud of, is the army—and not, for instance, the Weizmann Institute for Science, the Technion, the Archaeological Institute of the Hebrew University, or anything else you can be proud of.

On the other hand, and I don't think this is a contradiction, I'm aware of the fact that, in the present reality, we need a strong army. I'm aware of the fact that it's the army—and me as a part of it—that guarantees the continuity of the Jewish presence here. In order to fulfill my dreams for the Jewish people, I need a strong army at the moment. Now, this doesn't keep me from advocating a peace treaty—I think that it's inevitable. And, very slowly, we'll be witnesses to a process whereby the army will lose its privileged place. Because when peace breaks out, the army will be the big loser, in the end.

If you do your army service through Naḥal, you go through, like, a number of different parts: training, then active duty, then more training, then more active duty, then some time at a "military kibbutz"—something pathological, really awful—and finally, like, a period of a year back at the kibbutz where you have been assigned. Altogether, the track is four years and four months. Of that, two years and three months in uniform.

So once we were drafted, everyone came to the kibbutz where we were assigned, for, like, a month, as a sort of pre-basic training preparation, to get to know our new home here in the north, on the Lebanese border. We began working at the kibbutz, and there were, like, meetings and committees and cultural evenings. When the month was up, the guys would go to the army, to basic training. The girls would stay back on the kibbutz for another two months, and then they would come also.

But I wasn't there—I had been selected to go to the air force, to be trained as a pilot. I gave it a try. I began the preliminary training and selection pro-

[§] All Jewish men and women in Israel are subject to the military draft, with the exception of the ultra-Orthodox, who argue that military service is incompatible with their religious beliefs and distinctive way of life.

gram for pilots. It was, like, one big trauma. I'm a pussy cat! I didn't know what the hell I was doing as a combat soldier. I never knew. It wasn't for me. I'm not a fighter, I'm not a destructive person. And that's just the way it is. On top of everything, I was cut off from my group, and it was very difficult for me, suddenly to be alone, not knowing anyone. It was very difficult.

Finally the nightmare ended—I didn't pass the preliminary selection because of an intestinal infection. Because of that, they actually offered me another chance—I could have gone through the whole thing again, but I said, "Thanks, but no thanks." I understood, of course, that I had to tell my father that, like, I had "failed" the course. He wouldn't understand any other choice of words. But for me that wasn't a failure, it was a great relief. I couldn't take it any longer, I missed everyone so much it was killing me.

My father was disappointed in me—I was raised to believe that the army was a holy thing. And everyone is supposed to, like, dream of being a pilot. And I was supposed to be the successful son, impeccable. My brother was a little wild, my sisters are nothings, not, like, especially bright. But I think that my father felt that we had a lot in common politically, ideologically. And he wanted me to share his views on the importance of the army. These were the central subjects of our conversation.

But I left the air force, and was placed back with the rest of the group, at the kibbutz. And the moment I arrived, there was a battle outside. Terrorists. Awful. They had crossed the border from Lebanon. One of the first actions of the Ḥizballah, one of their first serious infiltration attempts.[§] It was the second I got here, like, six in the evening. I remember that the alarm sounded, the kibbutz alarm, and ʿAnat began screaming, and Meirav was also shouting, and they were competing who could shout the loudest, trying to, like, warn anyone who might be outside. And I had gotten there just in time, in uniform, my combat uniform, brand new! Only I wasn't armed—I didn't even know what a gun was yet. And we all sat in the room, I remember, and we locked the door, and we listened to the announcements on the kibbutz loudspeakers. At that point I decided that this kibbutz was my home.

In my view, socialism is reconcilable with Zionism, but not with the state. I'll explain. I do not believe that merely by having a state, merely by managing to secure our physical existence here, we are realizing the Zionist vision. A state is a tool, an instrument. It has no inherent value. No value. I'm willing to obey the laws of the state so long as this is the tool that exists. And I do believe that the State of Israel is a necessary step on the way to the assurance

[§] Ḥizballah: Iranian-supported Shi'ite Muslim militia based in Lebanon.

that the Jewish people really will survive. But, again, I think the state, the mere fact that there is a state, is not enough. I accept it within limits that I set.

For instance, I won't do my reserve duty in the territories any more. I won't go and serve in Gaza again, be a part of the continued holding of these territories, or the continued rule of a population that doesn't want us. I'm not taking part in this. I won't go to Gaza. And if that means that I'll go to jail, I'll go to jail. Because I think that our continued control of the territories is a threat to the continued existence of this nation here. Horrible, if you ask me. I'm not going to have anything to do with it. Yes, I personally am making my own deal. As an individual. And that's allowed, it's legitimate.

There is a very destructive trend in Israeli society—I think that a large portion of the young people here don't want to stay here. And I think that's awful. It's a failure of education. You could say that we've become "normalized" too quickly. I mean, there aren't too many people who are third-generation Israelis—they're the minority. And we're already "as the nations of the world," even though, like, the realization of the Zionist dream is still very far off. So long as there are such deep social and economic inequities, this is not enough. And so long as the state contributes to the perpetuation of these inequities, the state itself is anti-Zionist. This is not the Zionism I dream of.

I'm not loyal to the state. Because the state itself is worthless. And I'm certainly not loyal to the flag. I'm loyal, and I am willing to go to war and die, because I know this is the only thing that can guarantee the continued existence of the Jewish people.

So I went back to the kibbutz, and then my love affair with Liraz began. She was the ex-girlfriend of Eli, who was in my group, and from, like, a psychological point of view, you could say I was in love with him, and not her. But we began the long letters, telephone conversations, movies, hikes, the wind blowing through her hair, lifting up her skirt. I didn't know what the hell I was doing.

I mean, I knew at this point that it was men who physically interested me. But there's more to life than physical interest. Liraz wasn't especially pretty, but she was very sexy. She had, like, something I'm attracted to. Maybe not because of how she looks, but, rather, because of what she is. Only with men can I find myself thinking, like, "If only I could put a band-aid over his mouth or a blanket over his face, I would gladly molest him." But I was in love with, like, everything about her. I still am.

I stretched out this thing with her for a very long time. More than six months. Like, a nonrelationship-relationship. Very amorphous. And in the kibbutz that's ultimately impossible, because everybody begins asking questions. Everything has to be in, like, existing frameworks. This shapeless thing had to be immediately defined in some sort of rubric. People would ask us, "Are you a couple?" and we wouldn't answer.

At this point, the guys in our group went to serve in the Gaza Strip. There were no questions asked—orders were orders. The attitude was, like, we'll go where we are sent, and once we're there, we'll do our best to, like, keep to our own standards of behavior. As it turned out, two of us were kept back—one because he was an only son, and his father wouldn't agree to sign that he could be a combat soldier. And I was kept back because I had been chosen to be trained as a sniper.

After three months in the army, one of the girls, Hagar, left our group. I remember how difficult it was for her to make the split. And I remember asking myself, like, why the hell is she leaving if it makes her so miserable? She was a team commander in the army, a very responsible position. And one day, I remember that I was inside, I wasn't feeling well, and through my window I saw someone running from the communications tent. I didn't hear shouting, but I saw everyone all worked up, emotional. Hagar had committed suicide. For me, it was such a blow. She shot herself in the mouth—she shoved the rifle barrel into her mouth. They couldn't even identify her afterwards. Luckily, she had a picture with her. We had celebrated her nineteenth birthday a few days earlier. She didn't leave any kind of an explanatory letter. Today I'm very angry with her. She didn't leave a clue as to what was going on with her. No one knows.

So the other guys went off to the Gaza Strip, and I was sent to the snipers' course. And the situation was that, like, once again I was alone, and I was under a lot of pressure. Hagar had just killed herself. My parents had just decided to get divorced. And together with this, something happened with Liraz, suddenly, and that was it, it was over. We broke up. I felt so lonely.

And I remember, one Friday, a week or so afterwards, I went up to guard duty. I had to sit in this guard tower in some dark corner of the base where I was being trained, and it was totally desolate all around me. And, in the course of four hours of guard duty, I just screamed the whole time. Four hours, nonstop. It didn't make a difference, no one could hear me. I was in the middle of nowhere. But, like, somewhere inside, I felt a threat. And it was then that I began making plans to hurt myself. I really wanted terrorists to come, to shoot me. I wanted it. All sorts of thoughts ran through my head.

I began to convince myself that, when it comes down to it, I'm the living dead. On the one hand, I'm very much alive, I keep myself busy, and I have a lot of friends, I have a very full life, from morning til night, also on Shabbat when we go home, I always have things to think about, things to do. But on the other hand, something is wrong, because I'm repressing something. Something is on the back burner, all the time. And I decided that I didn't want to keep on living. A carefully weighed out decision. I just had to, like, choose the timing.

It was clear to me that I had to wait at least a little while because Hagar had only just killed herself. Even though it is very fashionable, statistically, in groups like ours, where there is one suicide, others immediately follow. Sometimes two or three. Or if someone is killed, two more will commit suicide. This happens. It's a system like that, I don't know why. Crazy.

But I was convinced that I wanted to die. I just had to choose the timing. I didn't have a shadow of a doubt that I would do it. I knew that I was not willing to live, I knew already at that point. I knew what the implications of these things were, like, of being gay, and I was not willing to live that way. I had the sense that it was irreconcilable with living on the kibbutz. And I was really worried about it, for instance, that if I wanted to be a teacher they wouldn't let me. Because there are no secrets on a kibbutz. There's no such thing. If a mother beats her children at home, like, she's not going to work with the kids. You know who hits their children, and who doesn't. And you know who has a drug problem. You can't hide anything.

So I thought there was a terrible contradiction here. And I said, if I can't live on the kibbutz, my life is meaningless. What, I'll go back to the city? That, in my book, is failure. The kibbutz seemed to me the best way, the most just way that a person could possibly live. The way where you relate to people because of what they are, and not because of their family name, skin color, years of education, or age. But back then, I also thought that equality was sameness, and so there could be no special cases on the kibbutz, no deviations. That's the way I thought. Today I know that the kibbutz is basically a collection of deviants. But then, something like that never even occurred to me.

The whole matter of accepting people who were different did of course come up in our discussions, but it didn't fit with my own preconceptions, and I heard what I wanted to hear. My interpretive framework could only allow me to see that I was different. I stood out—I was lonely and alone. Certainly no one would understand—talking to them would only, like, alienate them. And I felt guilty, because, I said to myself, they love me, and I'm cheating them. I'm showing them only one side, I don't show them the real me. If they knew who I really was, they wouldn't feel this way about me.

So I gave up on myself. I said, like, everything about me is a show. Because nothing from my dark side is ever expressed. I didn't believe that I was myself. I saw myself as a kind of a side-effect, produced by a performance. I began to distrust all of my friendships. Do you understand? I asked myself, what does it mean that Ran is a good friend of mine if he doesn't know anything about me? Do you understand? People flipped over me, people loved me. And I would tell them everything, the most intimate things, about my parents' divorce, and all sorts of personal, very personal things. And people interpreted it as, "Yossi is a good friend, he lets you in on his most intimate things." And to me it was all bullshit, because, like, everything was dwarfed by this terrible other thing, this burden I was dragging. That shadow, my other life.

So, deep inside, I had a total lack of trust. And it just kept on growing and getting deeper, until it became totally central. So I stopped and said, I can't live this way, and so, at the first opportunity I have, which I will carefully plan so that there will be no retreat, I will execute my plans. That's it.

The snipers' course ended, and I was sent to my brigade. We were all on the Golan Heights. January, 1990. I was twenty, already six months in the army. And I arrived at the brigade, and, like, suddenly there were days when there was nothing to do, nothing at all. And that was just what I needed. I just let my thoughts flow. How I was going to do it—poison, sleeping pills—and where I was going to do it, and if I would tell someone beforehand, and who. To write a letter, not to write a letter. I planned everything out. There was so much time. And time is a terrible thing in situations like that.

At this point, they gave us four days to go back to the kibbutz as a group to have some discussions. Snow—the first time in my life since Safed. And I said, like, that's it, it has got to be now. Now. This is the time. "If not now, when?" And then I said, OK, what do I do? So, on my way through Qiryat Shemonah, I bought some sleeping pills, forty of them. I planned to ask for a leave to go home, and instead of going home, to go to my friend Ran. I couldn't help but say goodbye to him, to see him, hear him, to be with him, so that this would be my last memory. I planned to sleep at his place that night. The next day he would go to the army, and I wouldn't wake up.

And that's it. The moment I knew how it would be done, and had already taken the first step, by buying those pills, apparently something was, like, visibly different about me. A sensitive person can notice. Back at the kibbutz, I didn't take part in any discussions, even on the most controversial subjects. There was a general meeting of the kibbutz, but I had no patience. I just wanted it to end already. And I checked over and over again whether the car that was supposed to take me to Haifa was still leaving on schedule.

The general meeting finally ended, and I ran to my room. I had all sorts of beginnings of letters to all sorts of people, and I didn't have a chance to finish them. I intended to keep on working on them at Ran's.

The word "homosexual" had never crossed my lips. I had never said the word in my life. Nothing that could link me to that matter had come up with any of my friends. Nothing. But now I began to write a letter to Rayiv, one of my friends from the group, about all sorts of things I was thinking, and what was happening, about, like, how I feel about him, and all sorts of things like that. And I wrote—I don't remember the sentence, it was in parenthesis at the end of the letter, I just couldn't believe that I had written it. I wrote something like, "If you haven't figured it out, maybe I should tell you that the time has come for me to come out of the closet." And I continued to write, "I don't believe I'm writing this." Close parenthesis. And that's it. I didn't write any more. I intended to continue later on.

I left the general meeting, and ran to my room to pack my things, to be alone. I didn't want anyone around me. And then my counselor called me over to him. I was like, "What, what, what, I've got to go." "You're not going anywhere." "Why?" "Because I said so. I decided not to let you. I talked to your commander in the army, he doesn't want you to go home." He was lying, of course. "He said that he wasn't willing to let discussion days be used for trips home. I'm very sorry, you're not going tonight. You can go tomorrow, to visit." I was totally shocked.

OK, so what do we do now? I thought that this was the end of the matter. But then he said, "Come to my room, I want to talk to you." And it was, you know, on his part, just, like, a shot in the dark. We sat down in his room, and he began to make coffee, and I was unbelievably pissed off. I was just thinking that, like, the moment this conversation was over I would find a corner somewhere, and end it all. Execute my plans. And he sat down and began to talk. I remember only the general outline of what he said, not the actual words. "Sometimes a person feels alone. He thinks that his problem is the most terrible thing that there could be in the world. And a person, thinking this way, can come to the conclusion that there's no way out." Afterwards, when I asked him if he knew anything for sure, he swore to me, and I believe him, that he didn't know. He didn't know.

And he talked about Hagar indirectly. He sort of touched on it, somehow, that subject. And that's it. That was when I just cracked. I was in shock, I said to myself, God, he read me like an open book. I asked him if, like, he knew why I wanted to do it. By this point it was clear to both of us that we were talking about suicide. And I asked him if he knew why. And he said no. And I was like, "It can't be that you know that I want to end my life, but you don't know why." It was important to me that someone come and toss it in my face. Say it to me. But he said to me, "No, I don't know."

I had created a very elaborate defense system, a network of lies, masks, self-control. I had actually practiced preventing myself from blushing—I exercised in front of a mirror. You couldn't catch me blushing. No way. People would make some sort of a comment, or something like that—nothing. Poker face. In retrospect it's clear to me that it was really very stupid, so idiotic. Because it's written on your forehead. The question is only how people relate to it. I just expected some sort of a reaction. Absolutely, if a person knows that I'm "like that," there has to be some sort of a reaction, I assumed. It can't be that it's just a natural thing, right? It's deviant.

So I was like, "It can't be that you don't know why." And he said, "No, I don't know why." And I said, "OK, I'm going to sleep." And he gave me a look, and I just went, "Yes, I'm going to sleep. And tomorrow when we meet I promise you to continue this conversation. If you don't trust me, we don't have anything to talk about." I turned to leave, but then, like, at the last second, I said to him, "Take this, maybe it'll help," and I gave him the letter I had begun to write to Rayiv. And it was written there, in black and white, with that sentence in parenthesis, about the closet.

What's funny is that I actually thought that this sentence wouldn't give it away, because I thought it was exclusively gay jargon—that stuff about the closet, doors, coming out. I thought everyone else thought about *The Lion, the Witch, and the Wardrobe*, C. S. Lewis, Aslan, Narnia, and all that, when they talked about closets.

And that's it. That night snow fell again. It wasn't that everything was, like, wonderful suddenly. But it had simply been halted. I felt like they had tricked me. I hadn't planned things this way. I had always been very careful to be in control of my life. And if I had decided to end my life, no one was going to stop me. I determine my own fate, not anyone else. My grandfather told me when I was little that there was no God, that God was invented by some people, to take advantage of other people. That's God. So the person who decides my fate is me. But now, you know, it didn't seem that way.

And the next morning, I was on pins and needles to see my counselor. He said to me that he wanted to talk to me again, and we went to his room. I said, "Well, did you figure it out?" And he said to me, "Yes," with this surprised look, as if to say, like, "Of course." And he went on, "OK, so most of society is heterosexual, and there are also some people who are homosexual. What else? What other problems do you have that made you want to do a thing like this?" I was, like, in shock. I was totally shocked. I basically said to him, "What are you talking about—this is the end of the world!"

And there was some sort of a conversation, I don't really remember it, only the general lines of it. He talked and I listened and cried. And he talked in way, like, totally the opposite of my earlier way of thinking. He talked about how, in a kibbutz society like this, he was surprised at how I could get myself into such a state over this. Because I'm in a society that has been designed, really, educated to handle exactly this kind of deviance. He said to me, "You know that you're not the first to come to this room. People come with all sorts of terrible things. So what's going on, what's your problem?" And he said to me, "Listen, I can call the brigade, and ask that you stay the night, and tomorrow you can see a psychologist. There's one in Qiryat Shemonah who can help you get a grip on yourself a little." I said to him that, like, there would be no need, and he insisted that there was. I said to him, "OK, but not now. Next Friday."

I mean, what the hell is a psychologist, anyway? Who are those strange people? I'm a mature person, I'm in control of my emotions, my actions. I think in a very particular way. "It'll be OK," I said to him, "We'll talk about it." He said, "I'm worried about sending you back, I'm worried." But I said, "Don't worry."

I insisted on going back again, primarily because I had forgotten what the army was like. What it is to be a soldier. I had, like, been in the sniper course for a while—it had been two months since I had lived the intensity of a combat soldier.

So I went back to everyone back at the base, and that very same night we had to do what they called an "Elephant Trek"—as a group, to hike all night long, nine miles in the snow, carrying all the equipment we would theoretically need for a battle where we would have no chance of being resupplied. Everything a soldier can carry, he carries—a frightfully heavy tent, uniforms wrapped in plastic to protect them against water, rocks, I don't know, like, everything, just so that it should be heavy. And the shoulder straps of our bags were an inch wide—they really cut into you. In addition, each person had the specific equipment that he used to fight. Everyone had a rifle, and then you had something additional. All I had was another rifle, since I was a sniper, and a second canteen.

Everything in my backpack weighed about eighteen or twenty pounds, and then my vest weighed, like, another eighteen or twenty pounds. My special rifle weighed four and a half pounds more than a standard rifle. Extra ammunition for an emergency was another, like, nine pounds, and my second water bottle was around another two pounds. This was the "Elephant Trek." Nine miles, through the night.

Now, Rayiy, from my group, he was the signal operator—he was responsible for carrying and operating the unit's field communication equipment. And the communications pack was fitted for him, so that he would be able to carry both his standard backpack and the communications equipment, like, on his back. But at the last minute, they notified him that he had to go for a special training course, for a week, so he wouldn't be able to go on the trek. Now, when we were in basic training, Rayiy and I would always fill in for each other. I mean, we were buddies. That's, like, what buddies do. So what do I do now? I did the stupidest thing possible. Fucking brainless. It was, somehow, clear to me that I should volunteer to carry the communications equipment. I volunteered. I don't know why I did it—I had never been so boneheaded before. This was the only time.

So we leave the base, by bus, and we're ready to start moving, but, like, we do an equipment check first. I was in an incredibly foul mood, like, unbelievable. And then they're like, "Where's Rayiy's equipment?" Nowhere. "Who was supposed to bring it?" They check: Yossi. "Yossi, where's the communications equipment?" And I was like, "What, who, huh?" "You goddamn fucking stupid idiot!" Terrible shouting. Terrible. Now, when I'm shouted at, I immediately just, like, turn myself off. So, really, all I heard was gibberish: "AEOU-AOUEOUOAE!" And I could see this person shouting at me, his mouth moving. It was already one in the morning. So. "Should I go get the equipment?" "AOEIAOEIOAIEOA!" I understood. I took the truck and went back to the base to get the equipment. When I came back, we were ready to go.

Forward march. Backpacks, special equipment, everyone panting. Unbelievable. There are, like, no words. And all the time the thought in the back of your mind that this was not a random exercise. This was not simply, like, to see if you could take it or not—if there's a war, this is the way you'll fight. It was a rehearsal for reality. I was bowled over by that thought. I was in shock.

So, like I said, this equipment was fitted for Rayiy. He had adjusted it for himself, so that it would rest on top of his backpack. But his backpack's shoulder straps were, like, lengthened, so that it would fall pretty low, from his rear to the middle of his back, and then this equipment would sit from middle of the back to the base of his neck, on top. But, like, I never had a chance to lower my backpack. So when I put the equipment on top, it pushed on the back of my head, and it created a situation where, like, I had to walk with my head bent down, my chin on my chest.

This wouldn't be so bad, except that the person carrying the communications equipment is also supposed to be in charge of communication—it was my job to, like, pass on messages from the platoon commander to the soldiers, to run to the very back to talk to the sergeant, and to egg on the soldiers in the middle. That was my job. But I can't do any of that. In fact, like, I need an ambulance. Immediately.

So, we keep on moving, and I can't see where we're going, I can't see what the hell's going on in, like, this dark, ice, and snow. Everything is white. Iced-over puddles. What's going on here? They're going straight ahead, and I keep losing my way, veering off to the side. And they have to drag me back. Because I simply can't see where I am going.

It was a matter of seconds—and everything that had happened with my counselor was erased. I said to myself, within seconds, OK, at the first opportunity, I'm going take my rifle and shoot myself. That's it, I've had enough, I'm through, there's nothing for me to do. And I started to cry again. But a lot of people cried, I wasn't the only one. It was difficult, so people cry—it's legitimate, like, you're allowed to cry.

I finally grabbed someone by his pack and he led me the entire way. At one point I fell, and cut open the whole side of my hand on the ice. I was irritated, depressed, and I said, like, as soon as we arrive, even before we set up camp, I'm going to take a shit, and I'm not coming back.

And we got there, and there was no time to shit. Who has time to shit now? "When the time comes, you can take a shit, in the meantime, pitch your tent." It was, like, five in the morning, and it was still dark as one of the ten plagues. But I began to calm down a little, and we pitched the tent. In spite of my plans, my tiredness forced me to sleep for, like, two hours. And then everyone had to go out for exercises, but someone needed to stay behind in the camp, alone, to guard. I volunteered. My hand was bandaged and I was too tired to see anything. So the platoon commander gives me a kind of suspicious look, he thinks for a moment, and then he says OK. Another little psychologist.

And then they left. I was on guard alone for, like, three hours. And then, the platoon sergeant came. He gave me all sorts of things to do for him. I asked him when he would be coming back, and he said, "I'm going to the platoon base camp. I'll come back with the rest of them." "When will that be?" "For dinner." That's it. I would have the whole day.

And I cry again. Tears, sun, a beautiful clear day, snow, everything is white. And that's it. I said, OK, it's now. My gun was a sniper's gun, an M-14, with a very high caliber. During my training course, I had seen movies about the kind of wound it inflicts, what levels of hell someone goes through before they die. But I didn't have anything else. So I loaded it.

Now, during basic training, a soldier hears a lot about not loading his gun when there's no officer present. This alone was a very grave action, very serious. And then I sat down. And that was also a serious violation of guard duty. You're not allowed to sit. In my entire life I never dreamed I would—I mean, these were very serious infractions. I can't explain, I can't explain it. These were not things I would do. I broke guard duty. I sat down. And I held the gun between my legs, the barrel pointed at my face.

The problem was that I couldn't reach the trigger like this. But if I, like, leaned a bit to the side, and rested my temple on the end of the barrel, then I could reach. I could sit that way and shoot—like, rest my head on the barrel and then shoot. The bolt was already back—I had already done that— *chak chak.* Now I just needed to release the safety and pull the trigger. I had to be careful, because you can create a situation where you pull the trigger with too much strength, and then the bullet can fly in the wrong direction, and not at me. That would have been bad. It was important to me that it be just right.

And then, I remember, I saw all these memories, thoughts, scenes. And I cried and cried and cried, more and more and more and more and more. It was more than I could take. I was, like, losing my mind. And suddenly I remembered that I hadn't written a letter to my friend Ran. I put the down gun, and quickly wrote him a letter. I put it into the electric razor case of someone from my group who uses his razor only on Friday. Before he goes home for Shabbat he, like, shaves with the electric razor.

And I went back to that position with my gun, and my mind drifted again, and suddenly it was the evening already. And they were back. I had missed my chance. Hours and hours had gone by like that, and suddenly they came back. I stood up as soon as I heard them coming. But my gun was still loaded. You just needed to shoot. And I, like, ran to someone and said,

"Look, you've got to relieve me, I have to take a shit. I've been standing up all day." So I went to shit.

There are lots of ditches there. And I, like, went down into one of them, and I said, this is it. I didn't do it like the first time. I stayed standing, and propped the rifle butt up on a stone. But then something happened to me. It was a thing like, it wasn't a blackout, I really can't explain it—it was like I was frozen in place. I was just standing there, not thinking about anything. I was just looking at the gun, waiting until I would pull the trigger. That was it.

And from far away, I could hear that they were looking for me. "Yossi, Yossi." And then quiet. I was standing there for, like, forty minutes. Forty minutes. Emptiness. I wasn't thinking about anything. Me. The gun. The ditch. The sound of the wind. I waited. I don't even know what for. And then suddenly, someone from the platoon found me. And as soon as I heard him coming, I put the gun down.

The moment I put the gun down, something snapped, and suddenly I understood what could have happened at that moment. I was totally stunned. I think I was really hysterical. Clinically, physically speaking. It was really hysteria. And he comes, and he says to me, like, "What are you doing here? We've been looking for you." I didn't answer him. I couldn't. He left, and when he came back, he brought the platoon commander with him. And the commander came and sat down next to me. He said to me quietly, "What happened?" And then I put the bolt back into the resting position, took the bullet out, and said to him, "Take this. It's better that I don't have this right now." I gave him the bullet.

I found out afterwards that if I had given him the gun, they would have kicked me out of the army. Because there are all sorts of degrees, apparently. There are psychologists who deal with this. And if a soldier turns over his gun, refuses to touch his gun, the procedure is to immediately discharge him. Immediately and permanently. I don't remember what my commander said at this point, but he brought me back to reality. It was like, "OK, that's that, that's done with, try to explain. You can't explain, OK, so what do you want to happen now? Do you want to go back to the regimental headquarters?" And I was like, "No, no way." And he said to me, "Do you want to stay?" And I was like, "Yes. I promise you personally," and I really looked up to him, and he knew it, "I promise you that you can forget all about this. This doesn't make a bit of difference. This didn't happen, and it will never happen again." And he said to me, "Look, I'm obligated to report this to the psychologists at the regimental base. But I can't report it now, so for tonight, just go back with everyone else." He gave me the bullet back, I put it back in the cartridge, I put the cartridge back in my vest, and I went back up to the platoon.

The next day I was sent to the psychologist. He asked me to tell him what happened. I told him that I couldn't talk about it. He said, "OK, then I'm going to kick you out of the company." And he said, "I'm asking again to hear about this, it's important." I said, "I'm sorry, but it's too difficult for me." And he said, "OK, go back and pack your things. You're leaving tomorrow." So in the morning, the next morning, I packed up, and everyone was like, "Where the hell are you going?" I was like, "I've got to go." I continued with my lies. "I've got to go to the infirmary."

So I was sent one more time, with all of my things packed up, back to the psychologist. My platoon commander also came. And we went in, and the psychologist was like, "OK, Yossi, what's the deal." And I didn't say a word. My platoon commander said to the psychologist, "Would you rather I left?" And I gave him a pleading look, like, don't you dare leave me alone with this schmuck. But the psychologist thought it was better that he leave. And then he says, "Listen you, I have no patience for nonsense like this. If you can't decide what your problem is by 2:00, when I have a meeting of the psychological staff at the regimental headquarters, that's it, you're history, you're leaving the company. Pure and simple."

And he knew that for me, that was something I absolutely would not have been able to bear. No way. Because I knew that if I didn't remain in exactly this routine, if I didn't work this through, then and there, then I was going to go through this whole scene, like, again and again, until at some point I would actually do it. So I had no choice.

I said to him, "OK, but I don't want to talk. I want to write." He gave me a slip of paper. But I couldn't even, like, write it, I just couldn't, I couldn't write the word "homosexual." That was impossible. I began to explain to him in hints. I don't remember how, but, like, one thing led to another, and in the end he understood. I conveyed to him that I was bisexual. I was afraid they might kick me out of the army if I said I was gay. And he said to me, "What are the implications of this, in concrete terms." Really! So I said to him, "When you walk down the street, you see a pretty girl, you look at her. But I look both at guys and girls." "Have you ever done anything about this?" I said, "No." "Do you want to?" "I don't know—I'm still thinking about it." "So what brought you to this state that you're in?" "I'm also having problems at home," and so on. I put together a whole sob story, and the fucked-up idiot, like, swallowed it, the jerk. "OK. I'll think about it, I'll talk to your counselor, we'll see what's going on."

My counselor got there as fast as was humanly possible. He took me aside, with this pissed-off look, like, really pissed off. You can just imagine. "I never expected that you would do a thing like this, after we talked, and you promised. We're going right now, right now we're going to Qiryat Shemonah to the psychologist there." I said to him "No, no way. I'm not going anywhere right now. If I don't stay here tonight, and if tomorrow I don't participate in exercises just like normal, then it's all down the drain. Nothing will do any good. After tomorrow, I'll do whatever you want." "But how can I trust you, after you already promised me?" "When I promised you, I didn't know what it meant to go back, now I know, and I don't want to leave everyone else." And that's it. I stayed.

Now my biggest problem was, like, to retrieve the suicide note I had left in my friend's razor case! I had forgotten about it until Friday afternoon, when I saw him taking the case out of his bag. And I ran to him and insisted that he let me borrow it and shave first. "No, no, no." "Come on, come on, come on." I took it, like, shaved, and with a slip of the hand the note was safely in my pocket.

Three days later I was wounded in a practice drill. Can you believe it? I got frostbite. They were worried that my spinal cord had been damaged, so I had to stay in the hospital for five weeks. I was so pissed off at myself that it happened, because it was, like, so close to everything else, it looked as if I had done it on purpose. It took me a long time to convince the psychologist, and my platoon commander especially, that I hadn't planned it. But I hadn't.

I was released from the hospital in the morning, and by that evening I was already in Rafiaḥ, on the Gaza Strip, on patrol, with my unit. I didn't even want to go home. While I was in the hospital, the psychologist from Qiryat Shemonah came to see me. We met, like, three, four times. Those conversations touched on the edges of what was going on. I didn't feel close to him at all. He wanted to talk about my parents, and I lied to him. I just lied to him all the time, because I couldn't talk to him. I had no patience for the whole thing. Afterwards I stopped it, because it was so expensive. It cost a hundred twenty shekels for every hour, for those meetings. I mean, the army was paying, but I just couldn't bear the thought that he was making so much money off of my problems.

In the end, it did help me though, because it was really then that I said to myself, OK, this is the way things are, this is the way you are, now you've just got to try to tell your friends, so that you can relieve some of this pressure, and get on with your life. We'll see what the future will bring. But it's OK, it's legitimate, nothing can happen, tell the first one, then the second one, we'll see what the crowd says, and based on that, we can decide.

The first one I told was Gili, from my group, shortly after I got out of the hospital. He knew that I had been seeing the psychologist. I remember that I was driving with him—we were going back to the kibbutz to see the movie version of *Hair* on television with a friend who was alone because her husband was on reserve duty. But when we got there, we could hardly see the movie because the power kept going out, there were problems with the electricity. It really got on my nerves. I really wanted to watch the movie.

Anyway, on the way back, I said to him, "Do you know why I'm going to the psychologist?" And he was like, "Because of Hagar." And I said to him, "Nope. Come on, you know the real reason why." And he said, "No, I don't know." But I insisted, "Come on, think, it has to do with something I'm sure you all, like, know about me, and you never talk about." How much more could I say? And I said to him, "What's with you, are you playing games with me? You know what I'm talking about." But he just didn't know.

I really don't remember how we moved on from this, I don't remember what I said, but somehow I got the point across. And then I asked him if he was surprised. And he said no. And I was like, "So you did know." And he went, "I thought it might be, maybe, but what difference does it make, what, what's the big deal?" So I said to him, "What, it doesn't make a difference to you?" And he was like, "Wait a second, I mean, are you someone different from the person I know?" So I said to him, "What do you think?" He went, "I don't think so. OK, so, to each his own, but what, do you want me to tell you the crazy things about me?" I said no, because, like, then I wouldn't be the star of the evening any more. The conversation was about me, not him. And that's it. I was very disappointed. Simply disappointed. This was not what I had expected.

My platoon commander had also asked me to tell him what was going on with me, and I promised him that I would. He knew that I had been seeing a psychologist in the hospital. At the end of our time in Rafiaḥ, I said to him, "Do you remember that I promised you to tell you?" And he said, "Yes." "I was meeting with the psychologist to treat a problem with my sexual identity." I phrased it, like, very gently, nicely. And he said to me, "I thought that it was either that, or you have a serious disease. Cancer or something like that." And then he said, "So, it's final, your decision, you can't change yourself?" As nicely and gently as I phrased it, he knew exactly, like, what I was talking about. So I said to him, "I think it's final." And then he said me, "Well, you know, in my own group," he had gone through the same army program, "I have in my own group these two guys who were, like, sleeping with each other for a while, but it turned out OK. I mean, now one of them has a girl-friend." I said to him, "No, I think that, for me, that's the way it is." To this day, he's the only person who I have ever said things so clearly to—that this is the way it is, absolutely. I had to see how that felt. Today I wouldn't say that things are so clear to me.

The army never made an issue out of what they knew about my sexuality. And I know that it reached the regimental commander. I remember, after my training accident, that my father went to talk to the commander. He wasn't satisfied with the way the matter was taken care of, something like that. He wanted to know some details. And after they met, I was very suspicious that maybe my commander had taken it upon himself to talk about the matter with my father. So I debriefed my father most extensively concerning every detail of the conversation, and I compared the results with another interro-gation I had performed, of Irit, from my group, who just happened to be the commander's clerk. And it emerged from my investigation that the only thing they talked about that touched on the subject was that the commander asked my father if I had a girlfriend. My father said to me, "He asked me if you had a girlfriend, and I said I don't know, but that there was somebody from your group, something like that." He had heard things from my sister, that little gossip-monger. And that's it. I understood that the regimental commander was a person who was not going to pass this information any-where. He just didn't let it influence anything.

In my group, we're a very physical group. We talk with our hands. When I'm talking to someone from the group, I have to touch him. I simply must, otherwise I can't talk to him. It was part of the general system—guys and guys, guys and girls, girls and girls. When we talk we touch. When we are sit-ting in a circle and having a group discussion, and I want to say something to a particular person, I get up, go over to him, and hug him, touch him, otherwise it's impossible. To this day. Kisses when we see each other, like, be-tween girls, between guys, between guys and girls, sometimes even on the lips. Even today. We touch each other all the time. The slap on the back and the hug are very important rituals. Everyone's like that. And it's not, like, a sexual thing, in my opinion. It's another way of expressing ourselves, we're used to it.

Of course, I made some basic rules for myself, and I kept to them. I tried very hard to keep from being attracted to someone from the group. Because it isn't healthy. Everything having to do with them is simply not healthy. That's the way I felt.

It was really funny in the military kibbutz, because the other guys, who weren't from my group, and would shower with us and see how we would, like, soap one another up and everything, they were freaked out at first. But we're just very free with one another. Somehow I managed to keep myself under control. Today, I don't know if I could do it. Because I've already come one more step, where, I feel, what's your problem, everyone is kosher—or, rather, I don't keep kosher anymore, there are no forbidden foods!

It was totally the norm for everyone to shower together—I would never shower alone. I mean, there was a time during our year of community service when both the girls and the guys would shower together. Not out in the open—there were stalls with curtains, so the guys would go in first, close the curtains, and then the girls would go into the empty stalls. Because otherwise there was no hot water, it ran out. Back then, I never had a problem in the showers. During most of the time in the army, you're so tired you don't even have time to fantasize. You fall asleep instantly.

Now that I think about it, of course, there were some gorgeous guys there, especially in the pilots' course. Not all of them, but most of them were beautiful. Shocking. An unbelievable selection, from all types, like, all the nations, smooth-skinned, hairy, blond, dark, whatever you want. But I didn't really notice them back then.

I remember one time, we all had a party at someone's kibbutz. And I decided that at that party I will get drunk. Two weeks earlier I had gotten drunk for the first time in my life. And so I drank and drank and drank and drank and drank. Now there was this guy Eyal, and I, like, really wanted him. And this was our last night in the same company. We were being transferred. So I told him that I wanted to talk to him later on in the evening. And I intended to make him an explicitly indecent proposal.

I began drinking that night so that I would have the courage to go through with this—but I drank so much, that I forget what the whole point was. I mean, I forgot who I was, I didn't know what was going on. Luckily, we were all supposed to, like, sleep on the floor in sleeping bags, and I hadn't brought mine. So I asked Eyal if he would share his bag with me—I said he should just leave it open when he went to sleep. The evening drew to a close, a lot of drunk people, darkness, guitars, singing sort of bluesy songs, without the words, just la, la, la, la, or something, da ba da ba da. And then that was it, people were going to sleep. And I go, like, prowling around—where's Eyal?

He was in a room with about ten people, and he had left the sleeping bag open like I had asked him, and was laying there in the middle. I climbed in, and, like, pushed him over to the side. We were back to back at the beginning. Because at that point, I was saying, like, "OK, that's it, stop this drunken nonsense." But he was sleeping only in underwear and an undershirt, and I felt, like, the heat of his back on mine, and I couldn't take it any more, so I turned around. And then I said, OK, I was thinking very foggily, and I said, OK, there isn't anyone else in the room, just him and me—there were, like, another ten very close by. And now I began, like, experimenting. Let's see at what point he is going to respond. I began to, like, stroke him, to lift up his shirt, stroke him starting only on his back, afterwards on his stomach also, and on his thighs, and his bottom. I was careful not to touch the truly holy places. And then I started in with, like, my lips and my tongue. And he didn't respond. I can't believe that he really didn't wake up. Could it be? I don't know. He wasn't very drunk. I wonder to this very day, if it can be that you can do these things to a person and he can keep on sleeping. And then I decided, enough. Again, I said to myself, enough, you're lucky he didn't wake up, don't do anything you'll be sorry about.

In the morning, when I was, like, totally sober, I didn't want to look him in the face. I was so pissed off at myself. I felt very uncomfortable. I wanted to avoid him. And at some point, it became clear that he was avoiding me also. He was avoiding me, and that got me even more worked up. We were supposed to leave in the evening. But around lunchtime I went into his tent, a big tent, there were all sorts of people there. And then they left, and the two of us were suddenly alone, and he said, "Come here, give me a massage, for the last time, because you're leaving." Now, I was the company's unofficial masseur. No one gave a better massage than me, it was universally acknowledged. OK, so I began with his shirt on, and then I said to him, "Take off your shirt, I can't do it through your shirt." I remember the look he gave me—he tossed me, like, one of those penetrating looks, straight in the eye, and he took off his shirt. And I didn't give him a massage—I stroked him and made him horny, that's what I did. And it was clear to him too. This went on for, like, almost half an hour, and then they came to call us for lunch.

I remember the look on the face of the guy who came in—he, like, stuck his head into the tent, to call us for lunch, and his eyes nearly popped out of his head. Eyal was lying on his stomach with his shirt off, and I was sitting on top of him. But the best defense, of course, is to look as if this was the most natural thing in the world, so we just smiled and I kept on going, as if to say, "Wipe that stupid look off your face, if you're trying to imply something, we can't imagine what it is." And then we said, "OK, we're on our way." I got up. And when he got up, you could see, like, beyond a shadow of a doubt what kind of a mood he had been in. But I didn't stare. I saw that he was trying to make eye contact for a second, but I avoided it. And then, when I went to leave, he said to me, "Hang on a second, will you," as if to say, "I've got to wait something out over here." And that's it. I never saw him again.

After Gaza, we went to Lebanon for four months, to the security zone, and when that was over, we were sent to the West Bank, the Judean Desert, for exercises, the whole company. So, OK, Yossi baby, we said that we need to give it a try, so forward march, find yourself someone, and—to bed. We'll see what the story is. I really wanted it. Very, very much.

We were stationed near Teqoᶜa, not far from Jerusalem. And I said, well, it's about time to begin to go to the dentist, and, like, all that crap, all the things that I didn't want to do when I was in Lebanon, so that I wouldn't be separated from the guys. Back pains that I had, all sorts of things. Every week I would find a new reason to leave the base.

And I began looking for a personal ad from someone in Jerusalem. It would be convenient, on the way home from one of my trips, if I could hook up with someone. To delay my return by two hours. And I found a really ancient ad, really old, from a six-month-old newspaper. I don't remember the wording. But it stood out. It grabbed my attention. I just looked in a newspaper we had lying around at home.

OK. I answered the ad. I wrote a long letter, five pages long. I had to do it, like, I said to myself, I don't even care who this is, this poor guy. I just let it all out. I used a pseudonym, of course. And I got a letter in return on stationery like this, like, a big white unlined sheet, written in the handwriting of, like, a retarded six-year-old. Absolutely hieroglyphic handwriting. I saw the way the address was written on the envelope, and I said to myself, oh God, it's probably some creep who's sending me pornography or something. I sat down in the park near the post office, and I read it, and I was absolutely glued to the page. I fell in love with him immediately. He was so different. A different way of thinking. He wrote damn well.

His name was Rami. He was twenty-five, four years older than me. His mother worked in sales for some clothing company, and his father was the head of the Jerusalem region for a big bank. A very, very upstanding family, with the kind of house that revolts me when I walk in. Rami himself is a businessman. He would open a business, it would succeed, and he would sell it. He doesn't do anything himself. He is, like, a parasite, the antithesis of everything I believe in. He lives off of other people's work. Don't worry, I've said all of this to his face, too.

So I wrote him back. I described what I was looking for. And he wrote, "I want just the opposite. I think the other way around. Let's get together." I loved it. He gave me his telephone number at his parents' house. I called, he wasn't home. Two weeks later, I called again, he wasn't home. Two weeks later I called again, and he answered. I was very worked up. It was very difficult for me to make these calls. I mean, like, I was in the army. It wasn't like there was a public telephone in the Judean Desert. And I knew that they tap the telephone wires and listen in on our conversations. It's beyond, maybe, I suspect that perhaps they tap the lines—every day I would see the soldier whose job it was to listen in on conversations. So it wasn't easy for me to talk.

But I finally reached him. I thought I would lay down and die right there, just from his voice. It just, like, blew me away. Fabulous. Unbelievable. That was it, I was in love. And then I went to see him.

I had said that I wasn't looking for a serious relationship. I just wanted to get a little experience. But he said, "I've been running around for a while. I need someone who will lock me inside, who will chain me to a post." I said to him, "I don't want to make any promises." What, I'm going to, like, sign a marriage contract when I don't even know who this is? I said, "Whatever happens happens. But I'm not planning on making any commitments, because I'm in the army, I have my own life, I don't want someone to come in and rearrange my whole life. I won't let that happen. I just want to give this a try. We'll see what happens."

I told him I smoke, and he said, "That revolts me." And he really trashed the kibbutz way of life. He wrote the word "socialism" with every possible spelling error, just so he could make it absolutely clear to me how much contempt he has for the concept—he said it couldn't even really be dignified by the word "concept," it was just, like, someone's hallucination. There wasn't even anything substantial enough about it to talk about. It was air, nothing. On the other hand, he was very enthusiastic about all sorts of things I had written him. It turned out that he has a terrific sense for literary Hebrew.

So we arranged to meet when I would be on leave. It was Sukot. I told my parents and friends that I was going to meet a group from Beit Shemesh, to talk to them about the movement. And there really was a group, and I really did set out as if I was going to meet with them. But before I left the base, I called Beit Shemesh and canceled the meeting.

We had arranged that I should call him from the central bus station in Jerusalem when I got there. He asked me, "How will I know who you are?" I said, "I'll be in uniform. You'll have to choose among the soldiers." And he said to me, "Just look around, I'll be the best-looking guy in the central bus station. Just come right up."

I smoked, like, two cigarettes while I was waiting, I was so tense. I was smoking a lot at that time. And that's it, suddenly he came. It's difficult for me to reconstruct the feeling. Very different from what I'd imagined. But it fit very well with the description—the best-looking guy in the central bus station. He wasn't beautiful, but he was very sexy. He had, like, a kind of a jump in his step. And that's it. Suddenly I was frozen. I couldn't move. I couldn't speak. He said "Hello," and it was clear to me that this was it.

We went back to his parents' house. They weren't there, and his brother was at a basketball game. Rami was really hoping that his brother's team would lose. And then he said to me, "Where do you want to go? What should we bring?" I said, "I don't know, take a bottle of wine." "And where should we go?" I said to him, "To the Dead Sea." He said, "Let's go."

So we, like, drive, drive, drive. He's driving at unbelievable speeds, hardly looking at the road, his hands off the wheel. And me, what do I care, this is peanuts. I mean, I almost shot myself—I should care if I die in a car accident? And that's it, we passed ʿEin Gedi, and we got out of the car at the southern part of the Dead Sea, where the hotels are. The sea really just glittered during the drive down. He said to me, "Do you want to go into the water?" And I said yes. We undressed. And I just, like, stared. I just wanted to look at him. And I really liked what I saw.

We went into the water, and I was, like, following him in, slowly. But then, all of a sudden, he turned around and grabbed me by the shoulder and threw me into the water, and we rolled around struggling, wrestling. And that's it. We kissed a lot, I remember that. I mean, we had written to each other a lot beforehand, and we had spoken on the telephone. I knew him already—this was a foregone conclusion. Everything I ever wanted to do with a man, we did then. Almost. He was nuts.

Due to, like, intensive activity, we didn't sleep the entire night. We stayed on the beach, in spite of the mosquitoes. He got salt in his eyes at one point, and he was blinded, and I had to drag him out of the water to the showers. I tortured him a little on the way—grabbing him in unexpected places, then abandoning him suddenly. He couldn't open his eyes. But that's nothing compared to what he did to me afterwards.

In the morning, we got back into the car, and we drove back to Jerusalem. He told me that he was moving, and wanted to go look at some apartments in Tel Aviv. So I waited for him in town, and he went home to change his clothes, and when he came back I didn't even recognize him. I really thought it was someone else. He was dressed like he had stepped out of a fashion spread. Slacks and leather shoes, a silk shirt and a tie, a briefcase and sunglasses. I was in shock. Wonderful. Really, fabulous. And I was like, still in my uniform, looking like something the cat dragged in.

I went with him apartment-hunting in Tel Aviv. And we talked and laughed. He was beautiful. And he spoke graceful, proper Hebrew. That was enough. At this point we already, like, felt free with our hands, and we were constantly touching one another. I was like, "You'll flip the car over if I do what I want right now." And he was like, "Not at all—I'll just be combining the two things I need to do right now—to drive, and to have sex." So, on the Jerusalem-Tel Aviv highway, with all the cars around, we had our way with each other, while driving. You have to understand what this meant for me. I totally let go. It was like, utter release.

So we got to Tel Aviv, we saw a few apartments, and then he said, "OK, where do you need to go now?" I said, "Home, near Haifa." And he said "OK, I'll take you, I've got to go to Acre, I've got a friend there who is doing some business for me." OK, fine, we begin driving from Tel Aviv to Haifa, but we don't make it all the way without a stop in Caesaria, where we move the seats to the recline position, and go at it again. I'm, like, totally dead already. I mean, we haven't gone to sleep yet. He's all energetic, and I'm like a wet rag. Eventually I did get home.

In the evening I went, just like every Friday night, to eat dinner with Ran's family, *qidush* and so on, and I was, like, dozing off at the table.[§] And Ran's mother just gave me this look like, "What happened to you?" After dinner, Ran and I were supposed to go out, but I just fell asleep at his house! A girlfriend of his and another two friends were on their way, but I couldn't wake up.

Later that night, Rami called me. "OK, I'm on my way to pick you up, we're going out." I was like, "Have you slept?" And he said, "No, I've been at the alternative theater festival in Acre." I said, "Tell me, are you insane?" I mean, I was having trouble gripping the telephone receiver.

[§] qidush: Literally, "sanctification"; the prayer said over wine, especially before the commencement of a festive meal on Shabbat and other holidays.

At this point in time, my army service demanded very little effort on my part, and what little effort was demanded of me, I tried very hard to avoid. So I took every opportunity to leave the base and go and spend time with him. I made a grand series of dentist's appointments for myself, for example. Of course, I never went to one of them, which only created a need for new appointments. And there were all sorts of other scams. But time was a real problem, because I was supposed to be on the base all week, and I never wanted to be with Rami on Shabbat—it was more important to me to go home, to be with Ran's family on Friday night, and spend Saturday night with my old crowd. And I didn't tell anyone about him, not one of my friends. This wasn't supposed to be a problem, so far as Rami was concerned, because we had agreed that there were no obligations here. Or at least that's the way things looked.

Rami had all sorts of games. Because I was so freaked out that no one should know about me, he would always, like, molest me in the street. All sorts of pinches and grabs. We would walk around Jerusalem a lot, and I remember once, we were walking in that neighborhood with the windmill, Mishkenot Sha'ananim, overlooking the Old City. There were people walking around, and suddenly he pulled me into one of the doorways of the houses, and had his way with me. And I was, of course, totally freaked out, and he loved it, and would laugh about the whole thing.

I entered into this relationship in order to experiment. I didn't want something too restricting. I never thought of him as my boyfriend, my partner. That was never the definition. There never was a definition, I didn't do any defining. But I knew from the start that he wanted something else, he wanted someone to rely on. And he said to me, "If you don't take advantage of me now, when I'm looking to commit, then very soon I'm not going to be interested any more, and you'll be sorry." Which did indeed happen very quickly. I became attached—I suddenly wanted a more stable relationship, deeper. I began, perhaps, to love. But he wasn't interested any more.

During this entire time, we continued to write to one another, we didn't give that up. It's strange that our correspondence didn't reflect our real-life relationship. We had two parallel relationships—one much more physical, in person, and one more emotional and intellectual, in letters. At first, I refused to bring the written relationship to life. From my point of view, it would create a totally full "relationship," which I didn't want. And when I decided that, yes, I wanted to try to add it all together, to talk about the things I had written, he was the one who refused.

In the meantime, he had found an apartment in Tel Aviv, a penthouse studio in the south, near the central bus station. Not a very nice neighborhood, but the apartment had a huge roof that you could walk out onto. Lots of antennas, but it was still a roof. These were crazy days—we spread out these huge sort of plastic mattresses on the roof, and we would fool around out there. We were the highest roof in the neighborhood, so no one could see us. But I thought the entire street would wake up from our yelling. We had a very nosy neighbor, across the street, one floor down. We would watch her watch us, and we would just, like, sit and talk. But then she would lose interest, and the moment she would look away, Rami would just begin to take my clothes off. And she would be totally freaked out. We laughed so much, we had some great times. Terrific scenes. I think that everything that I know about sex today is from what I learned experimenting with him. We had hours and hours set aside just for this, just for sex.

I've saved all our letters, and when you read them, the story of our relationship is very clear. I guess you could think of it as two lines that cross at a certain point—one is my expectations and the other is his. They start far apart, they get closer, cross, and then separate again, each one in its own direction, switching roles. And you can see, there is one letter that's the point of contact, and from that point on we began to grow apart rather than closer. And I began to hate every second of the relationship, but I couldn't get myself away from it. I was really addicted to him.

It began with his telling me that he had slept with someone else. We had talked about monogamy, as a concept. But of course, it didn't have anything to do with us—there was no question, because I refused even to define what we had as a relationship. I said, "So far as I'm concerned, as long as you promise me to protect yourself, I have no problem." And he ran to take advantage of this. But the truth is that it did bother me. And then he began doing all sorts of things which, I can see now, were very humiliating for me. Like, I would have to wake up at a certain hour and leave for a little while, because he wanted to get together with someone who he might want to bring back to the apartment. I would be able to come back, like, in an hour or so. And I agreed to this.

I didn't have a choice. I couldn't allow myself any other way, because now I had two separate, complete lifestyles. There was the army, my friends from the group, going home on Shabbat, and then there was my whole life with him. I couldn't imagine giving up that second life, like, leaving that space empty. Even at the price of a relationship that was clearly, unmistakably, becoming more and more fucked up. Somewhere inside, even I knew that it was fucked up. But I couldn't do anything about it.

The whole thing was, I mean, my whole motivation to answer his ad in the first place, was that I needed to find reasons for staying alive, and quickly. I felt that life is a collection of experiences. And I, as a person, needed to collect as many experiences as possible, to get to know as much as possible. I could tell myself that my life was worthwhile only if I could say, I'm having the experience of getting to know a person, someone who under normal circumstances I would never have met, never have even wanted to meet. And so I was dependent upon the relationship.

Then he went to Europe for a month, to Germany. This was right before the war, the Gulf War. While he was abroad he gave me a very special job to do—I had to call the stock market every day, and ask how a particular stock of his was doing, and then call him and leave him a message on his answering machine in Germany. Can you believe it? He left me the key to his apartment in Tel Aviv, fully equipped, video, microwave, television, refrigerator, computer, hot water, bed, books, everything a person needs. I would go there sometimes.

Around this time, my group was transferred back up to Lebanon. But the whole time that Rami was in Germany, I managed to find excuses to keep myself at headquarters, and didn't go up to the Lebanese border with everyone else. Because Rami was supposed to come back to Israel any day, and, like, if I went up to Lebanon then that was it, I wouldn't be able to come back to welcome him. I paid a very heavy social price for this in the group. Because the entire group went, except for me—everyone who was physically capable of going up to the border went, but I didn't. It didn't interest me at all. I was really addicted to him. But he waited until the very last minute. He came on a Thursday, and by Sunday I already had to go up, that was it. There were no more games to be played, I couldn't drag it out any longer.

When he did finally come back, we went to bed on Thursday afternoon, and we got out of it on Shabbat, in the evening. I never knew when it was evening, morning, afternoon, it was dark all the time, and he was awake the whole time, from Thursday afternoon until Saturday evening. I went to sleep, like, every now and then. But he didn't sleep. When I went to sleep he would, like, do some work on his computer. I remember that I helped him to write a few letters. He was planning on going back to Europe. One of the letters I helped him write was actually to the guy who would become his new boyfriend. Maybe they're still boyfriends. That was the last time I slept with him.

And that's it. I had to leave. I went up to Lebanon. And then the Gulf War began. Rami left Israel before the war, and I would go to the apartment from time to time. That was a real experience—one time there was a serious boom near the house. I was really happy it happened. I was worried I was going to miss that war, like, stationed up in Lebanon, where it was safe. And that's it.

After another little while he came back to Israel. I would call from time to time, and I knew that often there was someone with him. But like an idiot I kept on calling. I can't explain it. He's irresistible. It's impossible. And then he was supposed to go away yet again, and I decided that this was the end. He went to the Far East. I wrote him a few things, poems, a long letter that sort of summed things up finally, and sort of didn't. And that's it, he left.

Of course, we had lots of arguments about this whole German thing, about Jewish loyalties, which Rami totally rejected. But I believe in the continued existence of the Jewish people. It's a moral value, it's not rational. There is no logical explanation. But you know, those people who think that the world is heading toward unification are wrong. Maybe Europe is, but for me, Europe has always stood for all the evil in the world. I don't see why everyone shouldn't dwell with his own tribe—I think that's beautiful.

Nationalism doesn't necessarily lead to conflict. An Egyptian can be an Egyptian, a Palestinian can be a Palestinian, and an Israeli can be what he is, and it doesn't have to, like, cause a conflict of interests. I don't believe in borders, and I object to the instrument that is called the state, which already lost all its value the moment it created a bureaucracy. The state murders its citizens not through war, but through the thicket of bureaucratic entanglement. But you can have a different kind of nationalism.

You can have one large, general system, all-inclusive, and within that, like, culturally autonomous areas. That's exactly what I'm talking about. This fits with my conception of a city, with different communities, and in each community, congregations, and in each congregation, groups. And they will relate to one another however they want. And there will be no obligation to the state.

Jewish identity is important to me, even though I'm an atheist, and I always was. But there's a lot that I take from our tradition. Until I was seventeen, I didn't even know what making *qidush* on Friday night was. But when I was exposed to it for the first time, I saw how it had been missing for me. I missed it. Of course, for me it has a different meaning—like, as a group ritual.

My Yom Kippur is mine alone—*my* Yom Kippur, even though it is also the general Yom Kippur. I'm always on the kibbutz for Yom Kippur. Most people there eat, a few fast. And there's always a discussion on Judaism and Zionism, and we discuss the Holocaust and the Inquisition, all sorts of things having to do with Judaism. And I think that it's a great thing that Judaism provides that tool, of a day for spiritual accounting. And of course it's a very social message, that says that before you can go ask forgiveness from God, first of all go resolve the problems you have with your fellow man. I think that this is beautiful, a great concept.

There are other wonderful laws, especially from the Deuteronomists, the people who wrote the book of Deuteronomy. They have wonderful, like, communal laws. In my opinion, the people who wrote the Tanah knew there was no God—but that's another story. From the point of view of heritage, the Jews have brought beautiful things to the world, to human society. The fact that in all sorts of places people have, in my opinion, distorted them terribly is another story. But I feel very close to a lot of things in the Tanah. And as a free man, I choose what I want, and I add.

Four hundred years ago, five hundred years ago, a thousand years ago, two thousand years ago, people took responsibility, and they established all sorts of religious rulings that dealt with important things—not just whether it's permissible or forbidden to, like, shake the snow from one's umbrella on Shabbat. Serious things. But today no one has courage. The kibbutz, for instance, in my opinion is a natural development of Judaism. It establishes the relevant context for the holidays. For instance, Shayu'ot can only have meaning in, like, an agricultural or industrial community.[§] And for Passover, we include all of our favorite Hebrew poetry in the Hagadah. Things by Natan Zah, for instance, or A. D. Gordon, or Berl Katznelson or Rahel, things that are relevant to me, and that are important to me.[†] They all bring a message of liberty, of freedom.

After things fell apart with Rami, and I was feeling very blue, I began to tell more and more of my crowd from the group. The reactions were like Gili's—very understated, like, chilly almost. "That's the big secret? What, yes, we guessed, yes, we knew, yes, so what?" I would always start off with, "I want

[§] Shayu'ot: Pentecost; early-summer holiday celebrating the gift of the Torah; also an ancient harvest holiday.

[†] Natan Zah (b. 1930): Modernist Hebrew poet and literary critic. A. D. Gordon (1856–1922): Hebrew writer; political philosopher; manual laborer; spiritual mentor of the early Zionist pioneers. Berl Katznelson (1887–1944): Socialist Zionist leader and ideologue, writer and journalist. Rahel (1890–1931): *Nom de plume* of Rahel Bluwstein, manual laborer; author of lyric Hebrew poems of love for fellow pioneers and the land.

to talk to you about something," so immediately everyone would look at me like, "Yes, yes, what you want to talk about," and I would, like, drag it out, and drag it out, make it very dramatic—like I love to do—and when I would finally tell them, they would say, "Yes, OK, but what did you want to talk about?" They weren't surprised.

The most negative reaction came from Oran and his girlfriend Raᶜayah. He said, "What, really, you don't find any girls attractive? But what do you do with a man? What is there that you can do in bed? I'll tell you what I do with Raᶜayah—can you do any better?" Then he said, "Maybe you want to sleep with Raᶜayah, to see if you enjoy that more?" He just couldn't accept that, like, this was the way it was. I had a terrible conversation with the two of them at one point. I said to them, "If I move into an apartment with another man, will you come visit?" Oran looked at me and was like, "You know it would be difficult for me. But I love you, and you're the most important person in the world to me, there's nothing I can do, I'm stuck with you. You want to live with a man, with an Arab woman"—he's very nationalist, Oran—"you want to live with a sheep, what can I do?" I said to him, "Would you bring your children to visit me?" "No, no way." "Why?" "I don't want my children to be exposed to that." "What does that mean—if your children won't be exposed to it, will that mean that it won't exist? Where's the logic in this method?"

So at this point Raᶜayah jumped in and said, "No, it's dangerous." I said, "What does that mean, dangerous—are you talking about AIDS?" "That too." So I said to her, "You know as well as I do that, even though you haven't slept with anyone besides him, your boyfriend has had a number of lays on the side since you've been together—so why don't you go get tested, maybe he infected you. You two have never used a condom, right?" "No, of course not. But I don't want to get tested." And now I let her have it. "Why not? I, I'm aware. I get tested, I don't do dangerous things. And if I do things which are a little dangerous, then I'm very careful. And if someone wants to be with me on a regular basis there are a few things which he is going to have to guarantee me beforehand. And you, you're irresponsible." "No, no, no, no, no, it's not the same thing. Besides, you would be an influence on our children." I said to them, "Do you think I am going to seduce your children?" At this point, this almost got violent. Of course, like, nothing has been resolved with them. The conversation has continued to this day.

I would like to raise children—but only in the context of a cooperative group. For gay parents to raise a child in Tel Aviv really does seem like child abuse to me. I mean, I remember how they behaved in my nursery school, to kids whose parents were divorced. There were kids who suffered terribly because of this.

But it is very important to me to have children, I can't explain this rationally. It's just an innate drive, I guess. I'd really like to be a father, to follow the development of a child, to see what it would mean that another person is a part of me. I'd like to learn how to build a family on a different model than the one I grew up in. I'm curious about that blood connection, which I just don't feel with my own family. It makes me curious. It attracts me.

My fears about telling my friends in the group were totally baseless. Except for Oran and Raᶜayah, everyone reacted incredibly well. I mean, there wasn't anything to react to at all, it was totally meaningless to them, it was like nothing happened. I know that some of them had kind of negative views on the subject to start with. But when it happens to you, when you're dealing with a friend, you behave differently. Up to this point they guessed, or knew, and they kept their mouths shut. Now I was dying to make a sensation. But they refused to cooperate.

I didn't feel any change in my relations within the group. But in spite of that, it was difficult for me. It took me some time before I talked to everyone. The last one I talked to was Eli, and I'm sure he already figured things out. But even when Eli was the only one left who didn't know, no one went and told him. And when a bunch of us would be talking about the subject, and he would come in, we would stop talking. Because they knew that it was my thing, that I decide who to tell and when.

Today I see that this whole question of kibbutz gossip doesn't have to be something threatening. It's strange, because people stay away from the kibbutz because of this. But when you're already inside, you see how meaningless it is, in comparison to other things. I don't feel threatened by being the conversation of the day in the laundry room anymore. I know they talk about me. So let them talk.

But I have to say, I have gotten over the stage where I feel the need to tell people. Of course, if someone comes along, I won't hide him. But I won't go out and, like, put up posters, write a notice on the bulletin board, and put notes in the mailboxes of all the members either. I'm not the kind of person who goes in for public displays of affection.

I've never told my father or my mother. I'll never tell my father—I don't need his first heart attack on my conscience. I have my sisters, who will certainly give him one first. Besides, I have no interest in his dying—he doesn't really have much of an inheritance to leave me anyway. Seriously, I like him very much, he's a nice guy, but I will not go to him and make, like, a production out of this in front of him. I don't intend to tell my mother either. Look, I didn't even tell her about my girlfriends! My parents have no part in my private life. It doesn't interest them what I do. It has nothing to do with them. If it came up, at this point, it might be that I wouldn't deny it. But I'm not going to initiate the conversation. We aren't close, we have nothing to talk about. I have friends—they're the primary socializing force in my life. And that's it.

I've been becoming a little closer with my brother lately, so maybe I'll tell him sometime soon. He's in the army now, and he's having a hard time, so my father asked me to take matters in hand. I've been reviewing his file lately, trying to figure out who this kid is, besides the name. I knew him up to about fourteen—since then, I have no idea what's happened to him. I've found out that he's something of a Don Juan. One day I was at home, and, like, nine different girls called looking for him. It's amazing.

My sisters are closer to my age, and there was a time when we spent a lot of time together. They talk freely about their sex lives with me, so I talked to them about what was going on with me. One of them was very happy that she has a homosexual brother—she was, like, positively blissful. I'm serious. She's nutty, she's a photographer—well, she takes pictures, let's put it that way. Even before I told her, she would sometimes go to Independence Park and hang out, ask to photograph people. She would listen and talk to the men there. She's straight, but she slept with a girl once, just to see how it feels. She's drawn to the fringes. So she's very happy with me—"Yes! Yes! My brother is gay." She tries to set me up with people. Terrible. "You simply must meet someone I met, he's so nice," or "Who's Rami? I must meet him—give me his phone number." I don't even talk to the guy anymore, but she actually called him, and they went out! She's nuts. The other sister is much more, like, aristocratic—"Oh, really, OK, well, hmm. Interesting. No, no, don't tell me, I don't want to know. That one who was here, right? Hmm. I knew it, I knew it."

After things were over with Rami, and I had already begun telling people in my group, my second girlfriend, Irit, came into the picture, very unexpectedly. Back when things had ended with Liraz, my first girlfriend, right before I became so depressed, I had really decided to give it up, with women. But Irit made me want to try it again.

By this time, we had finished the military part of our service. The girls had been back on the kibbutz while we were in Lebanon and the West Bank, but now the whole group was reunited for our final year of service, which began with four months on a military kibbutz. I met Irit there.

She was the personal affairs officer on the military kibbutz. In my introductory interview with her, I felt that here was something out of the ordinary, really exceptional. I think she's very beautiful, although most people disagree. She's tall and freckled, with long hair. And that's it, I decided to go for it. I talked about it with some of my friends from the group, and they were very supportive. There were some who were kind of confused—they asked, "What happened?"

I still had this distinction that I made, between, like, physical attraction and the desire to build a relationship. While I might not be immediately physically attracted to a girl, I felt I could have a relationship with her. And I would find her more physically attractive once I got to know her and I loved who she was. So I began having very long conversations with Irit about kibbutz life. Her grandfather was one of the early leaders of the movement.

And then I felt that the next step was to suggest that we become "a couple," or something. I didn't know how to define it, I didn't know what I wanted. I was simply screwed up, I didn't know what the next step was, for God's sake. And then, I decided to just talk to her about the whole thing, because I felt that I was cheating her.

Now, when I think about it, I'm not sure I should have told her. I don't think I was cheating her—that's bullshit, total bullshit. Because it's like saying, if I weren't gay, but heterosexual, saying to her, "Irit, I love you—but I'm attracted to other women." You understand? It's like, if you love this particular person, what difference does it make what other kinds of people attract you also? Who cares if you're attracted, what's the point?

It was very difficult for me to talk to her about it. I finally did it, one time when I was on guard duty. I didn't have a lot of time to talk in general—it was the army after all—and I was very anxious to tell her. And it was a good opportunity, four hours of guard duty, you sit there like a corpse, at least you can talk.

I beat around the bush for a while. I talked about us, and I began to tell her that there was something she needed to know. I began with all those old games. And she finally was reduced to the point where she said to me, half seriously, "What have you done, knocked up an Arab girl?" It reached that point. And then I said to her "No," and she was like, "Are you sleeping with another girl, is that what this is about?" And I said, "Almost." And then she looked at me and went, like, "Another guy." And I said, "Yes." And then I remember the way she kind of went, "Oh." And it was suddenly very quiet.

I said, "What do you have to say?" And then she was like, "You know what? I knew." And I asked her how—I was really curious. I said, "I must know, I have to know how people know, how did you know, how?" So she said, "When we talked, when we began to get to know one another, I looked at you, and talked to you, and I said to myself, 'I want him.' I felt some sexual tension. But when I tried to deploy this tension, there wasn't anything on your side that reacted. And it really surprised me. It really confused me, I didn't know what you wanted. It hurt me. Because, like, what, he only wants a platonic relationship, he isn't attracted to me, I'm not pretty?" And I suddenly understood something about myself from what she said. When I thought about it, I saw how, like, erotic I could be when I was with guys, and how much I don't broadcast any sexual signals at all when I'm with girls.

It was clear to both of us that I had brought up the subject because I wanted to clarify what our relationship was. So we began a series of conversations about what love is, and what partnership is, and what meaning there is to partnership. We talked about whether a person can divide love among a number of people, and how you can express eroticism in that division of love, and what is faithfulness in a couple, and what is a relationship when it suddenly becomes an intimate partnership, beyond a deep and meaningful friendship.

And in the end, the argument circled around the fact that she didn't believe—even though I told her explicitly—that, while I'm not able to control to whom I am physically attracted, I can control to whom I make a commitment. "A soldier passes in the street and I'll look at him, exactly like you. You can't control it either, you'll look too. But you have to believe me that if I choose to be with you, and if exclusivity is important to you, the way you define it, I will be faithful. Because my relationship with you is more important than anything else. And there's no question of your not satisfying me." And I said to her that with all due modesty, I thought that I would be able to satisfy her. But she wasn't convinced. And this just, like, destroyed everything. After four months at the military kibbutz, my group moved on. And that was that.

We left the military kibbutz and became part of the national kibbutz movement. Our group was spread out throughout the country, everyone was a counselor in a different place. I insisted on being placed in the Tel Aviv area, because I knew that Tel Aviv was the center of the gay scene. I wanted to be close by. I knew that at this point I would go to a gay bar for the first time, maybe I would go to a gay disco for the first time, and I would put a personal ad in the city newspaper, *Haᶜir*. By this point, I knew what my options were. I'll live in Tel Aviv, I thought, because everyone lives there.

Three years earlier I thought I was alone, and after, like, six months I realized that there were another ten or so. A little while later I discovered that there were about a hundred. But now I realized that there were tens of thousands of gays—and most of them lived in the Tel Aviv area. So why not join them?

I was convinced that the only way you can really meet other men was through very commercial media, like an advertisement, or a bar. Up to this time I hadn't been to a gay bar yet, but now I went, like, once or twice. But I never believed that there could be a situation where you meet someone, discover each other, and become a couple. The classic getting-to-know-each-other, just like a guy meets a girl. That can't be. To this day, it is difficult for me to believe, I don't know why, there's no logical reason. But I'm screwed up, it's something about me that's screwed up. I know that it's a problem. A fucked-up approach.

And I know that I'm missing out, that it's a shame, that things are passing me by. Take hitchhikers, for instance. I mean, it's so legitimate, if a guy picks up a woman hitchhiker, and they get to talking, and he likes her, it's so legitimate to ask for her telephone number. And even if she doesn't give it to him, even if she says she has a boyfriend, it doesn't make a difference. You gave it your best shot. But I wouldn't dare do a thing like that with a male hitchhiker. Even though there were times when I really wanted to. I know people, I have one friend who does do it, like, that's the way he meets new people, by giving rides, to guys and girls, and he takes telephone numbers. He's straight, he's had a girlfriend for a long time, but he likes to meet people, and these are his friends. Do you understand? That's the way he meets people. But I can't even do that.

So at this point I once again decided to place a personal ad. And you know, you're coming into the story now, Amir. It's just a little difficult with the time, it's difficult for me to, like, place it all. Was it a year ago, a year and a half? A year after the war? Yes, give me a second. December, 1991. Yes, that terrible winter, right? Wow, a lot happened in the last year, it seems like ten years. Yes. So. Who put the ad in, I don't remember. Oh, this is very strange. It doesn't make a difference.

Either me or Amir put an ad in the paper, one of us put an ad in the paper, in *Magaᶜim*? *Haᶜir*? *Qol Ḥeifah*? Apparently I answered his ad, and I, like, got a letter, and then the telephone conversations started. And I remember that they were very dangerous conversations, because I was at the kibbutz, where there are some problems with the phones, especially in the winter, when the water gets into the telephone wires. To make a long story short, when someone would call a number in the kibbutz, the phone would ring on every phone, all over the kibbutz. And if the call was of interest to you, you stayed on the line, if not, you hung up. So it wasn't very hard to eavesdrop. I remember once, I was talking to someone, a girl who had just dropped out of the group, and we were talking about sex. And a friend from the group came running and banging on the door, "Yossi, Yossi! They can hear you! They can hear you!" Because she had just picked up her phone, and, like, there we were.

So we had these two or three very long telephone conversations, Amir and me. They were very, like, literary. I read him things that I had written, and he read me things that he had written, all very impressive. I was very confused. It came at a very bad time, because I wanted to be totally immersed in my guidance work, and I knew that anything else I did would make my work suffer. This was a recipe for failure both in my personal life and my work. But that's in retrospect. At the time I don't think I realized that.

We're going to skip the rest of this story. It's difficult for me now. Maybe, like, some other time. You understand. This is kind of weird.

In any case, when it was over, it ended in a very peculiar way. I got a letter from Amir, which had some explanation or another, and it was a big relief for me. Because it was beginning to become meaningful, and I would have preferred that my work come before everything. The kibbutz before everything.

But I guess I did kind of pity myself for a while. Amir told me in the letter about the guy he had met, who was now his boyfriend. American. And the only thing I could say for myself was, like, what a great day I had had with the kids in the group I was responsible for. Impulsively, it was sad. And I remember that I wrote a letter to myself that day—I said to myself, you know what, I need to respond to myself, above all.

For the last ten months I've been counseling a movement group in the central region of the country. It's a full-time job. I also work in the movement offices, and in the library. It takes the entire day, the entire week—and if there were another day in the week it would fill that up too. I'm responsible for the ideological education of these kids, but more important, I provide support for them, on the basis of my own experiences as a member of a group. I'm responsible for their spiritual, intellectual, emotional development.

I haven't come out to the kids I'm working with, and, at this point, I have no intention to do so. It's irrelevant. All of the counselors have decided together that our personal lives are out of bounds, they're not relevant to our counseling. Sure, things might be easier for me if I came out, but then that would become the most important thing about me, and I don't want that to happen. Because that's not my message to the nation. Period.

So after things didn't work out with Amir, I was pretty depressed for a while. And my work with the movement suffered. I got an ultimatum from my superior—shape up or ship out. "I'll get back to you in two days," I said. I actually thought about leaving the movement. And one of the most important decisions I've ever made was to stay on. To shake myself out of this funk, to get my act together, rub my eyes, straighten my shoulders, and forward march. There's work to be done, there's no time for bullshit. And this attitude has stayed with me to this day.

The idea of a gay ghetto seems ridiculous to me. Is there something attractive about a ghetto of people who like brown shoes? Does sexual identity have to be the dominant thing in the life of a person? I don't chose my friends on the basis of their sexual identities. Or because they have a certain color skin, or because they are of a certain religion. It's totally irrelevant. It has nothing to do with anything. What difference does it make, sexual identity? Of course, a kibbutz is also a kind of ghetto, for people with a certain worldview, people who want to live according to a certain worldview. But can a worldview begin and end in that people love members of their own sex? That's not enough for me. That isn't to say that my homosexuality is a marginal thing in my life. But my world doesn't revolve around it either.

I'm very confused about the campaign for gay rights. I don't see myself as a partner in that struggle, right now. I know that if I had some sort of problem, if I got discriminated against, or something, my group would come to my defense. And that's the way it should be. Look, I lost the motivation to struggle in the world as it is a long time ago—I mean, the class war is also a struggle in the world as it is. But we need to find a total alternative for life as it is now—and if you just try to, like, make switches within this Lego-block wall, you try to replace the block that says "homophobia" with one that says "homosexuality is OK," you haven't done a thing. But what we're doing is building a totally different, better world. I know it sounds naive. But the fact is, in the place where I will live, I'm not going to have to worry about discrimination. This is not going to be significant. And if, at some point, I'll need to stage a battle on my issue, outside of the kibbutz, there will be people standing behind me. And they won't be from the Agudah. Because what is the Agudah to me?

What the kibbutz has done is to establish a whole way of life, as complete as anything Orthodox Judaism ever imagined. I mean, why do the Orthodox see such a terrible threat in the kibbutz? Because there are ceremonies in the kibbutz, there's, like, a kibbutz circumcision, and there's a kibbutz wedding, and there's a kibbutz funeral. And kibbutz festivals, and kibbutz holidays. The kibbutz will give you a framework from the moment you're born to the moment you die, just like religion. And I feel that the homosexual problem is only one small part of the whole grand scheme of life. And I want to live life at its grandest, its fullest—and not only concern myself with, like, one thing.

By the time the summer rolled around—this was about a year ago—there was a little less pressure at work, and I felt that I was strong enough to try, once again, to meet someone, in spite of my previous disappointments. I thought I could keep myself from losing my sense of proportion. We had left the commune, and Eli, from my group, and I had just moved in together. It was a practical decision. Everyone else was counseling in the north—I'm the counselor for Jerusalem, and Eli was counseling in the northern Negev. So it was decided that we would share an apartment.

I put an ad in the paper, ʿIton Haʿir, did you see it? I remember that it was then that I understood to what degree that system, of meeting someone through commercial media, is terrible. Fifty or sixty people answered. I eliminated half of them for, like, no reason at all. No reason at all. Because you can't deal with those sorts of numbers. And I felt terrible about it. It's like marketing, it's like a store, everyone is selling himself. I thought it was terrible.

I remember I said, this is a thing that I have to do from beginning to end, to see what this really is, what it means to put an ad in the paper, what it is to meet someone and be let down, to meet someone, get into bed, and get out the next day feeling like shit. I said, OK, that's the way this month, two months are going to look, and afterwards, I can reach some educated conclusions. I typed a chart on the computer at the movement office, to keep track of the incoming data, to write it all down.

There were a few guys who I met through this ad who I was in contact with for a while. But they each told me in the end that they weren't interested, or only as a friend, blah, blah, blah. And it got on my nerves, because I have no time for that. Even if I really wanted it, I have no time. I just don't have time. I don't see my family, I don't see my friend Ran, I'm hardly ever at the kibbutz. It's a terrible thing when you have to make appointments with your friends, it's shocking. So one thing I don't need is any more friends. And that's it. This was a time when I had, like, very little self-confidence, low self-esteem.

And then there was the military policeman I met through the ad. I also talked with him on the telephone a lot. Also a wonderful voice. I have a weakness for voices, apparently. And then we met. And when I saw him, I said to myself, yes, but only for tonight. I said that to myself. He was gorgeous. Really. A dream man. Very well built. I really wanted him. But the next day I woke up, with, like, such a feeling—I was so disgusted with myself. I looked at him, I said to myself, who is this, and what is it doing here? What was the point of this? What am I going to do now? How am I going to get rid of him? How am I going to tell him 'bye, 'bye, have a nice day, without, like, driving him to suicide? Because he had already seriously fallen for me—he had been writing me love letters, and that was after only the telephone conversations, beforehand. I was certain that for him this was the beginning. I drove him home, and we talked and held hands, and he kissed me before he got out of the car.

I drove like a madman to work, very annoyed with myself, really very disappointed with the whole thing. And that's it. I called him, and I told him on the phone that I don't think that things between us will work out. I didn't hide anything from him. I told him that I think I ripped him off. He's a nice, clever guy. I felt terrible. I didn't know how to atone for this. Other people from the ad called, but I didn't return their calls. That was the straw that broke the camel's back.

But he didn't give up so easily. I don't know if it was connected, but I began to get anonymous phone calls. I would say "Hello, hello," but there was no answer on the other end. And one day he called me at work, at the movement offices. And I had never given him that number—he had to do some serious research to get that number. It made me very nervous. And then one day at, like, two in the morning, I was alone in the apartment, and someone knocked on the door. I was scared out of my wits. It really frightened me. I think I talked to you about it at the time. It really frightened me. I remember that I got up, and because it's the ground floor, I closed all the windows, quietly. I had trouble getting back to sleep that night. I was sure it was him, even though I have no way of really knowing for sure. And that's it. That was my last attempt to meet someone.

I'm afraid of a relationship. It doesn't fit into my life right now.

Up to now, Eli, my apartment-mate, hasn't been one of my closest friends in the group. When we moved in together, I still hadn't told him about myself. I mean, I always thought he was a good guy, at least as far as looks go, but he has the image of being, like, the sexpot of the group. He's always telling dirty jokes, his language is straight from the gutter. But at some point, after the military policeman had been over, we began to talk very honestly. I was basically trying to seduce him. We would spend a lot of time on my bed together, because my room is the one with the television, and I have a huge, huge double bed, twice the size of a normal one, just gigantic. And we would lie together in the same bed watching TV, and we were very free with our hands. One day, I turned to him and said, "You know why I'm doing this?" And he looked at me and was like, "What, really?" And I was like, "Yes, really." And he said, "OK, I'm going to sleep." And he got up and went into his room.

And the next day we agreed that we needed to clean up the apartment. It was as if nothing had happened, nothing at all. It's just that everything was, like, out in the open. That night, we went to a Chinese restaurant together to celebrate my birthday.

Eli found a girlfriend shortly afterwards. The whole group was happy, everyone, including me, that he had a serious relationship. But she wouldn't stay the night, and when she would leave in the evenings, he was ready to do just about anything. But I didn't want to. Because I knew that he would, like, destroy himself with guilt afterwards, and I didn't want that. Besides, I could see how much his girlfriend liked him—he was her first boyfriend. And I didn't want him to let off his sexual steam with me. I didn't want it to be like that.

It's a real relief that he knows that I would really like to sleep with him, that I'm very attracted to him. I don't have to hide it. And we still have lots of physical contact, within the limits that have been set, over time—through experimentation, you could say. There are places that are permitted and places that are forbidden. It's basically, like, just the groin itself that's off limits, everything else is totally fair game. In the group, when we began to talk more seriously about living together as a group, like, building our common future together, it's funny, because we said, "What's going to happen, there are more guys than there are girls in the group." And we would joke about it, they would say to me, "You've got to solve the problem, seduce someone, and we'll get another couple created, from within the group." So I'm doing my best!

A lot of my future depends on the future of the group, which is kind of up in the air at the moment. We have to decide whether we want to found a new settlement or not. This has a lot of significance for your personal life. It's clear to me, just as it's clear to the other people in my group who are single, that anyone who will agree to become my partner will have to essentially marry, like, the whole group—it's a package deal. I don't believe that anyone will be able to take me away from the group, from our plans. So it will have to be someone who, through a long, perhaps painful process, will have to accept that this is my future. I won't give this up. I don't believe that there's anything that's worth that. And I know, exactly like the other singles in my group, that it's very complicated. There's no difference between the fact that I am looking for a man, and the others are looking for women. In this matter, I'm facing difficulties that are not connected to sexual identity.

I want to build a world for myself where there's no place for power-mongering, there's no place for politics, where there's no administration, and no bureaucracy. Do you know a little about Kropotkin's anarchistic groups? It must be a social structure based on an "intimate group," however you define that. I dream of creating a new, cooperative factory, and eventually, a completely cooperative city. Conceptually speaking, I think I have a very serious alternative, which is both good and right, and I think that you could find support for it from every sector of the population.

The relations that take place within the group are of dialogue and democracy at its purest, which, for me, means consensus. Until everyone agrees to a certain decision, there is no decision. I'll give you an example. In my group now there's an ongoing discussion about what to do—if we're going back to the kibbutz or going to start a new settlement, where we'll be able to live in the way we choose, and to bring in other, similar groups. This discussion will continue until we reach consensus. Right now, we have a majority for going to start a new kibbutz. But because there's one who's not sure, and two who want to go back to the old kibbutz—no way, the proposition doesn't pass. It isn't like, who's for, who's against, OK, it passed, new business. Because it affects the life of every single one of us very personally, and until everyone is convinced, we don't do anything.

There isn't any pressure. We've gotten past that. We've come to the conclusion that, like, it's far better that you should say what you're feeling, and the entire group will stop and wait, than you should wake up one morning and find yourself in a place you don't want to be. And that's the foundation of everything.

I know there are lot of internal contradictions in this. Because, for instance, in order to realize our goals, we do have to choose someone from among us to be a representative, who will deal with political battles with the outside, with the Naḥal Section of the Defense Department, with the Jewish

Agency, with the Joint.[§] Someone who will talk to the Housing Department and the Histadrut.[†] I think that the selection of this person to represent us is, like, the beginning of the end. Because you can't act in a certain way outside, without having it influence, in some way or another, your behavior inside. I think it's impossible. I pity the person we choose.

Liraz, my old girlfriend from the army, has been abroad for a while, but she just came back to Israel. I've got to check things out with her. Maybe she's changed her mind. She's a wonderful girl. Exactly like Eli is wonderful. I'm not attracted to her the way I'm attracted to Eli, but I don't think that would bother me. I don't know.

I know deep down that I'm not going to find someone through a commercial medium. Maybe if I go back to school, or maybe through the movement. There's a new guy at work—wow, he's a real hunk. I just found out that his brother is married to another man. They live together on the same kibbutz, in the Galilee. But this guy is gorgeous, and he's such a gentle soul— very smart, a real child of nature, wonderful. A free spirit. This is something where I think I might have a chance. Maybe. But beyond this, it's all very, very unclear.

[§] American Jewish Joint Distribution Committee: Commonly known as "the Joint"; philanthropic organization of American Jews, traditionally providing emergency relief for world Jewry; founded in 1914.

[†] Histadrut: Literally, "Federation"; short for "General Federation of Workers in the Land of Israel"; founded in 1920 with the aim of building a "Jewish workers' society" in Palestine; the central institution of the Jewish community during the pre-State era; the most powerful organization and largest single employer in contemporary Israel.

OREN

It was Rafi Niv's lead that brought us to "Oren," who had achieved moderate fame among gay Haifans for, at the age of twenty-two, having been in a "committed relationship" for nearly two and a half years. Was he representative of the new generation of Israeli gays? We wanted to get the inside story.

Amir and I had to act fast, because Oren had, in fact, already left Haifa and moved to Eilat—perhaps the one city in Israel that was out of commuting distance from Tel Aviv and Jerusalem. Yet Oren was coming back to Haifa one last time, to move out of his apartment—with some careful synchronization, we might be able to speak with him during a free moment.

We made a special trip up to Haifa in order to catch Oren at the moment in question, and we found him willing to put himself at our service in spite of the fact that, to our eyes, his apartment showed no signs of being ready to be vacated. Oren's living room was meticulously appointed, the walls adorned with expensively framed, arty posters. The glassy cyclops eye of a perfectly monstrous color television seemed to dominate an entire wall. The apartment itself was modestly sized, but commanded a ravishing view of a lush, wooded landscape. Oren—slight, dressed in a t-shirt and long shorts, his blond hair cut very short—was a flurry of intense energy. His clipped speech, impatient manner, darting eyes, cynical laugh, and commanding presence gave me the persistent impression that he held a position of great power.

∾

I WAS BORN IN HAIFA. I'm the middle child—my little brother is now six-teen, and my older brother is thirty. Eight years between me and my older brother, six years between me and my little brother. My mother was born in Israel—her parents were from Hungary and Poland—and my father was born in Romania. My parents were divorced when I was six. My little brother was supposed to be the baby that would, like, save their marriage.

I remember very few arguments or shouting matches. I just remember a lot of peace and quiet when my father moved out. And I remember that all of a sudden I began getting a lot of presents from both my father and my mother. They each wanted me to live with them—so each one gave me pre-sents, each one was very nice. And I had to decide where I wanted to live, with Dad or Mom. They said I might have to appear in court, to tell a judge what I wanted. In the end, I didn't go to court. They, however, did spend a lot of time in court. All of the kids wound up staying with my mother. That was the best thing. I liked it that way—and I could still get presents from my fa-ther. He kept on, you know, trying, and I kept on getting presents.

I was definitely spoiled. We weren't a very wealthy family, until later on, when things got better, but we were in good shape. A two-salary family. I had everything I wanted, but, like, I didn't demand very much.

I was the kind of boy who would sit at home all day, read books, and play Lego. I wouldn't go outside at all. I only wanted to sit inside. But, at every point in my childhood, I always had a best friend. When I look back on it to-day, to be chosen as my best friend was very bad luck on that person's part, because I would totally glue myself to him. He was, like, a sort of an object for me. I would say, OK, this is my best friend. I'm going to do everything with him. You can go to my grandmother's house and look—she has pic-tures of me when I was four, with my best friend. At six, with my best friend. And so on. To make a long story short, I was always with somebody else, who was my best friend.

I don't know if it was, like, sexual—all we would do was play hide-and-go-seek and act out children's stories. But I was hysterically jealous. I wouldn't let him be anyone else's friend—my friend is *my* friend. And that's the way it is to this day.

I was the one in charge. Not dominant in terms of "you do everything I say." It was just that I was the one who decided what we would play. I had all the time in the world for my friends. We would get out of school, and we would get together right away.

The person I remember as my first friend, my first real friend, his name was ʿIdo. He was my neighbor, and we went to nursery school together, and apparently this was how we got to know each other. And of course I didn't let him have any other friends. He was only allowed to be with me. We would go to movies together, and watch television together, and no one else would be included. We were a couple. There really weren't other people who were allowed in this relationship. I was very mean to anybody who tried to get involved.

My friends would just replace one another in the course of time. For instance, with ʿIdo, the relationship ended when we moved. There was no choice. And then I became close with another neighbor, who to this day is a good friend of mine, named Erez. I was on the thirteenth floor, he was on the tenth.

I had a problem with Erez, because he was a very social type, so he had tons of friends, and I would argue with him. How dare you hang out with other kids? What do you think you're doing? What right do you have to do that? What is this? Really, very serious arguments. I remember that I would sit at home a lot in the afternoons, like, all angry, pissed off, because he had gone over to someone else's house. Oh, wait, if you can stop the tape for a second, I'll go get my diary—I'll read you something from my diary, something short having to do with this.

Here, this is it. Now that I look at it, I see that it isn't exactly what I remembered. First of all, it's February 15, 1983. I'm twelve years and three months old. I wrote, "Today was not the best day, because I had a fight with Erez about a movie. We were supposed to go to a movie, but just kidding around I hurt him, he gave me a punch back, and because of that we didn't go to the movie." That's that. Now, if we look ahead a little bit—just a minute—here it is—I wrote about how I might switch into Erez's class, and then I wrote "the big day has come, I switched classes, not into Erez's class, but nearby." To make a long story short, I was, like, very dependent on him. I was glued to his side.

To this day I write in my diary sometimes. It's very good. There are things in my past that I didn't write about, and I'm sorry that I didn't. There are events that you can't remember objectively if you don't write them down when they happen. There are a lot of things that I wrote only looking back on events, and I'm sorry about that.

Soccer, basketball, and all that, sports never interested me. I remember that people would get together to play soccer during recess. I couldn't understand why they wanted to go outside into that heat. Forget it. I was never interested.

It didn't really bother me very much, because I compensated for it in other things. I would read a lot of books. I would sit at home and devour books. I think they also saw it in school. The others would laugh at me in gym class, but I would laugh at them in other places, you understand?

Thanks to my older brother, I began watching pornographic movies at a pretty young age. I would watch the movies he would bring home—I remember that I would always be sure to, like, mark where he had stopped and to rewind the tapes to exactly that point. So that, God forbid, he wouldn't catch me. I would usually watch them with Erez, but we didn't do anything sexual together. Yes, I would wait for him to go home so I could jerk off. I wouldn't dare do it in front of him.

My brother brought his first girlfriend home at fifteen or sixteen, and I remember her well. I was about eight years old at the time. They would come home, and they would close themselves into his room for hours on end. I remember that. And I remember those terrible scenes where they would go into the bathroom together, and he had a lot of zits, and she would, like, pop them for him. I'm sorry—but it's true. They were very close, they were together all the time. She lived in the building across the street. He became very close with her parents, my mother became friendly with her mother, and so on. We would go visit them, they would come visit us. Ideal.

I remember that there were conversations about it, between my mother and her mother, because he, when he got annoyed, he would sometimes, like, hit her. He doesn't do that any more. But there were a lot of conversations, how dare he, what right does he have, my mother should stop him. But this girl stayed with him anyway. They were together for a long time.

Homosexuality was never mentioned at home, not even in jokes. Maybe if my father was in the house there might be some sort of reference, but with my mother and my brother, it really didn't come up. I didn't know what it was. My first encounter with it was at seventeen. I was, like, very innocent. Today I can't figure out what I was thinking.

My mother is a bureaucrat who has worked herself into a pretty responsible position by now. My father was a bank clerk and a taxi driver and a theater manager all at the same time. He worked at a city-run theater. Every Shabbat there would be a kind of variety show, and in the middle there was, like, a striptease act. I remember that I once tried to sneak in, and I was not very pleasantly received. I planned it all out—right before the preceding act had finished, I went to the bathroom. I meant to stay there until the striptease began, when I would come out and, like, blend inconspicuously into the crowd. But it didn't work. My father said to me, "Um, Oren, what exactly do you think you're doing here?"

Then my father got into a car accident, and received a lot of money in damages. So he quit working at the bank, and he used the money to open a restaurant, which was very successful, and which he developed into a whole chain. Then began the period where we had a lot more money. You can't mention the name of the chain—people will know who he is. You can say, "a well-known chain of restaurants in Israel." I'm sure it will sound just fine.

At thirteen, I went away to a boarding school. It was my idea. I thought it would be a good idea to be far away from home. I needed a vacation from my father and my mother. It was an agricultural school, a very cozy, warm atmosphere. It was very, very nice.

All the boys lived together in one dorm, and there were some interesting, kind of, episodes. We would shower together, and there was always the old question of who was the biggest. I remember that I always avoided that. Only one day, because everyone was saying, "You won't show it, that means you have the smallest one," what did I do, I tricked them—I made sure I got a little hard, and then I called them, "Come here, take a look." And they were like, "Wow, you've got a big one," and from then on they kind of left me alone.

To this day I really like to give massages. So I made sure, it was sort of common knowledge, they knew that in my room you can get a massage. But, you know, I have to get massages also, so it was my rule that if I give someone a massage, he has to give me one back. People really loved it, and I enjoyed the fact that they liked it. I don't think I was, like, plotting, like in pornographic books or movies, to try to touch them below the belt. I wasn't interested in seducing anyone.

But one time, there was a boy named ʿOmri. I gave him a massage and we talked and so on. And I don't remember exactly how it happened. First of all, I should preface this by saying that there was a very peculiar obsession in the school, where everyone had to know who was jerking off. They would try to catch the ones who would jerk off when they were doing it. And I, I swore to myself that I would just never do it in the dorms—I would make sure to go home more often, and so on, but my rule was that I wouldn't ever do it in the dorms. But there were people who, for instance, tried to show up at meals a little late. But the other kids figured out pretty quickly that if someone didn't show up on time to a meal, he was probably jerking off, and they would send someone to run back to the dorm to try to catch him. And if he was caught, they would really let him have it, and of course they would tell the girls, and so on, and it would become a running joke.

So there was this boy named ʿOmri. You're the first ones I've ever told about this. I remember that it was Tuesday, everyone had gone into town to see a movie and we were left in the room alone. I gave him a massage, and he gave me one. And then, I don't remember if he suggested to me, or if I suggested to him, but it was something like, "As long as you're already giving me a massage, why don't you just give me a hand job?" And he began to, like, give me a hand job, and asked me to give him one. But I didn't know what I was doing back then—I, like, put my hand on him, but I said to him, this isn't comfortable, I don't want to do this, but I'll keep on giving you a massage if you want. So he jerked off and he came.

The next day, he told everyone that I gave him a hand job. But I was no idiot. So listen to what I did—I immediately said it was true. I said, "Yes, that's right, I did it. Do you want me to tell about it? I'll tell exactly what I did." And because I said it that way, no one would believe him. Everyone called him a liar for trying to make me into, like, an outcast, and they really let him have it—"How can you do that, to try to get him like that," and so on. "What happened was really that you were jerking off and he caught you, and you're just trying to get out of it." To make a long story short, he was in hot water. And he left the school at the end of that year. Because of this. They really let him have it. It was like, they didn't let him hear the end of it. I mean, he tried to set someone up. He tried to make people think someone was fooling around with boys.

Later on, when I was in the army, I tried to get in touch with this ʿOmri. And I found him. I invited him to Haifa, he slept over, and I told him about me, and he, like, flipped. He just ran away. He ran for his life. He didn't remember anything about this incident. I said to him, "I'll never forget." He remembered that the others picked on him about something that made him leave in the end. Something with jerking off. But he didn't remember the scene with me. It might be that he just repressed it.

I never had a real opportunity with anyone except for ʿOmri. But I, of course, chose who got massages and who didn't, and I remember very clearly that I always got a hard-on when I gave massages to the guys in my room. Always. I remember that I always made sure that I wasn't wearing sweatpants or something like that, so they wouldn't see. You know, I can't believe I'm talking about this.

I left the boarding school after a year and a half. I wanted to go home. I wanted more time to myself—I don't like to be around a lot of people. There, I was in a very collective framework. Everything was communal, eating together, drinking together, sleeping together, all those people in the room. I didn't like it any more, and I wanted to be alone. I was with crowds of people all the time. I left in the middle of the year, and that made a lot of problems, but in the end it worked out. I went to a technical high school. Mechanics track. Again, I wasn't, like, cut out for it, but I went there. It was better than nothing.

So this is already 1986. I was almost sixteen years old. I wrote in my diary: "Seeing as I haven't written in this diary for a long time, I'll write a little more in depth now, and first of all I'll tell about two friends of mine, Sagiy and Gili." I described Sagiy—"black hair, black eyes, about my height." Then I wrote about Gili Friedman, because I was in love with him, "Brown hair, dazzling green eyes, a smile that can drive you crazy, a tiny pointed nose, about five centimeters taller than me, grades lower than low, but not stupid, very social"—and I have "horny" written in quotation marks. "He thinks he's good-looking" and I wrote in parenthesis "it's true, but it helps to be a little modest." And I will censor what comes next. Then I wrote, "In the area of girls he has a wide field of action, with a high percentage of success, and I'm pretty jealous." Now, I'm saying this after the fact, but I know that I didn't mean that "I was pretty jealous of his success," but rather, "I was pretty jealous of the girls who went with him." Let's see. That's all that's written about this.

Here, I'll read you something else, this was a few days later—"At the moment I really miss Gili Friedman. I don't know why, but I think I really love him." And then I add as insurance, I write to myself in parenthesis—"As a friend, of course." Got it? I go on, "This is the first time I really miss a friend," and so on. Do you understand? This is already when I began to think that, like, maybe something was wrong. Again, this is a sort of an explication looking backwards. But the way it's written, it looks that way, anyway. Here— "Yesterday I slept over at Gili Friedman's, and it was so much fun. He gave me a quarter-hour of massages, chills, and goosebumps, and I really flip over that. I was so sorry when he stopped." That's it. All sorts of scenes like that.

This is where you can see that I'm wondering, and I don't really know what's going on with me. I wrote, "Today I went out with a pretty nice girl. We went to a new movie. To make a long story short, as usual, I didn't make a single move, besides talking a lot. I probably gave her a headache."

Afterwards, I see what I wrote, here's something sudden—"Since I last wrote, I have a girlfriend, nice, friendly, named ʿEinat." And then I go on to write about something else. I hardly even mention her—just her name, nothing, no description. I go on to talk about the rock band I started with some friends. "The nicest, most sociable ones in the band are Naday and Dori. I get along with Naday the best. But the whole thing is, I never know what he thinks about me. He doesn't provide any feedback, and it's very annoying." But that was my first girlfriend back there!

I met ʿEinat through my friend Naday, from the band. I was with him a lot. Like a leech. I was with him hours upon hours, we would go out together, travel together, hang out together, every little thing together. And I know that at a certain point it began to be a real burden for him, and his mother began to object. I would sleep over at his house, he would sleep over at mine. She didn't like that. But we had no sexual contact. Not even massages. Nothing. And that bothered me. I wanted it.

Naday invited me to go on his annual school trip. Because we did everything together, you understand. So I went with him on the trip, and I met ʿEinat there—she was in his class at school. I talked about, like, all kinds of things with her, and we became close. I invited her to a gig that our band was playing, and I also invited her to a Gidi Goy concert. We left after the first half—and I never leave his concerts, I always sit from the beginning to the end, I'm hooked on him. But we left, and we went someplace and just talked. And I really enjoyed that. We found a lot of things in common.

We agreed to see each other the next day. And we became a couple. It was natural. I liked being with her, and she liked being with me. I don't think I was attracted to her. But we saw each other every day, we liked being together, we went out, we had fun. We would sit in my room. And then we began closing the door, locking the door. She made the first move. We didn't actually have sex—I kept my underwear on, and she kept hers on. But I would, like, definitely come. And I really liked it.

It became a ritual. She would come over in the afternoon, after school, we would go straight to the room, close the door so that no one could come in, and we would stay there until nighttime, so that no one would bother us. I was sixteen.

One day we went together to visit my father, to sleep at his place, and we did what we did, and I, like, stopped in the middle, all of a sudden, because I imagined that I saw Naday. I just stopped, because it frightened me. And I told her what had happened. And she said, "Well, what do you expect, you're with him all the time, so you're thinking about him now also." But I said to her, "No, I don't think it's like that." She said it was nothing to worry about. OK. We continued what we were doing. And it happened to me this way another few times, and I told her what was going on, and that I couldn't keep on like this. I told her that I was confused, that I didn't understand my relationship with Naday, that I had no idea what was going on with me, that I wanted to break up. I wasn't afraid to tell her all of this. This was what I felt. In the most natural way. It was like, that was what I felt, that was what I talked about. So I began seeing ʿEinat less, and we became just friends. The thing with her lasted a total of six months.

Our band kept on performing, and I switched from loving Naday to loving Dori, the drummer in the band. I don't know how. I don't understand it, but I switched to loving Dori. This is what I wrote at the time: "We had a gig in the Palace Disco, there were four hundred people there who bought tickets at ten shekels apiece. The gig was excellent, we played a forty-five-minute program." And so on. "Lately, there have been a few things that have been bothering me. For instance, I very much like him," and I have next a question mark and a sort of exclamation point next to the word. I'm referring to Dori. "In my opinion, he's very good-looking, but besides that, I'm really jealous of his success. For instance, after the gig, I found out that girls who saw him on stage want to meet him. And that really kills me. I mean, he can do whatever he likes, but I don't want to hear about it. Besides, I'm not sure that I only 'like' him. I really suspect that it tends toward"—and now there are three dots—"love." And I go on: "It really worries me, bothers me. I've decided that I have to go to a psychologist to try to solve my problem. I'll do my best to do that as soon as possible." That's it.

I didn't write anything for a while, but in my next entry I wrote, "I've begun to see a psychologist. The day after tomorrow will be my third appointment. We're trying to go over every detail about me in order to figure out what the story is. I myself suspect that I have homosexual tendencies." This, by the way, is November 27, 1987—one month before I turned seventeen.

The next time I write, I have this to say: "A lot has happened. I continue to see the psychologist. But it has become clear, contrary to my suspicions, that I'm not queer." And then I talk about my birthday, and then: "Me and Dori have become good friends, really close. He tells me the most personal things about himself and I do the same. And I'm totally satisfied with the relationship. This year, like last year, we will perform at the Scouts' festival." And so on. "At the first performance I met a girl named Ayelet. We talked and afterwards I got in touch with her. We went to a Gidi Goy concert together." You see, here also. "The next day we went to a movie, and now I feel like we are really good friends, but one of my problems is that I'm not brave enough to make the first move, and we're not going to get anywhere this way. Sometimes we find ourselves in situations where we're standing facing each other, and really feeling that here, this is it. But no. Because I just don't have the courage. Dori says I'm an idiot, as well as all sorts of things that I don't need to mention, but it just doesn't help, I'm not brave enough. Tomorrow there is another rehearsal, and Ayelet will come also, and afterwards in the evening we'll get together." That's it.

My next entry is like this: "A month has passed since I last wrote, and a lot has happened since then. To my deep regret, the psychologist's decision has still not convinced me. And, in my view, I am still in love with Dori. So my next step, if I have the courage, will be to cut off my friendship with Dori. On Thursday of last week we were talking, and we got to the question of why I am seeing a psychologist. After numerous attempts, I succeeded in convincing him to tell me why, in his opinion, I was seeing a psychologist. And he said to me that it was because of the matter of 'differentiation' between guys and girls. And I confirmed that it was true, after he let me know it wouldn't hurt our relationship. But the thing is that what Dori doesn't know is that the main problem is that I'm in love with . . . him."

I remember my first meeting with the psychologist. I said to her, "I think I like guys." That was the first thing I said to her. She was very nice. But, like, up to our very last meeting, she insisted that it wasn't true. She would say to me, "OK, let's say that Dori is here, what would you want to do with him?" And I said, "We would sit together, talk, have fun. I like to be with him." She said to me, "Would you kiss him?" No. "Would you want to kiss him?" No. "Would you want to hug him?" No. It was true—these things didn't seem like things I wanted to do with him. It wasn't until the first time I was with a guy that I figured out what it was that I wanted. It just, like, seemed too strange. To this day, when I'm with my boyfriend, I can't stand in front of a mirror. It just seems too strange. I can remember times when we've been dancing together in a disco, and I just couldn't dance with him in front of a mirror. Listen, maybe I really am, like, screwed up. Maybe something is really wrong with me, besides being a little nutty in general. But I kept on seeing this psychologist, and at every meeting, I would say that I was "like that," and she would say that I wasn't.

I remember something else—I can't figure out why I didn't write about it here. It was like this. I, at this very time, right when I began seeing Ayelet, was in a very close relationship with a guy named Raz. Now, at the same time, I wrote a song for a girl who was making her own recordings. And I wrote the music and lyrics, with a chorus. And I wrote it about Raz. For me it was forbidden love, and I knew it. So the chorus went something like, "This isn't just a puppy love / Like all the others think / I know that this is a painful, painful love." I don't know what the girl who sang the song thought, but I knew that it was really about forbidden love between men. Like, I love him, and he has no idea.

One day I was sitting in my room, and I was listening to the recording of this song, and my mother came in. Now, my mother has the habit of, if she finds a poem or a line from a song she likes, writing it on a slip of paper and putting it in her wallet. Her little quirk. So she came and asked me to write down the words to the song, and to give them to her. And as she was leaving the room, she went to close the door, and she kind of muttered, "Ayelet is a lucky girl." And I said to her, "Why?" And she said, "Because you write songs like that for her." And I said, "I didn't write it about her, I wrote it about Raz." And my mother left the room and closed the door.

And I said to myself, did she pick that up or not? I could hear her footsteps walking slowly away from the door, down the hall. And then all of sudden they stopped, and I could hear her coming back. Very quick steps. The door opened up, and my mother was standing there with a chair. Now, we live on the thirteenth floor. And I remember saying to myself, "If that chair lands on my head, I'm going to jump out the window." That's what I thought. But she took the chair, she, like, put it down dramatically in the middle of the room, plopped herself down on it, crossed her legs, and said to me, "Talk." So I talked.

It wasn't that I had made some sort of a decision to tell her. It just seemed the natural thing to do. She had said, "Ayelet is a very lucky girl," and it wasn't right, so I said so. I told her that I had a very close relationship with Raz, that I was unhappy when I didn't see him, much more than when I didn't see Ayelet. And I explained this to her. And I said to her, "I think I love him." And she said, "You'll get over it." I said, "OK, we'll see." I'm still waiting. That's it. That's all she said.

It just didn't make sense to me that, on the one hand, I had a girlfriend who I liked being with, and on the other hand, I had a friend who I would think about more than her. It just didn't make sense to me. And I didn't try to use the terms "good" or "bad." You understand? Nothing sexual happened with Raz. Nothing. And what's more—and this is important—I didn't even think about it. Sure I thought he had a beautiful body, but I never could picture to myself what I would do with it. I'm telling you, I never imagined in my wildest dreams that I would touch him, or sleep with him, or something like that. Absolutely not.

The next step was to tell Raz how I felt. It was very dramatic. We were sitting in my room, listening to music, and I said to him, "Raz, there's something I've got to tell you." And then I said, "Listen, we're together all the time, I'm with you all the time, and we're always trying to make sure that we have time alone together." And he interrupted me and said, "Alone? What do you mean alone?" And I said to him, "I really like being with you." And he said, "Yeah, I have fun being with you too." And I said, "No, it's not the same thing. Raz, I think that it's not just a regular friendship. I think I love you." And he sort of jumped backwards. We were both sitting on my bed, and he sort of moved away from me and said, "What the hell, what are you talking about?" And then we, like, got into some kind of an argument, I don't even remember about what, and he got up, and left, and that was that. The next day, he didn't talk to me. He totally stopped talking to me. And that's it. We lost touch with each other for a long time. Now we're talking again. He's totally straight. And he was just looking for a close pal, not anything more.

I was still with Ayelet through all of this. But the way I switched from boyfriend to boyfriend is just amazing. I write here that a few days before a gig, I met a guy named Eyal while clothes-shopping. "We talked, and we agreed to go out that night, he came to pick me up, and we went to the beach, I met his whole crowd, ʿOfer, who I know from school, Adir, Ziv, Yariv, Yoʾav, and Zohar. I wasn't very nice to him that day, because I hate smokers, but in the course of the following two days I got to know him better, and, as is my custom, I simply fell in love with him." You get the point? "He had a birthday, and I had a surprise party for him which was a real success." Blah, blah. "He was so happy he hugged me and almost kissed me. Since I've gotten to know his crowd, we've all gone out absolutely every night. We even went to Eilat for five days, we stayed in a hotel." And I mention the name of everyone who was there. "It was really terrific, we let loose and had a blast."

In the hotel in Eilat there was an interesting sort of scene. I don't remember exactly what happened. We were all kind of sitting in the lobby, and I wanted to go up to the room. I said to Eyal, "Come up to the room with me." And we were sitting with some other people also, and he said, "OK, let me just finish talking, and I'll go up." But I said, "No, you'll come up now." And he said, "I'm not going up now, I'm talking." "No?" "No!" I got very worked up. I remember how everybody was, like, looking at us, we were in the lobby and it was a respectable place. But I grabbed his chair and threw him onto the floor, and stormed off to the elevator. Then it really became clear to me how much I loved him, and how much it bothered me when he was with other people, when I wanted him to be with me, and he wasn't with me.

It didn't take too much, even at the time, to recognize a pattern in my relationships: "I write the following lines after having flipped through some of the earlier pages, reminding myself of some of the things I've been through. I've come to the conclusion that I really have nothing new to say. Every single time it's the same old story. I meet an object, I fall in love with him, we become friends, in a very short time become best friends, then there's some sort of short circuit, and it's over, as if it never happened."

My next entry begins like this: "Everything really began on," oh, this is good, I didn't remember that I wrote the date, "February 10, 1989." Wow, that's strange. That's later than what I thought—I thought it was at seventeen, but I was already nineteen. Oops. "A totally normal Friday night. But I decided after much hesitation to go to a gay club which I heard about from Erez." Now, I didn't write about this here, so I'll tell you what I remember about how it happened.

I went over to my old friend Erez's house at some point, and I said to him, "Erez, I've got to talk to you about something." We went into his room, we closed the door. And I told him that I had been seeing a psychologist— by this time, I had been going for a year and a half. I said to him, "Erez, I think I like guys." So he said, "OK, listen." He was a very worldly guy. He said, "I have a friend who is a lesbian." I said, "She's what?" "A lesbian." "What's a lesbian?" So he told me. And he said, "Listen, she goes to a place in Tel Aviv, it's called the Theater Club." And I asked him what it was, and he explained it to me, he told me, "I'll find out the address for you. You should go there and see that there are other people like you."

Now, I was still seeing Ayelet. It was a year and eight months at this point. We had never really, like, had sex. We kept our underwear on. She was young, seventeen, and I didn't pressure her. And I would come anyway, so I really didn't care if I penetrated her or not. Penetration is something I don't do with my boyfriend either—it's just not that important to me. I came, that was the most important thing, at this time. We had actually begun to, like, talk about really doing it, but it wasn't something I was dying to do.

So what happened was that there was a guy in my class, who we called Lifshitz. I don't remember his first name—everyone just knew him as Lifshitz. He couldn't stand me. He just couldn't stand me, this guy. And I said to my girlfriend, "Ayelet, come on, let's go to Tel Aviv, I've got my brother's car, we'll go out, we'll go to a club called Theater Club." She said, "What kind of a club is it?" I said to her, "I don't know, but Lifshitz told me it was a great place." "Lifshitz told you about a club?" I said yes. And she said, "He's probably trying to pull something on you." And I said "No, no, I'm sure it's OK, we were talking and all, I'm sure it'll be great. Let's go." OK. I convinced her.

But another friend of mine, ᶜOfer, heard that we were going to Tel Aviv, and he said, "Great, there's a girl I know in Tel Aviv, we'll all go out together, couples, it'll be great." So I had no choice—I said, "Great, cool."

So we got to Tel Aviv, it was our first time out alone in Tel Aviv. We went to pick up ᶜOfer's friend, and he said to her, "We're going to the Theater Club." And she said to him, "What? Where? The Theater Club?" And I tried to shut her up, to keep her from telling them what it was. She began to say, "But I heard that it was . . . " And I said, "Forget about what you heard, we've heard great things about the place, we'll go, we'll see what it's like, what's the worst thing that could happen?" And she said, "No, but . . . " And I tried to keep her from saying it, to distract her. I turned up the music, I made wrong turns, I tried everything. And somehow she kept her mouth shut.

So we got to the club. And I said, "OK, first of all, let's go down and pay the cover, then we'll go buy some ice cream, and then we'll go in." So we got to the club, the girls waited upstairs, me and ᶜOfer went down to buy tickets. And as we were counting our change, I turned to ᶜOfer and said, "ᶜOfer, ᶜOfer, you know, I don't see any girls here." And he said to me, "What are you talking about." And as we were walking upstairs, a couple of guys were coming downstairs, and one takes the other, and, like, gives him a big French kiss. And ᶜOfer grabs me, and begins shouting, "You're fucking nuts, where the fuck did you bring us? There are faggots here!" And he begins shouting, in the street, and people are beginning to arrive, because it's twelve-thirty already, people are beginning to come to the club, and staring at him, and he's shouting, "Homos, faggots, gross, yuck!" And the girls come running, "What happened, what happened?" And he says, "Oren and his crazy ideas." And I say, "It's not me, it's Lifshitz." And then my girlfriend joins in, "God, that Lifshitz, I could just kill him," and so on. The argument heated up, but the girls had already come to the conclusion that we had may as well make the best of it. "Let's go in. We'll see what homos are like." And I said, "No, no, no way," and they were like, "Yes, yes," "No, no," "Yes," "No," and I, finally was "convinced" to go in.

I'm telling you, from the second we walked in, I knew that this was what I wanted. The moment I went inside and I saw a male couple, like, sitting together and talking, sort of holding hands, I just knew that this was what I wanted. I was holding Ayelet's hand as we walked in, and I remember that, at that moment, I just kind of let her hand go. And then she took my hand back, and she kind of said to me, "Oren, what happened, what's wrong?" We sat down together, and I was looking at them, hypnotized, and she kind of said, "Oren, Oren, are you OK?" And it was, for me, a sort of confirmation. It was the first time that I had seen men kissing and touching, and it didn't even look so revolting. It even seemed interesting. After a year and a half going around in circles with a psychologist, it took me two seconds in the Theater Club to know that this was what I wanted.

The next day, me and Ayelet went shopping together, we bought some clothes. And I went over to her house afterwards, like, all dressed up, and I told her that I want to break up. And she said, "What happened? What landed from outer space all of a sudden, that we need to break up?" Everything was ideal, so far as she could see. And I said to her that, like, I had come to the conclusion that I was gay—well, I didn't use that word, but that's basically what I said. "How the hell did you come to that conclusion?" So I said to her, "I liked what I saw last night."

I told her that I thought I was in love with Dori. And she said to me, "Oren, listen, you like to experiment, to check everything out. So OK, go ahead, go out, meet some guys, do whatever you want, but let's not break up." But I couldn't do that. I wanted to break up.

Now I'll tell you about my first real night out in Tel Aviv. A week after we had all been out together at the Theater Club, I went back, by myself. I took my older brother's car—he had just gone abroad. I remember that, like, there was a long hallway you had to pass through to get to the dance floor there, and it sort of forked into two, with a column in the middle, and I was leaning on this column. And I suddenly felt tapping on my shoulder. So I, like, moved over a little bit, so that I wouldn't be in the way. But again, I felt tapping. So I moved again. And again. Finally I turned around and said, "Yeah, what do you want?" And this guy said to me, "Good evening." And I said, "Good evening."

I was very frightened, because I had really only come to look, to see what was happening, to open my eyes. And this guy said, "Nice to meet you, my name is Qobi." And I said, "I'm Oren." And he began to talk to me. I understood from the very first moment that I wouldn't be able to have a serious relationship with him, because he was older than me. Besides, I didn't think he was very good-looking. And I told him that. It really surprised me that I immediately knew what I was looking for. I said to him, "If I want anyone, it's someone my own age, not a day older than me. I want him thin, tall, smooth-skinned." That's what I said. I don't have any idea where I even pulled that from.

Here, my diary picks up the story: "In spite of that, he wanted to get together with me again, the next day." He was from Haifa. "I made it absolutely clear that it was with the exclusive goal of platonic friendship. We got together the next day," he introduced me to some of his friends in Haifa, and "we went to a restaurant. Afterwards, when I had dropped his friends off, he wanted to go to the beach with me. I declined. I explained the reason as being that I was perfectly aware of what happens when a couple goes to the beach at night. Yet, after Qobi promised me that he didn't intend to do anything beyond converse in a pleasant atmosphere, I agreed. Of course, he broke his word, and I, who had never in my life had any experience with a man, even a kiss, was revolted by him." I see that I didn't describe what happened.

We were sitting and talking, and all of a sudden I felt his arm around me. And I said, "Um, excuse me, what do you think you're doing?" And the second I said that, he grabbed me close to him and kissed me. And I was so revolted by him. I don't know whether it was because he was a man or because of who he was, but he just disgusted me. He also smoked. Ugh! Have you ever heard that saying, that kissing a smoker is like licking an ashtray? To make a long story short, "I started the car, I dropped him off at his house, and told him that I never wanted to see him again."

I kept everybody, like, up to date on what was going on. My mother also. She asked why I broke up with my girlfriend, and I told her that we had been to this club in Tel Aviv, and I liked what I saw. I didn't tell my father. It just didn't, like, work out that way. I was living with my mother. It wasn't that I was trying to hide it, I wasn't afraid or anything. It was just in the course of conversation. My mother talked to me more. She didn't have any reaction. It was like, "You should do what you want, if this seems right to you, then you should do it." I know it's very unique. I love her for that. She lets me do what I want. She's had questions, but she's never made any sort of scene, "I won't allow it," or anything like that, "I object." She has, like, treated me respectfully, and I've treated her respectfully.

This was when *Dynasty* was on television. And I remember that I told my older brother about what was going on, because I needed his car to get to Tel

Aviv. And he said, "Ah, we have a Steven in the family." That was, like, the re-action. Nothing more than that. And, don't get me wrong, it isn't that he's pleased. I know that he has a problem with it. But he just said, "OK, we've got a Steven in the family." That was his entire reaction. And he gave me his car keys to go to Tel Aviv.

I also told ʿOfer, who had gotten over the shock of our trip to the club by this time. And he really wanted to go back to Tel Aviv to see his girlfriend, and since I could get my brother's car, he was glad to take advantage of an-other free ride down to Tel Aviv the next time I went to the Theater Club. It was his suggestion.

On the way down, we picked up two hitchhikers, young guys, our own age. One of them got out before Tel Aviv—he was driving us crazy anyway, he had, like, diarrhea of the mouth. But the other stayed in the car, quiet as can be. As things turned out, he was to become my first boyfriend. I adjusted the mirror so that I could see him, and we just began talking. I said to him, "Where are you going?" And he said, "I'm going to the Theater Club." And I just went white. White. And ʿOfer, he immediately, like, jumped in and said, "Oh yeah, that's where *he's* going also—not me, I'm not going there—*he's* going there too." Now, the hitchhiker apparently thought that we were pulling one on him. So he asked us to just drop him off as soon as we got to Tel Aviv. But it began to rain pretty hard at this point. So I said, "Why should you get out, I'm going there in any case, I'll take you there. I'm going there also." But he refused—he wouldn't believe me. He insisted on getting out. So I said to him, "OK, you can get out here, and I'll wait for you at the entrance to the club." And that's the way it happened.

So we went in together, and began talking. And all of a sudden I hear someone shouting, "Hey, buddy." I turn around, and I don't believe what I see. It's that horrible guy Qobi. "What do you want from me, I told you I don't want anything to do with you." And he says to the other guy, "Hey, how's it going, I see you've met Oren, he's a cool dude." Qobi knew this guy also! So I turned to the hitchhiker and said to him, "That's one mark against you." And he said, "What is?" "That you know Qobi." To make a long story short, we went into the pub, and the three of us sat down. And I began try-ing to get rid of Qobi. Finally, the hitchhiker got up to go to the bathroom, and Qobi said to me, "Do you like him?" I said yes. And he said, "Do you know how old he is?" I said no. He said, "He's your age." And I said, "I'd def-initely like to get to know him better." And that's it, when he came back from the bathroom, Qobi, like, finally got the message and left.

We had a nice time together that night, just talking, and we exchanged telephone numbers. I took him back to Haifa. The next day I went to his house, and then the next day, and the next day. And then, we were sitting in his room, he, like, dimmed the lights, we were sitting on a kind of love seat, on opposite sides, far apart. And we got to the point where we didn't have anything else to talk about. Just twenty minutes, thirty minutes of, like, quiet. So I said to him, "Listen, if you don't do something, I'm certainly not going to do anything, because I haven't the slightest idea what we're supposed to do now."

So he got the message. He, like, undressed himself, and then he undressed me. He got out some hand lotion. I was in shock. I didn't understand exactly what it was that he was doing. He said, "Trust me." And I trusted him. And I really enjoyed myself. It was also the first time that I had, like, taken all of my clothes off with someone, the first time someone had really touched me. It was glorious, wonderful. I even kissed him afterwards. And that's it. I really liked it.

Unfortunately, what I found out afterwards, and this was the reason that I dumped him, was that he lived with someone who was paying his rent in return for sexual favors. Oh well.

Here's what I wrote in my diary: "That hitchhiker was my first boyfriend, who I slept with and kissed. Since then a lot of water has passed through the Sea of Galilee, and it has become clear to me that I really am, as I argued all along, gay. I went to the Theater Club another four or five times, but then it folded, and a new place called Metro opened up. And on Tuesday nights in Haifa, a place called Fever has become a gay club."

The Metro was also in Tel Aviv. I don't know if you remember it, but inside, there was a kind of platform, where you couldn't be seen, but you could, like, look at who was dancing and who wasn't and so on. Once, I was sitting on this platform, and I saw a couple, one of whom I really liked. It was clear that they were a couple, but I said to myself, that one is going to be mine. I made an oath to myself.

A few weeks later, I finally saw him alone. I went up to him, and we began talking, and I could tell that he was, like, kind of uncomfortable. I asked him what was wrong, and he said, "I'm here with someone else." I said, "Your boyfriend?" And he said, "No, not exactly," and he began stuttering and all. So I said to him, "I'm going outside, follow me out if you feel like it." And that's what we did, I went out, he went out afterwards, and he explained that, like, there was this older guy, he felt uncomfortable saying no to him, blah,

blah, blah. And I said to him, "You know what, take my telephone number, call me if you feel like it." He told me about himself also. His name was ʿAdi. He was in the army, stuck on some base in the middle of nowhere.

He called me, I invited him to come to Haifa, and we met, and we began, like, developing a relationship. He dumped the other guy. And we kept on meeting. He would come to Haifa on the weekends, whenever he could, once every two weeks, something like that. He was right at the end of his army service, and after about two months he was discharged.

I remember once, I called him on a Friday, and told him that I really, really wanted to go out with him and to paint the town red. Now, he lived in Jerusalem, and he had to return the car to his parents that same night. So this is what he did—I tease him about it to this very day. Not very nice of me, but I do it. He drove from Jerusalem to Haifa to pick me up, and then took me to Tel Aviv, where we went to the Metro. When we were done, he took me back home to Haifa, and then he drove back to Jerusalem by himself, to return the car to his parents. We had a great time together.

Around that time, I met a girl named Ayiyit. I had performed in a graduation concert at a high school, and I met her there. I was nineteen. We got to know each other, and we went out, and so on. And then I introduced her to ʿAdi, I told her what was going on between us, and she was, like, very thrilled by the whole thing. And after she had gone out with me once or twice, she began going out with him! And that's it. To this day I'm good friends with ʿAdi, but nothing more than that.

I had finished high school by this time, but every time I got a draft notice from the army, I managed to come up with a new excuse, so I hadn't been drafted yet. I didn't want to go into the army. It didn't really seem to fit me. I don't even remember what I said—I claimed to be enrolled in all sorts of courses, which wasn't true, but I could always get the papers, because I had enough friends. I was working in all kinds of jobs and I was playing the drums in all kinds of bands. I sang, things like that, nothing serious.

It was a very wild time. I went out every day, and every day I would come home with someone else. And it got to the point where one day I went out with a friend to the Metro, and we were kind of looking around. And he said to me about someone in particular, "Look, what a cute guy." And I said, "You won't like him." And he said, "How do you know?" I said to him, "I've been with him already." OK. A few minutes later, he said to me, "Wow, look, what a hunk." And I said to him, "Oh him, yes, you're right, he would be a good match for you." And he gave me a look, and I said, "I've been with him." OK.

So he said, "Oren, who else in this room have you been with?" And I was quiet for a some very long seconds, and then I said to him, "I think it would be easier for me to tell you who I haven't been with." At that point I think it came home to me how nasty I had been. The thing is, during this whole period, it was never just like, I liked someone and I said to myself, OK, I'll sleep with him and that's that. Every time I met someone, I was really hoping that I would develop a relationship with him. But it never worked. I wasn't very aware of AIDS, but you can't get AIDS from what I did—no penetration, I didn't even kiss. Nothing that could lead to AIDS. In spite of that, I would get tested every once in a while, every three months. It was kind of a waste of time, because, like, there wasn't any chance.

I remember one time at Fever, in Haifa—of course, there weren't a lot of people there, but I saw a guy there who I liked a lot, and I began to talk to him, and in the course of conversation he made it clear to me that he had a boyfriend. So I said to him, "OK, no problem, I'm not trying to pick you up or something, introduce me to your friend also." That wasn't really true, because I was really into him. And I was aware of what I had going for me—I was young. It was a tremendous point in your favor. So we just talked, and I gave him my telephone number, and he said that we would be in touch. That was Monday. And Tuesday and Wednesday went by, and I couldn't believe that he wasn't calling. Finally, he called on Friday. He said that he would come visit. He was in med school, he was in the middle of exams, pressure, and so on.

He came over, we sat and talked. He was very nice, he said that he would bring his boyfriend the next time he came. And they really did come, the two of them, and we sat and talked. In retrospect I know that both he and his boyfriend had crushes on me. But I didn't know that then. So we developed a relationship, he would come to visit and so on, and on one of these visits, when he came without his boyfriend, we just kind of slipped into bed. I was aware of what was going to happen, maybe he was less so. So we did what we did, and afterwards, when we finished, he went to take a shower, then I showered, I made a little something to eat, we went back to the room, and, like, it happened again. And that's it.

A few days later, his boyfriend called me up and invited me to come over for a serious conversation. He said to me, "I have something I want to talk to you about." It was late at night, so I said to him, "Listen, if I go over there now, that means that I'm sleeping over at your place." And he said to me, "OK, why not." I went over to his place, we sat and talked. He wrote poetry, and he read me some of the poems he had written. And you could understand, between the lines, that he had figured out what had happened between his boyfriend and me. And in my great innocence, when I heard how much he had been hurt—I certainly wouldn't react that way today—I began to cry. Because I had hurt him so deeply. And the next thing he did, apparently, like, overwhelmed by how deeply he had touched me, was he put his arm around me. You can already figure out what happened from here.

Afterwards, I just felt like a complete idiot. I said to myself, if there is such a thing as a slut, that's me. What, two days ago his boyfriend, and today him? He told me that from the first time he had seen me he had liked me, and so on. And two days earlier I had heard exactly the same thing from his boyfriend! And then I, to myself, weighed my options in a very cold, logical fashion. Which of them do I want to try to build a relationship with? I liked both of them by this point, and I didn't know which one I preferred. But this one had just gone to live in Kfar Saba, and I said, if he's going to Kfar Saba, how am I going to have a relationship with him—but the first one is already in Haifa, I'll choose him. And that's it.

We were together for about a month and a half. I moved in with him. He had his own apartment. I worked a little, but then I ran out of excuses, and I was drafted. I was almost twenty, there was nothing I could do.

After I had gotten my first draft notice, I found out that, according to the army, my physical and mental profile was good enough that I would have to be put in a combat unit. But I said no way, absolutely not, I'm not going to be a combat soldier. No chance. I was going to have that changed.

So I went to the draft board, and asked to see an army psychologist. And I told the psychologist that I was gay. So he said to me, "How do you know?" I said, "What are you talking about? I like men." And he said, "What do you mean 'like'? What exactly do you do?" I was convinced that he was "like that" also, the way he was looking at me. So I told him, more or less, what I do. And he asked if there was someone who could testify to this! It seemed like he didn't believe me, so I said to him, "What, you want to sleep with me— I'll prove it." And he just kind of gave me a look—but that didn't convince me that in fact, this wasn't exactly what he wanted. Of course, a few weeks later, I really did see him in the Metro. And we looked right at each other, and I understood that we had a kind of "pact of silence."

I really wanted to get out of doing the army. I was convinced that after I told them, they would send me flying out of the office. They didn't do that, but they did lower my profile. When I was finally drafted, I was sent to the absolute minimum basic training a person can do, if he hasn't already been totally disqualified from being in the army because of a physical handicap or something. As soon as I got there I began making trouble. The very first day I was drafted, when I got to the induction center, I already began making trouble.

There was supposed to be a lights out at the end of the day, right? But I went to my commanding officer, and I said to him, "I don't know what you know about me and what you don't know, but you can't turn the lights out here." And he said, "What are you talking about?" And I said, "I never sleep in the dark, I only sleep with the lights on. I'm afraid of the dark." So he gave me a look, and I said, "You apparently haven't read my medical history. Do you want to take this kind of responsibility on yourself?" To make a long story short, all the lights in the entire tent stayed on all night. Needless to say, the other soldiers hated me from that moment on.

The next day, they brought us to basic training, and at the first opportunity, I took my new commanding officer aside, and I said to her, "I don't know what you know about me, and what you don't know about me—but I just don't see how I'm going to manage in the same tent with so many guys. And then there are the showers . . . " and so on. I played the whole thing, like, very hysterical. And she didn't know what to say. I mean, she was younger than I was. What was she supposed to say? I said, "I don't shower with so many guys together. No way." And she didn't make any problems for me.

To make a long story short, in no time at all I had, like, compiled an astounding list of exemptions and special conditions—I didn't do guard duty at night, because I was afraid of the dark, I didn't do kitchen duty, because I thought it was gross, and so on. There was even one day, when the power was out, when they, like, made sure that I would have someone to come outside with me to pee, because I was afraid. Sure, I played up my problems because I wanted to get out of the army. I don't have any problem showering with other guys—but I really am scared of the dark. Anyway, that was basic training. None of the other soldiers knew that I was gay. I didn't tell them, and the officers didn't tell them either.

Afterwards, I found out that one of my commanding officers was lesbian. We even, like, went out together to the Metro once. She had become friendly with me, and then one day she took me aside and we had a big talk. She "confessed" to me—"What, you think I don't have my own things going on," something like that—"I've got an apartment in Eilat, a girlfriend," and so on.

I finished basic training, and then, oh God, it was a disaster, I was sent to the army's transportation base near Haifa. And there, the first day I got there, the commander of the base asked to see me. But the company sergeant major decided that there must have been some mistake—like, normally, you've got to make a special request to get an interview with the commander, so how can it be that all of a sudden a soldier walks into the base and five minutes later, the commander invites him for an interview? I mean, the company sergeant major himself probably hadn't ever had an interview with the commander. So he said to me, "You're not going anywhere. This must be a mistake." And I said to him, "What are you talking about, the commander of the base asked to see me." He said, "I'm sure there was a misunderstanding." But he called to make sure, and I could see the shocked look on his face as he was talking. And when he got off the phone he said, "Go."

So I went to the commander's office, and I was, like, shaking all over from fear. Back then, the whole thing with rank really made me very nervous. I hadn't even been in the army for a month. So I was trembling with fear, like, to have to go in to the commander of the base, to salute, and so on.

They brought me in to him, he said that I could sit down, calm down, make myself comfortable. He said to me, "Is what I read about you in your personal file true?" And suddenly I was back to my old self. I said to him, "I imagine so—what did you read?" I don't remember what we said next, but, like, we both knew what we were talking about, and he asked me what my expectations were and so on. And I said to him, "I can't stay on this base," where we wouldn't be going home at the end of the day. "I'm not going to sleep in the same room with other men, I'm not going to get dressed with them, I'm not going to undress with them, I'm certainly not going to shower with them." Of course, I presented it as a very urgent problem, which it wasn't. At this point, I didn't have any hope of being discharged from the army. I just thought that he would, like, give me permission to leave the base from time to time, once every two weeks or something like that. And he said, "OK, no problem, I'll make sure that you can go home every day. You won't have to sleep on the base."

Now, this itself, like, caused a lot of problems for me. Because we were all going through training together, all of the soldiers, doing exactly the same things, and all of a sudden, like, there would come a time each day when Oren would just get up and leave, go home. What the hell? And I wasn't about to explain to them why.

I was supposed to be taking a driving course on this base. It had been determined that I would be an army driver—but I made it clear to the commander that I wasn't cut out to be a truck driver. I was, like, only going to drive cars. And right from the start they exempted me from guard duty and from kitchen duty. I said to the commander, if I didn't do kitchen duty during basic training, what, you think I'm going to do kitchen duty here?

So there were a lot of problems. On top of everything, all of a sudden I split up with my boyfriend right about this time. And that meant that I had to get my stuff out of his place. So I had permission to leave the base every night now, but nowhere to go!

I spoke to the commander and explained my problem, and what they did was they separated me from the rest of the platoon, and they put me into the headquarters building, to sleep. So there was the commander, the vice commander, the company sergeant major, and me. We each had a room. And then there was the operations room, the war room. I lived in headquarters, the main building, the most important building on the base—I just moved into an office. I figure that my commander kind of thought, "Well, what do you expect from a queer anyway. What am I going to do, lecture him? It won't do any good in any case." That's the way I figure it. Or maybe he was just a good guy. I don't know. We got along pretty well.

So all of a sudden, all the other soldiers decided that, like, they wanted to be my best buddy, now that I had even better living conditions than the instructors. My room had a phone with an outside line. I had air conditioning. I brought a television. And I even got a cat onto the base—yes, there was a cat living in headquarters. It was pretty entertaining. One day it ran away and hid in the commander's room. Would you want to go in there and get her out? I had some pretty great stories there. But only in retrospect.

Now, the army has a certain hierarchy, right? And it's obvious that someone on the bottom of the ladder, who isn't even a corporal, has got to salute everyone who is of a higher rank—and certainly the commander of the base, right? But normal soldiers in training, like I was, hardly ever see their commander—of course, they're going to salute him when they see him, but, like, it's not a big issue for them. I, on the other hand, would run into my commander, like, a zillion times a day. I would see him all the time, and I would drive him crazy, because every time he would pass by me, I would, like, salute, and every time I saluted, he would have to put me at ease. Finally he said, "Enough already. You can't go on like this. Don't salute me—don't you dare salute me ever again. If you ever give me another salute, you'll be in very hot water." OK, so I didn't salute any more.

And this really drove other people up the wall. You know, if he came into the dining hall, everyone else would, like, stand up and salute, and I would just kind of go about my business. And it drove people up the wall. Including my sergeant major, who of course, had to salute the commander when he saw him. Everyone would be saluting him and I would be like, "Hi, how're you doin'?" and he would come over and, like, sit down and chat with me. And of course people were jealous, and they began to spread all kinds of gossip, and so on. People thought I was related to him, or that I had connections even higher up.

To make a long story short, I finished the drivers' course, and when I finished, the commander suggested to me that I be transferred off the base—he told me that I didn't fit in, that there were, like, all kinds of rumors, gossip. "I'll try to set something up for you. What do you want to do?" So I told him that the thing I most wanted to do was to go to the navy training camp, as a driver. So he said, "I'll try to work it out." And he did. I was transferred to the navy training camp.

Once again, as soon as I got there, I was called to speak to the base commander. "Is what's written here correct?" and so on. He wanted to know how this affected my ability to serve, so I told him, I don't sleep on the base, I don't do kitchen duty, I don't do this, I don't do that. And he said, "I'll do my best to keep your duties to a minimum, but when they come up, I imagine that you'll do your best to get by." And that was it. I was a navy driver. It was the kind of job where, like, you would come at eight, do what you're told, and go home at five.

It quickly became apparent to me that I had an unbelievably idiotic commanding officer. You know you're in trouble when you have to explain to your commanding officer what centrifugal force is—he'd never heard of it! I remember once, he was telling me about how he took his kids to the amusement park, and they went on a kind of a tilt-a-whirl, and if they hadn't had their belts on, they would certainly have fallen off. And he said, "Especially when they got to the top, they would have fallen off if they hadn't been belted." So I said, "They wouldn't have fallen, because of centrifugal force. They were spinning very quickly. Maybe they would have fallen if the ride had stopped moving when they were at the top, but since it was always turning, they couldn't have fallen." And he said, "No, no, you don't know what you're talking about." So, as if I was dealing with a slow child, I took a bucket, like, filled it halfway with water, tied a rope to the handle, and told him to swing it around. And he was absolutely amazed that the water didn't spill. Really shocked. It was like I had discovered America.

Anyway, this guy had a problem with me. He couldn't figure out why, when he needed to send a driver to point x in the evening, Oren would refuse to go. And when he would talk to the commander of the base, the commander would always take my side and say, "No, he's not going." "But he's the only driver I've got right now, you're ruining my operation, how can this be." And the commander would never give him an explanation.

From the base commander's point of view he was acting logically—he was exempting me from things he thought I was incapable of doing. But he didn't go and tell my commanding officer, apparently because he knew perfectly well that this guy was a bonehead and wouldn't know how to deal with, like, having a soldier who was gay. Especially among the drivers, all these macho guys. Sure, from the very first moment that I felt I was gay I had always been totally open about it—but that was up until the army. My commanders told me that it wouldn't be in my interest to tell anyone, because I was in not-very-sympathetic surroundings. So the high-ranking people knew, but they didn't tell anyone down below. And if they weren't telling, I sure wasn't telling.

So, for most of the time I was in the army, I had my evenings and my weekends to myself. I kept on making periodic Friday-night trips to Tel Aviv, going mostly to the Metro. One time, I saw an amazing-looking guy. I asked around about him, and found out that he was eighteen years old, from the Haifa suburbs. I liked that. He was dancing, but I went up to him, tapped him on the shoulder, he turned around and I said, "Can I talk to you?" So he said to me, "Can't you see I'm dancing?" So I said, "OK," and I began walking away, and then he shouted after me, "Hey, wait a minute, when the song is over, we'll talk." And I said, "OK, I'll wait for you outside." I went outside, after a few minutes he went outside also, and we began kind of chatting, do you have a boyfriend, do you this and that, and he said, "Well, if you want to meet me again, give me your telephone number." By this time I was renting an apartment of my own. So I said, "It's a waste of time for me to give it to you, you're not going to call." And he said, "If I take your number, I'll call." OK.

Needless to say, the following day I sat by the phone, like, all day waiting for his call, and at about eleven or twelve at night, the phone really did ring. He was on the line, and I was very happy to hear from him. I said to him, "I'd really like to see you." And he said "That's a problem, I'm in Tel Aviv now." "Are you coming back to Haifa today?" "Yes, but very late." And I said to him, "Whatever time you get here, call me up, I'll make sure you get taken here." And he said, "OK." I made a few calls, and I made sure a friend of mine would be standing by. So he called when he got here, and my friend drove to the suburbs especially to pick him up, and brought him to my place. I told my friend that when we were done talking, I would call him up so he could take this guy home. And that's it. This guy came over to my place, and we sat and talked. That night we really did only talk. It was summertime, he came dressed in, like, shorts and a tank top, and I said to myself, yes, this is exactly what I need. I really liked him. We said we would speak the next day, and the next day he really did come over again, and it was really a lot of fun. We were boyfriends for the next six months.

It was really a fabulous thing. A lot of fun. He didn't hold anything back, and I like that. We were totally open, even in public. We would go into straight clubs and really shock everyone. It would make people very uncomfortable. But what did I care? We would kiss in public, put our arms around each other in public. I didn't care. Movie theaters, bars, clubs, on the street, it didn't make a difference to me. And I loved people's reactions, just like in the movies—they would walk into telephone poles, things like that, it happened a lot. Jaws just dropped. And some people were just thrilled. We would be sitting somewhere holding hands, and some people would, like, walk by us five times—back, forth, back, forth, back. But we never encountered a really negative reaction. Not even one.

After six months, he decided that he didn't like me any more. I loved him, but he wanted to try being with other guys. It was very clear and easy with him. Today, we're very good friends, but it took a long time before that kind of friendship could develop. After we split up, I was unbelievably depressed, I couldn't look at other men, I didn't like anyone. I could only think about him, I cried all the time, it was a very difficult time.

Around this time, I began making some more serious trouble in the army. I talked to the army psychologist again. I told him I just couldn't take being in the army any more, having all these men around all the time. I did my best. I also made a big deal out of these back problems I had always had, and, to make a long story short, they finally discharged me. Once things got rolling, the whole procedure took less than a week. Very fast. And that was that. I had been in the army for only nine months. And now I got what I wanted—out.

At this time, I had a good friend, a straight, his name was Ran, and I would complain to him all the time about how I didn't have a boyfriend, poor me, I want a boyfriend, and so on and so forth. It had already been, like, six months. So Ran said to me, "What's the problem, why don't you put a personal ad in the paper?" So I said, that's an interesting idea. I want you to write the ad for me. And he wrote something like, "Twenty-year-old hunk looking for similar boyfriend, thin, eighteen to twenty," blah, blah, blah. That was pretty much the style.

I got a ton of calls. There was a number where you could get messages. I stopped counting at seventy. And I'm not counting the dirty messages, with heavy breathing and all that. These were serious messages—hello, my name is such and such, I'm x years old, physical description of course, I'd like to meet you, call me on such and such day, between this and that hour, at this number. It was usually a public phone, and usually a fake name. There were some people I answered, and others who, just by listening to their voice, I knew I wasn't interested in, and others who, after having a short conversation with them, I knew I was wasting my time with.

And then I heard a message that went something like this—"Hello, my name is Adam, I'm seventeen years old, my telephone number is . . . ," and he gave the number. I was in shock. I said to myself, this can be either a mental retard, or someone who's lying, or someone who's playing a practical joke on someone else—someone giving the number of someone else in his class to make trouble for him. But, OK, I said, let's see. So I dialed. "Hello," a motherly voice says on the other end. "Hello," I say. "Good evening," the voice says. I answer, "Good evening. May I please speak to Adam?" "Sure, just a moment." And then I hear in the background: "Adam, telephone." At this point, I already knew that my leg was being pulled. I mean, there was just no way, I mean, giving your home phone number like that. And then I hear a deep voice saying, "Hello?" And I said, "Hello." And he said, "Are you answering my message?" And I said yes.

And then I let him have it. Because then I realized, by the tone of his voice, that he really did leave his own phone number. And I said to him, "Tell me, are you crazy? You gave me your home phone number and your real name? What's the matter with you?" I bawled him out. And I didn't even know him. But we continued the conversation a little bit more, and I asked him to describe himself. But he said, "Tomorrow, there's a graduation concert for this high school," and he of course, didn't know that I was the producer for this concert. He said, "I'm going to be an usher there. I'll be wearing a gray sweater and a white shirt. If you want to, introduce yourself." I said OK.

And I was, of course, at the concert, but I didn't see him, I was too busy backstage and so on. And so the next day I left him a message with my home phone number, and he called me, and said, "Why didn't you introduce yourself? You don't think I'm attractive?" And I said, "No, actually, I didn't see you. I was busy." And he said, "Well, when can we meet?" I said, "You can come over now." I gave him my address. And he came over. And I opened the door, and I saw him and he saw me, and you know what? There really weren't any fireworks. We sat and made small talk for a while. He's always very shy when he first meets someone, he, like, sits in the corner, and you're lucky if you can get a word out of him. I said to myself, "My God, what have I done to offend him?" So we just kind of made small talk. But we've been together for two years and four months now.

I was working in a recording studio for a long time after I left the army. But let's just say there were some professional conflicts, and I left that job a few weeks ago. I've taken a job at a hotel in Eilat, as a reception clerk. We'll see. I'm only twenty-two. The important thing is to make a living, it doesn't make a difference what you do. Money is, like, a means and not an end—but it is a very good means. So I do my best to get it. I like the good life, I like to buy the best things, I like to go abroad. I like the good things in life. So right now I'm in the middle of packing up this apartment, and moving to Eilat.

Eilat is a wonderful city. And it doesn't make any difference what happens, whatever you're doing there, for me at least, you always feel like you're on vacation there. There are a lot of people who are "like that" there, but there isn't any real meeting place. Some people are interested in getting something going, though, so we'll have to see what we can do.

To me, being with someone means living together, going out together, having a joint bank account, going abroad together—doing everything together. Choosing the carpet and bed linens together. That's what I've always wanted. I don't know if the relationship I have with Adam right now should be some kind of model, some kind of example—but I know that there are a lot of people who envy us. A lot of people who look at our relationship and say, wow, this is what I want.

I think that what we've got is better than marriage. This is how I explain the difference between a guy-girl couple and a guy-guy couple to my straight friends—let's say you've got a husband and wife, OK? They're both always going to have needs outside of the relationship—the man has his best friend, who he tells all about his problems with his wife, and so does the woman, she has her own special woman-friends. You're always going to seek out these bonds with your own sex, like, to go out and have a few drinks with the guys, or invite your buddies over to watch soccer, or whatever. And when that's what you want—your wife, well, she'd better just stay in the kitchen.

But with us, there's nothing like that. With me, at least, my boyfriend is first and foremost my best friend—he is what I would be looking for outside of the boundaries of heterosexual couplehood. But in addition to this friendship bond, we love each other. So we're buddies first, and lovers after the fact. And that's how I explain it to my friends. That's, like, the way I see it at least. And I think, because of this, a relationship like this is much stronger. Because, I mean, at least from what I've had a chance to observe in this world, your best friend is always your best friend. From a certain age onwards, he's always there. You'll always have him—you can get married, divorced, have children, he'll always be your best friend, he'll always be there for you. And in my case, I don't need to look for anything else, because in addition to Adam's being my buddy, I'm in love with him.

I would be lying if I said that our relations are totally equal. I do my best to make them that way, but they aren't. At first, to be honest, I was a tyrant. And even today, if, like, there are decisions that need to be made, I'm the one who usually makes them. I can't explain why, because I don't think it's right, I can't defend it. But I see that, like, this is what happens. I don't know whether it's because I'm the older one, or because I'm the one who's usually supporting us. Adam is in the army now.

Of course, none of this has anything to do with what we do in bed. Like I said to you at the beginning, we don't, like, do anything at all that involves penetration. So in bed we are totally equal. Maybe it would be interesting to try someday, but not right now. There's no rush.

It's all about mutual consideration. For instance, I like to have a lot of sex. He likes it also, but let's just say a little less. His dream is that, just once, we can go to sleep without doing it. That's his dream. And me—no way. So a few days ago, we were in Eilat, on Friday night, we came home very early that night, 11:30, and we went to bed. And I had decided, today, I'm going to let him go to sleep. So we, like, got into bed, snuggled up with our arms around each other, and that was that. And I thought I was doing him a favor. But, he, he began to make things happen. And I said to myself, wow, this is great. And when we had finished, I said to him, "You know, I've got to tell you, I had planned not to do anything tonight." And he said, "Shit, really? I thought you wanted it." We try to talk about these things now. We're, like, constantly building our relationship.

I think this relationship will last. I think it mostly depends on me, if I can keep myself from doing anything stupid, and be faithful to him. He knows about my past stupidities. One time, I met a girl, and we went to Cyprus, the two of us. And I don't even know why I didn't tell him that I went with her, I thought it was clear. But he found out only when he saw the pictures, that there she was. We got into an argument and he took his things and moved out. Of course I immediately realized what a mistake I had made, but he wouldn't come back, and it was really like we had to start over from the very beginning. Courtship, flowers, dates, long talks. And I think that today we have a much healthier relationship than beforehand. I want to be with him forever.

I have a lot of respect for gay activists, but that sort of thing just isn't for me. I think it's very important that someone work to make sure we can get government aid for a first mortgage, just like straight couples, for instance. But I'm not going to go shout about it. It would mean, like, a sacrifice on my part that I'm not willing to make. I think that it could alienate my family, and I don't want that. I like to stay within the limits of good taste—although I guess that in many people's opinion I've already crossed those borders. I, from my point of view, so long as it doesn't hurt my family, I've got no problem. But when it comes to the wider public, and it could hurt my family, I draw the line. My mother doesn't need someone coming up to her and telling her, "You've got a gay son." She knows already, but, like, she doesn't need to hear it from other people.

I think that it's great that such a small country like ours can be so advanced in its attitude toward gays, especially now, with what's been going on with the army, as compared to the U.S. I mean, we draft gays without any conditions now. If you go and say, "I'm gay," they'll take you now without asking any questions. This is even better than when I was in the army. Before I was drafted, when someone would come and, like, say he was gay, they would refuse to draft him. Me, they drafted and lowered my profile. But now, they don't even lower your profile because of it—they won't automatically lower your profile because you're gay. I think that's great. More power to them.

I didn't go to the Pride Day "Happening" in Tel Aviv because it didn't interest me. It wasn't that I didn't want to be seen there. It just didn't interest me. If they had, like, gotten a big-name rock singer, I would have gone. You understand? When I was in New York, I went to the Pride Day March there. I went, I shouted, it was a blast—to hear, to see, to feel Fifth Avenue, like, exploding with people. That was something. That was much more interesting. But what can we do in Tel Aviv that would be even close to that? Do you want me to show you pictures from New York, so you can see the difference? I think you can figure it out for yourself, the difference between Sheinqin Street and Fifth Avenue. Oh sure, I'm, like, just dying to go to Sheinqin Street and stand around with one hundred other people—that would be great, it would just make my day. You know, if I had gone to Sheinqin I wouldn't have even brought a camera—what could possibly happen there that would be worth taking a picture of? Really, I'm serious. When you think about it, we're, like, a tiny, peripheral, provincial country. What could there possibly be to get excited about here? And I bet that people in Tel Aviv weren't really open enough either. They didn't really feel comfortable, free.

Of course, with Adam, doing things like that is out of the question. He's not just in the closet—he's, like, deep somewhere in the back corner of the sock drawer in the bureau in the closet. He's most at home when surrounded by mothballs. Our biggest arguments are about this—if we ever have something to argue about, this is it. He's, like, totally hysterical about this. Even though his family knows.

If I had something interesting to do in New York, and Adam wanted to go, then I would go live there. Why not? The same is true of anyplace else in the world. I am absolutely not a Zionist. I'm, like, enjoying myself here, and my life is good, so I want to be here. My friends are here, so I want to be here. But if I had acquired the same kind of friendships in a different place, I wouldn't mind living somewhere else. I think that people should live where they're happy.

I guess you could say that I keep certain Jewish traditions. I observe Yom Kippur, I fast, and I celebrate the holidays, Rosh Hashanah, and Śimḥat Torah, and Passover. And I think that this is a beautiful thing. But I don't do these things because I'm Jewish. It isn't that I say to myself—I'm Jewish, this is what I need to do. It's that I think these things are beautiful, distinctive. I like distinctive things.

I may have learned this in elementary school. I remember I had one teacher who would always say, "The religious Jews, they're the ones who have preserved the nation. If it hadn't been for the religion, the people of Israel would have disappeared long ago." And it's important that the Jewish people not disappear, because it is a beautiful thing.

I think our holidays are beautiful, although I do have to say that we're missing one holiday—Valentine's Day. This is missing. I mean, like, Ṭu Beʾav just doesn't cut it.[§] People just don't treat it the way they treat Valentine's

§ Ṭu Beʾav: Holiday marking the beginning of the vintage in the ancient Land of Israel. According to tradition, the women of first-century Jerusalem observed the holiday by dancing and singing in the vineyards. In recent years, some have revived its observance as a holiday for lovers.

Day abroad. How many people do you know who do get presents on Ṭu Be²aẏ? But people take Valentine's Day seriously in other places.

I think that gay synagogues are a stupid idea. Why would you want to make a group within a group? Isn't it enough that we're separated because we're Jewish—we need to divide the Jews between gays, lesbians, and then, who knows what, drag queens, and so on? What good does this segregation do? You're all Jewish, you should be together. I can see the point of having a dance club or a bar for people who are "like that"—these sorts of institutions have a certain function, as meeting places, for the kinds of meetings which, like, generally do not end with a handshake and the morning prayer. But this is not the function of a synagogue. And if that becomes the function of a synagogue, then things are very bad indeed. At least that's what I think.

Very few people don't know about me at this point. But I have different ways of telling people. I just came back from a few weeks in Eilat, and I had a roommate there. And we were sitting up late one night and talking, and I said to him, "You know that cousin of mine that was here?" Because I had told him that Adam was a cousin, and he said, "Yeah." And I said to him, "He isn't my cousin." And he said, "So what is he?" I said to him, "He's my boyfriend." And he didn't quite get it. So I said to him, "Do you remember that I talked about my girlfriend?" And he said, "Yes." And I said, "That's him." And he said, "What?" And I said, "Everything I told you I had done with my girlfriend, I did with him, everything she said, he said, get it?" And so then he says, "And what about your girlfriend?" So I said, "No, there is no girlfriend." And so on. Eventually he got it—although even when he understood, it took him a while to, like, believe I was telling the truth.

Moving to Eilat is going to be complicated, because we're going to be meeting a lot of new people, and we're going to have to find ways to tell all of them about us. Usually, I hold off a bit before I tell someone. If I, like, meet someone new at work, say, and he tells me about his girlfriend, and has all sorts of stories, I want to tell my stories too—to tell about our trip to Paris, about the things I've bought for Adam, and so on. If I don't say anything at all about myself, then the person I've met is going to stop telling me about himself, and we'll never get to know one another. But I can't say "my boyfriend." So I say "my girlfriend." And then, after a few days, I tell people. And I explain why I said what I said at first. And they understand.

ITZIQ

At some point in the autumn, Amir decided to make Dror—the tall, heavy-set, blond kibbutznik in his Roman history class—the subject of an experimental exercise entitled "Revealing One's Sexual Orientation to a Newly Made, As-of-Yet-Casual, Attractive Male Acquaintance." The experiment had reasonably encouraging results—Amir was met with a Proclamation of Heterosexuality, but many long conversations about sexual identity ensued. Amir told Dror about our interview project, and Dror mentioned that we would certainly want to speak to Itziq. "What, you've never heard of Itziq?"

Itziq was a reception clerk at the Laromme Hotel in Jerusalem, where Dror was working as a part-time security guard; Itziq had apparently been regaling Dror with stories of his celebrity among sexually sophisticated Jerusalemites. While Dror had apparently shared the fact of his heterosexuality with Itziq as well, this had not prevented Itziq from making repeated propositions that left little to the imagination. Dror insisted that Itziq had to be met. Why not?

Itziq greeted our request for an interview with a simultaneously breathless and blasé rehearsal of the student movies, essays, and experimental dramatic productions that had already featured his life story—but he supposed that one more couldn't hurt. We arranged an evening visit to his apartment for the following week.

Itziq is unremarkable in appearance—he has dark hair, he is not tall, and his swollen cheeks attest to his being a bit heavy. He lives in one of Jerusalem's many neighborhoods with a drop too much history—the two- and three-story buildings here were once the elegant family dwellings of Jerusalem's Arab middle and upper class. When the 1948 battle lines were drawn, these Arab build-

ings found themselves on the Jewish side, and their residents fled for their lives. There are no Arabs living in this neighborhood anymore. Today, the houses are divided into exquisite apartments, of an architectural richness sorely missed in the typically utilitarian cubes built for the new Hebrew nation of workers. The furnishings of Itziq's apartment hint at a haremlike atmosphere, but the walls are covered with striking oil paintings in a variety of semi-abstract styles— upon examination, wild brush-strokes in dark colors yield up tortured faces and disfigured human forms.

∽

I WAS BORN IN JERUSALEM, and I've lived here all my life.

I come from a religious family, a very warm family. My father is Romanian, and my mother Yemenite. So I can speak Yemenite Arabic and Romanian—and if you speak Romanian then you also know Spanish and Italian, and a little French. And then I've taught myself a drop of German. I wanted to learn German because I wanted to be closely acquainted with Schiller— and to study Schiller is like studying Shakespeare or Bialik, if you don't know the original language at all, there's no point.[§] It was difficult. But there are a lot of very difficult things that I've gotten through.

My father plays the saxophone, he's a musician. Actually, he's a laboratory assistant. But music is the real interest in his life. My mother used to dance. She's this tiny little Yemenite woman who dances in this totally hysterical manner. I have a cute brother, one year younger than me, and two sisters. My family was very close, very warm. That made it very difficult for me to move out—I'm thirty-three now, and I moved out five years ago.

My father immigrated in the middle of the war, World War II. My mother was born here, in Jerusalem. Her father was a rabbi, the head rabbi of a Yemenite religious court in Jerusalem. They've written two books about him, because he had connections with all sorts of early Zionist activists, mostly the Revisionists—Jabotinsky and his crowd. That's my only connection to fascism—that's really what it is, fascism.[†]

My mother's mother was actually born in Aden. Because that country

[§] Ḥayim Naḥman Bialik (1873–1934): "Father of modern Hebrew literature"; poet laureate of the Zionist movement.

[†] Ze'ev Jabotinsky (1880–1940): Zionist ideologue, journalist, and political leader; essayist; poet; novelist; translator; journalist; founder, in 1925, of World Union of Zionists-Revisionists, a breakaway movement advocating the use of force in response to both British and Arab opposition to national aspirations.

had been ruled by the British for a very long time, she spoke both English and Yemenite Arabic. What I know of English I learned from her, because she would talk to me when I was little, and she talked to me in English, not Hebrew. It's a very strange story, because my grandmother was my grandfather's seventh wife. The other wives died of all sorts of diseases, and he got divorced from two of them, or something like that. When he married my grandmother, she was sixteen, and he was sixty. It's an amazing story, his story. So there are I-don't-know-how-many cousins that I have, spread out all over the world. Because these wives of his just never stopped having children. Every time I go to New York I find out about all sorts of cousins that I never even knew existed. Most of my family is in the U.S.

I went to one of the government-run religious schools. I mean, it wasn't like my family was ultra-Orthodox or something. But tradition was very strong. And because of the very strong influence of my mother's parents, we were very religious. Today, my sisters and my brother aren't religious, none of them. I'm the only one who really has a strongly religious sense. I'm very connected to it, both because of my extreme sensitivity, and because I believe that there is something that is surrounding us, some power. This probably sounds a little strange to you.

I know it will sound funny to you, but I still put on my *tefilin* in the morning, and I don't use electricity on Shabbat. I do work on Shabbat though. The reason I don't wear a *kipah* all the time is in order not to desecrate the sanctity of God's name—so that people won't say, "Look at that fag in the *kipah*. All the religious men are 'like that,' you know." That's forbidden. Desecration of the Name is a terrible, terrible thing. So when I say grace before meals, or when I make the blessing over wine, I always put it on. But not outside. It must sound terribly strange, to fuck in handcuffs all night and then get up in the morning and put on *tefilin*. But I'm different—it's just part of the difference, you understand? Because it's a matter of faith. I know it sounds totally primitive, and that's really what it is, but, you know, ceremony is an integral part of faith, and you need some connection to it, and that's the way it is with me.

We lived pretty well. I grew up in a good home. You could really say that I got everything I wanted, as a child. Not that I had a lot of demands. Even today, I don't have a lot of demands.

At thirteen, my mother came to me and said, "Listen, Itziq, if you're feeling the need, masturbate." A few days later she sat me down and said, "How do you like it?" That was exactly how it happened. I think I was twenty-something when she patted me on the head one day and said to me, "You like men, right?" Since then we haven't talked about it. That's it. My father is OK. We don't talk about it. We aren't very close, like I am with my mother. My sisters and brother are also OK, they all love me.

At home, we were always open, but absolutely not to an extreme. There are certain blocks. You have to understand that you're in a traditional household, or at least in a home which believes in the Holy One, Blessed Be He. You have limits, and there's nothing you can do about them. Even now I have all sorts of hang-ups. For instance, I really want to get a tattoo, but I have a problem with this. According to religious law it is totally prohibited—absolutely not allowed. Of course, it's also forbidden to fuck someone in the ass, but not exactly. What I mean is, there are all sorts of interpretations in religion. You probably don't know all this very well. I mean, you can't make the forbidden into something acceptable, but—oh, it's terrible to talk about this subject, because it's something I deal with all the time. Faith is something very important, something above and beyond—it isn't something you can touch. It gives something to your soul. It gives something to my soul. And I'm not the healthiest man in the world—I need all the help I can get.

There were never comments about gays at home. It was apparently a very big issue with them, that they didn't want to hurt me. And I know they did it for that reason, because the Holy One, Blessed Be He, he didn't create me especially stupid. I figure they knew from when I was seventeen or eighteen, something like that. Maybe more, even nineteen.

As I child, I was entertaining, funny, chatty, intelligent, you could say. I always wanted to know things. I read a lot. I made puppets for myself because I really liked the theater. I only played with the girls. I wanted to feel like one of them, to play with them, to make dolls with them. And I really liked to dress up, to put on wigs, when I was very young. And that's what proves it, really, because every gay's story is very similar—it proves that a gay is basically born gay. Because eighty percent of the stories are the same. It's amazing.

My first sexual experience was when I was twelve. I was in the library in Jerusalem, and some ultra-Orthodox guy touched me, and I ran away. But I remember that I enjoyed the feel of his hand very much. When I began masturbating, I would always fantasize about men I had seen. I knew that other people didn't think the way I did, but I never felt guilty about it.

It was a television program that opened my eyes. The media has always been very obviously supportive, not because of any leftist leanings, but because of a certain social openness it has promoted. There was a kind of talk show, where every time they chose a different topic. And on this show, they decided to take the topic of homosexuals. They mentioned Independence Park in Jerusalem, that it was a place that gays went, to meet each other. And I remember, another thing they did was, they asked people in the street, "What is homosexuality?" Or, "What is a homosexual?" And no one could answer. No one knew. It was amazing. That was 1974.

That was the first time that I understood that I was not the only one in the world. Before that, I thought that I was alone.

So right after I saw that program, I went straight to Independence Park. I was thirteen and a half. It was the first night of Ḥanukah. You know, every year, on the first night of Ḥanukah, you say the *sheheḥeyanu*.[§] So that year, the blessing had two meanings for me. Now, every year, when I light the candle for the first night of Ḥanukah and I make that blessing, I give a little smile.

So I just went into that park, and I met someone there. He followed me— I went in and he followed me. We went into the bushes, and what happened happened, and that's it. That was my first time. "I saw that it was good." I knew. I did it for the first time and knew, it was totally clear that this was it. I needed sex. But not anything more than that, absolutely not.

I developed differently from the people around me. I saw things very differently. I began to paint at a very young age, and my work raised a lot of eyebrows. After I visited Yad Vashem for the first time, I went home and painted what I had seen.[†] I was twelve. And I remember that my teacher confiscated the painting, and gave it to the school authorities. They decided that I had a problem, and sent me to a psychologist. And the psychologist just said, basically, "Listen folks, this kid is just different. He's bright. Just leave him alone." They sent the picture to the museum in the end, and it was on exhibit there for almost seven years.

My father is a survivor, and I guess he would tell us about it sometimes. He did talk about it, but not enough. He got away from it all at a very young age. They were already beginning to take everyone away, so he came here. He has a few things, little hang-ups, left over, like never throwing out food, things like that. They lived on potato skins.

[§] *sheheḥeyanu*: Benediction traditionally recited upon undergoing a new experience, or upon undergoing an experience that one has been pleasurably anticipating: "Blessed are You, Lord our God, King of the Universe, who has kept us alive, and sustained us, and enabled us to reach this moment."

[†] Yad Vashem: National institution for the commemoration of the Holocaust, founded in Jerusalem in 1953, housing a historical museum, shrines of remembrance, and research facilities.

I remember that once, I put on some music by Wagner at home, and he screamed. I explained to him that I didn't understand what it meant to him. He told me to go learn about it. Today I know Wagner well. I know that even though he was born a hundred years before Nazism, there are great powers in music and literature that can have an influence. Wagner was a terrible, awful person, a terrible Jew-hater, who betrayed all of his best friends, and ran off with his best friend's wife. And a man like this, a grand intellect like this, can't create placid music. That means that in his operas, a singer can do one aria, and you'll need to get the whole fire department to douse her with water, to put out the inferno—such power, such strength. And the Nazis tapped into that. They used Wagner's power and strength.

When I went to Yad Vashem, I suddenly understood. I said to myself, maybe you need to be a survivor—maybe you need to go through all sorts of awful experiences in order to feel OK about yourself. So I put it all together, and decided that I needed to go through some sort of trauma, to make myself different, to be separated. And only then could I feel good. So I went to the park. To get out all of the—I won't call them aggressions, because that's not the right word, but to release all the sort of enervating pressures that I was feeling. I didn't know what an "enervating pressure" was, back then, but that's what it was—an enervating pressure.

And that's why, when I came out of the closet, I came out in a big way. Now, to come out of the closet in the mid-seventies, when you're fourteen years old, you have to be daring. And that's what I was. Outside of the domestic framework, I was a total slut. But at home, I basically respected my parents. Respect for your father and mother is a supreme value for me. To this day. Again, these are things which sound primitive to you, and I know that. But I don't preach.

I did have relationships, a lot of them. I began to have my first loves when I was fourteen. I was a kiddie. I let people take pictures of me in the nude. I liked it. I wasn't exactly innocent. I needed something strong—I had to feel that I was doing something bad. But, inside, I knew that it was good. Because I had support, I felt spiritual support that came from somewhere up above.

At fifteen I was already considered some sort of idol, some sort of God— I drew a lot of people around me. I was different, I was unique—I was one of the first men in Jerusalem to put an earring in his ear. I got beat up because of it. You know, today, the reason I don't wear an earring anymore is that so many straights wear earrings, I'm afraid someone will think I'm straight!

Of course, they called me all sorts of names at school. Look, I wasn't exactly the most masculine kid in the world—you could say I stood out a little. I looked a little different—I had very long hair, and I would fasten it with braids. I wore earrings, I wore some makeup. I had a sort of a wild look. But I couldn't have cared less. Do you understand?

I wouldn't wish it on you, to be openly gay in Israel in 1975. I wouldn't wish it on anyone. It means getting beaten up because you're different. I was endlessly bashed when I was young. By all sorts of people who didn't like the way I looked. A lot of incidents of punches and things like that. I remember a lot of incidents. But it upsets me, you understand? I don't want to talk about it. Because I forgave everyone. I forgive everyone.

When it came time for the army, I really wanted to go. When they discovered my color blindness, there was a problem with that, but it wasn't a serious problem. And then I remember, they called me for some kind of preliminary examination, I was about seventeen years old. And I got to the army, and the doctor who came to examine me said, "Take your clothes off." So I said to him, "You first, sweetie." It was just a joke—that was my sense of humor. I'm very funny, and I really enjoy that. But he was kind of shocked.

It so happened that this examination took place right after I had come back from a trip to London, and I was wearing a new pair of underwear I had just bought. They were lovely—red lace. And he took one look and apparently thought that I needed a psychologist. This guy showed me all sorts of little pictures, and told me to talk about them. Now, by the time I got to the third picture, I had had it—I was fed up. And I suddenly recalled a Woody Allen movie, where he made up all sorts of things when he was looking at the pictures. So I began to just make up all sorts of nonsense. And then the terrible problem was that I remembered it all—he reversed the order, and asked that I repeat everything I had said, and that was my problem, because I remembered everything. Everything I had said. And at that point, he decided that I needed a psychiatrist, that I wasn't army material. Just because my memory is good, because I knew how to bullshit! What a nightmare. So then I was sent to a psychiatrist, and from the moment he saw me he just understood that he was dealing with a different kind of person, but not someone who was nuts. Since then we're good friends. To this day.

In the end, they decided to postpone my service for another six months. They told me to come back in six months, but by the time my new draft date came around, I really wasn't that crazy about serving anymore. They let me put it off for another year, and then when that year was up, they said to me, "Listen, you're not fit for service." So I said, "Suit youselves—you've missed out on a fine potential officer."

Immediately afterwards, I was wounded by a terrorist bomb. It was on Ben Yehudah Street in Jerusalem—there was a boobytrapped bicycle. This was in 1979. I was nineteen. I was badly wounded, with burns on my body, and I almost had my leg amputated. The whole thing was very painful, and I got very discouraged, and began to take drugs, to drink. I slowly went downhill, over the course of the next year or so. My parents didn't know. And then I basically became a total junkie, until they finally had to put me in the Ṭalbiyah Mental Hospital, for drug rehabilitation.

Most of this time I was working here and there, living at home. I was acting in a theater, the Jerusalem youth theater. I was dancing, and I did some things on the radio—I have a very good voice for the radio. But after I was wounded, it was awful—I was very down about that fact that I couldn't dance anymore, because of my leg. And eventually I went into the hospital. I was there for five months.

After three months in the hospital I was already totally clean, and when I got out, I took the college entrance exams. I was accepted to four universities. But then they opened the Laromme Hotel. It was 1982. Instead of going to college I began working in the hotel as a bellboy, and then they said to me, "Listen, maybe you want to get ahead a little, you would be better at the reception desk." And I've stayed there to this day. Almost twelve years.

I've taken all sorts of little courses, I've read a lot, I even wrote a paper that they used in the university. I translate a little, and I've studied literature by myself. I love Oscar Wilde. But it would be difficult for me to be a full-time student. I earn a lot of money at the Laromme, and that gives me a pretty high standard of living. I live well, I'm happy, I like what I'm doing. I'm frighteningly optimistic, after all I've been through, aren't I?

I'm always trying to reach new heights. Collecting high points. So, naturally, I need new heights in sex. That's why, in the last few years, I've become a little involved in sadomasochism. A little. I think it's a terrible thing.

I haven't established any stable relationships with men, and I never will. I can't stand relationships with men. It gets very boring after two days. So I have lovers. I have four lovers—of course they're all straight, and they have girlfriends. Because otherwise I can't come. The moment I know that he sleeps with other men, I have a problem about that. That's part of my nuttiness. And that's it. That's why I go to bars that are only a touch gay, like

Shunra, where there's a mix—people are mixed within themselves, not that there is a mix of gays and straights. I guess you could say that I'm into "horny straights." Of course, I'm not at all into women. When they ask me if I'm bisexual I say, yes, I like men and boys.

Now don't get me wrong, I don't do "service and wash," or anything like that, really. But when I meet a straight guy, I just toss it all out in the open, and if he wants it, he gets closer. And if he leans that way, then we do get into bed. And it happens to me all the time. It's all a matter of approach. There's a large segment of the male population who aren't personally acquainted with homosexuality, with homosexual possibilities. But they're very open-minded, and willing to consider it. There's a tremendous openness, especially among young people.

I think that it's when you try to hide your homosexuality that you become a problem. I mean, you shouldn't kid yourself that you're fooling anyone. Don't think they aren't gossiping anyway. So what I do is to provide the gossip about myself. If I meet a new person, I immediately reveal everything. That way, he has nothing to suspect, and I have nothing to suspect. He'll accept me exactly as I project myself. Taking openness to an extreme always helps. It always relaxes the people around you.

It isn't accurate to say that this is a roundabout way of bedding straights. But it's close. And I don't see anything wrong with this, because I succeed in 80 percent of the cases. That is absolutely so: 80 percent. There are all sorts of psychological interpretations about the gay potential that is latent in everyone. That seems logical. All I know is that, when I get to having longer conversations with straights that I've met, they will often suddenly say, "Actually, it has crossed my mind." You understand? And when you come across a person who exposes everything about himself, totally, and is accepted by those around him, and he sees you, and draws closer to you, well. . . .

For a while, I was kind of involved in some gay political work, because they asked for my help. But afterwards I kind of lost interest. I didn't find it stimulating. I think a lot of bad things about gays. A lot of bad things—but you probably figured that out already. There are still some OK people in the gay community. But look at what happened with the editor of *Maga^cim*, I forgot his name—he was running a brothel in his house. My God! So don't give me all this shit about "communities" or "societies." I don't think I can change things, and it isn't my goal to change things, on a broad level.

But I've been fighting in my own way. And I do think that my method of action can influence things. All you have to do is to get things out in the open carefully and reasonably, and then they'll look at you differently. That's what happens to me. I've never gone out with flags, and I haven't gotten angry. I've just given of myself in my own way. I've informed people, I've given them a different look at the gay situation—always with a lot of humor. I've made people feel comfortable around me. Look, you know what telekinesis is, right? If we can use mental energy to move objects, then the easiest thing in the world is to use mental energy to move people.

I have a lot of friendships with women, of course. I have women friends from all sorts of backgrounds. I have a friend who's in college, but she's a prostitute, she lives close by. I have another friend who's a lawyer, but she only sleeps with Arabs. Another friend who's crazy about opera, and we talk about it all the time. But besides a tendency to gossip, gay men have nothing in common with women. My most important relationships are my relationships with my male friends, who, of course, I don't sleep with. I have one gay friend. But it's difficult to create a relationship with gays.

Of course, I think that stable gay relationships are possible. But there's always all sorts of cheating, unfaithfulness. You can't deny that. We are a nymphomaniac race, gays. Without a doubt. It's different from the straights. I mean, there are places for gays that are total meat markets—you go there especially to get flesh. You can just walk into Independence Park and get three men in a single night. Compare that to your straight friend, who, if he's lucky, may perhaps get the chance to drink coffee with a girl until one in the morning. Sex is much more available for us. If there were a park for straights, I can't even imagine how it would look, but it certainly wouldn't have the same sexual power as the clearly gay places. So for this and other reasons, I don't believe that gays are capable of being stable.

I won't get old. I'm not going to settle down. Look, I can't see what the future holds for me, but I sometimes get glimpses from my friends. And I know that it's very painful, lonely. But listen, at twenty I already decided that I'll never get married. To live with a man? That's not what I'm looking for—no way. I'm happy with the way things are. I mean, I'm alone but I'm not lonely. There are people all around me. Aging is one of the most difficult things about being gay, very difficult. It isn't easy, I know. But we'll deal with that too. How am I supposed to know how I'll deal with it? I can't know how.

I've always painted. You see those three pictures? Can you tell what they're of? They're pictures of soldiers beating Arabs—I made it into gay sex. Go take a look, the three pictures on the bottom, you see? This is a soldier hitting an Arab, that one is the same—but I gave it a gay touch. I did a large series, this is a part of it, a small part of a large series I did. Twelve pictures. They're in my parents' house.

Naturally, my political views are on the left. And it's because of my sexual situation. Because of the legitimately oppositional viewpoint I've developed as a result of society's treatment of me. I keep the pain of the '70s with me—that doesn't mean that I hold a grudge against anyone, but it makes me critical of society. And it's difficult to shake that off.

I respect everyone. I don't preach. When you look at everything, you understand that everyone believes in one God. It's just that the commentaries, the translations are different.

Look, if I sound satisfied and very optimistic, it is only because I keep my faith. When I'm feeling down, I naturally turn to the closest thing around, which is the Holy One, Blessed Be He, in my case. And you have no idea how much it helps. I mean, I don't know whether He helps me or not. But the mere fact of baring your soul to the other, the different, something you haven't met, something you aren't familiar with—this gives you a lot of power. And this power helps me a lot, a lot, to feel better inside when things aren't going well.

Of course Judaism is also a matter of commandments, of laws and regulations. But listen, there have always been arguments about these laws. You'll probably tell me, sure, you're only doing what is easiest for you, choosing which commandments to obey and which to ignore. But that isn't accurate, that's not fair. It's more than that. There's the matter of certain basic norms, like respect for your fellow human beings. The rabbis say that "social norms came before the Torah," you understand? And basic principles of Judaism are very clear to me, and they're more important than some of the commandments.

When it comes down to it, no, I don't believe that God is responsible for the prohibition on homosexual intercourse. No. He didn't write that. That was the commentators. Sure, it's written that "a man shall not lie with a man as with a woman"—but, really, what was given to the people of Israel on Mount Sinai was only the Ten Commandments. And the stories were built on this. There isn't any decisive proof that things were written in this or that order. For instance, it has been definitely proven that the Book of Job is not factual.

I try to help people around me as much as possible. It's important to me to help people who need my company. You could say that I've dedicated most of my life to this. I enjoy it. And so do they. Because I really like people, in general. I volunteer in a lot of places. Last Passover, together with a friend of mine, we organized a Passover seder for the homeless, it was really nice. It was difficult to find them, but I gathered them all together. And there's an old woman, she's alone, and I clean for her—but, oh, it's forbidden to say things like these. You know, it's forbidden to be proud of good deeds—charity should be done anonymously. I'm sorry, but I won't talk about good deeds I've done. It isn't important anyway.

I don't see *tefilin* as having anything to do with sado-masochism. I'll explain to you why. It would be the same thing, if I believed in the Indian holy books. Now, there are terrible things there—like lying on nails, walking on hot coals, terrible tortures. And in Islam, the self-flagellation there is really awful—the radical Muslims have a scene once a year where they just hit themselves until they bleed. And there are some terrible ceremonies in Christianity. And awful ceremonies in primitive tribes. But if you ask any of them if what they do has something to do with sadomasochism, they'll give you the same answer—it's part of faith, and it's part of ritual. And ritual is absolutely integral to your faith. It's inseparable.

At the hotel where I work, I'm a supervisor now. I work very hard, but I still have time to relax. Often, I'll do something like work from 3:30 in the afternoon to midnight, then go out to a bar, and if I'm lucky, even get laid or something like that. And then the next morning I have obligations of my own—to clean this old guy's house, to help this woman, and so on.

You define Zionism for me, and I'll tell you if I'm a Zionist, how about that? I don't want to sound too radical, but I think that these school trips, where they go to the German death camps and wave the Israeli flag around, they are really sick Zionist provocations. Ḥutzpah.§ And I think that, with this, I have described my entire problem with Zionism. I don't want to sound awful. I love my country very much, and I love my land very much. I would never give up Jerusalem—but I would give up other parts.

So far as the territories are concerned, I think that anyone could have predicted this mess a long time ago. I mean, you can't grow up in a hole, without water or electricity, under a terrible occupation, and not become radicalized. Those conditions lead to discouragement, which leads to verbal violence, and verbal violence leads directly to physical violence. And that's basically the core of the intifadah, at least as Professor Yeshaᶜyahu Leiboyich

§ ḥutzpah: nerve; gall; guts.

sees it.[§] I'm not totally comfortable with everything he says, but he did prophesy all of this ten years ago. He just foresaw it all, stage after stage.

Of course I wanted to serve in the army in spite of these views—one thing has nothing to do with the other. I think the army is a very important thing, and disobedience is a terrible, awful thing. But on the other side, it is clear to me that we need to do something about the oppression.

Homosexuality as a bridge-builder between Jews and Arabs? You've got to be kidding. What, where's the bridge? Jews and Arabs both run around in Independence Park—that's a bridge? Get out of here—total bullshit. Sex doesn't make anything happen—sex leads to nothing but pleasure and orgasm. It isn't a bridge to anything. You can save your hot air.

I travel a lot. I really like Amsterdam. It's the only city where there's everything. But I really like the Greek islands also, and the U.S., and all of Europe. If there are important things I go to see them—like a good opera or a big art exhibition or something like that. I go abroad twice a year. I'm wasting my wife and children's inheritance! There won't be anything left. But I need these trips. I need grandiose things all the time, I need new heights all the time. So if I go to the Metropolitan Opera in New York, it gives me the strength I need, that's enough for the next six months. But it's also just for fun. And of course, I also travel to see the gay life. I'm very careful to protect myself. I always use condoms.

I wouldn't live in New York. No way. First of all, I love Jerusalem. It's very important to me. I love the people here. I love the land. There is something in the atmosphere here, a certain kind of strength. To sit across from the Old City, in Liberty Bell Park, and to look at it, there isn't anything grander than that. I have a thousand-and-one reasons to stay here—I only go abroad to relax a little.

True, there are no gay bars in Jerusalem. But I don't know if I would want them. I really don't know. I don't go the bars in Tel Aviv. I have no patience for the Tel Aviv gays, that kind of flamboyance. Look, when I use the word "flamboyance," I know I myself am the worst offender, I know. But I have a problem with gay social life, it drives me up the wall. I don't have anything against them, but it's just not what I'm looking for. I'm not even curious. I don't think I would go to a gay bar if they had one in Jerusalem.

[§] Yeshaʿyahu Leibovich (1903–94): Anti-Zionist, Orthodox professor of chemistry and physiology at the Hebrew University in Jerusalem; best known for his vocal advocacy of the return of territories acquired in the 1967 Six-Day War, and for his opposition to the policies of the Likud under prime ministers Menahem Begin and Yitzhaq Shamir.

You do have Shunra—please, forget their official gay night, every night is gay there. Every night, you have straights there with a "touch." So I go there very often. I drink and dance, and sometimes I strip. I like to. I like the strength. You need to let loose sometimes. How do they react? Everyone else takes off their clothes too. It's always two or three in the morning, and the squares have gone home. It usually happens twice a week, or something like that. Everyone there is a little sick. And I get along with them the best. You can go in and do what you want and no one will say a word, so long as it doesn't hurt anyone else, of course.

Their "gay nights" are such a joke. Just to look at all those funny Jerusalemite gays, those squares—kind of like you guys, you know? But that's OK, I'm not laughing at you, I'm not criticizing, God forbid. But it's a real trip—a real laugh. It looks like, I don't know, a knitting circle or something like that. It's embarrassing. But I guess there's a certain grace to it. Because the gays in Jerusalem are certainly different from the ones in the great big world of Tel Aviv.

Of course I'd like to have a child—I'd like him muscley, and about nineteen years old. Send him over to me tomorrow night. But I definitely do not want to raise a child—I know that self-perpetuation would be a dangerous thing for me. I know that, and I don't want to hurt anyone, not my child and not the woman involved. Besides, I have no intention of sleeping with a woman. I know there are all sorts of other methods. But I'm not looking to propagate. Besides, children mean obligations, and I don't want that either. I don't think I could be a healthy father. No way. Not because I'm gay, but because I'm a nutty gay. I have unstable behavior.

Of course, my parents want me to get married. Everyone is putting pressure on me. I have one nephew, four months old. He's amazing, he looks exactly like I looked when I was his age. It's strange. My sister loves me a lot, and she told me that it wouldn't bother her at all if gays raised her son. Her husband nearly fainted, but he didn't say anything, because he likes me.

There's infatuation, and love is what comes afterwards. I've had lots of little infatuations. And I've also had my great loves. But they really destroyed me. They were all straight. They did sleep with me, of course. And then I couldn't give them up, and I was afraid. But the powers above helped me, and these men are still among my best friends. Everyone is my best friend. But now love is out of bounds for me. I have a hard time with it. I really try not to fall in love, even though you can't control those feelings. But I really try not to.

Now that you've met me, I know that you're thinking that I seem different from every other gay you've met in your life. I think that my approach to life may influence you, but of course I don't know how—that will depend on you, not me.

Tonight I've got a million people to meet, a million social obligations. I'll probably get to Shunra at some point. I've already drunk two bottles of wine and half a bottle of vodka. Before you came. Now I'll have another half-bottle of vodka. Then I'll take a little time to get my balance. I won't get drunk. And that's it. Some people would call it a terrible problem, but with all the complicated interconnections between things, I need something calming. And this settles me.

THEO MAINZ

Shortly after I first arrived in Israel, I paid a visit to the Tel Aviv office of the "Agudah," the Society for the Protection of Personal Rights for Gay Men, Lesbians, and Bisexuals in Israel. There I met Theo Mainz for the first time. The diplomatically elegant European-accented English with which he addressed me made a memorable impression, but so did his silver hair—he seemed a good thirty years older than anyone else for miles around. Who was this gentleman?

The preparation of this book seemed an excellent opportunity to find out who Theo really was. It was important that we speak to people of a wide range of ages, and it also seemed essential that we speak to someone who could give us an inside perspective on the Agudah, which was Israel's only gay, lesbian, and bisexual political and social organization for years.

Theo was not enthusiastic about the idea. When I called him, he said that he would be willing to cooperate, but he warned me that his life story was dull. "You would be far better advised to find someone more interesting, I should say." This was a novel objection, and one for which I was not prepared. I asked that he allow us to take our chances, and we agreed that, on the following Friday night, he would stop by my apartment in central Tel Aviv.

After an additional phone call, in which Theo gave us another opportunity to reconsider, the appointed night arrived, sweltering in Tel Aviv's inimitable manner. I had bought some cookies to serve to my guest, but Theo outdid me, arriving with a home-baked cake in hand. Since my apartment lacked anything so extravagant as a living room, I had no choice but to invite Theo into my bedroom. He settled into one of my two chairs, I sat in the other, and Amir perched himself on the bed. I made sure that every window was open to the absolute maximum, poured myself another glass of water, and the interview began.

In spite of Theo's fluent English, we spoke in Hebrew. It just seemed the natural thing to do, especially since Amir was the one doing most of the questioning. German Jews are known in Israel as yeqehs—*the term is related to the German word for a formal jacket, and conveys a sense of stereotypically Teutonic fastidiousness, a quality somewhat unusual on the Israeli scene. Theo was a classic* yeqeh, *and his Hebrew was* yeqeh *as well: slow, precise, slightly old-fashioned, and completely devoid of the slang that formed such a large part of our other interviewees' stock of expressions.*

$$\backsim$$

MY NAME IS THEO MAINZ. I was born in 1924 in the city of Frankfurt, in Germany. The Jewish community there was large and very well established. My father was from a very old and well-known family—on his side, I can trace my roots in Frankfurt three hundred years back. Everything is on record there. My ancestors were all respectable merchants who traded in wool in that same city.

My parents were what you might call upper middle class. That didn't mean the same things back then as it does today—we didn't have our own house, we didn't have a car, that was very rare then. But we had three servants in the house—a cook, and someone who cleaned, and a governess for the children. Except for my sister, who is younger, my parents didn't send us to nursery school. You didn't really do that then. They were very frightened of children's diseases, and there were no antibiotics yet. I went to a private Jewish school for the first four years of my education. And my problems began there, really.

You see, all my life I've been different. At this school, I was different because my parents weren't as religious as other people's parents. There were two large congregations in Frankfurt, one more religious and one less religious—but this isn't the place to go into details. My ancestors were involved in both congregations, but somehow I got put into the more religious school, and that was not the place for me. My family was more modern—we would light lights on Shabbat, and the boys didn't have to wear a hat all the time. Of course, in all other respects, we were an Orthodox family. I always went to Jewish schools—I was never in school together with non-Jews. And the governess was always Jewish. But my parents, for some reason, maybe because of Hitler, put me into a school that was too religious. I remember that I was afraid that the other kids would beat me up if I walked in the street without a hat. I was afraid of the Jewish kids.

I have to say in my parents' favor that they didn't just leave us to the servants, which happened in some other families. My mother always took care of us and she always helped us with our lessons. She didn't leave that to tutors or something like that. My father was a little distant, though. He was a banker and he would come home late at night. He was only at home on Friday, Shabbat, and Sunday, so we didn't see much of him. The rest of the week, he would come home at nine in the evening, and even then, he had to deal with the news from the stock market in America.

So that's how I grew up. I can't say that life was difficult. Life was good.

When I was eleven, in 1936, my father could no longer go to the stock market—they forced him to sell his business to a German non-Jew. And we emigrated to Holland. We had lived in Germany under the Nazis for a total of three years, but I was very insulated from it all. I was very young. I had no contact with non-Jews at all. I didn't know a single non-Jewish boy. I remember one time, I went to a city swimming pool with my mother, and there were other boys there, and they undressed, and I saw that their "things" looked different. I had no idea that this was possible! I knew there were non-Jews in the world, but I really didn't understand—the difference between Jews and Christians wasn't very clear to me.

Of course, I was always aware of antisemitism. We shouldn't do this, and we don't do that. Why? Because that causes antisemitism. Don't stand out! It was always like that. And I also remember that my mother had a particular movement she would make with her hand when she was worried—she would lay her hand against her cheek, like that. One time I heard my mother talking, and she used the German expression, "*es wird Mord und Totschlag geben*"—"there will be bloodshed and murder," she said, in this conversation, and she put her hand on her cheek. When I heard that, I went to my brother, who is three years older than I, and I said to him, "Who is going to kill whom?" He said to me, "The S.S. is going to kill the S.A.," and that quieted me down for a while. But eventually I heard more talk about the S.S., and the S.A., and I went to my brother to ask him what they were—I had no idea.[§]

[§] S.S. and S.A.: Abbreviations for *Schutzstaffel* [Protection Squad] and *Sturmabteilung* [Storm Troopers]; elite Nazi military orders. The S.S., originally a corps of bodyguards, ultimately assumed responsibility for the administration of the mass murder of European Jewry. The S.A. was the division of the Nazi party responsible for undermining democracy and eliminating opposition.

For me, they were the people who walked around dressed like mailmen—it was a kind of school uniform that they wore, only they also had a swastika. And how was I supposed to know what a swastika meant?

As time went on, I heard more. Suddenly there were the Nuremberg Laws, and Christian servants couldn't work in Jewish houses any more.[§] But our servant, who had been with my family for many, many years, was over forty-five, so she was allowed to keep on working with us, it was permitted. But everybody found their own ways of getting by—if you couldn't have Christian servants then you got Jewish servants, you could make all kinds of accommodations. And then all of a sudden you couldn't perform kosher slaughtering in Germany, you had to get meat from abroad. But it wasn't something shocking. At least, I didn't feel it.

What was interesting was that in the Jewish schools, all of sudden there appeared children who weren't at all religious, who didn't know anything about Judaism. They couldn't study in the other schools anymore, so they all had to transfer to the Jewish schools. Or, for instance, there was a family that I knew from a village where we had been on vacation a few times, and suddenly that family appeared in the city. The Jews couldn't stay in the villages anymore, so they all found their way to the larger cities. Yet, as a boy, I didn't really feel the threat very seriously. I felt it when the time came to leave.

My father's business was kind of a personal bank, and his clients also all emigrated at a certain point, so we eventually left also, and went to Holland. I entered school there, and my life was a lot like that of Anne Frank before she went into hiding. We lived in an area where there were a lot of German Jews, and my father had an office near a sort of canal. If we hadn't left Holland in time, my fate would have been exactly the same as Anne Frank's—maybe we would have tried to go into hiding in the office building where my father worked, like the Frank family.

So I began school in Holland, and of course, once again, I was different—I had a German accent. I took a short course for children of immigrants, and I learned Dutch very quickly, in a few months. Children learn very quickly. But I was definitely in culture shock. It was quite difficult.

I had other problems as well. They wanted to leave me back a year in the Jewish school, so instead, my parents sent me to a very elegant private school, which didn't really suit me. They were real snobs. I wasn't used to

---

[§] Nuremberg Laws: Approved by German Reichstag on September 15, 1935; deprived all Jews of German citizenship; prohibited sexual relations between Jews and Germans; forbade Jews to employ Gentile domestic servants; forbade Jews to fly the German flag.

that. Terrible snobs, with their ties, and school trips, and a special yearbook, and all sorts of things like that. All the children there were from very wealthy homes, everyone was sent to school in private cars. In my German school, boys would dress in short pants. But there, at twelve, I had to go to school in long pants and even a tie. I had no idea how to tie a tie! Or, in Germany, for instance, we could just say "yes" or "no" in answer to a teacher's question. But in Holland, the convention was to say "yes, sir" or "madam" or "no, sir" or "madam." And I wouldn't say that, and they would say that I was a rude child, instead of explaining it to me. But I got over it. I did learn a lot there— at twelve, I spoke German and Dutch and was studying Greek, Latin, French, and English. I learned them all.

There were a lot of Jews in Holland, but they were very integrated into Dutch society. Things weren't nearly as segregated as they were in Germany, even among the religious. And because I didn't know how to recognize Dutch Jewish family names, it took me a long time to figure out that half of my class was Jewish. How did I find out? They built a new sports hall, and there were showers there, and all the boys had to shower together. And, of course, Theo looked at what interested him and, ah ha, they were circumcised. Later on, I learned to recognize the names. Or I found out by chance. When I had my bar mitzvah, someone said to me, "I did that too, a week ago."§ It never would have occurred to me that he was Jewish. On Shabbat I didn't go to classes. But I never knew how many other students didn't come to classes. I didn't talk about it with the other students—they knew I was Jewish, it wasn't something to hide, but it wasn't a subject for discussion there. In Holland it was so unremarkable that they didn't talk about it a lot—maybe it was similar to America, in that way. Later on, though, there was also some antisemitism, sometimes you felt something.

Now, I remember that when the war began, and pogroms began to take place in Germany, we were suddenly under a lot of pressure to get people out. My family was constantly talking about certificates to go to America— "affidavits," they called them. I heard it all the time, they talked about it non-stop. Some people lived with us in Holland while they were in transit, either to America or here. We had a big house, there were seven rooms, so we were never cramped. My parents were very worried, and they wanted to get grandmother and my two unmarried uncles out of Germany. But the three

§ Bar mitzvah: Technically, "of age." Commonly used to refer to the synagogue ceremony and celebration marking a boy's thirteenth birthday and his initiation into the religious responsibilities of Jewish manhood.

of them couldn't decide what they wanted to do, and they didn't get out in time, and they died there.

Now, when the war first began, Holland was neutral. I still remember the day when war first broke out, in Poland, in 1939. But Holland was neutral until May 10, 1940. I didn't understand it at the time, but my father was a smart man. He had money, and he already saw that this was not the place for us, we had to leave. And I know that he looked into America, and New Zealand, and so on. In the end, he got a call from Palestine. Back then it was very rare to get an overseas phone call, but a good friend of his, an accountant, had settled here, and he telephoned to say that he could get a visa for us. They called it a "certificate." There was still the British Mandate then, and they had a quota. There were a specific number of certificates available for "workers," for "pioneers," and for "capitalists." Capitalists had to invest a thousand pounds sterling in stocks in order to be allowed a certificate. With the outbreak of war, German Jews were considered "enemy aliens" by the British, and were barred from immigrating to the Mandate altogether. But German Jews who were living in neutral countries were allowed to come.

So my father got the call, decided quickly, and we left Holland only a month and a half before the Germans invaded. My father paid the thousand pounds sterling, it wasn't very difficult for him. We arrived here, I remember, on March 23, 1940. I was exactly fifteen. We lived in a boarding house in Haifa for a few weeks, and afterwards we settled in Ramat Gan, a suburb of Tel Aviv.

You know, I find a lot of parallels between the Jewish fate and the fate of gays. Were you born in Israel? I think that people who were born here can't understand at all. Being different. Having to cope with being different. Nowadays, Jews are used to—how do you say it?—"flaunting" their Jewishness. But it wasn't done then, not in Germany and not in Holland. You wouldn't walk with a *kipah* in the street. Absolutely not. And not in school. I already felt, even in Holland, that I wasn't religious, but I did it all, because it was what one did. I put *tefilin* on every morning, went to *selihot* at five in the morning, whatever it was you were supposed to do.[§] It made me feel very virtuous. I felt virtuous if I got up so early to go to synagogue, even though it was deathly boring, and I didn't understand a single word. But even if I had understood it, it would have been boring, all of that medieval religious poetry.

I remember when I first came here, and we were in that boarding house, in Haifa. And I put my *tefilin* on while standing outside on the balcony. There

---

[§] *selihot*: Literally, "penitential prayers"; used with reference to hymns recited during daily morning prayer services for the month preceding Rosh Hashanah.

was nothing wrong with that. Here, everybody knows what *tefilin* are—they can see them, you don't have to hide them. And from that day onwards, I never touched my *tefilin* again. I had no need for something special to make myself into a Jew. When I was abroad, you see, I needed it for my identity—I wasn't Dutch and I wasn't German. As soon as I opened my mouth you could tell that I was from Germany, but I wasn't German. I was a Jew.

When I was a boy, I read books about the Indians, about the Wild West. By Karl May, maybe you know the name. Of course, I especially liked the parts where they described how everybody stripped and went into the water, or something like that—I always thought about how much I'd like to be there. But I couldn't totally identify with the protagonists. There was always a barrier keeping me from being one of them. Because what would I do on Shabbat? I can't ride a horse on Shabbat. And they ate buffalo meat. But that's not kosher, I can't eat that. I would actually think about these things. These were problems.

On the way here with my family, we stopped in Paris, we had relatives there, so we went to Paris for Shabbat. And for the first time, we traveled, we rode a train on Shabbat. It was because it was a sealed train, and once we got on, we couldn't get off, not before Paris. Something having to do with enemy aliens. Once we got to Paris, we talked about how much we wished we could go to the opera while we were passing through. And I said, "I'll buy the tickets." It was still Shabbat—you're not even allowed to touch money on Shabbat. "We'll see what happens," I said. And nothing happened. And since then, I'm no longer observant. My parents pretty much gave it up also.

Once we got settled, I was put into school in Ramat Gan. I sat in class for the first month and didn't understand a single word that was spoken. Afterwards I began to learn, and eventually I became just another student. I always understood just about half of the lesson on Hebrew language and literature. To this day I know English better than Hebrew, because I didn't learn Tanah here as a child, and Mishnah, and all that.[§] But I finished high school with a degree that made me eligible to attend university, somehow. How I passed the Hebrew language part of the exam I have no idea. But I had one big advantage, that I knew grammar very well. In Holland, I learned Hebrew grammar with a special teacher, who was wonderful. So I knew grammar before I knew the language. And because of that I can still spell every Hebrew word there is correctly, and I know how to punctuate with the proper vowels. In any case, I graduated high school, and that was quite an achievement.

[§] Mishnah: First- and second-century codification of Jewish civil, ritual, and moral law.

I certainly wasn't one of the gang here. I was alienated. I was never a part of the mainstream. In Germany I wasn't religious enough, in Holland I was German, and here—well, I came here from Holland in a suit. You can just imagine! They told me that it was undemocratic, that it wasn't socialist. I was a strange boy, in their eyes. So they were frightened of me. Once, a girl asked me if I wanted to join a youth movement and go on hikes, learn to use a compass, and so on. I was supposed to understand that she was inviting me to join the Haganah, which was a secret organization at the time.[§] Of course, I didn't understand. I said no, thank you, it didn't interest me. So they left me alone, they didn't ask me any more. I think they were frightened of me, that I would tell someone. Later on I knew exactly what was going on, but they didn't ask me again. I would volunteer in the Red Magen David medical corps, that was also part of the Haganah then. But I was always an outsider.

My father found work here in Tel Aviv in a bank, as a midlevel administrator, and we lived in Ramat Gan. There was a very big drop in our standard of living. But it wasn't so awful, because everyone lived that way here. You have to understand what the atmosphere was like. Sure, some Jews came straight from Germany in 1933, with money. But in 1936, the disturbances began here, there was the Arab uprising, and the economic conditions for everyone here became very, very poor. People just couldn't make ends meet. A lot of people had to make their living cleaning houses. For the German Jews it was a problem, but the German Jews adjusted to the circumstances. Even professors were willing to work as gardeners, and everyone got by. I'm sure you've heard stories about this time. But because no one had anything, everyone was in the same situation, it wasn't so awful.

Without a doubt it was difficult for my parents. My mother suffered terribly. It was so very hot, there were barely even any fans, and she had to do all the housework alone for the first time. There wasn't any gas for the stove, we had one five-gallon gas cylinder, there was no washing machine, and she didn't know how to light the Primus stove, all sorts of things like that. Sure, we complained to each other, we said, "Why didn't Moses bring us to Switzerland," and all that. But there wasn't any choice. The atmosphere was such that—I mean, there was a war, you know, and over there, well, they were killing all the Jews in concentration camps. We would have been happy to be

[§] Haganah: Literally, "Defense." The main underground military defense organization of the Jewish community in Palestine under the British Mandate. Upon the creation of the State of Israel, the Haganah became the organizational base of the Israeli army—the Israel Defense Forces.

anywhere, even though we had nothing. Sure, some food products were being rationed, but you could always get bread. It wasn't so awful.

I graduated high school in 1943. And even as late as this, no one realized what was going on in Germany. Of course, we tried to keep up with events. Through the Red Cross, we got some letters from grandmother and one of my uncles. But then we didn't hear anything more—you couldn't make contact. They all died in concentration camps. One uncle was involved in some kind of scandal—a skeleton in the closet that I couldn't get anyone to tell me about. He had been a very popular and successful high school teacher, and he studied law and literature, and his house was full of books. He lived in the same city as we did, and would always eat lunch with us. There was some kind of story having to do with him which I never found out. My mother was a very reticent woman, and you just couldn't get anything out of her.

I remember once, I asked about some cousin of my father's, who had married a very wealthy man who was apparently insane, or something like that. I said to my mother, "What was wrong with that man?" So she said, "I can't tell you. I can only say this—to a man like that, you don't get married." That was all I could ever get out of her. That was all she would ever say. So you can understand that it never occurred to me that I could talk to her about my sex life. We never exchanged a single word about it. And neither she nor my father ever asked why I didn't marry. One doesn't ask a question like that. Even of your own son. But you have to remember that I had two unmarried uncles. They were used to it—in Germany there were a lot more people like that. It was commonly accepted, like in England also. It was an acknowledged status. I have no idea if it had anything to do with homosexuality. I don't know what they were thinking. We never talked about it.

Actually, I remember one time the subject did come up, but not in connection with my uncles. My father had a good friend, who was from a smaller city in Germany, and had gone to the United States, and became rich there. Maybe you've heard of him, he made a business out of raising canaries—he called his company "Hartz Mountain." And afterwards he had a chain of stores, of pet food and all sorts of things. A vulgar man with a lot of money. I think my father advised him on some investments, I don't know, but they were friendly, and the family would always come to visit when they were in Israel, after the war. And once—this man always spoke in a vulgar fashion—he said, when we were all sitting at the dining-room table—we never ate in the kitchen—he said that he had just had an operation, a hemorrhoids operation. They had fixed his bottom, and "now all the queers will like me." He used a vulgar German expression for gays—the "hot brothers." I doubt they still use this expression today. Now, my mother was a real lady, and I remember how she just froze in her place when he said that. I remember looking at the expression on her face. Now that I think about it, it may well be that she had no idea what he was talking about, even though she had studied a great deal.

My mother was an attorney. She had studied law—but that was before she got married. It was unacceptable that a banker's wife should work. And very soon after she got married she became pregnant with my brother. It was also unacceptable that a pregnant woman be seen in public. You couldn't even use the word "pregnant"—you never used the word at all. You would have to say "expectant," like in English.

Once, when I was nine or ten years old, it was Purim, and my brother and I wanted to dress up. So we looked in the Book of Esther for ideas, and my mother said, "Why don't you dress up as eunuchs?" Now, we were looking at the German translation, but even in German, there is only one meaning to the word "eunuch." How does a woman in her right mind tell a boy to dress up as a eunuch? But she thought the word just meant "servant." To me, this is a sign of a very general ignorance on her part about anything having to do with sex.

Of course, by the time I had finished high school I had become aware of what was going on with me sexually. But you didn't talk about such things. I thought I could just repress it all. I didn't think that if you feel something, you also need to do something about it. It didn't even occur to me.

When I was very little, men's bodies interested me more than women's. I said to myself about women, "There's nothing to see there." I didn't know that it was all inside. I remember that my father was a very handsome man, and I remember that my parents' bedroom was next to the children's bedroom. And you didn't really have modern showers then. It was a very old house, and my parents had added a washroom, where you could wash in the morning with a sponge. The maid would bring in big ceramic jugs with hot and cold water. And I remember that I would stand there and watch my father wash. I thought he was lovely. I was very young, maybe three years old. I know how young I was because there was a sort of full-length mirror, and I wasn't even tall enough to see myself in it. One day my father saw that I was watching him, and he closed the door. I felt like Adam and Eve must have felt when they were expelled from the Garden of Eden.

I also remember what I thought to myself when I saw my father's underwear on the laundry line. Back then they had the sort of underwear that was one piece—it went from your neck to your ankles. It was terribly cold in the winter. And I remember thinking, "I'm jealous of father's underwear, it gets to be so close to his body." And how I loved it when he took me onto his lap, which happened very little. Later on, the first men I had real crushes on always looked like my father did when he was younger, the way I remember him. I always knew that I felt this way. But I thought everybody was like that.

If there was a boy who I thought was attractive, I wanted to see him without his clothes on. I remember that when I was in Holland, I think I had a nonstop erection—this was at twelve, thirteen, fourteen years old. I thought the teachers were so good-looking, I would undress them with my eyes. And there, in Holland, the atmosphere was really what the English call "prudish"—I don't know how you would say that in Hebrew. Growing up, I never saw a naked man. I thought that grown mens' penises looked different. I never saw them! I remember, for instance, in the changing rooms at the swimming pool, people would always do something, like putting on a long shirt first, anything, just so no one should see your penis. It was a sort of brainwashing. It got to the point where it was a real experience just to see someone wearing short pants.

When a boy is bar mitzvahed in Holland, he first of all receives all the sacred writings. So I got the Gemara and Mishnah and all that.[§] But I also got art books. And I loved to look at those books, because there were naked men there. They were made of marble, but it was better than nothing. And everybody marveled, the boy is so interested in art. But I wasn't in the least interested in art. I was interested in the naked bodies of those statues.

I remember also, we would always go to synagogue on Śimḥat Torah.[†] The person who gets the honor of reading the last passage of the Torah is called the "Bridegroom of the Torah." And whoever reads the first passage in Genesis is called the "Bridegroom of Genesis." And the readers would stand together on the raised reader's platform, together with other prominent members of the synagogue, and they would all be dressed in their best

[§] Gemara: The central text of traditional Judaism, structured as the record of third- through fifth-century debates in the great Babylonian and Jerusalemite academies on the meaning of the Mishnah. The Mishnah and the Gemara together make up the Talmud.

[†] Śimḥat Torah: Autumn holiday marking the completion of the annual reading of the entire Torah in synagogue; on this day, the Torah scroll is also rewound to the beginning and the reading is begun again.

clothes—very formally, traditionally, with top hats and everything. And I remember that once, I completely fell in love with the "Bridegroom of Genesis." He was such a gorgeous man. I couldn't stop looking at him.

In Holland, I had a close friend who I would play with during vacations and all that. But he was only interested in girls. He also came here. We did not keep in touch. He got married, and I think he must have about ten grandchildren by now, or even great-grandchildren.

I never considered acting on my thoughts. And it wasn't until I was maybe sixteen or seventeen that I even realized that I was different from other people in what I was thinking. You have to remember, they didn't write about homosexuality in the newspapers back then. I had an encyclopedia that I had received, something like the *Encyclopedia Britannica*, in German, which formed a basic part of my education. But when I became curious, I couldn't really learn very much from it about homosexuality. It wrote that homosexuality was a tendency towards one's own sex, and in Austria it is punishable by this, in Germany by that, in Switzerland by this and that. Most of what was written was about the law. So it was hard to see myself as a homosexual. The pre-Hitler "gay" movement in Germany had no influence on me. I was a boy. There wasn't any television then, and I didn't begin reading the newspaper until 1935, and I never remember coming across anything about it. I didn't even know.

Once I was settled in Ramat Gan, I began going to bookstores, to read all the books I could on psychoanalysis. And that was how I found out that gays meet each other in public bathrooms—it was written in a book. Otherwise I never would have known. But all sorts of other, less useful things about homosexuality were also written in these books.

I made a friend in high school here in Ramat Gan, a very nice-looking guy. He was Dutch. He would sleep over at my house, and I would sleep at his—this was because he lived pretty far away. He lived in Giyʿatayim, and there was no road then. You had to go through the sand and all that. In the evening, we would play around with each other. And that's how, at fifteen, I first learned to masturbate. We also tried to suck each other, but I don't think we thought it tasted very good, I don't remember exactly. He later got married—I think he's been married about four times now. He went back to Holland after the war. But we didn't think that what we were engaged in was homosexuality. We thought like the Evil Son in the Passover Hagadah, who says, "What is all this to you?" To *you*, and not to *us*. I thought that gays were only "them," and not me. So it took me a very long time to feel that I was gay.

I became really conscious of it all only when I was eighteen, nineteen, or more. I can't tell you what exactly I was thinking before that.

My parents put no sexual pressures on me. We didn't talk about sex. It was as if it didn't exist. I never got any sexual education. I, until I was fifteen, thought that babies come out of the belly button. In the encyclopedia, they had descriptions of the female sexual organs, but only from a sort of internal perspective. And, for the life of me, I couldn't figure out how the description fit the way things looked. It was all very theoretical. I believed that sex was something sort of magical that only married people could do, and even then, only a few times in their lives. I couldn't conceive that it could be true that making love is the world's most popular indoor sport.

When I finished high school, there wasn't any money to send me to study in a university, and I didn't know what I wanted to study, in any case. So I had to learn a profession. I had always thought that I was interested in hotel management. So my parents sent me to study hotel management. There was a hotel then, Qalyah, on the Dead Sea. It doesn't exist anymore. It was a luxury hotel, and people like Abdallah, the king of Jordan's chief general, would come there. I was there for one season, at the reception desk, as an intern. It was pretty interesting.

There were gays there, and some of them were extraordinary. I remember one of the people I worked with, the only one who treated me nicely—Mr. Paul. He was a tennis teacher there. It was only afterwards that it became clear that he was gay. At the time, I thought that gays were strange people who you had to be a little scared of. There was a gardener there, who was actually a poet—we were all immigrants, you know, doing any kind of work we could. And there was a place where the British soldiers would go to bathe, and this gardener would go there, and kind of wander around. I also wandered around there, and I would look. But it didn't even occur to me that I could come on to the soldiers. I didn't even know how men have sex with each other.

There were also two Arab employees there, workers from Jericho, who no matter where I was were always trying to put their arms around me. They would say things to me in Arabic. But I didn't understand them, and I didn't find them attractive. There were also some servants from Sudan there, and I did find them attractive—gorgeous boys, who worked as waiters and bellhops. They definitely tried to come on to me, but I didn't get it. I didn't know anything—I didn't know what it was or how you did it. It didn't occur to me.

At one point, I was trying to find a temporary room in Jerusalem, and this gardener said to me, "I'll send you to someone who knows a lot of people, and you can find a room with another young man." And he wrote a letter for me and sent me to Mr. Rosenstein, a well-known man who had a bookstore in Jerusalem. Later on I found out that Rosenstein was also a well-known gay. I knew that the gardener wrote to Rosenstein about me, "He's one of ours." But I didn't understand at all—I thought he meant that I was a German Jew like them!

From my time down at that hotel, I learned that the most important person in a hotel is the chef. So I went to Jerusalem planning to study cooking. Rosenstein helped me find a room. The other guy in the room was a student and a member of Etzel—Etzel is the Likud today, but during the Mandate they were an underground organization, they were considered terrorists.[§]

It was in Jerusalem that I had my first gay experience, which was very unpleasant. I had been working until late on Friday night, and the buses had already stopped running. So I caught a cab with an Arab driver—this was before the War of Independence. I was sitting next to the driver, and all of a sudden he began groping my crotch. And I began to grope him back. He was a beautiful guy. It was pretty pleasant, but then he decided that he wanted to screw me. He brought me someplace, but I didn't want to—I mean, sure, there was something going on between my legs, but this was not what I had in mind. I remember that he demanded a tenth of a pound for the fare afterwards. And back then, I could pay my whole month's rent with two pounds! This was a really unpleasant experience. But I just had to learn to live with it—I couldn't tell anyone. You couldn't talk to a single person about something like that. But I couldn't get it out of my head afterwards, this experience.

After I finished my course in Jerusalem, I moved to Tiberias, on the Sea of Galilee, where I spent one season as an intern chef. It was very uneventful. I didn't even let myself think about sex. And afterwards I went to work as a chef here in Tel Aviv, in a hotel on Hayarqon Street. I worked on Hayarqon Street for five years, from May 1945 to May 1950.

I remember the first Independence Day, in 1948. It was terrible. Such a very difficult time. I remember every moment. All of a sudden they began

[§] Etzel: Abbreviation of the Hebrew name of the "National Military Organization." Founded in 1931 by Ze'ev Jabotinsky as the military arm of the nonsocialist Zionist political parties of the Jewish community in Palestine under the British Mandate. Engaged in violent attacks against those who were perceived as violently impeding progress toward Jewish independence, including both the British military and local Arabs.

bombing Tel Aviv. I saw it from the roof of the hotel. If you go to Independence Park in Tel Aviv, there is a monument there, an eagle, in memory of an Israeli plane that was shot down. I saw that plane, as it crashed into the sea. The park is, of course, "Independence Park"—it's dedicated to those who died fighting for independence.

I remember that all the journalists were in the hotel with us during the war, and I had to work day and night. My parents were living in Ramat Gan, on high ground, and all of sudden the army came and gave them twenty-four hours to leave the house, because they wanted it for the chief of staff—he had been in the army headquarters, but the Egyptians had bombed it. There was very strict food rationing, and it was so very hot. Not a happy time.

I never went into the army. I suffered from serious asthma. When the War of Independence began, before the establishment of the state, the Jewish Agency and the Haganah had their own draft boards. And I would always be called and they would always send me away. Now, I never missed a single day of work because of my asthma, and I told them that. But they didn't want to take me. It was very unpleasant. I remember one time very clearly. The doctor used a Yiddish word—I remember that doctor, he knew me from Ramat Gan—he said, "We're at war, we don't need *kalikes*." A *kalike* is a man who is physically worthless. It hurt me very much. I said, "But I've never missed a single day's work because of this." My attacks would be at night. And if I can cook for a hotel then I can cook for the army. But it didn't do any good. It wasn't that I particularly wanted to go to the army, but it was very unpleasant for me that everyone else was going, and here I was, staying behind. I didn't think that the army would be a terrific amount of fun or anything, but I thought I should have to go like everyone else.

Later on, when I was twenty-six, twenty-seven, they decided that they wanted to draft me into the army—but at that point I really didn't want to go. What, in the middle of my life, to start my army service from scratch, when they didn't even want me back during the war, when they really needed me? Also, I had heard about all sorts of people who had been thrown out of the army for being gay, some of them officers. And I didn't want that to happen. If my personal life was against the law, which it was back then, would that mean that I would have to hide this for three years? I didn't want that. So I went ahead and told them in the army that I was gay. And with that, and my old asthma, they stopped bothering me. I don't remember if it was 1953 or 1954. So I've never even held a gun.

Across the way from the hotel where I worked in Tel Aviv was London

Park. During the years right before independence, there were always a lot of British soldiers around, and a lot of them would go to this park to look for prostitutes. And there was also a public toilet in the park, where men would cruise one another. It was there that I began to cruise for the first time. I didn't really know what to do at first, but I learned. Every night, there were all sorts of men in the bushes, in the entrances to buildings, just sort of lurking. And every night I would say to myself, I have to, but in the morning I would swear I would never do it again. It was a little dangerous—there were all kinds of unsavory types there. And I didn't want to be like that. But it was all pretty open, and there were so many men there. And some of them were very attractive men indeed.

It was already clear to me that I was gay, and that this was an intolerable state of affairs. So I entered psychoanalysis. Then there weren't psychologists like today. If you wanted treatment, you had to go to a psychoanalyst. I had another problem as well—I was nineteen years old, and still wet my bed. So I spoke to a friend of mine, and she sent me to a certain psychoanalyst, a terrible man by the name of Dr. Wolf. He was famous. Now, you have to remember, I was incapable of talking about homosexuality. I couldn't even say the word. And he sat with me at our first interview, and didn't say anything. Not a word! So we just sat there in silence. I didn't go back. I went to someone else, who was also very cold, until I finally got to a female doctor, Dr. Smilansky. She lived not far from here, on Gilboʿa Street. Her brother was a famous writer, Moshe Smilansky.[§] She was blind. She had studied in Berlin. And she talked to me, asked me what I had studied, what my hobbies were, what books I read, all sorts of things like that. She drew me out. In the end, she said, "If you have such an interesting life, why have you come to see me?" And that way, she got me to say why I had come to see her. She was such a nice woman. I would go to her four times a week.

I wasn't getting along very well with my parents at the time, and I didn't want to ask my father for money, so I paid her with my own money. It was very difficult. It was fearfully hot, and you hardly even saw a fan anywhere back then. I would work through my break in the hotel kitchen, and then I would leave a little early, at four o'clock, and bicycle over for a one-hour session of analysis. I was so tired, sometimes I would doze off on the couch. And the poor woman, who was blind, thought I was experiencing a "block" or something. She thought I was resisting, but it was just that I had fallen asleep!

§ Moshe Smilansky (1874–1953): Writer of Hebrew fiction deeply influenced by Tolstoy; agricultural laborer.

After three years, the sessions with her did have a really positive effect. I became more independent. I was able to decide to quit my job, which I hated, and do what I really wanted to do. And I also decided that I wanted to be gay. She didn't have any direct input into that decision. Back then, they were very strict about not saying anything. They worked with free association. This isn't the time to go into it—I think they do the same thing today. I think that it's a sort of religion, psychoanalysis. A sort of cult. In any case, it helped.

After analysis, I had this realization that restrictions like, "It's forbidden to have sex," or "It's forbidden to be gay," are imaginary, and I am not obligated to take them upon myself. People take them upon themselves because they want to, but I am permitted to live my life however I want. I learned this from psychoanalysis—my analyst didn't say it, she never said anything. But it came from inside myself. It might be that without her I would have come to the same conclusion. I don't know.

After the war, and after my analysis, I decided that I wanted to quit my job at the hotel. It was very difficult work. We had no contract, and we would work ten hours a day, in primitive conditions—I don't want to go into it. And it was work devoid of, how do you say—let's just say it wasn't a vocation. We have something, the religious German Jews, we have a sense of social responsibility. A person can't do things exclusively for his own benefit. You have to do something for the public good as well. So I thought to myself—I thought then that forty years old was very old—I thought to myself, when I'm forty years old, what will I have done with my life? I'll have nothing to show for myself but steaks and cutlets for rich people, the nouveau riche of Tel Aviv. I didn't want that to happen.

Around this time, there was an advertisement in the newspaper that Qupat Ḥolim was looking for a hospital chef.§ So I went to see what the conditions were like. And I was very impressed. First of all, the kitchens were big and well-ventilated, and they had eight-hour days, and you didn't work in the evenings. All sorts of things like that. So I went to be a chef at Qupat Ḥolim.

My first season, in 1950, I spent at Safed, in Beit Bussel, a spa. A beautiful place with a gorgeous view, but from a sexual perspective, a totally dry well. I didn't even have anyone to talk to. Nothing. I thought that this was the way it should be. It didn't occur to me that it could be different. There was a nurse who fell in love with me there. I didn't know it at the time. But the first time my name was in the newspaper in a homosexual context, two

§ Qupat Ḥolim: Health insurance organization of the Histadrut, Israel's general labor union.

years ago, she called me up and told me. She said now she understands why she couldn't get anywhere with me. I hadn't the slightest idea what was going on at the time.

In any case, afterwards, I worked for another season at a spa in Motza, near Jerusalem. There was only one bus a day to Jerusalem. It was also very isolated, but wonderful for getting away from it all. I was very affected by that, such a beautiful place, and such good air, but I was out of the mainstream of gay life. When I could get there, I did go to the beach in Tel Aviv, in the evening—what you find today in Independence Park used to go on then on the boardwalk behind the Dan Hotel. And on Roṭshild Avenue, not far from where the Agudah community center is today. And on Betzalᵓel Yafeh Street—some people would stand on the sidewalk. I knew all of this already. Of course, it wasn't like today, there wasn't action like today. It was all kind of on the sly.

I remember the first time I slept in a bed with a man was on Independence Day, 1951. I was exactly twenty-seven. I had been at a party in Tel Aviv, and I was deathly bored, so I left. I went outside and sat down on a bench, and someone just came along and picked me up. He took me home with him. He had a boyfriend also, and the three of us were together. I didn't really like his boyfriend, but I liked this guy so much that I didn't wash for two days afterwards, because I wanted to feel his smell on me. But in general, I thought my sexuality was something to repress, to kick to the side. I was not going to plan my career around it.

After a little while at Qupat Ḥolim, they could see that I was a little exceptional, because I was the only chef with an academic high school degree. And I spoke excellent English, a little French, and I could read the professional literature. So they put me in a course to learn to be a food service manager. Back then, it was an exclusively female profession. They were offering a course in Beilinson Medical Center. Soon, I became a food service manager near ᵓAfulah, another isolated place. There were two buses a day from the hospital to ᵓAfulah, and that was all. Once again, I was totally cut off. But from there, they transferred me to Reḥoyot, to Qaplan Hospital, which had just opened. I was the kitchen manager there, and afterwards the institutional director, and from there, they sent me abroad to study. To Switzerland.

In the meantime, I was traveling to Haifa often, during vacations, because I had a very good friend there who had gone to school with me in Ramat Gan, and his parents were good friends as well. They had moved to Haifa. He wasn't gay, at least, in any case, I don't think so. He once asked me, at eighteen, when we were walking together, "What do gays do in bed anyway?" I said, "I have no idea." By that time, of course, I did at least have a general idea, but I said I didn't know. It never occurred to me that I could sleep with him—he was like a brother to me. In any case, I never said a word to him about my sexuality.

Eventually, he went to England, to study at the London School of Economics, and since his little brother had been killed in the Battle of Laṭrun during the War of Independence, I would often go to visit the parents on Shabbat, so they wouldn't be alone. It was a very interesting house. His parents were very interesting people. His mother was a painter and a smart woman, who knew how to relate to young people.

I would go, and sort of absorb the talk there. I learned a lot about art, and all kinds of interesting people would come to the house. And one day the mother said to me, I was twenty-two or twenty-three at the time, "You have been very withdrawn lately." And she was right. Because at a certain point, I saw that I could never talk about what I really wanted to talk about, so I stopped talking altogether. I got used to not talking about myself. I knew that most people really weren't interested in me, and what really interested me, I couldn't say to anyone.

At one point, my friend's parents had a tenant who was a Viennese psychoanalyst, very elderly. I once consulted with him as to whether I should go back to analysis. Because I thought I hadn't done enough about myself, that I was still gay. He said, "After three years of psychoanalysis, you know yourself well enough to make your own decisions. But you should remember this, if you decide to live as a gay man, you will need a very strong sense of self-worth." It's very true. Because a gay man always tends to think that he is worth less than others. From the very start he "knows" that his behavior is not good, that it's forbidden. And he has to overcome that.

In Haifa, I would sometimes go to Binyamin Park in the evening. It was the only place where you could meet people there, in Haifa. They hadn't yet opened Memorial Park. Binyamin Park was behind the theater, although I don't think there was very much of a theater there, at that time. It was pretty dark, there were bushes and so on, and there was a fair amount of traffic there. I met all sorts of people, some nicer than others, and we would go into the bushes. Once I met someone who had come from Tel Aviv. He offered me a ride back to Tel Aviv the next day, and I accepted. He was a German Jew, older than me, he was maybe fifty, or something like that. His name was

Karo—he's still alive, he's eighty-eight or something like that now. He was really the unofficial dean of the gays in Israel—he was what you would call in English a "screaming queen." In any case, I said I would go with him, and another fellow was in the car also, by the name of Rosenzweig, also older than I was. On the way we stopped to drink coffee. They had a container of instant coffee. And that was really something—if someone had instant coffee back then, it meant that he was very high class. Most people didn't have coffee at all.

I learned from them that there was a gay social life, that people would meet in private houses. It had never occurred to me. I had no idea. This was in 1950, 1951. So I went to Karo's house in Tel Aviv, and I met other people, and then things really began to happen. My brother had had some mental problems, and, at Karo's house, I mentioned the psychiatrist who had treated him. I liked him very much. I remember that I once said to Karo, "I really like that fellow, it's a shame he's not 'like that.'" Because he wore a wedding ring. And Karo said, "What are you talking about, he is too 'like that'!" I was suddenly finding gays everywhere. I was making all sorts of little discoveries. I had the sense that I had found my way into a sort of mafia or something. I still had the feeling that this was something not very good, but at least there were people to talk to now.

When I was working in ʾAfulah, it was very difficult. People were awful. I remember that I, as a young man alone, didn't have anyone to talk to at all. They were such snobs, such an exclusive group. Staff members would come into the kitchen and take their food and ignore me, like I was a piece of furniture, when I would be working there preparing their meals. They would never say hello or anything like that. But there was a pediatrician who came, who had been quite famous in Germany. And the first time his wife came into the kitchen, she went right up to me and said straightaway, "Hello, I'm Mrs. So-and-so, and I'd like some bread please." It was amazing. Such a thoughtful, polite person. And I would talk with her at times. She, I realize now, in retrospect, tried to set me up with her son. She asked if I was married, and I said no, and she said, "Yes, you know, not everyone needs to get married." We spoke in German. She said, "My son is also single." And she would often invite me to their house. They were the only ones who would invite me in, and most often her son was there. Of course, I only realize all of this in retrospect.

I did my work well, so eventually, Qupat Ḥolim sent me abroad, in 1954, to study nutrition. They were preparing me for a position at Beilinson Medical

Center, which was under construction at that point, and they sent me to a similar hospital in Switzerland. And in Switzerland I began to live a little more.

When I was getting ready to go abroad, I said to one of my friends, "How do you pick someone up outside of Israel? How do you know where the meeting places are?" So he said, "Go to a public toilet, come on to someone, and ask him." And that's what I did in Switzerland. So I found my way to a cafe, Zaehringer, they called it. It still exists. It was in Zurich, where I was studying. And I went there almost every evening, but I didn't meet anyone. I was young, and I really needed it, to touch a man, but no one would even talk to me. In the end, I figured out that they were even shyer than I was, and that if I was going to meet someone, I was going to have to make the first move. So I had to force myself.

I remember that one time, it was very crowded there, I put my arm on the jukebox and I said out loud to myself in Yiddish, "*A yid getzikh an etze*" ["A Jew finds a way"], as a way of summoning up my courage—and someone heard me, and all of a sudden someone began talking to me in Yiddish there! As things turned out, I met some very interesting people, and I found my way to a club, a political organization something like our Agudah, which was just starting out. I met some pretty interesting and nice people, I began to live a little more.

I remember that I met one guy there, he was Dutch, an educated man, a lawyer in the U.N. He loved straight men. His hobby was to go to cities in Germany where there were a lot of American GIs, and he would walk around the red-light districts and invite them to come with him, for money. Everyone would be happy—I mean, my friend would get what he was looking for and the soldiers would get what they were looking for, and instead of wasting money on a prostitute, they would even make a few bucks! He had a lot of clients.

So once I got to Zurich, I began to live a little. The course went well, and afterwards, I was sent to London for a short while. In London I didn't get by very well, because I just don't understand the British mentality, with all of their pubs. They don't say a word there—they don't talk to one another, not a single word. And only when they finally get a little drunk do they begin to wake up a bit. I don't drink, I can't stand alcohol. So I didn't fit in very well there. But often I would meet people in the street. I lived off Finchley Road in London, a place with a lot of Jews. And if I walked in the street, around eleven or twelve at night, when the last underground of the day arrived, I could pick people up on the street without any problem. I became more skilled, and I didn't have any inhibitions. I didn't know anyone in London, and no one knew me, so I didn't care what people thought. I went totally nuts. Sometimes I would be with four or five men in a single evening. It became something compulsive, like with a lot of gays, compulsive sex—you run up numbers, like a stamp collector. You must have sex at every available opportunity. And it's there on demand.

I once met a guy on the street, and he said to me afterwards, "Isn't it marvelous being queer!"—they didn't say "gay" then, they said "queer." I said, "What's so marvelous about it?" He said, "Well, I've just come from Belsize Park," which is a beautiful public garden, "and I chewed sixteen people there." "Chew" is to "suck," that's what they said then. I still didn't see what was so marvelous about it. But that was what he thought.

Actually, there was a family that I knew in London, and I stayed with them when I first got there, for about a month. They used to be neighbors of ours in Frankfurt. There were ten children in this family, but in particular I remember a girl, two or three years younger than I, named Judith. I knew her as a young girl. At this point she was working as a midwife. She had been to Israel, and studied at Shaᶜarey Tzedeq Hospital in Jerusalem. While she was here, she fell in love with a Yemenite guy and wanted to marry him. In the end it didn't happen. I know all this because her aunt wrote to my father at the time, asking him to please find out who this man was, and what sort of family he came from. In any case, while I was staying with her family in London, Judith fell in love with me. She really was very nice, and we understood each other well. We came from such similar backgrounds, and she spoke Hebrew and German and English, and we would go on trips together. But she wanted to marry me. She had fallen desperately in love with me. So I had no choice, I had to tell her that it was impossible. And you couldn't talk about such things then. But there was an actor then, John Gielgud, who had been arrested for "loitering"—cruising in public toilets—and it was in all the papers. And I said to her, "I'm like John Gielgud." And, as you say in English, she "professed understanding," but she really thought that she, through love, could change me. She said, "I'll not make any demands of you." Those were her exact words. "I'll not make any demands of you." But I didn't want to get married.

In spite of that, we went together on a hitchhiking trip to the Isle of Skye, in Scotland. It was very interesting, a very remote place in Scotland, where they make wool. They were so Protestant there that there were no buses on Sunday. We stayed in youth hostels and so on, and it was a terrible burden for her, because she wanted to be close to me all the time, and all I wanted was to be close to some of the beautiful fellows we would see all over the place. But we stayed good friends.

Later on, she came back here to live. She had met a Vietnamese man who was married to someone else, and had become pregnant by him. And she had come to Israel to raise her half-Vietnamese child! Once she got here, though, she had an abortion. She became a nurse. A very successful nurse. She was very understanding. For instance, she would never kiss me when we were inside alone—only in public. For the neighbors, you understand. She tried to set me up with some men she knew a few times. She died of cancer a few years ago.

In the end, I was in Switzerland for six months, and London for five months. I came back from London by way of Amsterdam. It was a real experience for me to see Amsterdam again, and there I went to what they called the "C.O.C.," the "Center of Culture," a gay social club. And it was such a wonderful thing for me, I compare it to the children of Israel who finally came to the Holy Land after forty years in the desert. Such a spacious place, and everyone there was gay. I stayed in a gay hotel, too. You didn't need to wear a mask. It was such a liberation, I didn't want to leave. And I didn't run up numbers there, almost none. It didn't interest me at all. I just wanted to be there. I've seen similar reactions when young people have come into the Agudah's community center in Tel Aviv for the first time. I see it in them.

I remember once, when the Agudah was just starting out, there was a guy who came to the office when I was working there. And he was so pleased that he called his job and told them that he wasn't coming to work. He just wanted to hang out at the office, just to be there. His eyes were shining. I saw myself all over again. It was also the same feeling I had when I put my *tefilin* on while standing on the balcony in Haifa—you don't need to hide it here. And I still have that feeling. One of the reasons I am so active in the Agudah is that I love to be around gays. I really feel comfortable only among gays.

I have a distant cousin from England, who got married while I was in Amsterdam. He married a girl from the old Portuguese-Jewish community there. The Portuguese Jews had a fabulous synagogue, and they were wealthy people, but they've all disappeared. Now nothing is left of them but the synagogue. It's very sad. In any case, my cousin got married in Holland and I kind of stood in for his father, who had died many years before. I escorted him seven times around under the bridal canopy instead of his father. And in place of the bride's father, her brother accompanied her, an adopted brother. Now, the funny part is that the night before the wedding, I had met the bride's brother *and* sister at the gay club—it was so amazing, and there was no one I could tell about it. Such a coincidence! And afterwards there was a sit-down reception at a hotel and they of course called me over to sit with them. We had a grand time. An aunt came by and said, "Oh, I see you're sitting at the singles' table." It really was very funny.

When I was in Amsterdam, I ran into the Jewish secretaries who worked in my father's office until 1940. That was fourteen years earlier. They were so happy, just thrilled to see me, and they invited me to stay with them and so on. Now, I wanted to stay in Amsterdam, but hanging out with elderly secretaries was not what I had in mind. So I had them escort me to the train. They thought I was starting on my way back to Israel, but I had secretly bought a ticket for only one station. We said our goodbyes, I rode one station out of Amsterdam and then turned around and came back. I stayed there for another month. And it was wonderful.

During this time abroad, I learned how to live as a gay man, and I saw that it might be possible in Israel too. But when I came back to Israel, I went back to my routine, only occasionally meeting a few people here and there. I wouldn't just say that I went back into the closet—I went back into the refrigerator. At first, I moved back in with my parents, and afterwards, in 1956, 1957, I got my own apartment. But I was very closeted, and I never said a word to my parents about anything. I went to see a psychiatrist again, but it became clear very quickly, as he said, that while I did have problems, homosexuality was not one of them.

I had also passed through Italy on my return trip. There, I would also meet people on the street, or in the squares, by making eye contact, and beginning to talk, and so on. I remember one evening in Tel Aviv, after I got back, I was in Dizengof Square. And there were a lot of people, there were two large movie houses there, and all sorts of people were wandering around. It wasn't like today, we didn't have television yet, so everyone would go to the movies. But everything was in short supply then, even tickets to the movies. I remember looking around, and feeling amazed at how many people were returning my glances, making eye contact. I thought that maybe they had learned to do this here, like in Italy. But it turned out that they all thought I had a movie ticket to sell. You've got to be very careful.

Once I got back to Israel, after my European training, I got ahead very quickly in my work. I reached the top of my profession, in large part because I could stay in touch with international developments through the latest professional literature. I've never needed to go abroad again. I don't have any desire to, either. And in spite of that, I know what's going on in the profession better than a lot of others, who are always traveling. I went back to school again when I was fifty, over fifty. I went to get an academic degree. And I reached the top of my profession.

One day in March 1957—it was a Friday night, a night like this, I remember—I was walking along the beach here in Tel Aviv, hoping to meet someone. And I did run into a fellow, and we sat on a bench together and began talking. He liked to talk a lot, and he told me his story. He told me that he was born in Germany, and grew up in France, that he had a Vespa, but he had recently had an accident, all sorts of things like that. This was Yiśraʾel Zehavi. Do you know him? A man a little younger than I, today he's very active in the Agudah and in the AIDS Task Force. And as it turned out, we were both from the same city in Germany, from Frankfurt. His uncle was one of my father's best friends. This uncle of his had married my father's cousin, so we even had some common relatives. The religious families of good standing were all connected by marriage somehow or other. Of course, I knew all of his cousins, who were also from the same city, and included the family I had stayed with in London.

We've never had sex, Zehavi and I. I don't find him attractive, and he doesn't find me attractive. Besides, you don't do things like that with family. But we became close, and would go all sorts of places together. When we first met, he had no sexual experience at all. I taught him what I knew about how things are done. There was a real social scene, in the meeting places, the cruising areas.

The terminology was different then. There was a sort of gay slang. They called it *strich*—does that mean anything to you? *Strich* is a word that the gay Germans brought. Should I explain it? *Strich* means line. And in German, you refer to a male prostitute as a "*strich* boy," or a woman might say, "If you don't give me a raise, I'll have to walk on the *strich*," meaning, to be a prostitute. Before the First World War, prostitution in Vienna, which was the metropolitan center of Central Europe, was legal, but the prostitutes were forbidden to go onto the main street to hunt clients. They could only work on the side streets. And the city put a yellow line on the pavement that they were forbidden to cross. And they would walk on the line, to be as close as they could be to the crowds on the main street. And that's where the word comes from—or at least that's what I was told.

We used all sorts of slang. A lot of gays would talk to one another using the feminine forms of verbs, for instance. And, of course, there was the expression "like that" referring to someone gay, which is still used today. And "she's a whore," meaning that a man was a bottom. That was the terminology. I was kind of repelled by the set that talked that way.

Zehayi soon became known as "Madame Vespa," because very few people had Vespas then. He loved to be around people, he loved to talk, and through him I heard a lot of news. I wasn't so social. But it was very convenient, we would go on trips together, and spend our vacations together. To this day we are close. We speak on the phone every single day.

Now here's a spicy little story. Zehayi's uncle, my father's friend, he's one hundred years old now, he's still alive. He has a birthday coming up. I visit with him sometimes. About a year or two ago, I was with him, and we were talking about pollution or something like that, and he said, "Yes, I remember once, on a summer night, it was very hot, your father and I were boating on the Main River." This was the river that passed through Frankfurt, and there was a lot of industry there, chemical plants and so on, and I remember that the water really stank. And he said, "I remember that all of a sudden your father undressed and jumped into the water, and began swimming." And I said to Zehayi's uncle, "How can you go into that dirty water?" The story isn't that important—but it got me thinking. So I said to Zehayi the next day, "Do you think that there was something between your uncle and my father?" And he said, "I don't know—but I know other people who had something with your father." Other people had told him, but he had never dared to say anything to me about my father, through all these years. But at this age, I guess you take everything in stride.

I'm certain that something was going on with my brother also. He later married twice. But before he got married, he had a good friend with whom he lived, and they were inseparable. When he started dating women, he stopped talking to this fellow. And I've seen this friend of his a few times since then, both in the toilets at the Central Bus Station and also elsewhere, cruising. Years later. But we've never exchanged a single word about it.

My mother and father never once asked me why I never married. All sorts of neighbors would offer to set me up with all sorts of people all the time, but my mother never said a word to me about it. She only told me much later, when she was already a little bit confused, and she told me all sorts of things that under normal circumstances she never would have said.

Another person I met at that time was a government minister. Maybe you've heard of Giora Josephthal? He was housing minister or something like that for a while in the fifties.[§] He was a charming man, big and fat. He was married—I don't know if his wife was lesbian or what, but people have told me that she knew before they got married that he was "like that." They had some kind of an agreement. They were members of a kibbutz.

He had heart disease, and I am a professional dietician. So I was asked to advise him on his diet. Now, I had always heard lots of talk about him. He was the treasurer of the Jewish Agency for many years, and he gave his lovers positions there. To this day there are still two people who are there thanks to him. I don't know their real names—one of them was known as Yossi Jewish Agency, and the other was Moshe Jewish Agency! They're people my own age, but they were Josephthal's boys, in their day. So Josephthal arranged that I should come to his house in Tel Aviv, on Hayarqon Street, for a consultation. Apparently he had heard talk about me as well, because when I got there, he was alone, wearing only a bathrobe, and he just ravished me. But you know, anything for a minister! I was young. And he was a charming man, and very smart. He said to me, "Tell me, do the boys know about me?" We spoke in German. So I said, "Yes, of course." I said, "You're a role model queer." And he said, "That's how you talk to a minister of the Israeli government?" It was grand!

Afterwards, I introduced Josephthal to someone else, who was even from the same city in Germany as he was. A certain Ḥayim, Ḥayim the Kibbutznik. Ḥayim only liked older men. Josephthal called me at work to tell me he wanted to meet Ḥayim—I didn't have a phone in my apartment yet. I was working in the Qupat Ḥolim Center in Tel Aviv at the time. I said, "OK, I'll send him a note." Because Ḥayim didn't have a telephone either. Josephthal said, "Be careful." So I wrote Ḥayim a note—I wrote, "Auntie wants to see you." He immediately understood what I meant. Josephthal died not long afterwards, but his wife is still living, she's the general secretary of Hakibbutz Hameʾuḥad, I think. She was also the general secretary of Mapay for a time. A woman with a lot of power.[†]

[§] Giora Josephthal (1912–62): Politician, diplomat. Secretary general of Mapay (see below); minister of labor (1960–61); minister of development and housing (1961–62). Mapay: Abbreviation of the Hebrew name of the "Party of the Workers of the Land of Israel." Founded in 1930 through the union of two previously existing socialist Zionist organizations, it immediately became the dominant party in the pre-state Jewish community, and played a leading role in the early history of the state; party of the first Prime Minister, David Ben-Gurion. Merged into the Labor Party in 1967.

[†] Senta Josephthal (b. 1912): Leader of kibbutz movement; prominent political bureaucrat. General secretary of Iḥud Haqevutzot Vehakibbutzim 1963, 1967–70; member of Secretariat of Labor Party; member of Executive Committee of Histadrut.

I never actually kept a count of my partners. I remember once, a friend of mind said to me, "I've had miles of cock in my life." I took care of him when he had AIDS. I remember, we first met many years ago in Ramat Gan, in the park. I would go almost every day to visit my parents in Ramat Gan. I had a moped. And so I would pass through the Ramat Gan park twice a day, coming and going from my parents. And I would always take a look at what was going on. There was a clique there of mostly Iraqi guys, people who all gave each other women's names—this fellow I was referring to was called "Riyqaleh." He really was a person who had sex compulsively. I wasn't quite like him, but I also, I did it compulsively. I wasn't as daring, but I had that compulsion to go out and find someone too. I can't even explain it. Why it was. But with a lot of gays it's a very big problem. I know that in the United States there are even groups to help people overcome sex addiction. Maybe AIDS has changed things a little.

It never occurred to me to look for a long-term gay partner. It just never occurred to me. The experience was looking for someone to have sex with, and a place to do it. That was first and foremost. So I've never had a real relationship. I can't say why. But I can never maintain my sexual relationships. I've made some of my "numbers" into very good friends, but after a few times, they just don't interest me sexually. I don't know why. Either I'm just not the type, or the taboo is so tremendous, that I don't indulge myself. Maybe I'm too much of a narcissist, and I can't find a person who is exactly, like Truman Capote wrote in one of his books, that "one, inseparable friend." Someone who is my own reflection. I don't know. I am a very territorial person. I very much like my privacy, and to be in a close relationship, I would need to sacrifice my privacy. And since I haven't gotten used to it at a young age, it's impossible now. It's like a student of mine who became widowed, and could have easily remarried, but she said to me once, "What, at my age, I'm going to wash a strange man's underwear?"

Nowadays, I am of the opinion that maybe the burning desire for couplehood is a romantic fiction. Among heterosexuals too. Everyone thinks, especially people from Polish or Russian backgrounds, they think that getting married solves all your problems. But they don't realize that your problems only just begin when you get married. It's very rare that you find people who really live their lives together, and not just in close proximity. Of course, it's never too late. But I've been at peace with myself ever since I came to the conclusion that for me, sex and friendship do not go together. Maybe that's sad, but it's a fact. And maybe I'm too old to change it. Besides, at this point, sex isn't very important to me anyway.

I am alone much of the time, but I wouldn't say that I'm lonely. It doesn't bother me. Loneliness is a state of mind. Because I've always felt different from other people, I actually feel most comfortable when I'm alone. Besides, I can change things if I want to. Once someone said to me, he was very upset that no one had invited him to a Passover seder, and I said, "Look, you've got an apartment, you can cook, why don't you invite people? Cook a good meal, invite people, and you won't be lonely. You can change the situation." I can decide what I want. But a lot of the time I just feel the physical need to be alone. I've gotten used to not talking. It might be that it's because of all the years when I couldn't talk about what I wanted to talk about.

It's not just a gay problem for me, it's a cultural problem. For instance, the person I can talk with the most easily is my brother. Such an educated man. And, like me, he knows German and English and Hebrew and Dutch, and he still reads a lot. Culturally speaking, we are a perfect fit—we understand every word the other says. You know, there are sometimes little words that only someone from the same cultural background can understand. But I can't talk with him about homosexuality at all. I don't know whether he knows. I've never spoken with him about it. I figure he knows. He doesn't live in Israel, he lives abroad. We speak twice a week on the telephone. But we never talk about this.

So for years, the park was the only place I would meet people. I didn't have another place. I would bring them home from the park. I really couldn't say how often I did it. There were evenings when I brought two different people home, one after another, and sometimes I would be with just one person for a few weeks running. It depends. Something in me hated that world of cruising, pacing the byways. I would say to myself, OK, I'm going to go home when my feet begin hurting, when I get cold, or when I've found someone to talk to. For me, it didn't always have to do with sex—sex wasn't always what I was looking for. Often, once I had spoken to someone, I was satisfied.

That's one of the reasons that I'm so active in the Agudah now. For me, to see that people can sit and talk—without drinking alcohol—that they can sit in a room and talk and meet one another, it's like a dream come true. I always dreamed of this. I would daydream of starting a sort of cafe in the park, where people could meet, or something like that. Now I don't need to do that, we have the Agudah. When the office was on Beit Yosef Street, we had tables, I set it up like a cafe, and I brought the coffee from home. To this day I'm responsible for the Agudah's kitchen. I really love it. Often, when there's a lecture, or a movie—we show movies now—afterwards people can stay around and sit and talk, and I'll let them stay as long as they want. I don't care that I need to close up and go home. I can go at midnight, I can take a taxi home. I find it very gratifying. A dream come true.

I don't remember exactly what year they founded the Agudah. It was at the beginning of the 1970s. There were some people, mainly English-speaking women, who had seen this kind of thing, a gay and lesbian social and political organization, where they came from, and wanted to do it here. I don't remember exactly how they began organizing. And then there was Yonatan Danilovitch, and there was Uri Aviram, and Naḥum Landsman—they have all totally distanced themselves from the Agudah now. They keep their distance. I don't know why. And there was Dani Laḥman also. I wasn't involved with that group, but it was really very exciting for me. It was like Moses had brought us to the Holy Land. I was thrilled. That there could be a thing like this.

I remember, it was 1976, I think, when we hosted the International Congress of Jewish Lesbians and Gay Men. No hotel wanted to rent us a hall. But when we had services on Friday night in Independence Park, it was something else—you could see that people were just flabbergasted. That something like that could happen here. There were also people who got a little crazy because of it, out of excitement. I remember one fellow from a religious family found an American guy that he fell for, and they hugged and kissed in front of the television cameras. Afterwards, this poor guy had some very big problems at home. Of course, this love didn't last, as you might expect.

Even afterwards, I wasn't very active in the Agudah. I was busy with other things. My father died, and then suddenly my sister died, and I was left with my elderly mother, who was eventually institutionalized. I went to visit her every single day, and twice on Shabbat. At this point they called me from the Agudah and asked me to be on the board, because there was no one else. It was very difficult to find candidates then. So I became more involved.

Today, I'm very active at the Agudah, but not in management. I don't have the patience to manage anymore, because it's too big a responsibility. I do little, daily tasks. I take care of the coffee and the toilets. I don't want the people on the board, who have to make important decisions and do complicated work, to concern themselves with whether or not there is toilet paper, and whether we're out of coffee. They don't even know where the toilet paper comes from, or who takes care of it. They can leave that to me. That's my profession—institutional management! When I'm at the Agudah, every evening before I go home, I sweep the entrance to the building. Because people go out there, smoke, and they toss the cigarette butts on the floor. And I can't stand that. So what am I going to do, argue with everyone? I sweep them up. It takes no more than a minute. Likewise, when, for instance, this Tony Kushner fellow came, and we had a reception for him, they said to me, "We need hors d'oeuvres."[§] And I asked, "How much money can I spend?" And I took care of it. I like what I do.

I never felt like I missed out on something by not having children. It never really bothered me. I saw in Germany as a boy that there were a lot of unmarried people. It was very acceptable. I don't think about it a lot. I can't explain it. Maybe I'm too egocentric for it. Because I'm also a very realistic man. Children are a very big nuisance. Most people are so vocally proud of their children, but they suffer terribly with them. It limits your personal freedom, it takes a huge chunk out of your salary, and a lot of children make terrible trouble for their parents when they don't develop the way their parents would like. It never bothered me. I have no rapport with little children. I get more gratification from them when they're a little older, and they can learn.

Young people need a little help at times, either material or verbal, and I do find it very gratifying to help other people in this way. It can be very difficult for kids who don't come from a background like my own, with a stable home and a good income. And now I've got a very nice pension. So, when I come across young people who need a little help to get over a troubled time, I'm glad to listen to them, or to help them out with fifty shekels or something like that. If, at this age, I had grandchildren, wouldn't I sometimes slip a few bills into their pockets?

I can't really say what I think about gay couples who raise children. I'm sure that gay parents can be much better parents than the regular macho ones—they can be more understanding. But a child really does need a mother and a father. It's more of an ethical problem. If gays or lesbians already have children, then it's obvious that they have the right to raise them. And, for instance, when you talk about lesbians who want children, you can't tell a woman that she can't have a baby. But on the other hand, society has the obligation to defend the rights of children. For instance, if a woman wants a child, she can sign a contract with the father that she won't demand

[§] Tony Kushner (b. 1956): Jewish-American playwright, author of *Angels in America: A Gay Fantasia on National Themes* (1993).

anything from him. But the state can come and say, on behalf of the child, that the mother does not have the right to forfeit the support of the father—it's the child's right. I don't know if a woman has the right to decide that a child will grow up without a father. I'm only bringing up the problem, I can't give an answer. If there are already children, I'm sure that gays can raise them exactly like heterosexuals, maybe even better. I can't decide anything for anyone else, but this is the way it seems to me.

In my opinion, homosexuality is a defense mechanism to prevent the overpopulation of the world. Among the wolves, there is a defined role for "uncles" and "aunts" who don't have partners. They help raise the children. A smart social planner would encourage more gays as an essential economic resource, to help raise children, as more women enter the workplace. And for governments that want to keep their populations down, in places like Egypt and China, what could be more natural than to encourage homosexuality? People won't reproduce, but they'll be able to live as couples. As they say in English, "you can make a virtue out of necessity."

My sister married a guy from Vienna, a backslapping type. The kind of guy who likes to be in the army. He was never very interested in his son, when he was young. And this son, when he was ten or eleven, was driving his mother crazy—he didn't want to go to day camp in the summer, and she didn't know what to do with him. So one day, I was on vacation, I bought a book of origami, which I had learned when I was a boy, and I sat with my nephew on the porch at my parents' apartment in Ramat Gan. They had a big porch, and the children were often with her. And I taught the boy all sorts of games, and he was very pleased, he made all sorts of things. But I would only see him at my mother's, on Friday night and Shabbat afternoon. There was always good food and a lot of newspapers. It was very nice. He always wanted to be around me.

But one day, my brother-in-law came to see me—he had to pick up something from me—and he said, "I've got to talk to you about ʿAmi," that's the boy's name. And he spoke very indirectly, I had no idea what he wanted to say, so I said, "Tell me, what are you talking about?" And he said, "Homosexuality." I was about forty years old then. I said to him, "What do you know about my personal life?" He said, "Nothing." "So why do you think this?" He said, "OK, I'm from a big city, I see things in the army, I've seen a lot of the world," and so on and so forth. One thing led to another, and it became clear that he thinks that every unmarried forty-year-old-man is a homosexual, and every homosexual chases children, including his own sister's children.

When he saw how shocked I was, he said, "I've apparently said something incorrect." And I said to him, "What you've just said is the first correct thing you've said this whole conversation." And we've never talked about it again. We've never said another word about it.

My sister, his wife, died a very sudden, untimely death, and left my brother-in-law alone when ʿAmi was an eighteen-year-old boy, and their girl was only nine. And after a little while, my brother-in-law began trying to remarry, dating women. At this point, the boy was away in the army, and the girl would be left home alone for entire evenings. All by herself. And I could have been there. I had every evening free. But I never dared say a word, because he could accuse me of trying to start something with his daughter. And he never once asked for my help. So I saw her only at my mother's. Never alone.

ʿAmi later married, and he has a lovely wife, and they have three daughters. They live in Ramat Aviv, just north of downtown Tel Aviv. The daughter has married also. We have an understanding. The daughter let me know one time, when we were talking about a certain play, which was a little homophobic. She said, "I don't like that play." She didn't say why, but it was clear. It's understood, and they don't ask any questions.

I'm so sorry I could never talk to my parents. It put a barrier between us. The real dialogue between us was when I was little and they took care of me, and later on, when they were very old, and I took care of them. At both of these times, we couldn't even talk to each other—but there was direct physical communication, kisses, embraces, and all that. This took place only during those times. In between, when we could talk to each other, there was no communication of any kind. You just can't be close to someone from whom you're hiding more than half of what interests you. And so I think that it's important for people to share their lives with their parents if they can.

The Agudah's support group for parents is a very important thing, once they do know. The same for the religious mens' support group. I respect the religious. They have a very big problem with their conscience. From the very first meetings of this group, I paid for the refreshments out of my own pocket, took responsibility for inviting them, and all that. Now I don't need to any more, but I make the phone calls, and I open up the building for them. I give them my home number, everything I can do. That's in spite of the fact that I think my *tefilin* must be pretty moldy by now. I'm not even sure I remember how to put them on. I don't even know if I've still got them.

The gay stereotype always bothered me. You know—a young Barbie doll, with unusual clothes, and an earring, which used to be very unusual, and so on. So when, in 1975 or 1976, I don't remember, they came from the television station to the Agudah to ask if we had volunteers who would be willing to appear on camera in a show about homosexuality, I said that I would do it. People should know that there are also older gays.

This was back when television was something very new. They were only broadcasting in black and white. I don't even think they were broadcasting every day, it was three days a week. The show was called "The Third Hour Program," and the host was Professor Yirmiyahu Yoyel, a professor of philosophy, a very capable man.

There were only two people in the country who were willing to allow their faces to appear on television. I wasn't one of them—my parents were still alive. They didn't have a television, but in any case, I wasn't ready yet. Ayi Engel, who afterwards totally distanced himself from the Agudah, because he demanded that everyone come out of the closet, was one of those who appeared. He was on army reserve duty at the time, and he said that when he went back to the base the next day, everyone in the mess hall gave him a round of applause. And the other was a Dutch guy, who was visiting Israel, studying theology or something like that.

In my case, they came to my house before the show, and I said on a tape recorder what I wanted to say—I compared gays to Marranos, in that we need to hide our tendencies from the people who are closest to us, and so on. I said I was older than I was, I said I was fifty-eight—I was forty-eight, something like that—and I said that I was from Switzerland. When I went to the studio, they promised to show only my silhouette on the screen, and I wore a wig. They made a script out of my earlier recorded remarks, and I read sections out loud. I was told that my voice would be distorted so as to be unrecognizable. I thought the show went very well, but afterwards, as I was leaving the building where it was taped, I took off the wig—it was very hot, very uncomfortable. And sitting right there in a car was one of the nurses who worked in the hospital with me. I didn't know this at the time. As it turned out, her husband was a technician at the station, and she had come to pick him up!

Now, when one nurse knows something, the whole hospital knows something. So already the very next day after my bewigged shadow with a fake voice had appeared on television, everyone knew! I found this out only later, from someone who worked in the same division. But it was clear to me at the time that something was going on. Everybody stared at me for a few days, like I was walking around the hospital wearing nothing but women's underclothing. Their attitude was, one doesn't talk about homosexuality, except maybe to a psychologist. So I had the feeling that they were waiting for me to burst out in tears at any moment.

Years later, I found out that the students in the Nursing School didn't want to take any classes from me after this. Their advisors had to call a special meeting. But a number of people became much nicer to me as a result. It's very interesting. I got some presents from a few nurses. They didn't say anything, but I figured out that it was because of this. Why should they bring me presents all of a sudden? There were a few people who made comments, of course, in the kitchen, but I just ignored them. I remember once there was a kitchen supervisor, I went into her office, and her assistant said, "Don't come in, she's changing." But the supervisor said, "Don't worry about it, Theo's not interested." This was OK. She said it in a warm manner.

I think it was in 1982 or something, when a black man with AIDS, from San Francisco, came to Israel with his partner, because they had heard a rumor that someone in the Weizmann Institute had found a cure for AIDS. Of course, this was totally unfounded. This man died here, in Qaplan Hospital. But when they got here, some organization in San Francisco got in contact with the Agudah, and asked us to look after the couple. So I got involved, I invited his partner to my home, and I went to visit the hospital, and I spoke to the dietician there, who had studied with me, and we worked on feeding him through a tube, and so on.

It was after this that the AIDS Task Force was founded, and they made a course for volunteers, who were all gay. I enrolled in the course, but I needed to take a day off to go there. Now, I worked with a certain assistant, a very nice woman. We worked together from 1969 onwards in the same room. We were always together. And I never talked to her about this. So in a case like this, where I wanted to take the day off, it meant that I was going to have to make up some kind of story. But I got fed up with hiding it, and I said to her, "Do you know anything about my personal life?" She said, "I know everything." And she began to cry. This was years after I had appeared on television. She said, "Every day since then I've been waiting for you to say something, but you've never said a word." I'm not used to talking. Of course, she didn't know *everything*—she didn't know that I would sometimes run up five numbers in a single day, for instance. But she didn't really need to know that. It was very pleasant to talk to her at last.

Afterwards, I helped a little to organize other courses with the AIDS Task

Force. I would bring social workers and medical specialists to lecture, and so on. On the second day of one of the courses, a doctor who worked in my hospital came to lecture. He was an expert on infectious diseases, and had just come back from the United States, where he had treated many AIDS patients. And, of course, he saw me at his lecture. Now, every day at ten o'clock the doctors sit and have coffee together, they review all the files with the head nurse and the interns, and they gossip. I don't know what this doctor said, but the day after his lecture, I had to go into the room during this meeting, to ask something about a patient. And in front of everyone, the head nurse got up, came over to me, and gave me a gigantic kiss on the cheek. Without saying a word. It was apparently a demonstration of sorts. I thought it was very nice.

I retired on January 31, 1989. They made a party for me and two hundred people came. So apparently it didn't do me any harm, that everyone knew I was gay. But I don't think you can use me as an example. By the time they found out about me, I was in great demand—they needed my services. I was at the top of my profession, and unlike most of the dieticians who are entering the profession today, I was patient-oriented. I provided service. I don't know whether, if I had been just starting out, or not so successful, or not so nice, it might have been that people wouldn't have reacted quite so well.

I'm usually a very reticent person. It's because I'm different—not because I'm so modest. So how did it happen that, after I retired, I was willing to be interviewed in the newspaper using my full name? And I appeared on television talk shows twice this year? Well—I think that we are considered deviant. And people do not like deviants—I think it's something biological. Someone of a different color, someone who dresses differently, it bothers, it frightens people. We can't change human nature. But we can be so persistent in bringing to the public's attention the knowledge that we exist, for better or for worse, that things reach a saturation point, and we are no longer thought deviant. So that's why I do it, not because I like to be in the spotlight. That isn't very pleasant for me. I do it because I have nothing to lose. I'm not such a hero—what can happen to me now?

When I was working, the worst thing that could happen would be that if someone didn't like the fact that I was gay, he would stop sending me his fat kid for treatment. But nothing at all can happen now. I have a pension. And my neighbors—some of them I couldn't care less about, and some of them know about me and treat me very nicely indeed. And I'm not interested in anyone else. Someone in a support group once said to me, "You are totally cut off from this society." I think that's a very positive thing. It empowers me not to care what people say. They can all kiss my behind. It has very often been my sense that I walk around in the middle of society, but that I'm not a part of it. Christopher Isherwood said it best, in the name of his book, I think it was *I Am a Camera*—have you read it? I see, I hear, but I stand on the side. At times, it's a very positive characteristic. Not to take everything to heart. It doesn't have anything to do with me, I'm just observing. So, because of that, I can indulge myself, and do what I think is important. Most young people can't do that. And the people who do it, sometimes they do it wrong, and sometimes they're not the right people.

After I appeared on television recently, without any disguises, most of the phone calls I got were from people who wanted to discuss their diet with me! Women whom I had treated in the past called me to discuss their present situation! I got only positive reactions. But I guess that's natural—you don't hear the negative ones. For instance, not far from where I live there is a hardware store. Two married men work there, both of them in their midthirties, Sefardim. They run the store with their father. The day after I was interviewed, I went in there, and one said to me, "You were the tops on television yesterday—hats off to you." And since then, he treats me much more respectfully when I go into the store, and he calls me by my name—he never knew my name before I went on television. The same thing in the health food store where I always shop. All of a sudden the clerks call me Mr. Mainz—they never knew my name before. And also in the place where I develop film. And a few days after I was on television I went to a supermarket where I don't usually shop, and the cashier said to me, "Weren't you on television a few days ago, on that talk show?" And I said yes. And she said, "Well done—if only there were more people like you." It's very encouraging. One neighbor's daughter said to me, "We're proud of you." But I still think that it's very difficult for young people—you should think it over a thousand times before you come out of the closet.

It used to be that we didn't have anywhere else to go besides the park. It was something social. Like I said, if I just found someone to talk to, I already didn't really care if I ran up another number that night or not. I could go home. Now, it's a very big problem, I think, today, that a lot of gays, in social situations, even today, act like they're in a cruising ground—if you don't want to have sex with someone, you don't talk to him. And that's something very complicated. You've really got to educate people. And I'm not the only one who says that. You've really got to teach them.

For instance, there was the poet Ilan Schoenfeld's discussion group at the Agudah. I went for about six months, I did a full cycle of discussions. There, for the first time, I saw gay men sitting together and talking about poetry. But, I'll tell you, living all those years as an unusual person, a deviant, is good preparation for being an older man in a group of young gay men. Because young people don't like older people—this is true of everyone, but more so with gays. I have no complaints—when I was young I was the same way. But when an older man finds himself in gay surroundings, he becomes a nonperson. It's like he doesn't exist. And this is one of my biggest challenges. I saw in this poetry group, at first, that they just pretended that I didn't exist. But as time passed, and I participated in discussions—I've become more assertive now that I'm older, I don't care what other people think—I began to make contact with the other people. Suddenly they gave me a nod when I came, or talked to me, and acknowledged my existence. But I had been prepared.

I learned a lot about people from a certain cat I had. Actually, it's more accurate to say that the cat had me—she adopted me, and lived in my apartment for eight years. The cat craved my physical presence. When I got into bed, she also wanted to get into bed. She knew it wasn't allowed, but it didn't make a bit of difference to her. Every morning I would find her curled up next to my head. And if I wanted to watch television, she sat herself down on my lap. She didn't want me to screw her, and she didn't want to screw me. And she didn't care whether my penis was big or small, or anything like that. Just like this cat, a person really needs physical closeness to another person. But in our society, it isn't simple to get that. Physical closeness, unfortunately, is interpreted as sex, especially in the gay community. If I don't want to sleep with someone, I won't even talk to him, let alone touch him. And this is a very big flaw, and it causes suffering.

Once, at the Agudah, there was a guy who I wound up talking to about whether or not to tell his parents. He was under a lot of pressure, with his parents, with money, and he was sick as well—I think he had cancer. What he really needed was a kiss on the forehead, and some hugs. But there was no way I could do that. Because he could take it the wrong way and think that this old man was coming on to him, which was the last thing in the world I was thinking about. All he needed was to be hugged, but I couldn't do that for him. It's a pity.

I don't have a problem with getting older. I enjoy the fact that I can wake up in the morning, and I don't have to go to work. I find my satisfaction and my entertainment in daily life. I think my attitude toward life is something that runs in my family—we're easygoing people, we like to enjoy life. We always enjoy ourselves. I enjoy the winter and the summer. I love to eat and prepare food—and you need to eat three times a day, so that's already three times a day that I enjoy myself, right off the bat. I have a very positive attitude toward most of the little things in life. It might be that it comes from a kind of desperation—I don't ever expect that anything good is just going to happen to me. When I was young, I always thought, something good is going to happen to me any minute now. But I don't think that anything else good is going to just happen to me in my life, without my making it happen. Because of that, I have to enjoy what I have now. And I do enjoy myself.

I could write poetry about it, how much I enjoy seeing all of those young beautiful people who wander around Tel Aviv, so free and easy. Or all the trees and flowers there are outside. Or the beautiful view. Or the sea. Everything. Sure, it's just looking from a distance, but seeing beauty is my great joy. Paintings, beautiful architecture—sure, you can't sleep with them, but there's more to life than that. That's also something you learn when you get older. I'm no longer the slave of my penis. That's a very positive thing. It's still there, it does what it's supposed to, but I'm not its slave.

Now, let's say I go to Works, that club, and there are a lot of beautiful men there. Even in the best of all possible worlds, I couldn't sleep with every one of them. I couldn't do it. So how many will I be able to lay? How many cocks can I suck, tell me, before it gets boring, mechanical? It's like the pornographic movies that they have in America. It's deathly boring. How many times can you see a person doing this? I mean—have you ever bought flowers? You buy them to look at, right? Why do you raise houseplants—to look at them, right? That's enough. It's totally legitimate to look. And it's like with food, too. If I eat an orange, first of all I smell it, and I look at it—I love the color of oranges—and then I cut it in half. I take my time. And every time I eat an orange, I remark to myself that God, or Nature, call it whatever you want, is certainly the greatest artist there is. But how many oranges can I eat? One, two, and that's it. I'm full. But to look at them—I can do that all day long.

In the last few years, things have been changing much more quickly for gays in Israel. And that's thanks to a few people who have taken matters into their own hands. I think that the present board of the Agudah is the best one it has ever had. They're not the only ones responsible for the change that is happening, but they helped make it possible, they built the foundation. There are two excellent people there, Avi Sofer and Li'ora Mori'el, who is very good, a great diplomat. She is very interesting to listen to, and when she finishes talking you can't remember what she said, but you agree—and I think that is a very positive point. Abba Eben was the same way.[§]

We had a meeting recently with some people from the gay and lesbian synagogue in San Francisco, after the Knesset passed the laws against discrimination in the workplace, and after the changes in the military regulations. They asked us, "What's your new agenda?" I think that in the area of social change we haven't done enough. In the legal arena, we've made so much progress, I don't know if we can do more than we've done. I'm not concerned about Professor ʿUzi Eyen—his situation can be changed by changing the law, or the army regulations. But what happens to the rank and file gay soldiers? That interests me. What happens to the common soldier? And this can only be changed by educating the public as much as possible. And that demands a lot of money, and public relations experts, and some brave people who can take to the streets.

Personally, something like Gay Pride Week seems ridiculous to me. Idiotic. But it is a means to an end. We need to get out in front of the public eye. This is one of the means. In and of itself, I don't like it. I think that the Agudah's goal should be that one day the very organization will be obsolete— just like you don't need an organization to defend redheads, or left-handed people. Our goal should be that, if there are once again rumors that the military chief of staff is gay, people will say, "So what?"

I think that the "gay community" is something artificial. It doesn't really exist. It's a community only because there are people who share a common fate. The ties are not really that strong. My ideal is that there should be no gay community, no need for it. It's something temporary, I think. Just an attempt to copy America. The Agudah has three or four hundred members, but there are probably hundreds of thousands of gays in Israel. And it's the same thing in America. Some people insist that things are different there. But in the New York area, there are even more Jews than there are in Israel— so what, if three hundred people come to the gay and lesbian synagogue there on a Friday night. That's not any more than the number of people who come to our activities. It's just that, from here, it looks like a lot.

But Jewish community is not temporary. Even if I want to forget about it, they remind me. Look at what happened in Germany—they even killed the ones who didn't even know they were Jewish. Besides, Jewish community is

[§] Abba Eben (b. 1915): First representative of Israel to the United Nations; Israeli ambassador to the United States (1950–59); foreign minister (1969–74).

something beautiful. I'm not at all religious—I'm antireligious. But religious tradition is our cultural heritage. Just like the British tradition—they have all sorts of holidays and all sorts of things that they do which may be religious in origin, but they have nothing to do with religion anymore. They do things because that's what you do in Britain, that's what they've always done. We need to keep in touch with our past, in the same way, and that may be actually easier for us than for the British. If you read the Tanaḥ, you read the language that we speak today. But if you read English from more than four hundred years ago, you can't understand a word—you need a translation for Chaucer, you can't understand him!

There are a lot of reasons why I don't want to travel anymore. During this long trip that I had in Europe, I saw that I am incapable of being a member of more than one minority. Here in Israel at least, I am a member of only one minority. I am gay. There, I'm both Jewish and gay. Not to mention, within the Jewish community, I'm also either too religious or too secular. At one time I was offered a position overseeing food preparation for the El Al airline in Heathrow Airport. But there, look out if anyone sees me traveling on Shabbat, because they would take away the certification of kashrut for my food. So I would need to be careful about that. Not to mention that they shouldn't see me in a gay club. And with the British in general, as soon as I open my mouth they can tell that I'm either Jewish or German. So I said, no way—it's better to be here.

In Amsterdam I met a gay Jewish man from America, and we became friendly. He told me about how he went to a museum one day, and he met a man, and he said to me in English, "He gave me the Jewish eye." Do you understand? He knew immediately that this man was Jewish. Now, to be in Europe, I need to keep track of two kinds of eyes, the Jewish eye and the gay eye. That's too much for me. The gay eye is enough for me. I've never left the country since then. I'm not a traveling person, I like to be in one place. I have a more interesting life here, even if I walk a few blocks in Tel Aviv, from here to my apartment. There is beauty in every place, you just need eyes to see it. I once wrote a poem about that, after I saw that ʿAmos Guṭman's awful, negative movie about gay life in Tel Aviv, Amazing Grace. What's so horrible? Why be so pessimistic? I only open my eyes, and I see beautiful things. But that's the way I am.

There's another reason I don't go abroad. It's because I'm ashamed. We are doing things here which will be a lasting disgrace, for generations to come. What we are doing to the Arabs. We have a million people with rights like those of the blacks in South Africa under apartheid. Our law doesn't protect them. This is a scandal about which I wouldn't be able to answer people. I have nothing to say. I'm ashamed. It's better not to go. There are all sorts of things here, with human rights. It's just that most of the people here in Israel aren't aware of it. And when I hear what they did now, in "Operation Accountability," that they made 250,000 people flee their homes in Lebanon, because two people were killed in Qiryat Shemonah by missiles fired from across the border—they could have found a better way.

Without intending it, we have become a country like South Africa. I'll give you an example. The natural law of justice says that if you want to punish a person, you need to make a trial for him. Under all circumstances. But there are some people who are in jail in the territories who have never been given a trial. If such a thing were to happen here in Israel, inside the green line, would we tolerate it? But because it's in the territories no one says a word. But it's against natural justice—already eight hundred years ago they had a rebellion in England because of this. The right of *habeas corpus*—you can't punish a person without a trial. It's not allowed. But it happens in the territories.

The Arabs in the territories have been totally denied the right to determine their own fate. It's like in South Africa under apartheid—the blacks had to live in certain places, they could work in the cities but they couldn't sleep there, they needed to go back to their townships. And, just like in South Africa, the people from Gaza who work inside Israel, they can't sleep here. And, for instance, I read in the newspaper, that mayors of towns on the West Bank wanted to meet, but they weren't allowed to. We, inside the green line, can tell a group of people who want to meet that they're not allowed to? Who ever heard of such a thing? But suddenly, we're allowed to do absolutely everything there. No one says a word.

I want to know whose idiocy is responsible for getting us into a situation where we are shooting at children with tanks. There's a saying—the clever man gets himself out of every situation, but the wise man doesn't get himself into situations he needs to get himself out of. I don't go to demonstrations, but I donate money to Peace Now, the Association for Civil Rights, and the Citizens' Rights Movement.

I'm not someone who likes Arabs very much. I came here to live among Jews. But I'm ready for a smaller, Jewish Israel—I think that we need to get out of the territories. We need a DeGaulle to just get us out of there already. We can't tolerate this situation anymore, because in the end it will blow up in our faces, this injustice. It will come here too. You see it in the violence of the police and Border Guard. They're used to it there, so they do it here too. It's a disgrace for us. I remember during the Lebanon War, when they concentrated all the residents of Tyre on the shore, and they wanted to bomb the city from the air. A nurse said to me, "Now I can understand the Germans who said they didn't know." What could we do when our army up there was doing the same thing the Nazis did, by forcing everybody out of their houses and concentrating them in another place? You can't justify it. And if our army was doing worse, up in Lebanon, and we had known, what could we have done?

Politically speaking, of course, what we are doing now isn't even smart. All of those who want us to rule over the Arabs refuse to learn from history. The British brought Protestants to Northern Ireland in Cromwell's time— how long ago was that, five hundred years, four hundred years?—and they're still killing one another. The Turkish have been in Cyprus for five hundred years, they still can't live together with the Greeks. In Bosnia, people lived together, married one another, and now they're killing one another. So do we Jews really need to rule over the Arabs? Must we be together? No—we need to be separate. A state for them and a state for us. It can't be that we rule over them against their will.

I was in the supermarket once, and the person before me on line had a lot of bags and he needed to have them delivered to his apartment. So the cashier said to him, "The Arab will deliver it to you." I saw that this cashier was a new immigrant. So when it came my turn, I asked her where she was from. She was from Vilnius, Lithuania. And I said, "In Vilnius, if someone said, 'The Jew will do this,' you would say that he was an antisemite, right? Why don't you say 'the man,' 'the gentleman,' instead of 'the Arab?'" She said, "You're right."

It's very difficult for Arab gays. I know three people who have boyfriends from Gaza. And it's a very big problem, because these men aren't even allowed to be inside the green line. They're not allowed to sleep here. And these couples love each other very much. Now I'm in touch, on the phone, with a guy from Bethlehem. Somehow, he found the phone number of the Agudah, and I spoke to him there. A Christian Arab boy. Utterly isolated. I gave him my number at home, because it's difficult to talk in the office. He doesn't dare take a step in Bethlehem, not that he has anyplace to do anything. There doesn't seem to be a meeting place there—the problem is that everyone knows everyone else. He doesn't know what he's going to do. He needs a permit to cross the green line right now, and to get a permit he needs to explain where he is going. Over there, he can't talk to anyone and he can't get mail. So he talks to me. I gave him my home phone number, and he calls me and masturbates on the telephone sometimes. It's a very complicated situation. I know an Israeli Arab who is a member of the Agudah, and some of his family know about him. He's supporting them all, they're not working, so they keep their mouths shut.

I hope you're not disappointed by my life—I warned you before we started that I'm not a very interesting person. I've had no great loves, no broken hearts. There's nothing dramatic about me. Maybe the lack of drama is itself dramatic, in retrospect. If there's something I regret, it is all those years when I thought one wasn't allowed to do the very things I wanted to do. You know, I once treated an elderly woman, she was over seventy, and she told me about how she emigrated from Poland in the 1930s, as a widow with three children. And she said, "I was too respectable to be courted. I guarded my honor. And what do I have to show for it today? Not even memories." And that's how it was for me. Until I was twenty-seven I had never slept with a man in a bed. And even afterwards, for years I didn't let myself enjoy it. All the guilt, the dark places. I thought I had to go to doctor after doctor to cure myself of this disease. It's a pity. I could have started enjoying myself at sixteen!

AFTERWORD

A LIFE STORY IS A DYNAMIC THING: not only because new chapters continue to be added as long we are alive, but also because, as our understanding of ourselves changes over time, so does our understanding of our past. If Amir and I were to sit down with these twelve men today, most of them would tell different stories, from a different perspective, with a different attitude—not only about their current lives, but also about their distant past. Of course, if Amir and I were to sit down with these twelve men today, we would also ask different questions. We too have changed. It would be nice if this book could track, in "real time," the modulations in self-conception that develop over a lifetime: dampening an optimism that can no longer be sustained, accreting insights born of distance. In the absence of this option, we offer this Afterword—a news brief, a mere "postcard" from each of these men, mailed in the autumn of 1998. This will have to suffice as a reminder of the always-provisional and ever-unfolding nature of all self-understanding, and of every life.

The Shabbat following our meeting, Shaḥar went back to the moshav and came out to his parents. And remember that "somebody new" he mentions that he's just met? They now live together, on Moshav Tzoran, outside of Tel Aviv. Shaḥar's lover has a son from his first marriage, who often visits. Shaḥar himself is working as a Web site designer, and, in the summer of 1998, walked with a flag in the first Tel Aviv gay pride march.

No‘am, now a grandfather, is still married and still religious. Lately, he has been seeing another older man—also a grandfather—twice a month.

They often meet at the Hebrew University for sex in a bathroom stall. Noʿam has become more daring lately—"because time is running out." He is very, very pleased with recent social changes. "If I were ten years younger, I would have lived my life different," he says.

About a year after our interview, Rafi Niy and his partner, Asaf, split up. Rafi moved to Tel Aviv and now works as an administrator at a government mental health center. He has since organized a popular gay men's discussion group at the Agudah.

ʿAmit moved to Los Angeles, where he is studying for his B.A., majoring in economics, spending lots of time in the gym, and continuing to have sex with men for money. He plans to stay in the U.S.

At the very end of our interview, Andrei mentioned that he had just begun seeing a "guy from Leningrad." Well, they wound up staying together for five years. Andrei still lives at home—he never discusses his boyfriends with his mother, but he is certain that she knows he is gay. He left his job as a waiter last year, and is now looking for work as a travel agent. Andrei does not feel at home in Israel—he says, "If you haven't been born in Israel, you can never be Israeli."

Eli is single now—he and Moṭi broke up after four years together. (Moṭi now has a girlfriend, with whom he lives.) Eli has completed his M.B.A. and is working in management at a high-tech firm. He has not come out to his family, and, as he sees it, "I'm only gay in bed."

Dan and his wife now live closer to Tel Aviv, and Dan continues his involvement with the gay and lesbian community, working with the support group for gay married men and with the AIDS Task Force. Dan's wife recently began a therapy group for wives of gay men.

Walid is now working as a marketing consultant in Tel Aviv. Since our interview, he has told his parents that he is gay, and he has had two serious relationships—one for two years. These days, he likes to go out to the clubs—"a lot."

Yossi's group decided to join an existing kibbutz, and not start a new settlement. A year ago, Yossi met a guy, a member of a different kibbutz, who is now his "life partner." Their relationship is not monogamous, but it is committed, and they divide their time between their two kibbutzim. Yossi is working as a youth group counselor and is "happy and satisfied."

Oren's boyfriend ended their relationship after they were together for more than four years—as Oren tells it, because of parental pressure "to become straight." Oren spent two years in San Francisco, working as a D.J. and living with a new beau. Oren moved back to Israel in the summer of 1998, and, although the San Francisco beau isn't Jewish, he is considering following Oren back to Israel.

Itziq quit his job at the Laromme Hotel and went back to school, finishing his B.A. He is now "self-employed" and goes out on the town less often—but, he cautions, "At 38, things don't change."

Theo Mainz is reading lots of poetry, even working on some translations of homoerotic verse from Dutch into Hebrew. And he is still a familiar face at the Agudah. Theo notes that he is no longer quite so interested in sex—"but you wouldn't believe how many people are attracted to an old man such as I."

GLOSSARY

Agudah Literally, "Society" or "Association"; the commonly used name for Israel's first—and for many years its only—gay social and political organization. The Agudah was founded in Tel Aviv in 1975, as the Society for the Protection of Personal Rights. After Israel's dormant antisodomy law was repealed, in 1988, the Agudah added the phrase "for Gay Men, Lesbians, and Bisexuals in Israel" to its name. The organization opened a community center in downtown Tel Aviv in 1993. The Agudah voted in 1995 to change its name to the Association of Gay Men, Lesbians, and Bisexuals in Israel; in 1999 it added "Transgendered People" as well. On procedural grounds, the government agency responsible for the registration of nonprofit institutions has refused to acknowledge the above name changes.

Ashkenazi Jew of Central or Eastern European origins. The majority of the economic and academic elite of Israel remains Ashkenazi.

Conservative Judaism One of the three major branches of contemporary American Judaism, with roots in nineteenth-century Germany. Conservative Judaism acknowledges traditional religious law as binding (unlike Reform Judaism), but accepts the possibility of its self-conscious modification by contemporary rabbinic authorities (unlike Orthodox and ultra-Orthodox Judaism). There are very few Conservative Jews in Israel.

Dayan, Yaˤel (b.1939) Member of Knesset for the Labor Party; daughter of Moshe Dayan, the legendary general; for many years the most consistently outspoken pro-gay voice in the Israeli political establishment. See the Introduction.

Eyen, ˤUzi (b.1940) Gay activist; professor of chemistry at the University of Tel Aviv; former senior researcher for military. Instrumental in the 1993 campaign to remove all restrictions on the service of gay men and lesbians in the Israeli army. (See the Introduction.) ᶜUzi Even and his spouse, Amit Kama, are also the first same-sex couple in Israel to be officially acknowledged as foster parents.

Golan Heights   Formerly Syrian highlands occupied by Israel during the 1967 Six-Day War; officially annexed by Israel in 1981; never ceded by Syria. Under Yitzḥaq Rabin, Israel entered negotiations with Syria regarding the return of this territory.

Ḥadashot   Israel's first daily tabloid newspaper; published from 1984 to 1993.

Hagadah   Literally, "telling." Compilation of biblical texts, rabbinic prayers, medieval commentaries, poems, songs, and stories read annually at the seder on Passover.

Haᶜir   Weekly Tel Aviv city newspaper; similar in format and style to New York's *Village Voice.*

intifadah   The uprising of the Palestinians of Gaza and the West Bank against Israeli military control, beginning in December 1987. Characterized by strikes, violent attacks against Israeli soldiers and civilians, and murders of Palestinians accused of collaborating with Israeli authorities.

Jewish Agency   The executive and representative branch of the World Zionist Organization, headquartered in Jerusalem; an international charitable organization with the status of a quasi-governmental agency in Israel, involved in issues of Jewish immigration, settlement, education, and quality of life.

kashrut   The condition of ritual purity; see **kosher.**

kibbutz   A communal colony of socialist Zionist workers engaged in agriculture or manufacturing. Although kibbutzim have never been home to a substantial percentage of the Israeli population, they have played a major role in pioneering the Jewish claim to outlying areas of Palestine before statehood and in defending national borders since then. Kibbutznikim have traditionally been overrepresented in the Israeli military, political, and intellectual elite.

kibbutznik   Member of a kibbutz.

kipah   Small skullcap worn by some men in accordance with traditional religious law, identifying them as Jews who are at least nominally observant of the law's authority. Knitted, colorful skullcaps are generally worn by the Orthodox; black velvet skullcaps, often covered with larger black hats, are usually worn by the ultra-Orthodox.

Knesset   The Israeli legislature, organized on the model of the British House of Commons. One hundred and twenty members are chosen in general elections held every four years. There are no electoral districts for the Knesset—the electorate votes as a single national constituency.

kosher   Literally, "ritually pure"; often used to describe food that is permissible for consumption according to traditional religious law. "To keep kosher" is an English idiom meaning "to observe the dietary laws."

Labor Party (Ha ʿayodah) Nominally socialist party of the largely Ashkenazi establishment; founded by merger of parties in 1968; party of former Prime Ministers Levi Eshkol, Golda Meir, Yitzḥaq Rabin, and Shimʿon Peres. The Labor Party and its predecessor parties governed uninterruptedly from independence until 1977.

La'ishah "For the Woman"; a weekly women's magazine of tremendous national popularity; akin to a hybrid of *People* and *Cosmopolitan*.

Lebanon War Initiated in 1982 as an Israeli operation—"Peace for the Galilee"—to drive the raiders of the Palestine Liberation Organization (PLO) out of their bases in Lebanon, on the northern border of Israel; developed into an extended war, ultimately involving Syrian troops and leading to both the Israeli occupation of Beirut and a three-year struggle against Shi'ite Moslem guerrillas in the south; concluded in 1985 with the relocation of PLO headquarters to Tunis and Israeli withdrawal from most of Lebanon.

Likud Literally, "unity"; political party formed by merger of parties of the opposition in 1973, advocating capitalist economic reforms and the retention of territories conquered during the 1967 Six-Day War. Menaḥem Begin formed the first Likud government in 1977; later Likud governments were formed by prime ministers Yitzḥaq Shamir and Binyamin Netanyahu.

Maʿariv One of Israel's two major mass-circulation daily tabloid newspapers. See also **Yediʿot Aḥaronot**.

Magaʿim Literally, "Contacts" or "Touches"; a magazine for gay men, printing personal advertisements, black-and-white pornographic photography, and news and feature articles; published with varying frequency from 1987 to 1995.

Meretz Literally, "vigor"; political party formed by merger in 1992, advocating the return of territories conquered during the 1967 Six-Day War, defense of human and civil rights, and social justice.

Operation Accountability See A Note to the Reader.

Orthodox Judaism Views traditional religious law as binding and unchanging (unlike Reform and Conservative Judaism), but accepts the possibility of attempts at accommodation with modernity (unlike ultra-Orthodox Judaism), for instance, in dress and in secular education.

Passover Seven-day spring holiday celebrating the exodus of the Israelites from slavery in ancient Egypt. See also **seder**.

Purim Early-spring holiday celebrating the victory of Esther and her uncle, Mordecai, over the evil plotting of Haman to destroy the Jews of the ancient Persian empire, as recounted in the biblical Book of Esther. Observed by masquerading and engaging in generally carnivalesque behavior.

Qol Ḥeifah Weekly Haifa city newspaper; defunct.

Reform Judaism   One of the three major branches of contemporary American Judaism, with roots in nineteenth-century Germany. Characterized by a willingness to view traditional religious law as non-binding (unlike other major movements in Judaism), and an emphasis on the moral law as opposed to ritual.

Rosh Hashanah   The solemn two-day early autumn holiday of the Jewish New Year; one of the most widely observed festivals.

seder   Festive meal marking the start of the Passover holiday, traditionally a time of family gathering. See also **hagadah**.

selihot   Literally, "penitential prayers," hymns. Especially those recited during the month preceding Rosh Hashanah.

Sefardi   Literally, "Spanish" or "Iberian." Jew from Spain or Portugal, or, in common usage, from any of the Mediterranean Jewish communities to which the Jews of Spain fled after their expulsion in 1492, including all of North Africa, modern Italy, and modern Turkey.

Shabbat   The Jewish Sabbath, observed from Friday night until Saturday night. According to traditional religious law, travel and the direct use electricity are forbidden during this day of rest. Even among secularist Israelis, the gathering of family for a large Friday-night dinner remains a widely observed tradition. Saturdays are often devoted to napping, eating, hiking, and visiting with friends and family.

shekel   Israeli currency, technically the "New Israeli Shekel." At the time of writing, there were approximately three shekels to a dollar.

Six-Day War   On June 6, 1967, Israel embarked on a preemptive strike against the armies of Egypt and Syria, resulting in Jordanian retaliation. Six days later, the bulk of the Arab militaries had been destroyed, and Israel was in possession of the Sinai Peninsula and Gaza Strip (formerly Egyptian), the Golan Heights (formerly Syrian), and the West Bank and East Jerusalem (formerly Jordanian). The question of how best to dispose of these territories became the central preoccupation of Israeli politics during the following decades.

Tanah   The Hebrew Bible, including the Torah, the Prophets, and the Writings.

Technion   Israel Institute of Technology, located in Haifa; oldest institution of higher learning in Israel; leading university of the applied sciences.

tefilin   Phylacteries; small sealed leather cases holding slips of parchment inscribed with biblical passages. Worn daily during morning prayers by Jewish men who are observant of traditional religious law; leather straps hold one case on the forehead, the other on the left arm.

Torah   Literally, "teaching"; the Five Books of Moses (Genesis, Exodus, Leviticus, Numbers, and Deuteronomy). According to Jewish tradition, God presented the

Torah to Moses, as the representative of the Jewish people for all posterity, at Mount Sinai. Traditionally, every synagogue is in possession of a Hebrew Torah scroll, hand-copied on parchment, that is read publicly during certain prayer services.

ultra-Orthodox Judaism   Views traditional religious law as binding and unchanging and (unlike Orthodox Judaism) aggressively rejects many aspects of modernity. In Israel, such Jews refer to themselves as *ḥaredi*; in the United States, they are commonly grouped together as "Hasidic." Ultra-Orthodox Jews are usually distinguished by their appearance (black suits, hats, beards for men; long skirts, long sleeves, and head coverings or wigs for women) and by their political quietism, which leads many of them to reject the propriety of the Zionist movement and Jewish statehood.

Weizmann Institute of Science   Institute for graduate study and research in the sciences; south of Tel Aviv, in Reḥoyot.

Yediᶜot Aḥaronot   Israel's most widely read mass circulation daily tabloid newspaper. See also *Maᶜariv*.

Yom Kippur   Literally, "Day of Atonement"; solemn early-autumn holy day; according to traditional religious law, a day of fasting and prayer for God's forgiveness of the sins committed by the Jewish people during the previous year; the most widely observed holy day.

Yom Kippur War   On Yom Kippur 1973, Egyptian and Syrian forces attacked Israel simultaneously, with the intention of recapturing territories conquered in 1967. The attack caught the Israeli army by surprise, and casualties were high on all sides. Although it ended in stalemate, the war shook the faith of many Israelis in the competence of the military.

Library of Congress Cataloging-in-Publication Data

Independence park : the lives of gay men in Israel / Amir
    Sumaka'i Fink and Jacob Press.
        p. cm. — (Contraversions)
    Includes bibliographical references.
    ISBN 0-8047-3619-7 (cloth : alk. paper). — ISBN 0-8047-3854-8
(paper : alk. paper)
        1. Gay men—Israel—Biography.   I. Fink, Amir Sumaka'i.
II. Press, Jacob.   III. Series: Contraversions (Stanford, Calif.)
HQ76.2.I73I54   1999
307.76'62'095694—dc21   99-39611
                                                                    Rev.

⊗   This book is printed on acid-free, recycled paper.

Original printing 1999
Last figure below indicates year of this printing:
08   07   06   05   04   03   02   01   00   99

Designed by Sandy Drooker
Typeset by James P. Brommer in 10/14 Minion